# Introduction to Cloud Computing

Michael Wufka • Massimo Canonico

# Introduction to Cloud Computing

 Springer

Michael Wufka
Douglas College
New Westminster, BC, Canada

Massimo Canonico
University of Piemonte Orientale
Alessandria, Italy

ISBN 978-3-032-07150-7        ISBN 978-3-032-07151-4   (eBook)
https://doi.org/10.1007/978-3-032-07151-4

© The Editor(s) (if applicable) and The Author(s), under exclusive license to Springer Nature Switzerland AG 2026

This work is subject to copyright. All rights are solely and exclusively licensed by the Publisher, whether the whole or part of the material is concerned, specifically the rights of translation, reprinting, reuse of illustrations, recitation, broadcasting, reproduction on microfilms or in any other physical way, and transmission or information storage and retrieval, electronic adaptation, computer software, or by similar or dissimilar methodology now known or hereafter developed.
The use of general descriptive names, registered names, trademarks, service marks, etc. in this publication does not imply, even in the absence of a specific statement, that such names are exempt from the relevant protective laws and regulations and therefore free for general use.
The publisher, the authors and the editors are safe to assume that the advice and information in this book are believed to be true and accurate at the date of publication. Neither the publisher nor the authors or the editors give a warranty, expressed or implied, with respect to the material contained herein or for any errors or omissions that may have been made. The publisher remains neutral with regard to jurisdictional claims in published maps and institutional affiliations.

This Springer imprint is published by the registered company Springer Nature Switzerland AG
The registered company address is: Gewerbestrasse 11, 6330 Cham, Switzerland

If disposing of this product, please recycle the paper.

Michael Wufka • Massimo Canonico

# Introduction to Cloud Computing

Michael Wufka
Douglas College
New Westminster, BC, Canada

Massimo Canonico
University of Piemonte Orientale
Alessandria, Italy

ISBN 978-3-032-07150-7     ISBN 978-3-032-07151-4   (eBook)
https://doi.org/10.1007/978-3-032-07151-4

© The Editor(s) (if applicable) and The Author(s), under exclusive license to Springer Nature Switzerland AG 2026

This work is subject to copyright. All rights are solely and exclusively licensed by the Publisher, whether the whole or part of the material is concerned, specifically the rights of translation, reprinting, reuse of illustrations, recitation, broadcasting, reproduction on microfilms or in any other physical way, and transmission or information storage and retrieval, electronic adaptation, computer software, or by similar or dissimilar methodology now known or hereafter developed.
The use of general descriptive names, registered names, trademarks, service marks, etc. in this publication does not imply, even in the absence of a specific statement, that such names are exempt from the relevant protective laws and regulations and therefore free for general use.
The publisher, the authors and the editors are safe to assume that the advice and information in this book are believed to be true and accurate at the date of publication. Neither the publisher nor the authors or the editors give a warranty, expressed or implied, with respect to the material contained herein or for any errors or omissions that may have been made. The publisher remains neutral with regard to jurisdictional claims in published maps and institutional affiliations.

This Springer imprint is published by the registered company Springer Nature Switzerland AG
The registered company address is: Gewerbestrasse 11, 6330 Cham, Switzerland

If disposing of this product, please recycle the paper.

# Foreword

Cloud computing in its modern form arguably started in 2006, when Amazon began to offer public cloud computing resources. One of the consequences of this rather young age is that significant innovations are still occurring at a rapid pace. In turn, this means that books on the subject tend to become obsolete quickly.

Universities started to offer courses related to cloud computing in the middle of the 2010s when the popularity of this platform was already high. Unfortunately, about ten years later, it is not easy to find a good textbook on the subject. Most introductory books that offer an overview of cloud computing to a technical audience are either of a low quality or already significantly outdated. It seems that the size and complexity of the topic has led most authors to focus on specific areas of cloud computing. For example, there are great books on topics such as cloud security, how to program cloud native applications, or specific tools such as Kubernetes. For an introductory college course in cloud computing this is a challenge, as it is unreasonable to ask students to buy and read a number of expensive textbooks for a single course.

This book aims to fill the void described above—to serve as an introductory textbook on cloud computing, usable as the primary resource in cloud computing courses at the undergraduate or graduate level. But even outside of the use in post-secondary education, any reader with some technical background or interest who wants to achieve a deeper understanding of cloud computing should find this book helpful. While practical and hands-on examples are primarily based on the Google Cloud Platform, the principles covered in the book are equally relevant to other cloud platforms.

# How to Use This Book

The book breaks the topic down into nine chapters. While we generally expect the reader to work through the topics in the order in which they are presented, the different chapters are for the most part independent from each other, allowing users to jump to topics that they are particularly interested in, or to skip topics they do not care about or already understand. The exception to this is that all readers should read Chapter 1 (Fundamentals) before proceeding to any of the remaining chapters.

To help students learn the material, each chapter features a brief summary, a list of key terms, some review questions and hands-on laboratory exercises.

The hands-on lab exercises contain questions prompting the user to write down answers or take screenshots of key points of the exercises. It is recommended that the reader records their answers in a file for future reference. If the book is used in the context of a college or university course, the instructor might use some of the laboratory exercises as assignments. In that case, the instructor will typically ask students to submit their answer files (often in a specific format) as a basis for grading the assignments, where the links will become footnotes as in the rest of the book: "Some of the hands-one exercises in this book are losely based on different Google Codelabs (https://codelabs.developers.google.com/), which are licensed under the Creative Commons Attribution 4.0 licence (https://creativecommons.org/licenses/by/4.0/), and provide excellent material for additional hands-on practice in Google Cloud.

Moreover, google provides additional resources, including credits to use on the Google Cloud Platform for educational purposes at https://cloud.google.com/edu?hl=en."

The field of cloud computing is constantly changing and progressing and, as new technologies are introduced, the steps to take in the hands-on exercises may change somewhat over time, for example due to minor changes in the cloud provider's web-based user interface, added options, etc. While the basic steps will likely stay stable for quite some time, the reader might have to slightly deviate from some of the instructions. If significant modifications become necessary, supplementary instructions will be posted at cloudbook.uniupo.it. Please feel free to contact us to report problems with the hands-on exercises or any other questions or suggestions at cloudbook@uniupo.it.

> **Additional Details**
>
> In several places throughout the book, we provide additional in-depth content on specific topics. This content will be presented in boxes like this one and is not required for an understanding of the rest of the book. Therefore, these boxes can be read later or skipped altogether if the content is not of interest to the reader.

# Acknowledgments

*I could not have completed this work without the ongoing support and encouragement of my wife Karina and son Andreas.*

**Michael**

*I have to say thanks to my wife Manu, my son Jacques, and my dog Mia, all of them supported me or asked me for a walk. I really appreciate both aspects during this year since most of my free time was dedicated to this book.*

**Massimo**

We thank the "Google Cloud Faculty Experts group" which brought us together and allowed to start this useful collaboration. We also thank Susan Grove and Springer Nature for putting the trust in us to write this book. Special thanks also goes to Luisa Fernanda Barrera Leon for her work on the figures.

**Massimo and Michael**

**Competing Interests** The authors have no competing interests to declare that are relevant to the content of this manuscript.

# Contents

| | | |
|---|---|---|
| **1** | **Fundamentals** | **1** |
| 1.1 | What Is Cloud Computing? | 1 |
| | 1.1.1 Cloud Service Models | 3 |
| | 1.1.2 Cloud Deployment Models | 3 |
| 1.2 | Benefits of Cloud Computing | 7 |
| | 1.2.1 Elasticity | 7 |
| | 1.2.2 Cost Savings | 8 |
| | 1.2.3 Increased Reliability | 9 |
| | 1.2.4 Increased Performance | 10 |
| | 1.2.5 Reduced In-House IT Needs | 11 |
| | 1.2.6 Provider Benefits | 11 |
| 1.3 | Drawbacks and Challenges of Cloud Computing | 12 |
| | 1.3.1 Security and Privacy | 12 |
| | 1.3.2 Vendor Lock-in | 13 |
| | 1.3.3 Cost and Cost Management | 14 |
| | 1.3.4 Lack of Expertise | 16 |
| | 1.3.5 Performance Concerns | 17 |
| | 1.3.6 Organizational Issues | 18 |
| 1.4 | History | 18 |
| | 1.4.1 The Era of Mainframes | 18 |
| | 1.4.2 Personal Computers and Client-Server Systems | 20 |
| | 1.4.3 Grid Computing | 23 |
| | 1.4.4 Virtualized Data Centers | 23 |
| | 1.4.5 Cloud Computing | 24 |
| 1.5 | Summary | 25 |
| 1.6 | Key Terms | 26 |
| 1.7 | Review Questions | 27 |
| 1.8 | Exercises | 27 |

|  |  | 1.8.1 | Elasticity in Public Cloud | 27 |
|---|---|---|---|---|
|  |  | 1.8.2 | Cloud Pricing | 28 |
|  |  | 1.8.3 | Cloud Computing vs. Other IT Services | 28 |
| **2** | **Technical Foundations** | | | **29** |
|  | 2.1 | Networking | | 29 |
|  |  | 2.1.1 | Network Stack | 30 |
|  |  | 2.1.2 | Network Layer and IPv4 | 32 |
|  |  | 2.1.3 | Shortage of IPv4 Addresses and IPv6 | 34 |
|  |  | 2.1.4 | Transport Layer | 35 |
|  |  | 2.1.5 | Session, Presentation and Application Layers | 36 |
|  |  | 2.1.6 | Important Networking Commands | 36 |
|  | 2.2 | Virtualization | | 40 |
|  |  | 2.2.1 | Virtualization Technology | 40 |
|  |  | 2.2.2 | Virtualization Guarantees | 43 |
|  |  | 2.2.3 | Benefits of Virtualization in Cloud Computing | 44 |
|  | 2.3 | Linux | | 45 |
|  | 2.4 | Modern Data Centers | | 52 |
|  |  | 2.4.1 | Data Center Design | 52 |
|  |  | 2.4.2 | Modern Server Design | 55 |
|  |  | 2.4.3 | Modern Storage Approaches | 55 |
|  |  | 2.4.4 | Cost and Other Considerations | 57 |
|  | 2.5 | Summary | | 58 |
|  | 2.6 | Key Terms | | 59 |
|  | 2.7 | Review Questions | | 60 |
|  | 2.8 | Exercises | | 60 |
|  |  | 2.8.1 | Install Ubuntu in Virtualbox | 60 |
|  |  | 2.8.2 | Basic Linux Commands | 64 |
|  |  | 2.8.3 | Networking | 72 |
| **3** | **Cloud Computing Platforms** | | | **77** |
|  | 3.1 | Introduction | | 77 |
|  | 3.2 | Features to Compare | | 77 |
|  |  | 3.2.1 | Application Programming Interface (API) | 78 |
|  |  | 3.2.2 | Availability Zones | 78 |
|  |  | 3.2.3 | Fault Tolerance and Failover | 79 |
|  |  | 3.2.4 | Migration | 79 |
|  |  | 3.2.5 | Monitoring | 80 |
|  |  | 3.2.6 | Cloud Federation and Open Virtualization Format | 80 |
|  |  | 3.2.7 | Elasticity | 81 |
|  |  | 3.2.8 | User Management | 81 |
|  |  | 3.2.9 | Services Provided | 81 |
|  | 3.3 | Architecture | | 82 |
|  | 3.4 | Commercial and Open Source Cloud Platforms | | 83 |
|  |  | 3.4.1 | Amazon Web Services (AWS) | 84 |

|  |  | 3.4.2 | Microsoft Azure | 85 |
|---|---|---|---|---|
|  |  | 3.4.3 | Google Cloud Platform (GCP) | 86 |
|  |  | 3.4.4 | Alibaba Cloud | 87 |
|  |  | 3.4.5 | OpenStack | 87 |
|  |  | 3.4.6 | OpenNebula | 89 |
|  | 3.5 | Summary | | 90 |
|  | 3.6 | Key Terms | | 90 |
|  | 3.7 | Review Questions | | 91 |
|  | 3.8 | Exercises | | 91 |
|  |  | 3.8.1 | Install and Use Nextcloud in Virtualbox | 91 |
|  |  | 3.8.2 | Start a VM in OpenStack | 96 |
|  |  | 3.8.3 | Elastic Block Store (EBS) in AWS | 102 |
| **4** | **Types of Cloud Services** | | | **111** |
|  | 4.1 | Levels of Abstractions | | 111 |
|  | 4.2 | Types of Cloud Services | | 114 |
|  |  | 4.2.1 | Computational Services | 116 |
|  |  | 4.2.2 | Network Services | 120 |
|  |  | 4.2.3 | Storage Services | 123 |
|  |  | 4.2.4 | Big Data | 127 |
|  |  | 4.2.5 | Machine Learning | 130 |
|  |  | 4.2.6 | Management Services | 132 |
|  | 4.3 | Summary | | 134 |
|  | 4.4 | Key Terms | | 134 |
|  | 4.5 | Review Questions | | 136 |
|  | 4.6 | Exercises | | 137 |
|  |  | 4.6.1 | Using the Cloud Vision and Translation APIs | 137 |
|  |  | 4.6.2 | Deploying WordPress on a GCP VM | 142 |
|  |  | 4.6.3 | Cloud Storage | 151 |
| **5** | **Cloud Architecture** | | | **157** |
|  | 5.1 | Architecture Goals | | 157 |
|  |  | 5.1.1 | Performance | 157 |
|  |  | 5.1.2 | Reliability | 158 |
|  |  | 5.1.3 | Low Administrative Overhead | 158 |
|  |  | 5.1.4 | High Level of Control | 159 |
|  |  | 5.1.5 | Support Modern Software Engineering Approaches | 160 |
|  |  | 5.1.6 | Cost Effectiveness | 160 |
|  |  | 5.1.7 | Goal Conflicts | 160 |
|  | 5.2 | Architectural Principles | | 161 |
|  |  | 5.2.1 | Infrastructure as Code | 162 |
|  |  | 5.2.2 | Automation | 163 |
|  |  | 5.2.3 | Microservice Architectures | 165 |
|  |  | 5.2.4 | Hybrid Cloud Architecture | 168 |
|  | 5.3 | Architectural Building Blocks for Cloud Applications | | 169 |

|  |  | 5.3.1 | Infrastructure as a Service | 169 |
|---|---|---|---|---|
|  |  | 5.3.2 | Platform as a Service | 171 |
|  |  | 5.3.3 | Functions as a Service | 173 |
|  |  | 5.3.4 | Containers | 174 |
|  | 5.4 | Summary | | 178 |
|  | 5.5 | Key Terms | | 179 |
|  | 5.6 | Review Questions | | 180 |
|  | 5.7 | Exercises | | 181 |
|  |  | 5.7.1 | Infrastructure as Code with GCP Using Terraform | 181 |
|  |  | 5.7.2 | Auto-Scaling Load Balancer | 186 |
|  |  | 5.7.3 | Using Containers with Kubernetes | 189 |
| 6 | **Cloud Security** | | | **195** |
|  | 6.1 | A Brief Review of IT Security | | 195 |
|  |  | 6.1.1 | Common IT Security Risks | 196 |
|  |  | 6.1.2 | General IT Security Measures | 198 |
|  |  | 6.1.3 | IT Security Limitations and Tradeoffs | 200 |
|  | 6.2 | Impact of Cloud Computing on IT Security | | 202 |
|  |  | 6.2.1 | Cloud Security Risks | 203 |
|  |  | 6.2.2 | Cloud Security Opportunities | 205 |
|  | 6.3 | Cloud Security Best Practices | | 207 |
|  |  | 6.3.1 | General Considerations | 207 |
|  |  | 6.3.2 | Access Control | 210 |
|  |  | 6.3.3 | Encryption | 214 |
|  |  | 6.3.4 | Network Security | 216 |
|  |  | 6.3.5 | Security Monitoring and Logging | 220 |
|  | 6.4 | Summary | | 222 |
|  | 6.5 | Key terms | | 222 |
|  | 6.6 | Review Questions | | 224 |
|  | 6.7 | Exercises | | 225 |
|  |  | 6.7.1 | Encryption in GCP—Key Management | 225 |
|  |  | 6.7.2 | Access Control | 229 |
|  |  | 6.7.3 | Network Security and Firewall Configuration | 235 |
| 7 | **Multi-Cloud Systems** | | | **243** |
|  | 7.1 | Approaches to Use Different Clouds | | 243 |
|  | 7.2 | Introduction of Multi-Cloud Systems | | 245 |
|  | 7.3 | MS from Academia | | 246 |
|  | 7.4 | Commercial MS | | 248 |
|  | 7.5 | MS Current and Future Trends | | 249 |
|  | 7.6 | Summary | | 251 |
|  | 7.7 | Key Terms | | 251 |
|  | 7.8 | Review Questions | | 252 |
|  | 7.9 | Exercises | | 252 |

|         |       | 7.9.1 | Deploy a New VM on AWS Using Apache Libcloud | 252 |
|---|---|---|---|---|

 |       |       | 7.9.2 | Deploy a New VM on OpenStack Using JCloud | 258 |
|         |       | 7.9.3 | Deploy a Basic Flask Web Server by Using Terraform | 272 |

# 8 Cloud Operations ... 279
## 8.1 Cloud Management ... 279
### 8.1.1 Service Level Agreements (SLA) ... 280
### 8.1.2 Organizational Measures ... 280
### 8.1.3 Risk Management ... 281
### 8.1.4 Workload Management ... 284
### 8.1.5 Mobile Device Management ... 285
## 8.2 Cloud Monitoring ... 286
### 8.2.1 Introduction ... 286
### 8.2.2 Monitoring in GCP ... 287
## 8.3 Cloud Migration Strategies ... 288
### 8.3.1 Perspectives to Consider ... 289
### 8.3.2 Migration Assessments and Prioritization ... 290
### 8.3.3 Migration Strategies ... 292
## 8.4 A Critical View of Cloud Computing ... 295
### 8.4.1 Common Cloud Computing Challenges ... 295
### 8.4.2 Cloud Computing Limitations ... 296
## 8.5 Ethical Issues in Cloud Computing ... 297
### 8.5.1 Introduction to Ethics in Computing ... 298
### 8.5.2 Amplification of Existing Negative Effects of Technology ... 298
### 8.5.3 Privacy Risks ... 299
### 8.5.4 Environmental Impacts ... 301
### 8.5.5 Market Concentration Risks ... 302
## 8.6 Summary ... 303
## 8.7 Key Terms ... 303
## 8.8 Review Questions ... 304
## 8.9 Exercises ... 305
### 8.9.1 Cloud Monitoring ... 305
### 8.9.2 Cloud Logging ... 309
### 8.9.3 Cloud Migration Center ... 310

# 9 Edge Computing, Internet of Things and Cloud-to-Edge Continuum ... 315
## 9.1 Introduction ... 315
### 9.1.1 Internet of Things ... 316
### 9.1.2 Edge Computing ... 317
### 9.1.3 Cloud-to-Edge Continuum ... 318
## 9.2 Key Benefits and Challenges of Edge Computing ... 318
## 9.3 Edge Computing Architectures ... 320
## 9.4 Future Trends and Opportunities ... 320
## 9.5 Summary ... 321
## 9.6 Key Terms ... 321

| | | | |
|---|---|---|---|
| 9.7 | Review Questions | | 322 |
| 9.8 | Exercises | | 322 |
| | 9.8.1 | Streaming IoT Data to Cloud Storage | 322 |
| | 9.8.2 | Self-driving Cars Using Donkey Car: Training the Model on a Chameleon Node | 335 |
| | 9.8.3 | AWS IoT Core Quick Connect | 343 |

**Glossary** ............................................................. 349

# List of Figures

| | | |
|---|---|---|
| 1.1 | Service models | 4 |
| 1.2 | Deployment models | 4 |
| 1.3 | Cloud evolution | 19 |
| 1.4 | 2-tier architecture | 21 |
| 1.5 | 3-tier | 22 |
| 2.1 | The 7-layer OSI model | 30 |
| 2.2 | The 7-layer ISO model vs the 4-layer TCP/IP model | 31 |
| 2.3 | Classes of IP networks | 33 |
| 2.4 | The iterative DNS resolution | 37 |
| 2.5 | Sample output of the command ipconfig | 37 |
| 2.6 | Sample output of the command ping | 38 |
| 2.7 | Sample output of the command nslookup | 38 |
| 2.8 | Sample output of the command tracert | 39 |
| 2.9 | Sample output of the command netstat | 39 |
| 2.10 | Hypervisor types | 41 |
| 2.11 | Raised floor | 53 |
| 2.12 | SAN | 56 |
| 3.1 | How to start a VM | 80 |
| 3.2 | Cloud platform architecture | 82 |
| 3.3 | Market trend | 85 |
| 3.4 | GCP services | 86 |
| 3.5 | OpenStack components | 88 |
| 3.6 | OpenNebula architecture | 89 |
| 4.1 | Pizza-as-a-service | 112 |
| 4.2 | The Google cloud resource hierarchy | 115 |
| 4.3 | Different families of machines types available on GCP | 116 |
| 4.4 | Different cloud run options | 119 |

| | | |
|---|---|---|
| 4.5 | Different load balancer options in GCP | 122 |
| 4.6 | Different cloud armor protection levels offered in GCP | 123 |
| 4.7 | Different CloudSQL options offered in GCP | 125 |
| 4.8 | Example of a query in a sample data set in BigQuery | 128 |
| 4.9 | Different options when creating a Dataproc cluster in GCP | 129 |
| 5.1 | Ansible architecture | 164 |
| 5.2 | Istio architecture | 167 |
| 5.3 | App engine | 172 |
| 5.4 | Containers and VMs | 175 |
| 5.5 | Docker architecture | 176 |
| 6.1 | DMZ Architecture | 217 |
| 6.2 | Default subnets created in the default VPC | 218 |
| 6.3 | Explicit default firewall rules | 219 |
| 6.4 | Example of the GCP logs explorer | 221 |
| 7.1 | Use of multi-cloud architectures by all organizations. Source: Flexera 2025 state of the Cloud Report | 249 |
| 7.2 | Use of multi-cloud tools. Source: Flexera 2025 state of the Cloud Report | 250 |
| 8.1 | Fog computing | 297 |

# About the Authors

## Michael Wufka

Michael Wufka is a regular instructor in Computing Studies and Information Systems at Douglas College in Metro Vancouver, Canada. Prior to earning his PhD in Information Systems and Business Administration at the University of British Columbia, he completed his undergraduate degree in Computer Science at the University of Technology in Darmstadt, Germany, and worked for Accenture in a range of different roles on several IT projects for four years. His main research interests include cloud computing and agile software development. He is a member of the Google Cloud Faculty Experts Group since 2020.

## Massimo Canonico

Massimo Canonico is an associate professor of Computer Science at the University of Piemonte Orientale (Italy). His research interests lie in different areas. Concerning distributed computing systems, his current research activity is focused on cloud computing with emphasis on performance and energy-efficient resource management. He has also worked on fault-tolerant scheduling algorithms and efficient overlay-based data transfer techniques on various families of distributed systems (in particular, Grid Computing systems). In 2020, he has been selected as a member of the Google Cloud Faculty Expert Group and as an AWS Educate Cloud Ambassador by Amazon.

# Chapter 1
# Fundamentals

This chapter gives a broad overview of cloud computing. The definition of basic concepts and terms is followed by a discussion of advantages and disadvantages of cloud computing. A brief history of computing paradigms from mainframe computers to modern cloud computing concludes the chapter.

## 1.1 What Is Cloud Computing?

The *National Institute of Standards of Technology* (NIST) of the U.S. Department of Commerce defines cloud computing as "a model for enabling ubiquitous, convenient, on-demand network access to a shared pool of configurable computing resources (e.g., networks, servers, storage, applications, and services) that can be rapidly provisioned and released with minimal management effort or service provider interaction."[1] This rather dense definition contains a number of important characteristics of cloud computing:

- **Ubiquitous [. . . ] network access:** Cloud computing is accessed over the Internet. This makes it accessible wherever Internet connectivity is available.
- **On demand:** Cloud computing is inherently on demand—i.e., you are not required to plan ahead how much of a resource you will need at a specific time in the future. Instead, you can use as much of each resource as you spontaneously need (as long as you can pay for it), and you are only billed for how much you actually use.
- **Shared pool of configurable computing resources:** In order to allow the previous point, cloud service providers have a large pool of computing resources (such as servers, storage, network capacity etc.) that is dynamically allocated to their customers on demand.

---

[1] Peter Mell, Timothy Grance: "The NIST Definition of cloud computing", NIST Special Publication 800-145.

- **Can be rapidly provisioned and released:** Not only can resources be used and released dynamically—this can happen very rapidly (typically within a few seconds, or at most, minutes).
- **With minimal management effort or service provider interaction:** The allocation and release of resources happens in a self-serve manner, e.g. through a few mouse clicks in a web interface or through an API call, and does not require any manual actions by the provider (which is an important prerequisite for the 24/7 availability of rapid provisioning)

A few examples[2] might make this definition easier to understand. To begin with private cloud use: If you own a smartphone and occasionally take photos on it, odds are that you are using storage in the cloud. Typically, photos taken are automatically uploaded into a cloud (e.g. by Google or Apple) so that they are not lost if you lose your phone, and so that you can save storage space on your phone by removing old photos that have already been synchronized in the cloud. Another computing resource that is commonly used is applications. It is increasingly common to not install all the software one uses on one's computer, but to instead use software in the cloud. This might be typical office software (e.g. Google Docs or Microsoft 365) or design, image processing etc. software (such as the Adobe Creative Cloud).

Using cloud based software applications instead of locally installed and managed software is also increasingly common in organizations—everything from simple accounting packages to complex *Enterprise Resource Planning* (ERP)[3] systems can now be rented in the cloud. Another typical example of cloud use by organizations is to replace physical servers with virtual ones hosted in the cloud.

All these examples have in common that users do not have to commit to how much of each resource they will use in advance. Instead, use is on demand, with additional resources (more storage, more copies of cloud software for additional users in the organization, additional servers etc.) available virtually instantaneously, without any interaction with service provider personnel. And users are only charged for the amount of resources they consume.

For each type of resource, the cloud service provider typically defines a relatively fine-grained basic unit of use, and the cost associated with the use of that unit. For example, storing a GByte of data for a month might cost $0.026, or running a virtual machine with 16 CPUs and 64 GByte of memory for an hour might cost $0.53. The total charges for a cloud user are calculated simply by multiplying the number of units used of these (and many other[4]) resource types and their individual unit cost.

Cloud computing has different service and deployment models that are discussed in detail in the next two sections.

---

[2] More examples are discussed in Sect. 1.2.1 on elasticity.

[3] More info here: https://en.wikipedia.org/wiki/Enterprise_resource_planning.

[4] For many more examples of cloud resources, their basic units of use, and respective price, see e.g. the Google Cloud Platform price list: https://cloud.google.com/pricing/list.

## 1.1.1 Cloud Service Models

Cloud services are typically categorized into three main types of service models: *Infrastructure as a Service* (IaaS), *Platform as a Service* (PaaS) and *Software as a Service* (SaaS).

In **IaaS**, the cloud service provider offers virtual machines, networking and storage capacities. Everything on top of these bare resources (e.g. configuring and maintaining operating systems, applications etc.) is the responsibility of the cloud service user.

**PaaS** shifts more responsibilities from the cloud service user to the cloud service provider. In a certain sense PaaS is the most vague of the three service models (simply because not everybody exactly agrees on what a "platform" is). In practice, different cloud service providers offer different kinds of platforms at different levels of abstraction. To use a simple example here, a provider could define the *LAMP* stack as a platform. LAMP stands for Linux, Apache, MySQL and PHP, and consequently represents the combination of a very popular operating system, web server, database and programming language. There are many applications that can be directly deployed on the LAMP stack—the content management system Wordpress which is used by millions of blogs is a good example. In PaaS, the cloud service provider is responsible for maintaining the platform, and the cloud service user can focus on deploying and maintaining their application(s) on the basis of the platform.

**SaaS** moves even the responsibility for the application itself to the cloud service provider. Common examples include software packages such as Microsoft Office 365 or Google Docs.

Figure 1.1 illustrates how common tasks are distributed differently between cloud service providers and users in the different service models.

Note how certain responsibilities always lie with the cloud service provider (specifically, the underlying facilities and hardware), while user management typically lies with the cloud service users. The responsibility for everything in between—operating systems, platform components like application servers, and the actual application software—depends on the cloud service model. Chapter 4 discusses cloud service models in more detail.

## 1.1.2 Cloud Deployment Models

The discussion so far implicitly assumed the public cloud deployment model, in which a (typically large) organization such as Amazon, Google or Microsoft acts as the cloud service provider for a large number (typically many thousands) of client organizations. This is probably the most common cloud deployment model, since all of the benefits discussed in the next section apply. In the rest of this section we present the other cloud deployment models illustrated in Fig. 1.2.

**Public Cloud** computing inherently has multitenancy—which means that customers of different organizations share the same physical hardware. For example,

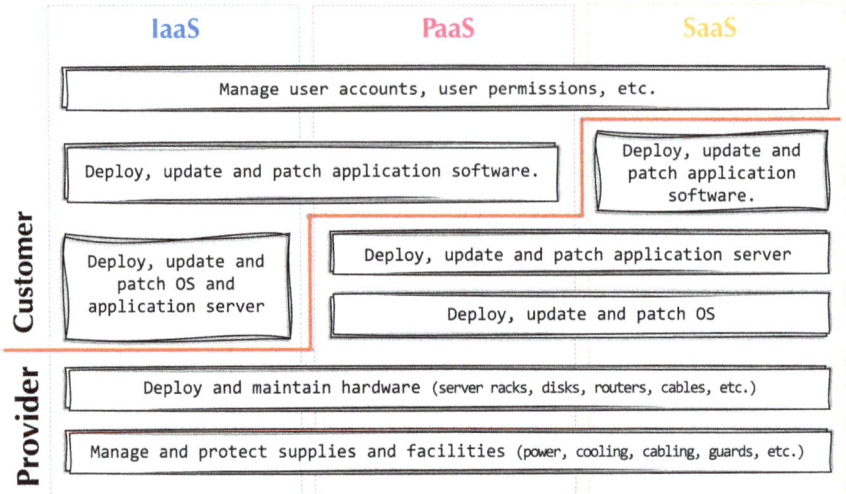

**Fig. 1.1** Customer and provider responsibilities in different service models

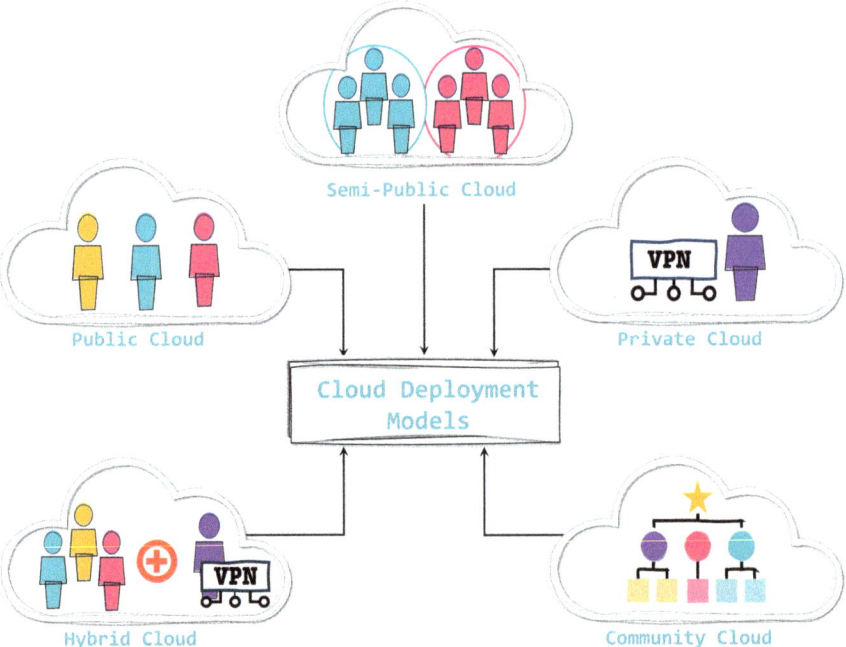

**Fig. 1.2** The cloud deployment models

data of multiple customers might be stored on the same physical hard drive, and virtual machines of multiple customers can be hosted on the same physical server.

Theoretically, multitenancy should not be a problem—if everything works as intended, the virtual resources of different customers are strictly isolated from each

## 1.1 What Is Cloud Computing?

other. In practice, this is mostly the case. However, bugs in the implementation of operating systems, virtualization software or even hardware (see e.g. the Meltdown and Spectre website[5]) can break this isolation. Therefore, public cloud use always comes with a small risk that the confidentiality of data might be violated. This is one of several reasons why public cloud use might be unwise (or prohibited by government regulations) for organizations that handle particularly sensitive kinds of data.

If this is the case, there are two main alternatives to public cloud use: Semi-private or private cloud. **Semi-private cloud** is actually quite similar to public cloud, in that a service provider typically hosts the virtual resources of many different customers. The key difference is that there is no multitenancy. In other words, physical resources are strictly separated between customers. The obvious advantage to public cloud computing is that it is more secure—the isolation between different customers is stronger. The main disadvantage is that costs are higher, since the cloud service provider cannot maximize the utilization of physical resources as well as it can in public cloud use. For example, if the cloud provider uses servers with 64 CPU cores, then four different customers who all want to use virtual machines with 16 CPU cores each can share the same physical server in a public cloud setting. In a semi-private cloud setting, the provider has to have (at least) one server per customer, which in this example means four servers, and consequently four times the cost.

Another problem with semi-private cloud is that it still carries security risks. In particular, the customer has to trust the cloud service provider, who hosts (and consequently has access to) all the virtual resources of the customer. Either negligence/incompetence or malevolence of the (public or semi-private) cloud service provider could put customer data at risk. This is one of the reasons why some organizations choose (or are forced by regulations) to host their own private cloud.

In a **Private Cloud**, the cloud service user and cloud service provider are the same organization. The NIST definition of cloud computing from above still applies—"a shared pool of configurable computing resources [. . . ] that can be rapidly provisioned and released with minimal management effort" . So rather than having separate physical servers for different IT systems, the organization has a number of physical servers on which all IT systems run in a virtualized way, e.g. as virtual machines. Within the limitations of the physical machines, this has many of the benefits of public cloud computing as discussed in the next section. For example, the virtual hardware of individual IT systems can rapidly be scaled up and down based on demand (as long as the physical servers have capacity left).

The main advantage of private cloud computing is that the organization has full control over its IT resources. It does not have to rely on a service provider to keep its data secure. This is closely connected to one of the main disadvantages—the organization has to create, run and maintain its own cloud infrastructure, which requires a significant amount of expertise and effort. Another key disadvantage compared to public cloud computing is that the scalability is strictly limited by the physical hardware that the organization has (while large public cloud providers

---

[5] Meltdown and Spectre: https://meltdownattack.com/.

typically offer virtually limitless resources—in other words, it is safe to assume that an individual customer will run out of money to pay for resources before the provider runs out of resources to offer).

It should be noted that an organization choosing a private cloud has different options of doing so, with different levels of required in-house expertise. The private cloud platform OpenStack distinguishes three approaches of running a private cloud:[6]

- a managed cloud, where a service provider helps to create and manage the private cloud infrastructure;
- the use of a supported private cloud distribution which takes care of tasks such as testing, bug fixing and packaging of the cloud infrastructure software;
- a *Do It Yourself* (DIY) approach in which all these tasks fall to the organization itself.

The **Hybrid Cloud** model combines some of the advantages (and disadvantages) of private and public cloud computing. In the hybrid model, IT resources are normally hosted in a private cloud. However, if a peak in resource use occurs, the system is set up to fulfill the demand that exceeds the locally available resources by accessing a public cloud provider. This is sometimes also called cloud bursting. It might seem as if the hybrid model mostly combines the disadvantages of both the private and public model—the organization has to maintain its own cloud infrastructure, and if cloud bursting is required, the data is no longer completely under the control of the organization. However, it should be noted that steps can be taken to mitigate the resulting risks. For example, cloud bursting could be limited to applications with less critical data. Some of the main advantages of using a hybrid cloud model are that an organization is not completely dependent on a provider, that it can maintain significant IT expertise in house, and that often already available physical IT resources can be continued to be utilized without running the risk of running out of capacity.

There is one more cloud deployment model: **Community Cloud**. In a community cloud, a number of organizations share cloud infrastructure that is privately hosted by one or several of them. This model is often used by similar organizations that do not compete strongly against each other. For example, a number of school boards or a number of colleges and universities might decide that privacy regulations in their jurisdiction make public cloud use impractical for them. On the other hand, each individual organization might not have (or might not want to spend) the resources to host their own private cloud. In such a situation, it makes sense for them to run a shared community cloud, which allows them to run the cloud in a way that follows all the regulations in their industry and jurisdiction. An example for a community cloud in the Canadian province of British Columbia is EduCloud.[7]

Deciding which cloud deployment model is best for an organization is no trivial task. Factors to consider include:

---

[6] "OpenStack: The Path to Cloud": https://www.openstack.org/assets/path-to-cloud/OpenStack-6x9Booklet-online.pdf.

[7] https://www.bc.net/service-catalogue/educloud-server.

- **Regulatory and compliance requirements:** Privacy and security requirements by government regulations might allow certain models such as public cloud computing only under very specific conditions.
- **Financial considerations:** The required initial investment amount and the ongoing costs differ significantly between the different deployment models.
- **Elasticity of resource demand:** High fluctuations in IT resource needs tend to favour public cloud use, and make private cloud use less efficient.
- **Geographical access patterns:** If accesses are only from one geographic location, then a private cloud data center in that location might offer the lowest latencies. However, if accesses are from all over the world, using the worldwide network of server centers operated by large public cloud service providers might be preferable.

## 1.2 Benefits of Cloud Computing

Two of the main benefits usually associated with cloud computing are elasticity (i.e. the ability to scale resource use up and down rapidly) and cost savings. However, there are additional benefits that might be even more important in certain circumstances, including increased reliability, increased performance, and a significant reduction of in-house IT needs. The following subsections discuss these benefits (which are all from the perspective of the cloud user) in some more detail. The end of this section then discusses the main benefits for cloud service providers.

### 1.2.1 Elasticity

The concept of elasticity can easily be visualized with a rubber band that can be stretched to get longer, but that also returns to its previous length rapidly if it is no longer stretched out. Cloud computing offers great elasticity of resource use—a cloud user can rapidly increase or decrease resource use, and only has to pay for the actual resources that are used over time.[8] Elasticity in public cloud computing is even better than in the rubber band analogy—while rubber bands usually break when they are stretched too far, the resources that public cloud service providers offer are practically unlimited: While a rubber band probably breaks when it is stretched to say ten times its usual length, a cloud user can easily scale from a single virtual machine to hundreds or even thousands of virtual machines within minutes, as long as they can afford the cost.

Elasticity is very useful in many different scenarios. For example, online stores have significant peaks and troughs in demand throughout the day (e.g. most people

---

[8] In contrast to scalability, which is about the ability of a system to handle a higher workload if it is run on more powerful hardware, elasticity refers to the ability to scale resources up and down dynamically in response to the workload.

shop in the evening, some during the day, but very few at night) and throughout the year (e.g. very busy for a few weeks before Christmas and on certain days like Black Friday or Boxing Day, but much less busy at other times of the year). For example, the website of the online retailer BestBuy has an annual peak traffic in the Christmas shopping season that is more than seven times as high as the average traffic.[9] If the IT infrastructure behind the website was run on servers owned by BestBuy that were only used for this purpose, three quarters of the capacity of these servers would be idle for most of the year.

Another example for the usefulness of elasticity is if demand peaks suddenly. This might happen if a previously not very well known website is mentioned on a popular website or even on a TV show. In such a case, the number of accesses can suddenly grow by orders of magnitude, overwhelming any single server.

A final example for the benefits of elasticity might be a system that allows senior managers to run complex analyses of large amounts of data. When such an analysis is run, it is highly desirable to have the results available within a short period of time (minutes or hours). This requires massive computational power. However, since managers will only spend a fraction of the time running such analyses (and only do so during the day on work days), the underlying IT systems will be idle for the vast majority of the time. Once again, the elasticity of cloud computing can solve this problem—when an analysis is run, dozens of powerful virtual machines can be spun up to solve the problem in parallel. Once the analysis is complete, they can be shut down equally rapidly, leading to a quick result at a low cost.

## 1.2.2 Cost Savings

The benefit of cost savings is closely related to elasticity. Given that a cloud service user only pays for the actually consumed resources, the more resource use fluctuates over time, the more money can be saved by using resources in the cloud. This is because if self-owned IT resources are used instead, they have to be powerful enough for the peaks of resource use, and consequently sit partially idle during all other times.

But how is it that cloud service providers can offer IT resources at rates that are low enough to actually lead to cost savings? There are two main factors at play: Firstly, the peaks of different cloud service users occur at different times. While certain types of systems (e.g. e-commerce systems) will likely have high resource demand at the same time (e.g., on big shopping days like Boxing Day or Black Friday), cloud service providers typically host many other kinds of systems as well. For example, many customers host their corporate IT systems (e.g. accounting systems, HR systems, ERP systems) with public cloud service providers as well. These systems typically have their peak loads at other times—during normal working days, when the demand for e-commerce systems is lower. Another reason for different peaks is that peak usage

---

[9] Joel Crabb, "The BestBuy.com Cloud Architecture", IEEE Software, March/April 2014, pp. 91–96.

typically occurs at certain times of the day. For example, streaming video services are most in demand in the evening hours. Since these types of services are hosted and used around the globe, the peak demand occurs at different times in different locations due to time zone differences, once again smoothing out peaks. The end result of these effects is that cloud service providers are able to run their servers at a much higher utilization than any individual organization could, significantly reducing their cost compared to individual organizations running their own IT.

Another important reason why cloud service providers can typically offer IT resources at very competitive rates is simply down to economics of scale. The data centers of the the big cloud service providers are massive—probably containing hundreds of thousands of servers[10]. Not only does this mean that the big providers can procure servers, networking equipment etc. at a discount due to the volume they purchase, but it also means that many relatively fixed costs can be spread across a very large number of paying customers. For example, a data center needs physical security measures such as surveillance cameras, security personnel etc. While a large data center probably spends more on these than a small data center, the costs scale much slower than the number of servers. For example, a very small data center with a hundred servers can be managed by a single security guard at a time. A large server center with 100,000 servers probably needs several security guards (to account for the larger size of the center), but likely significantly fewer than a thousand security guards at a time. Hence, the cost per server for physical security gets lower the larger the server center gets, giving the massive data centers of public cloud service providers a significant cost advantage.

### 1.2.3 Increased Reliability

Using a public cloud service provider can significantly increase reliability. Public cloud service providers host data centers in multiple locations globally.[11] Hosting an application redundantly in multiple data center locations makes it resilient in the face of natural disasters such as major storms, floods or earthquakes.

The elasticity of cloud computing can also increase reliability significantly, as it can be exploited to thwart *Denial-of-Service* (DOS) attacks, in which an attacker floods an application with fake requests in an attempt to make it unresponsive for real requests by actual customers. Given the ability and willingness to spend the necessary amounts, DOS attacks can be made ineffective by scaling the system to as many servers as are necessary to respond to all requests. Additionally, public cloud providers have network-based mechanisms to detect and mitigate DOS attacks.

---

[10] Details are generally not published by the big cloud service providers, as they represent proprietary and competitive information. The following video "Inside a google Data Center" gives a good idea of the scale of a modern cloud data center https://www.youtube.com/watch?v=XZmGGAbHqa0.

[11] For a map of locations of Google Cloud, see https://cloud.google.com/about/locations#regions.

A final argument for increased reliability is that the expertise in fields such as IT security is likely higher in a public cloud service provider than in most other organizations, especially if they are from industries other than IT.

Some of these benefits (such as increased reliability at reduced costs) are particularly strong for small companies. Imagine a small startup company that offers a specific service online. Because the customer base is initially very small, a single server might be capable of hosting the service. Therefore, the service could be hosted very inexpensively by dedicating a single machine (possibly just an inexpensive PC) in the office of the startup to running it.

One massive disadvantage to this approach would be that reliability of such a service would be poor. A number of problems could lead to the service being unavailable for customers: For example, a technical failure in the single server, a network component (e.g. router or switch) failure, a power outage, an outage of the internet service provider, a disaster such as a fire in the office building etc. The obvious answer to all these risks is redundancy. So instead of a single server, at least two servers should be used, so if one fails, the other one can continue to respond to customer requests. Similarly, all networking equipment should be redundant as well. For extra resilience, the two servers should actually be in two separate locations, so that a single disaster (such as a fire or localized flooding) cannot bring the whole service down. On top of this, it would be preferable to have redundant power supply by two independent providers, if possible, or at least uninterruptible power supply infrastructure (battery packs and diesel generators) as well as redundant internet connections.

It should be clear that such a setup would be very expensive to implement for a small startup company. However, there is an alternative: renting two small virtual machines in two separate data centers of a public cloud service provider gives the same level of reliability as the expensive setup described above, at a very small fraction of the cost.

## 1.2.4 Increased Performance

Using cloud computing can lead to a performance increase in the hosted service. This is mainly due to two reasons that have already been discussed in this chapter: Elasticity and the fact that the big public cloud service providers operate multiple data centers across the globe.

If a cloud application is designed to automatically scale up the number of servers it runs on as requests increase, consistently high performance (e.g. measured in short average response times) can be ensured much more easily than with a system that is hosted by an individual organization. The global distribution of data centers by the big cloud providers is not only for redundancy and regulatory reasons, but also to reduce the network latency for end users. For example, if a globally operating company responds to requests from around the globe with a website that is only hosted in their own data center in North America, then performance in e.g. Australia is significantly worse because of inevitable network latencies. However, if hosted

1.2 Benefits of Cloud Computing                                                                11

e.g. in Google Cloud, then requests in that region can be routed to Google's data center in Sydney, drastically reducing latencies.

It should be noted that increased performance is only achieved if the cloud systems are well designed. Incidentally, this is true for all the other benefits as well—a badly designed cloud application that does not use redundancy well is consequently not particularly reliable, one that does not scale automatically does not take advantage of elasticity etc.

## *1.2.5 Reduced In-House IT Needs*

A final major benefit of using public cloud computing rather than hosting all IT in-house is that it reduces how many in-house IT personnel are needed. The magnitude of this reduction depends on a number of factors, including the service model that is used: If the predominant model is Software as a Service, then very limited in-house IT staff is needed. On the other hand, if Infrastructure as a Service is the main approach, a wide range of in-house IT specialists from various kinds of system administrators to software developers are still needed, and only roles directly involved with the underlying hardware are eliminated.

Reducing in-house IT staff can be advantageous in several different ways. It often comes with cost savings, because (e.g. due to economics of scale) a public cloud service provider can typically perform the same work more cheaply. Additionally, it allows companies, especially those that are not in the IT industry themselves, to focus on their actual business. A related point would be that such companies often have difficulty attracting and retaining highly qualified IT personnel.

This concludes the discussion of some of the main benefits of cloud computing from the perspective of a cloud user. The arguments above implicitly assumed the use of public cloud computing. However, to a lesser degree, many of the points above still apply in other cloud deployment models such as private cloud. For example, while elasticity in the private cloud model is strictly limited by the number of physical machines the organization has, using a private cloud platform still allows the different applications of the organization to scale up and down flexibly, as long as their total resource needs do not exceed what is available. The main exception to the rule that the benefits of public cloud computing apply similarly (if to a lesser degree) to private cloud computing as well is that running a private cloud can be highly complex, which implies that it still requires very significant in-house IT expertise.

## *1.2.6 Provider Benefits*

The most obvious benefit of a cloud service provider is that offering cloud services can be highly profitable: For example, in the first quarter of 2025, Amazon Web

Services (AWS) posted revenues of over 29 billion dollars (up approximately 17% from the previous year) with profits (operating income) of over 11 billion dollars.[12]

These numbers are remarkable in a number of ways: Not only is the size of the cloud computing business significant, but also its growth rate and its profit margins. And the latter is true even though there is strong competition between the big cloud service providers (AWS, Microsoft Azure and Google Cloud). These numbers in their own right can serve as an indication that cloud computing is beneficial—why would customer organizations spend so much on services that they did not find useful?

Besides the profitability of the business, there are other benefits for cloud service providers. For example, most cloud service providers need significant IT resources for their own IT needs. Offering spare capacity to cloud service users allows them to increase the utilization of IT resources they already have. Additionally, offering cloud services can be a very effective strategy to retain customers. This observation leads directly to the drawbacks of cloud computing.

## 1.3 Drawbacks and Challenges of Cloud Computing

Even though the large economic success of cloud computing hinted at in the last chapter is a strong indication that the advantages of cloud computing often outweigh its disadvantages, there clearly are drawbacks or challenges related to the use of cloud computing. This section discusses some of the most important ones, including security and privacy concerns, vendor lock-in risks, cost and cost management issues, lack of expertise, performance concerns and other organizational issues.

### *1.3.1 Security and Privacy*

Security and privacy are probably the most commonly quoted concerns around cloud computing. They are really two distinct issues, but strongly related, so we discuss both together here. More details are discussed in Chapter 6 about security.

Security can be defined as the combination of confidentiality, integrity and availability. For example, for a database to be secure, access to its contents must be limited to people authorized to access it (confidentiality), nobody unauthorized must be able to delete or change data in the database (integrity) and the database must actually be available to authorized users (availability). Availability might sound like a non-security issue, but without it, the other two are trivial to achieve (lock a hard drive with the data in a big safe, and confidentiality and integrity are achieved). Similarly, in practical terms, an organization can get into trouble if either of the three

---

[12] Amazon Q1-2020 Earnings Release: https://s2.q4cdn.com/299287126/files/doc_financials/2025/q1/AMZN-Q1-2025-Earnings-Release.pdf.

components is violated—if customer data is disclosed, if it is manipulated, or if it cannot be accessed.

Privacy has an even wider range than security, and how much it is valued strongly depends on the laws and cultures of different countries. For example, while a disclosure of a complete list of movies watched by a person on a streaming service might not cause any direct (e.g. financial) harm, most people would consider it a violation of their privacy if such information was publicly accessible.

With regard to both security and privacy, a cloud service user has to trust the cloud service provider. Since (irrespective of the cloud service model) the cloud service provider operates the physical hardware on which the applications and/or data of the cloud service user ultimately reside, they have physical access to these applications and data. Consequently, a cloud service user has to trust the competence and benevolence of the cloud service provider, meaning that it does not accidentally or intentionally expose confidential data to unauthorized parties etc.

A related point is that countries often have regulations limiting cloud use for certain industries that handle particularly sensitive data such as the health care sector. For example, colleges and universities in the Canadian province of British Columbia are generally not allowed to store data with cloud service providers that might be hosted outside of Canada, since data protection and privacy laws e.g. in the USA are less stringent than in Canada. Compliance with such regulatory requirements can be challenging for organizations.

Security and privacy questions should carefully be analyzed by any organization that wants to use cloud computing. There are many measures that can be taken to mitigate risks. In particular, the use of strong encryption can reduce the risk that sensitive information gets disclosed due to e.g. a provider error. Additionally, it should be pointed out that the use of cloud computing can also increase security if it is done properly—for example, high availability can more easily be achieved by using a cloud provider with multiple secure data centers. Finally, it is important to recognize that cloud computing is not appropriate in all situations. For example, the control software of a nuclear power plant should not be run in any cloud system that can be accessed from the outside, since its security is of such critical importance.

## *1.3.2 Vendor Lock-in*

Vendor lock-in describes the situation that an organization which hosts IT resources at a cloud service provider tends to be locked into that provider, meaning that the level of difficulty of switching to a different provider would fall somewhere into the range from hard and expensive to practically impossible. This might not be a problem as long as the organization is happy with its cloud service provider. However, this dependency on a specific provider can become very problematic if there are significant disputes about e.g. provided services or billing, if the provider goes out of business, or simply if better and cheaper other providers become available.

Vendor lock-in is nothing new in the IT world. For example, most organizations store their data in commercial relational databases. These databases typically follow the SQL standard, and should therefore be easily interchangeable. However, practically all commercial database vendors have their own proprietary extensions of SQL. The justification for these extensions is typically that they add useful functionality that has not (yet) been standardized in SQL. However, customers who utilize these extensions will find it significantly harder to switch to a different database vendor.

In cloud computing, the degree of vendor lock-in experienced depends on several factors, including the service model chosen. Because there is very little cross-vendor standardization in cloud computing overall, a (slightly oversimplified) way to judge the severity of vendor lock-in could be to look at how many responsibilities lie with the cloud service provider vs. user. For example, if "Infrastructure as a Service" is used, the responsibility for operating systems, platform, applications etc. lies with the cloud service user. Therefore, switching to a different cloud service provider would probably be easier (as long as it offers similar virtual machines etc.) than for an organization that uses "Platform as a Service", which might have to change its applications significantly because no other cloud provider offers exactly the same platform.

There are different strategies to deal with vendor lock-in, and they all come with difficult tradeoffs between flexibility, cost etc. For example, an organization could decide to host its IT resources with multiple public cloud providers. While this creates significant extra effort and cost, it makes it much easier to shift resources away from a provider if necessary. Another approach (probably more suitable for smaller organizations, who cannot or do not want to afford using multiple cloud providers) would be to wisely choose the cloud features used, and refraining from using features that are not offered in a similar form by other providers.

### 1.3.3 Cost and Cost Management

The attentive reader might be surprised to see cost as one of the disadvantages or challenges of cloud computing, after it was listed as one of the main advantages earlier. Just like with many other aspects of cloud computing, the answer here is "it depends".

While it is generally true that cloud service providers offer IT resources at cheaper rates than their typically much smaller customer organizations can achieve when running their own IT, this really depends on several assumptions. In particular, if an organization already owns a lot of IT resources (servers, networking equipment, but also server software licenses) when it decides to move to the cloud, then the ongoing costs of cloud computing might exceed the cost of operating the already owned equipment. This is especially true if the IT needs of the organization are very constant, allowing high resource utilization and implying no need for spare capacity that sits idle most of the year.

## 1.3 Drawbacks and Challenges of Cloud Computing

In fact, Cloud Repatriation (i.e. the process of moving IT resources that are deployed in a public cloud back into on-premise data centers) is an increasingly popular topic (see e.g.[13]). This is only an anecdotal trend, especially in face of still (as of writing) strongly growing revenues of large public cloud providers, and more data and research is needed in this area. However, there are good reasons why companies might in fact overspend on their IT resources in the cloud, and could consequently benefit financially from bringing at least some of their IT back in-house. The ease of allocating cloud resources requires significant organizational discipline to avoid unnecessary spending. For example, if the performance of a web-facing application deployed in a public cloud begins to suffer under increasing traffic, it is very quick and easy to simply make the underlying virtual hardware more powerful to fix the problem. If the same system runs on a number of allocated physical servers in-house, the same approach (adding more hardware) typically requires lengthy procurement processes that also require management approval. Hence, in the in-house situation, other solution approaches such as attempts to optimize the performance by for instance adding database indices or optimizing bottleneck code are much more likely taken, ultimately making the application more cost effective in-house than in the cloud.

Another issue is not the absolute level of cost, but the fact that costs are much more volatile in cloud computing. An organization that owns and operates its own IT has very predictable and fairly stable IT costs—besides some extra electricity consumption, servers (and the personnel operating them) cost roughly the same whether they are running near peak capacity or idly. In contrast, costs in cloud computing are highly volatile. Since users only pay for what they use, if an application has four times the load in the busy Christmas shopping season than it has in say February, then the costs will also differ by a factor of four. Even if the overall costs for the whole year are typically lower if cloud computing is used, this volatility can be problematic for organizations that are not used to it.

A final point is that costs can spike unexpectedly, either due to misconfigurations that scale systems up unnecessarily, or because of applications that correctly respond to an unexpected volume of requests (e.g. due to a denial of service attack) by scaling up massively. This is also a potential issue for learners who want to try out a cloud computing platform by using the usually available trial accounts that provide a number of free credits, but require a credit card that is automatically charged if those credits are exceeded: It occasionally happens that students forget to turn off e.g. a group of virtual machines, in which case the costs can build up to hundreds of dollars in just a few weeks. Thankfully, some cloud providers have apparently recognized this issue and are now offering special accounts for educational purposes that can be used without entering a credit card, and which simply deactivate services once the provided funding runs out.

In summary, while cloud computing is often cheaper than operating ones own IT infrastructure, all the costs (initially and ongoing) should be analyzed carefully upfront. If cloud computing is used, its ongoing costs should be monitored closely

---

[13] https://techcrunch.com/2023/03/20/the-cloud-backlash-has-begun-why-big-data-is-pulling-compute-back-on-premises/.

to avoid surprises. Management also has to be on board and move away from traditional thinking in fixed budgets. If for example a well configured online store incurs increasing hosting costs by the cloud service provider, this is not a bad thing, but actually desirable, because the reason should be that the online store is busier (and consequently hopefully generates more revenues and profits).

## 1.3.4 Lack of Expertise

Lack of cloud expertise is another often quoted issue that organizations considering cloud computing face. This is not particularly surprising, given that cloud computing is still relatively new, and growing at a rapid rate. Only quite recently did the first universities and colleges start offering degrees or specializations in cloud computing. The fact that cloud expertise is in short supply can be illustrated by the fact that cloud computing was the most sought after hard skill on the platform LinkedIn in 2019,[14] and by an analysis showing that cloud computing professionals earn among the highest average salaries in the IT function aside from IT executives.[15]

Not every organization using cloud computing needs the same level of cloud computing expertise. Both the number of employees with cloud computing skills, as well as the specific knowledge required depend strongly on the cloud deployment and service models used. For example, an organization that chooses a hybrid cloud computing approach to run different applications with a range of different cloud service models obviously needs significantly more employees with high levels of cloud expertise than an organization that primarily uses *Software as a Service* in a public cloud setting.

Still, irrespective of the models chosen, to get the full benefit from using cloud computing, it is highly desirable that employees in many different job functions understand cloud computing, from specific technical expertise in technical operators to strategic understanding of the business opportunities afforded to an organization by the flexibility of cloud computing in executives.

There are several ways how organizations that do not have the cloud computing expertise they require can mitigate this situation, including training their current employees, hiring additional employees and temporarily using outside consultants. Additionally, deployment and service models that make sense with the given level of existing expertise should be chosen.

---

[14] https://www.linkedin.com/business/learning/blog/top-skills-and-courses/the-skills-companies-need-most-in-2019-and-how-to-learn-them.

[15] https://www.crn.com/news/global-it-salaries-hit-new-high-2019-it-skills-and-salary-report.

## *1.3.5 Performance Concerns*

Performance concerns specifically about public cloud computing come primarily from two main sources: Network limitations and performance implications of shared physical resources.

With regard to network limitations, the main issue is generally network latency. The further away a server responding to client request is located, the longer the time signals have to travel, and, usually even more importantly, the more "network hops" have to be performed, i.e. the more intermediate switches, routers etc. that each add a little bit of delay are involved. It highly depends on the situation whether these latencies are problematic. For some applications (e.g. transfer of large files), delays of even a few seconds hardly matter to users, while for other uses (e.g. video conferences) even delays of just a few tenths of a second are highly inconvenient. Network bandwidth is usually less important, unless massive amounts of data have to be transferred. If that is the case, and if the Internet connections of some of the involved parties are not high speed, cloud computing might in fact be not suitable.

The second performance concern comes from the fact that physical resources such as servers are usually shared by multiple virtual resources such as virtual machines of the same or different organizations. Consequently, it is at least theoretically[16] possible that the performance of an application is degraded by other applications (possibly belonging to other organizations) that run on the same server. Another concern is that most cloud providers do not guarantee the immediate availability of resources in the requested location. In times of generally high resource utilization it is possible that requested resources take a significant amount of time to become available, or are only available immediately in different geographic locations, which could impact the performance of an application that needs to scale up due to high load.

Two ways to address these possible performance issues is to measure performance continuously, and to automatically scale systems up as needed if performance dips. It should be noted that, just as with many other points discussed here, cloud computing can both be a source of and a solution to performance issues. For example, it is quite possible that the average network latency experienced by end users is lower if a public cloud service provider is used, since the provider operates multiple data centers across the globe. Consequently, the average user might be "closer" to a data center of the chosen public cloud provider than to the in-house IT resources of the organization.

---

[16] Technical details on this point are beyond the scope of this introductory chapter. However, it should be noted that modern virtualization and cloud computing platforms generally offer effective means to isolate different virtual resources that share the same physical resources in such a way that the load on one does not affect the guaranteed minimum performance of others.

## 1.3.6 Organizational Issues

The final challenge in adopting cloud computing discussed here can be summarized as organizational issues. Often times, companies starting to use cloud computing find that their organizational culture is causing issues. It is beyond the scope of this introduction to discuss all the possible obstacles and their solutions. Instead, the following just gives an example.

A very common obstacle would be resistance to change, which often affects other types of IT projects as well. Such resistance to change can have many different causes, from psychological factors to rational considerations. For instance, an IT manager might resist moving internal IT resources to a public cloud provider because they are not sure that they (and their employees) possess the necessary skills. An additional concern might be that the IT department would likely shrink, since a lot of work maintaining physical IT resources in house would be eliminated. This could result in undesirable layoffs, and also reduce the size of the IT department, which could make the manager afraid of losing status and power in the organization. Finally, the manager could be afraid that their performance evaluation (e.g. as a function of how smoothly the IT operates) could increasingly depend on factors outside of their control (and instead under the control of the cloud service provider).

Given that organizational obstacles to cloud computing are different in each individual case, no single approach for mitigation can be described here. However, achieving buy-in into cloud computing plans by all affected stakeholders is a critical goal, and a lot of honest (two-way) communication is likely an important means to achieve it. Also, getting external know-how will likely help, be in the form of training, new hires, or the use of consultants.

## 1.4 History

In order to understand the appeal of cloud computing for organizations, it is beneficial to briefly review the history of computing paradigms. This evolution of IT from mainframe systems to modern cloud computing is illustrated in Fig. 1.3.

## 1.4.1 The Era of Mainframes

We begin with the earliest Turing-complete computers, i.e. computers that could not just execute predetermined computations, but execute general purpose programs. Such computers first became commercially available in the 1950s, and became more widely used in the 1960s. These computers initially did not use integrated circuits yet, but had to be built from combining individual transistors. Consequently, they were very large (think—room sized) and very expensive.

1.4 History

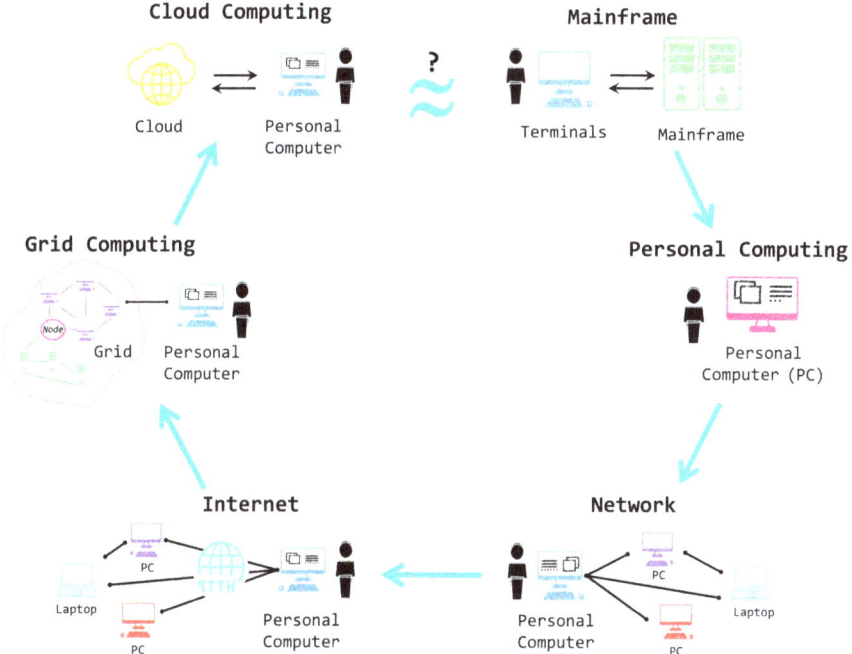

**Fig. 1.3** The evolution of cloud computing

Initially, these computers had to be programmed by manually inputting whatever program one wanted to run, often using sets of buttons or switches to directly manipulate the contents of memory cells. Needless to say, this was a lengthy and error prone process. As a consequence, typically much more time was spent entering (and fixing) the program than actually executing it, resulting in very low effective utilization of these very expensive machines.

Not surprisingly, better approaches to perform I/O were invented in the 1950s, and the first precursors of operating systems appeared. These simple batch systems typically had one (or multiple) punch card readers through which programs could be loaded semi-automatically, so that at the completion of a program the next program was ready to run. This improved the effective utilization of the computer significantly. The usual way to use these machines was to manually punch the correct holes for the desired program into multiple sheets of paper, drop them off at the operator of the computer, and to pick the results up at a later time (often hours or days later, depending on how many other programs were ahead in the batch queue) once the program had been executed.

These simple batch systems significantly reduced the time wasted between programs by eliminating lengthy setup time of programs, and removing the need to schedule specific time windows for access to the computer in advance. However, CPU utilization remained low, because the CPU had to sit idle during I/O operations. Consider a typical batch program that might be run in a large organization such as processing hourly payroll. In such a program, the program logic might consist of a single loop over all hourly employees. For each employee, the relevant information such as hours worked, hourly rate, factors influencing payroll deductions etc. would be read in from some input device (a card reader, a tape, or even a disk drive). Once the employee data was loaded, all the necessary calculations were performed in memory, and then the result (e.g. a printed check) was output. Now assume that the CPU runs at 10 MHz, the calculations for each employee on average take 1000 instructions, and the read and write operations for each employee take a total of 10ms. Under these assumptions, the time spent on CPU processing for each employee is 0.1ms, and consequently the CPU sits idle waiting for I/O to complete about 99% of the time.

To alleviate this issue, and to significantly increase CPU utilization, multi-programmed batch systems became common in the 1960s. In these systems, the computer keeps multiple batch programs in memory. Once a program needs to do I/O, its execution is paused, and another program is executed. Once the I/O operation is complete, the program becomes ready to be executed again, and is scheduled to be resume execution once the CPU becomes free (e.g. once the other program needs to perform I/O itself). Such multi-programmed batch systems were used for a long time (and in fact, are still in much more widespread use than one might suspect).

The next major innovation in computing was the invention of time sharing systems, which began to be widely adopted in the late 1960s . Just like multi-programmed batch systems, time sharing systems keep multiple programs in memory. However, rather than typically running an individual program until it cannot continue (e.g. due to an I/O operation), with a focus on maximizing CPU utilization and system throughput, these time sharing systems performed each program only for a short time period (called time slice) at a time. For example, assume that each program is executed for 100 milliseconds at a time, and that there are ten active programs. In such a scenario, each program gets to execute for 1/10 of a second every second. Even at a CPU speed of just say 10MHz, this means that each program can execute one million instructions per second. Consequently, for each of the ten programs, the computer effectively performs as if it had a CPU on its own that has the performance of a 1MHz CPU.

A computer running such a time sharing system was usually shared by many users in a company, or a large department in a company, and accessed from so-called "dumb terminals", consisting of not much more than a (single color, text only) screen and a keyboard that were connected directly to the computer in the same building.

### *1.4.2 Personal Computers and Client-Server Systems*

Significant technological progress made more and more complex integrated circuits possible. In the late 1970s, this led to the emergence of Personal Computers (PCs). These machines were typically significantly less powerful than the mainframes used in time-sharing systems. However, their price was also so much lower that it became

## 1.4 History

affordable to purchase a computer for each employee, or even for hobby use at home. When IBM introduced the IBM PC in 1981, the adoption of personal computers grew massively. Initially, these personal computers were often not connected through a computer network. Instead, they ran standalone applications such as spreadsheets or word processing. Data was typically exchanged using physical media such as floppy disks.

Of course, for many applications, data needs to be exchanged between multiple different users. A typical example might be a database system that stores inventory information of a manufacturing company. Such a system typically needs to be accessed by multiple employees in different departments such as the warehouse, purchasing, sales, product assembly and accounting. Such applications can be implemented following the client-server paradigm: One (or multiple) centralized servers, running on more powerful computers, are accessed by a number of client PCs. Application-specific software runs on both servers and clients which are connected through a computer network, such as Token Ring or Ethernet (the latter of course becoming the de facto standard for wired computer networks in the 1990s).

**Fig. 1.4** The 2-tier architecture

There are two main architectures for client-server systems: 2-tier (see Fig. 1.4) and 3-tier (see Fig. 1.5) architectures. The difference lies in how the different parts of the application—user interface, business logic and storage, are distributed between client and server. While at least part of the user interface (processing user inputs, displaying information) always has to be at the client machine, and at least part of the storage function (actually storing the data that is shared between all the clients involved) has to be located at the server, the business logic can be on one or the other, or distributed to different degrees between both. An example for business logic might be the calculation of prices, which often follows complicated rules for discounts, applying taxes, shipping rates etc.

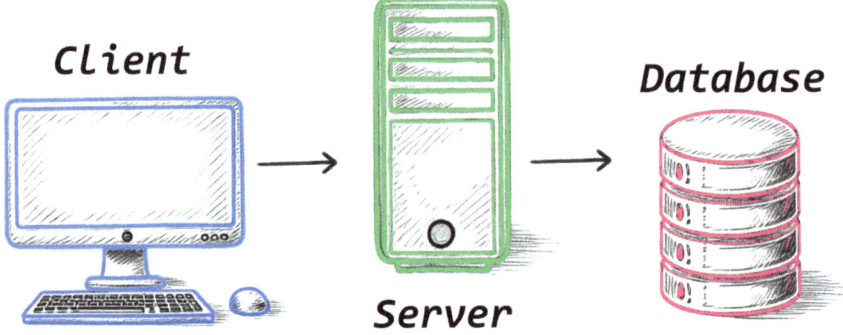

**Fig. 1.5** The 3-tier architecture

A disadvantage of 2-tier systems is that having business logic on the client side makes the client component rather heavy (often called fat clients), which might require powerful client PCs, and can easily cause problems if different users running different versions of the client software try to work together. On the other hand, keeping most of the business logic on the server side tends to overload the server, which of course also has the responsibility to store the data, and therefore can become a performance bottleneck for the whole application. 3-tier architectures address these issues by introducing an additional server-side tier, so that the client only has to deal with the user interface, one server tier is only responsible for the business logic, and the second server tier only takes care of storage.

No matter which architecture is chosen, various problems remain. Client computers typically use custom software that has to be updated regularly to fix bugs and to implement new features, creating potential issues if such updates are not performed on all the client computers of an application at the same time. The server side faces additional issues. In particular, in order to ensure that the failure of a single machine (a server) does not make the whole application unavailable for all its users, all the components on the server side have to be implemented redundantly. Additionally, many systems do not have a constant workload, but one that fluctuates over time. In order to work without interruptions, the server side has to be powerful enough for the highest required performance level, and is consequently partially idle for the majority of the time, wasting additional resources (in addition to the often idle redundant systems). And this is true for each of the applications used in an organization. Since organizations typically have multiple different applications that are used by different corporate functions (such as sales, purchasing, finance, accounting, research and design etc.), and that are created at different points in time, using whatever approaches and technologies are considered state-of-the-art at those times, this often results in highly complex, hard to maintain and under-utilized IT landscapes in organizations. For example, it is not uncommon for a company to have a few applications running on legacy UltraSparc servers running Solaris Unix, some Windows Server based applications (typically using different, often obsolete versions), in addition to several other applications running on various Linux platforms.

To ensure sufficient scalability and fault tolerance, several physical servers for each application have to be maintained.

### 1.4.3 Grid Computing

At the end of the 1990s, we have seen a considerable increase in commodity computer and network performance, mainly as a result of faster hardware and more sophisticated software. Nevertheless, there were still problems, in the fields of science, engineering and business, which could not be solved effectively with the generation of supercomputers used at that time. In fact, due to their size and complexity, these problems were often numerically and/or data intensive and required a variety of heterogeneous resources that were not available from a single machine. A number of teams had conducted experimental studies on the cooperative use of geographically distributed resources conceived as a single powerful computer. This new approach was known as *Grid Computing*.

The main problem about running tasks on this platform is related the heterogeneity of the machines involved in terms both of hardware and software (including the operating system). At that time users/developers who wanted to submit their tasks had to write applications able to face various kind of failures (hardware, software and network) that also had to be compatible with the operating systems and libraries provided by the computers involved in the grid. As a matter of fact, modern virtualization techniques were not available at the time, so for example, developers had to write two version of their application, one for Unix machines and one for Windows machines, if they wanted to exploit machines from both operating systems.

Once virtualization had reached good levels of both performance and stability, the Grid Computing platform was gradually abandoned in favor of cloud computing, where developers can decide in which operating systems their application must be executed.

### 1.4.4 Virtualized Data Centers

Virtualization technology, which makes it possible to run multiple so-called virtual machines on a single physical computer, became widely used in the 2000s. Each virtual machine has its own (often different) operating system installed, and for each operating system and its applications the virtual machine behaves as if it was a separate physical machine. For example, a physical server with 16 CPU cores and 64 GB of physical memory can run four virtual machines with 4 virtual CPUs and 16 GB of memory each. For the software (operating system and application software) in each virtual machine it appears as if it was running on its own physical machine with 4 cores and 16 GB.

Virtualization has three key aspects—isolation, encapsulation and compatibility. Isolation describes the fact that virtual machines on a single physical server behave as if they were in fact on separate servers—for example, errors in one VM do not affect other VMs. Encapsulation describes that the entire state of a virtual machine (including virtual hardware, installed operating system, installed applications and all their data and state) are simply a (large) file on the machine hosting the VM. This makes it easy to create backups of VMs and to move them between servers. Finally, compatibility means that the operating system and software in a virtual machine is decoupled from the underlying hardware. Whatever virtual hardware the virtualization software supports it can offer on any physical hardware that it supports. This means that it becomes possible to host legacy hardware in virtual machines on modern physical servers.

These advantages make so-called virtualized data centers very attractive. In such a data center, the servers running business applications do not run directly on physical hardware, but in virtual machines that are hosted on physical servers. This has multiple advantages: Due to VM compatibility, different kinds of servers can be hosted on a single, homogeneous server platform, which reduces complexity and maintenance costs. Encapsulation allows virtual machines to be moved easily between different physical machines, and isolation makes it safe to host multiple different applications in different VMs on the same physical server. Together, these properties significantly reduce costs, as they allow for a higher overall utilization of hardware resources and more efficient server management.

## *1.4.5 Cloud Computing*

While cloud computing data centers extensively use virtualization, cloud computing is more than just using virtualization. In non-cloud virtualized data centers, assigning VMs to physical servers and making decisions about moving them (e.g. due to load changes) are not automated, but typically manually done by operators. Cloud computing adds another layer of abstraction on top of the virtualization layer.

In cloud computing systems, users do not need to know about the underlying physical hardware. This is true no matter what cloud deployment model (e.g. private or public) is used, and irrespective of the cloud service model (e.g. IaaS or PaaS) chosen. The fact that there are different service models is a feature of cloud computing—in simple virtualized data centers, Infrastructure as a Service (i.e. using virtual machines instead of dealing with the underlying physical hardware directly) is the standard mode of operation.

Modern cloud computing depends on fast, reliable and affordable computer networks and mature and efficient virtualization. Consequently, it only became feasible in the last approximately 20 years. It has been argued that cloud computing is in fact just "old wine in a new bottle", implying that it is essentially no different than the first time sharing systems on mainframes over 50 years ago. While it is true that there are some superficial similarities between then and now—such as centralized computing (then on a mainframe, now in a large data center) that is accessed from remote devices (then simple computer terminals, now just about any device with a web browser). However, this architecture back then was based on necessity—if you could only afford a single computer, you had to share it. Modern cloud computing is not a necessity, just (typically) an improvement over more traditional, in-house IT. Also, modern cloud computing platforms offer a wide range of very powerful computing resources—from simple virtual machines to powerful AI-driven programming interfaces.

A discussion of the history of cloud computing would be amiss without mentioning the first public cloud provider. On August 24, 2006, Amazon (then "only" a large online retailer) announced the "Amazon Elastic Compute Cloud". How Amazon decided to not just get into, but invent this new business of cloud computing is an interesting story.[17] In simple terms, executives at Amazon realized that they were very efficient at running the large IT infrastructure they needed to support their e-commerce business. They concluded that it might be a profitable business model to offer access to their IT services to other companies (who were probably less efficient in running their own IT). It probably did not hurt that Amazon's business (and consequently their internal IT capacity needs) fluctuate significantly over the course of a year—with e.g. the Christmas season being very busy for a retailer, while other parts of the year are much less busy. Hence, it made perfect sense to offer the part of their IT resources that sat idle for a lot of the year to outside customers for a profit. The history of AWS is discussed in more detail in Sect. 3.4.1.

## 1.5 Summary

In summary, while cloud computing can be used in a number of different deployment (public, private etc.) and service (SaaS, PaaS, IaaS) models, its main characteristic and common feature is that computing resources (e.g. storage or virtual machines) can be allocated and deallocated very flexibly from a large pool of such resources. This ability gives cloud service users agility and often makes cloud computing the preferred approach to implement applications, especially since additional benefits such as cost savings and increased reliability can often be realized through cloud use as well. However, cloud computing is no magical solution to all IT problems either—it comes with its own sets of risks and challenges, is not suitable in all situations, and only delivers its potential advantages if implemented well. How to do this is one of the main subjects of the remaining chapters of this book.

---

[17] More info here: https://techcrunch.com/2016/07/02/andy-jassys-brief-history-of-the-genesis-of-aws/.

## 1.6 Key Terms

**Cloud Computing** is a practice where a network of remote servers hosted on the internet are used to store, manage, and process data, rather than a local server or a personal computer.

**Cloud Service Model** Cloud service models describe different ways of how the responsibility to operate the different levels of an application (from the underlying operating system at the bottom to the actual software application itself at the top) is broken down between cloud service provider and user.

**IaaS** Infrastructure as a service is a cloud service model that provides on-demand access to computing resources such as servers, storage, networking, and virtualization.

**PaaS** Platform as a service is a cloud service model that allows user to deploy their applications without worrying about the underlying virtual infrastructure.

**SaaS** Software as a service is a cloud service model that offers users ready-to-use software applications hosted in the cloud.

**Cloud Deployment Model** Cloud deployment models describe who operates the cloud infrastructure for cloud users.

**Public Cloud** A public cloud provider offers cloud infrastructure to a range of paying customer organizations.

**Private Cloud** In a private cloud, an organization operates its own cloud infrastructure in-house.

**Hybrid Cloud** An organization that uses hybrid cloud combines both private and public cloud resources.

**Semi-private Cloud** A semi-private cloud provider hosts cloud infrastructure for a range of paying customer organizations. In contrast to a public cloud, this deployment model typically exhibits no multitenancy, i.e. physical resources (such as servers) are not shared between multiple customers.

**Community Cloud** A group of organizations that combine their financial and other resources to host a shared cloud infrastructure exclusively for members of the group operate a community cloud.

**Multitenancy** describes the situation in which for example a public cloud provider hosts virtual resources (such as virtual machines) of multiple different client organizations on the same physical server.

**Elasticity** is the property of a cloud to grow or shrink capacity for CPU, memory, and storage resources to adapt to the changing demands of an organization.

**Vendor Lock-In** describes the situation in which an organization finds it hard to switch from one service provider to another one, for example because the services are not compatible. In cloud computing, this is generally not a contractual lock-in, but one that is created by the practical difficulties or costs from switching providers.

**Grid Computing** describes the practice of combining computational resources from a distributed number of computers to solve complex computational tasks.

**Virtualized Data Center** In virtualized data centers, individual applications are not run directly on physical servers. Instead, virtualization software is deployed on the physical infrastructure, and applications are deployed in virtual machines.

## 1.7 Review Questions

1. What is cloud computing?
2. What are the different cloud service models?
3. What are the different cloud deployment models?
4. Discuss the benefits of cloud computing.
5. What are some common challenges of cloud computing?
6. What is vendor lock-in and how can it be avoided?
7. What is the difference between Grid computing and Cloud computing?

## 1.8 Exercises

The following laboratory exercises contain questions that require written responses and, in some instances, accompanying screenshots. If the exercises have been given as an assignment, please ensure that all answers and requested screenshots are compiled into a separate document for submission to the instructor, as specified by the instructor.

### 1.8.1 Elasticity in Public Cloud

Consider 3 different organizations A, B and C that each could host their main IT application in a public cloud or in-house. Organization A is an online retailer, and their online store can be handled by one server most of the time, except it requires two servers between 12pm and 2pm and four servers between 5pm and 11pm. Organization B is a streaming platform, and its online streaming service requires one server most of the time, except two servers between 5pm and 7pm and four servers between 7pm and 11pm. Organization C is a manufacturer business, and its ERP system requires one server most of the time, except six servers between 9am and 5pm.

If each organization hosted its system in-house and had exactly as many servers as it needs during its peak period, what average server utilization would each achieve? Hint: Break down how many servers are used during each hour of the day.

If all three organizations hosted their systems with the same public cloud provider, which hosts only the systems of these three organizations, and has exactly as many servers as are needed during the combined peak of the three organizations, what average server utilization would the cloud provider achieve?

The difference in average utilization between a public cloud provider and individual organizations is likely even bigger than illustrated in this example. Why do you think this is the case?

### 1.8.2 Cloud Pricing

Based on the Google Cloud Platform (GCP) compute engine price list as of October 2024, a regular virtual machine with 4 CPU cores and 16 GB of memory costs approximately 20 cents (US) per hour, which is equivalent to about $144 (US) per month of uninterrupted use. Given that desktop PC with similar specifications can be purchased for less than $1000 (US), would you consider the virtual machine to be (too) expensive?

Hints:

- Consider different uses of the machine. Is it used continuously, or only at certain times? Do you need a single machine, or is it sometimes better to use several machines for a brief period of time?
- Is purchasing a computer really equivalent to using a virtual machine in the cloud? Are there other costs (besides the purchase price of the hardware) that are included in the cloud service cost? Does the importance of some of these differences depend on what the machine is used for? Consider factors like fault tolerance and reliability here as well.

### 1.8.3 Cloud Computing vs. Other IT Services

Assume a university makes an agreement with an IT service provider, in which the service provider commits to hosting ten servers for the university (used for various purposes, such as learning system, web site hosting etc.) for a year, with an annual renewal option for the university. How (if at all) is such an outsourcing appointment different from public cloud computing?

Hint: Consider to what degree the different aspects of the NIST definition of cloud computing are met in this scenario!

# Chapter 2
# Technical Foundations

The purpose of this chapter is not to give readers all the background necessary to fully understand all aspects of cloud computing—this could fill multiple books, as a basic understanding of a range of topics including computer programming, software design and architecture, operating systems, computer networks and several more would be necessary. Instead, it highlights the main technical foundations that made the widespread adoption of cloud computing possible and looks in some more detail at some technologies that are crucial for cloud computing.

## 2.1 Networking

Arguably, the single most important technical factor enabling modern cloud computing is the availability of high-speed networking. Moving IT resources (e.g. computing power, storage, or whole applications) to the cloud (i.e., a remote location) is clearly only sensible and desirable if sufficiently high bandwidth and low latency networking connections are available.

For example, in the days of 56K modems, which could only transmit 56 KBit (i.e. 7 KBytes) of data per second, synchronizing local storage (even if it might have only amounted to tens or hundreds of MBytes of data) with a location in the cloud, or running applications in the cloud in the case of Software as a Service, and transmitting the whole user interface across the network was clearly not technically feasible. In contrast to this, while data volumes have grown significantly (as have screen resolutions, which are often Full HD or even 4K now), end-user Internet speeds have grown by an even larger factor of around a thousand since those days. This is true of both cable or DSL based Internet access as well as wireless access (be it through wifi networks or 4G and 5G connections).

Similarly, *Local Area Network* (LAN) speeds to connect servers in data centers, which used to be for instance 10 MBit Ethernet can now easily reach or exceed 10 GBit per second. The bandwidth of wide area networking (WAN) connections, which typically use fiber optical cables, has grown in a similar way.

Network latency is primarily determined by the numbers of "hops" (in particular, routers) that a networking package has to pass through from its source to its destination. This number of hops primarily depends on the geographic distance. Consequently, sufficiently low latencies especially for interactive applications can only be achieved by reducing the distance that network connections have to travel. Public cloud service providers are able to provide most of their customers with fairly local network connections because they have data centers in multiple locations globally.

In order to use cloud computing effectively, a basic understanding of computer networking is necessary. The following sections summarize the most important aspects for cloud computing.

### 2.1.1 Network Stack

The most frequently used framework to describe the network stack is the 7-layer OSI model (see Fig. 2.1). From the bottom to the top it consists of the following layers:

| Layer | Function |
|---|---|
| 7. Application | Support for application |
| 6. Presentation | Protocol conversion, data translation |
| 5. Session | Establishes, manages, and terminates sessions |
| 4. Transport | Ensures error free packets |
| 3. Network | Provides routing decisions |
| 2. Data Link | Provides for the flow of data |
| 1. Physical | Signals and media |

**Fig. 2.1** The 7-layer OSI model

1. **Physical Layer:** Deals with networking hardware, such as cables, the RJ45 connector for twisted pair Ethernet cables etc.
2. **Data Link Layer:** Specifies communication between devices directly connected to each other in the same network. Ethernet is the most common standard. At this level, MAC-addresses that uniquely identify individual devices are used by switches to send Ethernet frames to the intended recipient only.
3. **Network Layer:** Enables devices in different networks to communicate with each other. The IPv4 or IPv6 protocols are used to create different networks and subnets, and routers use these addresses to send packets to remote hosts.
4. **Transport Layer:** Protocols like TCP allow reliable end-to-end communication between two hosts, with features such as error detection, automatic retransmission of lost packets and flow control. Ports are used to allow network traffic to reach

the correct application even when multiple applications communicate over the network on the same host at the same time.
5. **Session Layer:** Creates the ability to organize network communication into sessions, keeping track of state between individual network messages.
6. **Presentation Layer:** Specifies how characters, photos and videos are encoded and decoded between sender and receiver, allows for compression and encryption of data etc.
7. **Application Layer:** Defines the communication protocols of the specific network application, such as file transfer, hyper text transfer or email.

| OSI Model Layer Number | OSI Model Layer | TCP/IP Protocol Suite Layer |
|---|---|---|
| 7 | Application | Application |
| 6 | Presentation | |
| 5 | Session | |
| 4 | Transport | Transport |
| 3 | Network | Internet |
| 2 | Data Link | Link (or Network Access) |
| 1 | Physical | |

**Fig. 2.2** The 7-layer ISO model vs the 4-layer TCP/IP model

Note that while the 7-layer ISO model is widely used when teaching about the networking stack, in practice the 4-layer TCP/IP is predominant (see Fig. 2.2). It combines the bottom two layers of the ISO model (the Physical and Data Link Layer) into one layer called Link (or Network Access) layer. The Network layer (ISO layer 3) is equivalent to the Internet layer in the TCP/IP stack, while the Transport layer (ISO layer 4) is the same in the TCP/IP stack. Finally, the top three layers of the ISO model (Session, Presentation and Application) are combined to the Application layer in the TCP/IP stack.

Network communication happens top down at the sender and bottom up at the receiver. For example, when a user clicks on a link in a web browser, this might initiate a request sent to a web server using the http protocol. This request is passed down to the transport layer, where, if this is the first interaction with that server, a three-way handshake[1] between the sender and receiver is performed to establish a TCP connection. Each TCP message is then handed down to the network layer,

---
[1] https://en.wikipedia.org/wiki/Handshake_(computing).

where it might be put into multiple IPv4 packets. These IP packets are passed down to the Data Link layer, which results in Ethernet frames, which, at the physical layer, might leave the computer over a twisted pair Ethernet cable.

To reach the destination, multiple Switches and Routers are typically traversed before the final destination—the web server—is reached. The network interface card at the server passes the traffic from the physical layer up to the Data Link layer, which determines that the destination MAC address is identical with its own MAC address, and consequently passes the data up to the Network Layer, which in turn passes it up to the Transport Layer, which checks the incoming packets using the integrated checksum, reassembles multiple packets in the correct order and passes them up to the web server software listening on the http port 80.

The most commonly used networking devices to connect different hosts and networks are switches and routers. Switches connect multiple hosts in the same network and send messages directly from the sender to the receiver, as long as they are both in the same network. If a host wants to send a packet to a host in a different network, it will send it to its default gateway, which is typically a router. Routers connect different networks together. They have a routing table, based on which they make a decision for each incoming packet as to the port to which they should be forwarded to get closer to their final destination.

## 2.1.2 Network Layer and IPv4

Cloud service users mostly work in the network layer and above, because the lower layers (physical and data link layers) are typically handled by the cloud service provider. At the network layer, the most commonly used protocol is still IPv4. In it, individual hosts have 32 bit network addresses. For convenience, addresses are usually broken down into four 8-bit numbers separated by dots. For example, the IP address 10.1.1.128 stands for the binary value 00001010.00000001.00000001.10000000.

In IPv4, hosts are placed into networks. In each IP address, a specific number of leading bits is used to identify the network, while the remaining bits identify the host within the network. The number of bits that identify the network is usually specified using a network mask, which is the decimal notation of a sequence of 1s followed by a sequence of 0s. For example, the network mask 255.0.0.0 would signify that the first eight bits of an IP address identify the network and the remaining 24 bits identify the host.[2]

The IPv4 standard defines different classes of IP networks. In class A networks, 8 bits are used to identify the network and the resulting 24 bits are used to identify the hosts. In class B networks, 16 bits each are used for both the network and the host, while class C networks reverse the allocation of class A networks by using 24 bits to identify the network and 8 bits to identify the host. Figure 2.3 shows the allocation of the IPv4 address range to these three classes of network.

---

[2] Note that 255 in binary is 11111111.

2.1 Networking

| Class | First Octet decimal (range) | First Octet binary (range) | IP Range | Subnet Mask | Hosts for Network ID | # of Networks |
|---|---|---|---|---|---|---|
| Class A | 0 - 127 | 0XXXXXXX | 0.0.0.0-127.255.255.255 | 255.0.0.0 | $2^{24} - 2$ | $2^7$ |
| Class B | 128 - 191 | 10XXXXXX | 128.0.0.0-191.255.255.255 | 255.255.0.0 | $2^{16} - 2$ | $2^{14}$ |
| Class C | 192 - 223 | 110XXXXX | 192.0.0.0-223.255.255.255 | 255.255.255.0 | $2^8 - 2$ | $2^{21}$ |
| Class D (Multicast) | 224 -239 | 1110XXXX | 224.0.0.0-239.255.255.255 | | | |
| Class E (Experimental) | 240 - 255 | 1111XXXX | 240.0.0.0-255.255.255.255 | | | |

**Fig. 2.3** Classes of IP networks

Class D networks in the figure are used for multicasting, while class E network were reserved for future extensions of IPv4 and are not actually used.

Often, an organization wants to break a network into smaller subnets. This is especially true for the larger class A and B networks, but even a class C network with 256 different addresses is usually larger than necessary. Breaking networks into subnets has multiple purposes and advantages. For instance, smaller subnets suffer less performance degradation from necessary broadcasts within the network. Furthermore, networks are often used to group users who need access to the same resources such as server applications together. For example, an organization might have a subnet for all employees of the accounting department. All computers in this subnet would then have direct network access to the accounting servers which would be in the same network, while other employees would be in different subnets from which they would have no direct access.

For example, an organization might decide to break a class C network into eight subnets. Instead of having a subnet mask of 255.255.255.0 (the default mask for class C networks), they would instead use the subnet mask 255.255.255.224. Note that 224 in binary is 1110 0000. Since three bits are used for subnetting, eight different subnets are possible—subnets 000, 001, 010, 011, 100, 101, 110 and 111. This leaves five bits for the actual IP address, so $2^5 = 32$ different addresses within each subnet are possible. Since by definition IP addresses with all zeros in the host portion are used to identify a network, and IP addresses with all ones in the host portion are used as the broadcast address for a network, each of the eight subnets would in practice contain 30 available IP addresses for hosts. Note that there is also a shorter CIDR (classless inter-domain routing) notation. Rather than using an IP address like 192.168.1.0 together with a subnet mask like 255.255.255.224, this subnetting approach would simply be denoted as 192.168.1.0/27, to indicate (equivalently to the subnet mask notation) that 27 bits are used to identify each subnet and 5 bits are used to identify individual hosts. With this classless approach, any desired number of bits of IP addresses can be allocated for the network and host portions, going beyond the fixed allocation into class A, B and C networks. This allows for more efficient use of the available IPv4 address space,

## 2.1.3 Shortage of IPv4 Addresses and IPv6

When the IPv4 protocol was originally devised in the early 1980s, the number of networked computers (in the absence of smartphones etc.) was small enough to make the available address space of approximately 4 billion IP addresses ($2^{32}$ = 4, 294, 967, 296) seem plentiful. However, once the Internet became successful and the personal use of networked devices became widespread, it quickly became clear that the number of devices would soon be larger than the number of available IP addresses. This problem was made even more acute by the inefficient allocation of IP addresses in the early days of IPv4, where some organizations were assigned class A networks with over 16 million IP addresses, usually resulting in a large number of unused IP addresses.

Two main approaches were devised to deal with this IPv4 address shortage: Private IP addresses and IPv6.

Out of the overall IPv4 address space, three address ranges were dedicated for internal (private) IP address use in organizations. These address ranges are all IP addresses beginning with 10, all IP addresses from 172.16 to 172.31 and all IP addresses beginning with 192.168. These addresses are not routable, i.e. a router will discard any IP packets that have any of these addresses as a destination. Together with the concept of Network Address Translation (NAT) this means that these addresses can be used by anybody (and consequently many times over). A typical use of this in private households looks as follows: A home router (a device that combines the functionality of a router and a switch) is assigned a single public IPv4 address by the provider when online. The home router creates an internal network using a private IPv4 address range (such as 192.168.1.0 to 192.168.1.255) in which all devices with Internet access in this household are placed. In multi-person households this can easily be ten or more devices (smart phones, tablets, laptops, desktop PCs, smart TVs, other smart devices etc.). The home router translates back and forth between the internal (private) IP addresses of each device and the single external IP address, which is the only IP address visible outside of the network (e.g. to web servers that are accessed). This way, the single public IPv4 address can be shared by multiple devices, reducing the shortage of IPv4 addresses.

The second approach to overcome the limited number of IPv4 addresses is the use of the IPv6 protocol, which was first standardized in 1995.[3] IPv6 uses 128 bit long addresses, which allows for vastly more IP addresses than IPv4—to be specific, for $2^{128}$ or approximately $3.4 \times 10^{38}$ ones. The need for backward compatibility and the inability to update many legacy applications made a direct switch from IPv4 to IPv6 infeasible. Instead, dual stack approaches (in which networks and devices use both IPv4 and IPv6 simultaneously) and tunneling (in which IPv6 traffic can be "tunneled" through legacy IPv4 networks) are typically used.

While the shortage of IPv4 address has become more acute in recent years, which is reflected in the increased charges for public IPv4 addresses by public cloud providers, mitigation approaches such as the use of private IPv4 addresses with NAT

---

[3] https://datatracker.ietf.org/doc/html/rfc1883.

have been so successful that a full transition from IPv4 to IPv6 in the near future is generally not considered likely by experts (see e.g. [4]).

## 2.1.4 Transport Layer

The IP protocol on the Network layer enables the addressing and routing of network traffic between hosts on any connected networks. The Transport layer builds on this to allow for reliable transmission of data. The two most commonly used protocols for this purpose are the Transmission Control Protocol (TCP) and the User Datagram Protocol (UDP).

TCP allows for the reliable transmission of data and is used for instance to transmit emails or web pages. TCP breaks data into smaller segments, transmits them over the network and reassembles them again in the correct order at the destination. It uses checksums to verify that no information was corrupted in transmission, and automatically retransmits any incorrect or missing segments. TCP is the protocol of choice when correct data transmission occasionally delayed is preferable over prompt but occasionally incorrect data transmission—which is the case e.g. for emails or web sites. In contrast, in some applications such as video streaming or digital phone calls minor transmission errors are barely if at all noticeable (e.g. a few pixels in a video that have the wrong color for a fraction of a second). For such uses, waiting for retransmission of slightly corrupted segments of data would be counterproductive, because the consequence—an interrupted video stream—would be much less desirable. Therefore, for these applications UDP is used.

Irrespective of the protocol at the Transport layer, the concept of ports is used to allow multiple applications on each host to send and receive data over the network simultaneously. For example, a server might want to offer web server and email server functionality at the same time. In order to make sure that the network stack delivers incoming network packets to the correct destination application, different ports are used, for example port 80 for the http protocol to reach the web server and port 143 for the IMAP protocol to reach the email server.

Ports can also be used by firewalls, which are one of the key tools for securing computer networks. Firewalls are typically placed between different networks and apply a set of firewall rules to decide for each in-and outgoing network packet whether it should be allowed to proceed or filtered out. For example, if a specific network segment only contains an email server but no web server, the firewall could be configured such that it allows traffic on all ports used by the email server (such as the IMAP port 143), while traffic on all other ports is filtered out.

---

[4] https://blog.apnic.net/2024/10/22/the-ipv6-transition/.

## 2.1.5 Session, Presentation and Application Layers

The higher layers of the ISO stack are quite dependent on the specific application—aspects such as encryption, the encoding of different character sets or image files and the use of sessions in multi-message communications highly depends on what is sent over the network and for what purpose, which makes a more in-depth discussion here impossible.

One exception to this is the Domain Name System (DNS) protocol, which is used across many different applications to allow for the use of more user-friendly names instead of comparatively cryptic IP addresses. The DNS system resides on layer 7 (the application layer of the network stack) and is essentially a hierarchically organized mapping system between domain names and IP addresses. In it, an organization owning a domain such as example.com maintains an authoritative DNS server that knows the names and IP addresses of all servers in this domain, such as www.example.com or mail.example.com. One level higher, Top-Level Domain (TLD) servers know how to find the authoritative severs of all the subdomains within a top-level domain such as ".com", ".ca" or ".de". At the top of the hierarchy, DNS root servers simply know how to reach all the top-level domain servers.

When a user tries to access a server by its domain name, a local DNS client called resolver can resolve any DNS name such as www.example.com by first contacting a root server to find the correct TLD server for ".com", which it can then in turn query to find the authoritative server for "example.com", which in turn can return the correct IP address for "www.example.com" to be used at lower ISO protocol levels. This multi-step name resolution can either be performed by the resolver itself, which is called iterative DNS resolution (see Fig. 2.4), or it can be performed on its behalf by a resolving name server if recursive DNS name resolution is used.

## 2.1.6 Important Networking Commands

A brief discussion of some of the most important networking commands completes the discussion of networking. The commands are discussed in their Microsoft Windows version—the same or very similar commands exist in different platforms such as Linux. To run any of the commands, simply open a command prompt on a Windows computer.

The **ipconfig** command outputs information about the network configuration of the local machine. Here is its syntax:

    ipconfig [options]

## 2.1 Networking

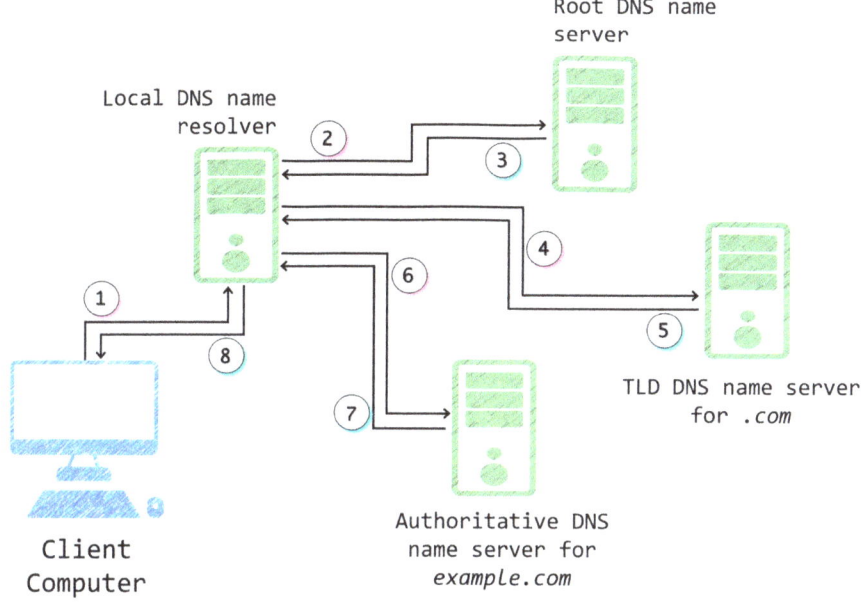

**Fig. 2.4** The iterative DNS resolution

```
Link-local IPv6 Address . . . . . : fe80::9467:1911:bb22:7152%10
IPv4 Address. . . . . . . . . . . : 192.168.1.185
Subnet Mask . . . . . . . . . . . : 255.255.255.0
Default Gateway . . . . . . . . . : fe80::ac7:f5ff:feb6:a4c4%10
                                    192.168.1.254
```

**Fig. 2.5** Sample output of the command ipconfig

Figure 2.5 shows an excerpt of the output of the command ipconfig, listing both the local IPv4 and IPv6 addresses as well as the corresponding default gateways.

One of the most important options is **/ALL**, which shows additional information, including the physical (MAC) address of the network interface.

The **ping** command attempts to reach a specified host using the Internet Control Message Protocol (ICMP) . Here is its syntax:

   ping [options] target

```
C:\>ping www.google.com
Pinging www.google.com [2607:f8b0:400a:80a::2004] with 32 bytes of data:
Reply from 2607:f8b0:400a:80a::2004: time=10ms
Reply from 2607:f8b0:400a:80a::2004: time=10ms
Reply from 2607:f8b0:400a:80a::2004: time=9ms
Reply from 2607:f8b0:400a:80a::2004: time=9ms

Ping statistics for 2607:f8b0:400a:80a::2004:
    Packets: Sent = 4, Received = 4, Lost = 0 (0% loss),
Approximate round trip times in milli-seconds:
    Minimum = 9ms, Maximum = 10ms, Average = 9ms
```

**Fig. 2.6** Sample output of the command ping

Figure 2.6 shows an application of the ping command to test whether the local machine can reach the server www.google.com.

By default, the command tries to reach the target four times, and displays statistics about the time (in milliseconds) the response took, as well as potential packet loss.

The ping command offers numerous options, for example, allowing users to specify the number of desired pings, the size of the data packet used in the pings or the timeout interval to use.

To find out the mapping of a domain name to an IP address, the command **nslookup** can be used. It has the following syntax:

nslookup target

```
C:\>nslookup www.google.com
Server:   node-1w7jr9phx8n9y6vatptukcc78.ipv6.telus.net
Address:  2001:569:504e:c500:ac7:f5ff:feb6:a4c4

Non-authoritative answer:
Name:    www.google.com
Addresses:  2607:f8b0:400a:807::2004
          142.250.217.68
```

**Fig. 2.7** Sample output of the command nslookup

Figure 2.7 shows sample output of the command.

With the command **tracert** (short for trace route), users can track the path a newtwork package takes from the local system to its destination. It also shows the latency betweent he different routers on the way, which can make it a helpful command to figure out the cause of network latencies. It has the following syntax:

## 2.1 Networking

tracert target

```
C:\>tracert www.google.com
Tracing route to www.google.com [2607:f8b0:400a:807::2004]
over a maximum of 30 hops:

  1     4 ms     4 ms     4 ms  node-1w7jr9phx8n9y6vatptukcc78.ipv6.telus.net [2001:569:504e:c500:ac7:f5ff:feb6:a4c4]
  2     5 ms     6 ms     5 ms  node-1w7jr9mlwgv1iufk9jmh2t43q.ipv6.telus.net [2001:568:f002:2::6]
  3     8 ms     8 ms     9 ms  node-1w7jr9fenjgbk2vrqtjijbdph.ipv6.telus.net [2001:568:1::525]
  4     8 ms     8 ms     8 ms  2001:4860:1:1::16fc
  5     8 ms     8 ms     8 ms  2607:f8b0:832f::1
  6     8 ms     8 ms     8 ms  sea30s10-in-x04.1e100.net [2607:f8b0:400a:807::2004]

Trace complete.
```

**Fig. 2.8** Sample output of the command tracert

Figure 2.8 shows a sample output of the command.

Finally, the command **netstat** can be used to display current TCP/IP network connections and network statistics. It has the following syntax:

netstat [options]

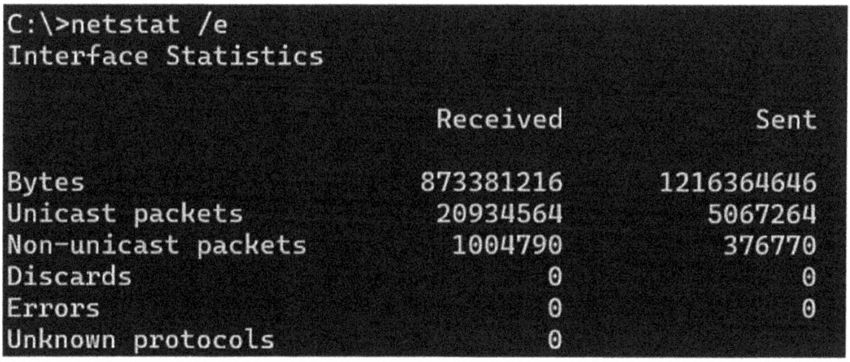

```
C:\>netstat /e
Interface Statistics

                          Received            Sent

Bytes                    873381216      1216364646
Unicast packets            20934564         5067264
Non-unicast packets         1004790          376770
Discards                          0               0
Errors                            0               0
Unknown protocols                 0
```

**Fig. 2.9** Sample output of the command netstat

Invoked without options, netstat displays a list of all open TCP/IP connections. Examples of useful options are /e, which displays Ethernet statistics, and /r, which displays the contents of the IT routing table.

Figure 2.9 shows an example of output of the netstat command.

## 2.2 Virtualization

Besides inexpensive and high-speed networking, modern virtualization technology is arguably the second major enabler for cloud computing. The development and usefulness of server virtualization depends on another factor—the availability of inexpensive servers with multiple CPU cores and large amounts of memory.

The idea behind virtualization is pretty simple: Computing resources (primarily CPU cores, main memory, storage, networking bandwidth) can be virtually partitioned into a number of virtual machines. For example, a server with 64 CPU cores and 128 GByte of main memory could be partitioned to host 16 virtual machines with 4 CPU cores and 8 GBytes of working memory each. The software (including the operating system) running within each of these virtual machines could not distinguish this situation from one where it runs on an actual physical machine with only 4 CPU cores and 8 GBytes of memory.

Virtualization is beneficial in many different contexts and for a number of reasons. For example, a web developer might use a number of virtual machines to test the application under development on different operating systems and browsers. Without virtualization, a separate physical machine per test system would be required, significantly increasing cost and space requirements. Similar benefits apply in data centers, where consolidating a number of different servers, which, especially if they are older, can easily be run as multiple virtual machines on a modern server, can significantly reduce cost factors such as server maintenance needs, space requirements, power consumption etc.

### 2.2.1 Virtualization Technology

In virtualization, a hypervisor (also called virtual machine manager) is used. The hypervisor is a piece of software that sits between the physical hardware and the virtual machines. To each individual virtual machine it presents a possibly different virtual hardware interface. Any hardware access from the operating system or software running within each virtual machine, such as the use of CPU time, allocation of memory, access to storage or networking, is mapped to the underlying physical hardware.

As illustrated in Fig. 2.10, two types of hypervisor are typically distinguished: Type 1 and Type 2 hypervisors. Type 2 hypervisors run on top of a separate operating system. The open source hypervisor VirtualBox[5] is an example. Users install VirtualBox on their normal computer operating system (such as Windows 11, Linux or MacOS), and can then create virtual machines running whatever (same or other) operating system is required. An advantage of Type 2 hypervisors is that they do not require a separate computer dedicated to the hypervisor. For example, a software developer can install VirtualBox on their normal development machine, alongside with

---

[5] https://www.virtualbox.org/.

## 2.2 Virtualization

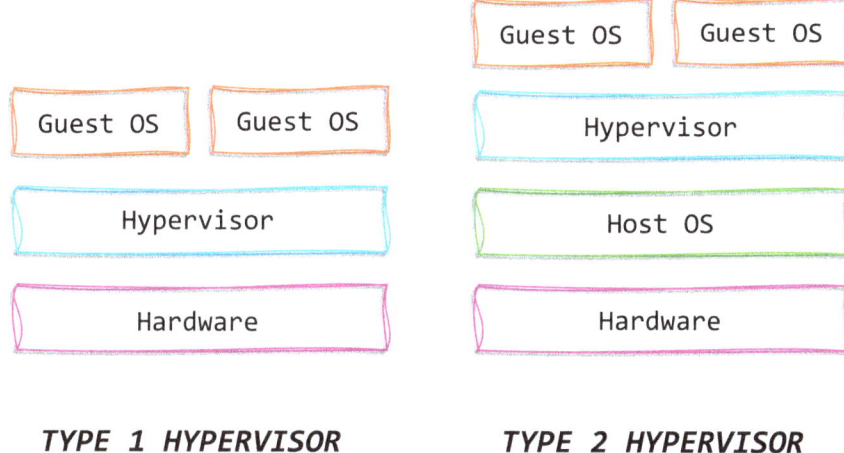

**Fig. 2.10** The two hypervisor types

their normal development environment, to try out the software under development under different operating systems in different virtual machines.

A significant disadvantage of Type 2 hypervisors is that they do not have direct access to the underlying hardware—they are managed by the underlying operating system themselves. Therefore, for high performance requirements, Type 1 hypervisors are better suited. Type 1 hypervisors such as the Citrix Hypervisor (formerly XenServer[6]) run directly on the physical hardware, without the use of a separate operating system. Therefore, Type 1 hypervisors have full control of the hardware, which generally allows them to achieve higher levels of availability, security and performance.

Modern virtualization software offers many powerful features to achieve these properties for their virtualized systems. It is beyond the scope of this book to explore them all in detail, or even to examine virtualization in more depth.[7] Instead, we discuss just one advanced feature that is of particular importance in cloud computing: Live migration of virtual machines.

A data center that uses virtualization, especially a cloud data center, does not just use virtualization on a single physical server, but instead has a large number of physical servers running virtual machines on the chosen hypervisor. Live migration (sometimes also called hot migration) of virtual machines describes the ability to move a virtual machine from one physical server to another physical server with practically no interruption of the operating system and other software running in the virtual machine. For example, assume that the web server of an online retailer runs

---

[6] https://xenserver.org/.

[7] Interested reader might refer to e.g. "Virtualization Essentials" by Matthew Portnoy.

in a virtual machine on a specific physical server. There are many reasons why it might be desirable or necessary to move the virtual machine to a different server—for example, the server might be decommissioned to be replaced by a newer, more efficient model. If this is the case, an administrator would trigger the live migration of the running virtual machine to the hypervisor on a different physical machine. While this overall migration would take several minutes or even hours to complete, there would only be an extremely short period of time (probably a fraction of a second) during which the web server in the virtual machine would not respond as usual.

Live migration is performed in multiple steps:

1. The hypervisor on the source server contacts the hypervisor on the destination server and creates a new virtual machine with the settings of the source virtual machine.
2. The source hypervisor transfers the secondary storage of the virtual machine to the destination virtual machine.
3. The source hypervisor copies all read-only pages in memory to the destination VM.
4. The source hypervisor copies all read/write pages to the destination VM, and marks them as "clean" (i.e. already moved).
5. While the previous step happened, since the source virtual machine is running uninterrupted, it is likely that some of the read/write pages have been changed (e.g. because a customer put a product into their shopping cart in the meantime). Therefore, step 4 is repeated.
6. Note that step 5 should have taken much less time than step 4, because the number of "dirty" (i.e. modified) pages that have been changed during step 4 is likely rather small. If necessary, step 5 is repeated until the number of dirty pages becomes very small.
7. Once only a very small number of pages is "dirty", the source virtual machine is frozen, and the remaining dirty pages are transferred to the destination virtual machine.
8. Finally, it has to be ensured that all current users of the virtual machine are automatically (and transparently) switched over to the new VM instance on the new physical server. In typical configurations in which users connect through a proxy or load balancer, this can be realized by simply changing a destination IP address. Now the target VM is started, and the source VM can be turned off.

> **Common Hypervisors**
>
> There are numerous different virtualization software products available. They can be categorized into type 1 hypervisors, which run directly only a server without any operating system in between and are primarily intended for the use in data centers, and type 2 hypervisors, which run on top of host operating system and are more likely to be used by end users such as software developers on their PC or laptop computers. Common type 1 hypervisors include:
>
> - VMware ESXi, one of the leading commercial hypervisor platforms
> - Xen Server, an open source hypervisor often used in cloud environments
> - KVM, an open-source hypervisor integrated into the Linux kernel
> - Promox VE, a virtualization platform based on KVM
> - Microsoft Hyper-V, integrated into the Windows Server operating system
>
> Since type 2 hypervisors run on top of a host operating system, they can additionally be categorized by the platform they support. Common products include:
>
> - VMWare Workstation, a popular commercial hypervisor for Windows or Linux host systems
> - VirtualBox, a common opensource hypervisor that supports Windows, Linux and macOS
> - VMWare Fusion, a commercial hypervisor for macOS
> - Parallels Desktop, another commercial hypervisor for macOS
> - QEMU, a very flexible open source hypervisor for Linux

## 2.2.2 Virtualization Guarantees

Modern virtualization software offers the following three guarantees:

- **Isolation:** A virtual machine is strictly isolated from the underlying physical machine and any other virtual machines that might run on the same physical server. This isolation is crucial for security—a software bug or malware infection in the software running in a virtual machine does not put other virtual machines on the same physical server or the software running directly on the physical server at risk. This isolation even extends to system performance, because modern virtualization software can limit the allocation of hardware resources such as memory, CPU time or network bandwidth to virtual machines. In other words, a virtual machine cannot use up so many system resources that it slows down other virtual machines on the same server.

- **Encapsulation:** An entire virtual machine (including the installed operating system and applications with all their data, the contents of main memory and the state of all virtual devices) is contained in a single file. This has multiple benefits. For example, the state of a virtual machine at a given point in time can be captured easily by copying that file, which allows the restoration of the virtual machine to its state at that point in time, as well as the creation of an identical clone of a virtual machine on a different copy of the hypervisor. Similarly, pre-configured applications can easily be shared in the form of a virtual machine export.
- **Compatibility:** The virtualization layer isolates the virtual machines (and all the software that runs in them—operating system and applications)—from the underlying hardware. This allows users to run software that would otherwise require legacy hardware on modern servers, as long as the hypervisor supports the virtualization of the legacy hardware. For example, a company might still have an application that requires an obsolete version of Unix that is no longer supported by current hardware. This application can be run in a virtual machine if the hypervisor supports the required legacy hardware as virtual hardware. Additionally, changes to the underlying physical servers do not affect the software installed in virtual machines, as long as the hypervisor is compatible with the new server hardware, because it would continue to expose the same unchanged virtual hardware to the virtual machines.

It should be pointed out that while these virtualization guarantees are generally met by modern hypervisors, significant configuration errors or software bugs (in the hypervisor) or even hardware bugs (e.g. in the CPU) can break them. The most famous example for the latter are the Meltdown and Spectre vulnerabilities[8] that affect most current server CPUs, and that allow sophisticated attacks that can circumvent the strong isolation guarantees of hypervisors, allowing attackers to gain access to memory outside of their own virtual machine.

### *2.2.3 Benefits of Virtualization in Cloud Computing*

Even though both hardware and software vendors have come up with mitigations for side-channel attacks like Meltdown and Spectre, a certain level of vulnerability remains. However, for practical purposes, if a malicious user manages to use the fairly sophisticated attacks to break out of their virtual machine and successfully accesses memory that belongs to a different virtual machine on the same physical server, not too much is generally gained, because users have no control over which other tenants they share the same physical server with. Therefore, in practice, other kinds of attacks are generally more promising, making vulnerabilities like Meltdown and Spectre not very relevant. Hence, the isolation guarantee between different virtual machines on the same physical server can generally be considered to still apply.

---

[8] https://meltdownattack.com/.

This directly leads to the first benefit of virtualization for public cloud service providers: It allows them to use multitenancy, i.e. to put the virtual machines of several different customers on the same physical server. Doing so lets public cloud service providers maximize their hardware utilization, because "left over" hardware resources on a physical server can be used for virtual machines of any other customer. In other words, there is no need to reserve physical resources for individual customers.

The fact that the state of a virtual machine is completely encapsulated in a single file makes it significantly easier for cloud service providers to achieve fault tolerance. Encapsulation (especially in combination with VM live migration) makes it easy to take snapshots of virtual machines that can be used as backups of VM state at a given time, or to move a virtual machine from a server with hardware issues (e.g. the failure of a disk in a RAID array) to a different server. The ability to move virtual machines between different physical hosts also allows cloud service providers to maximize the utilization of their servers. One frequently taken approach is to overprovision hardware resources. For example, a provider might choose to allocate more total memory to the virtual machines on a physical server than the server actually possesses—say, run ten virtual machines with a promised allocation of 8 GBytes of memory each on a server with only 64 GBytes. Most of the time, not all virtual machines actually utilize all their allocated memory. If the required memory ever exceeds the physically available amount, some of the more memory intensive virtual machines can easily be moved to a different physical server with spare capacity, without the user even noticing.

Finally, compatibility of virtual machines allows cloud service providers to run very homogeneous data centers, even though their customers might require heterogeneous virtual machines. For example, customers might want to run applications on a wide range of operating systems, including different versions of Windows Server, several Linux variants and versions, and numerous other Unix systems, many of which might require legacy hardware. Rather than having to maintain a diverse collection of different servers supporting these operating systems and applications, virtualization allows cloud service providers to host all these different systems on hypervisors that run on whatever modern server platform is deemed to be most cost effective. As is be discussed in more detail in the next section, this homogeneity significantly reduces complexity and costs for the provider.

## 2.3 Linux

While cloud infrastructure and applications running in the cloud can operate under any operating system, the most frequent choice is Linux.[9] Linux is a very versatile open source operating system that can be used for many different purposes, from

---

[9] One significant exception is Microsoft's Azure Cloud, in which Windows Server is also often used, especially in the context of Windows based applications and infrastructure elements like Exchange servers or Active Directory. However, even in Windows and Azure, Linux is available and a common choice as well.

small embedded devices to large servers. Modern Linux distributions designed for the use on desktop or laptop computers typically offer easy-to-use graphical user interfaces. However, when used on servers and in a cloud context, server-optimized distributions without graphical user interfaces are usually chosen. This has various benefits, ranging from a smaller memory footprint to a reduced risk of security vulnerabilities—a non-existing component (such as a graphical user interface) does not take up space and cannot be attacked by malicious software.

A comprehensive introduction into using Linux is beyond the scope of this book. However, the following lists a number of frequently used commands as a refresher that the reader might find useful for the hands-on exercises in later chapters. Before individual commands are discussed, it is important to note that Linux is case sensitive, which means that the command "cp" cannot be written as "CP" or "Cp", and that "names.txt" and "Names.txt" are two complete different files.

The **ls** command lists the content of a folder, including files and directories. Here is its syntax:

ls [options] [directory_or_path]

To list items inside subfolders, add the **-R** option. Other useful options include **-a** which lists all files and directories, including "hidden" ones starting with a dot, and **-l**, which lists in a long format, showing not just the file name, but also other metadata like its size, access permissions etc.

The directory or path portion of the command can be left empty, in which case the content of the current directly is displayed. It can alternatively be a path relative to the current location (any path not starting with a slash), or an absolute path, which is a path beginning with a slash, in which case the full path starting at the root directory of the file system is specified. Additional common ways to specify a path include ~, which refers to the home directory of the current user, a simple dot (.), which refers to the current directory, or two dots (..), which refers to the parent directory of the current directory. For example, if a user is currently in the directory "/home/mary", the parent directory could be specified either with its relative path by ".." or with its absolute path "/home". These different ways of specifying paths are also useful for several of the commands below, including to move around the directory tree or to copy files.

The **pwd** command outputs the full path of your current working directory. Its syntax is as follows:

pwd [options]

The **-L** option prints environment variable content, like shortcuts, instead of the actual path of your current location.

## 2.3 Linux

With **cd** users can move between different directories. The syntax of the command is

cd [directory_or_path]

Just like with the ls command above, the directory or path can be specified in a relative or absolute way.

To create a directory, the command **mkdir** can be used. The syntax of the command is

mkdir [options] [directory_or_path]

A common option is **-p**, which automatically creates parent directories as necessary if a whole directory structure is specified.

Directories can be deleted with **rmdir**. The syntax of the command is

rmdir [options] [directory_or_path]

If the directory is not empty, the command will by default display an error message. This can be prevented by first deleting all the files in the directory with the command "rm" explained below, or by simply using the option **-r** which recursively deletes the directory with its content.

Files can be copied with **cp**. The syntax of the command is

cp [source_file] [destination]

The destination can be a file name, in which a copy of the source file with the destination file name is created in the current directory. If the destination is the name of an already existing file it is simply overwritten. Alternatively, the destination can be a directory or path, in which case a copy of the file with the same name is created in that location.

Wildcards are a highly useful addition to the copy command. There are two main wildcards, the asterisk ("*") and the question mark ("?"). The former matches any number of characters (from zero to many), while the latter matches exactly one character. A common use of this is to specify the source file of the cp command as "*", which copies all the files in the current directory. If a user wants to copy all files ending in ".txt", they can simply specify this with the source "*.txt". A source file specified as "receipt?.txt" will match for example to files with the names receipt1.txt and receipt2.txt, but not to receipt.txt and receipt10.txt because the former does not have a character that matches the question mark in the pattern while the latter would need to match two characters to the question mark. In contrast, "receipt*.txt" matches all these files, because the asterisk matches zero, one, two or more characters.

These wildcards can be used with other Linux commands as well. For example, files can be moved instead of copied with **mv**. The syntax of the command is

    mv [source_file] [destination]

The "mv" command works very similarly to the "cp" command. The destination can once again be a directory, in which case the file is moved (rather than copied) there. If the destination is instead just a different file name, the file is effectively renamed.

Wildcards are also often useful to delete files with **rm**. The syntax of the command is

    rm [options] [files]

For example, to delete all the files ending in *.txt in the current directory, the command "rm *.txt" can be used. Common options include "-r" with which subdirectories are recursively deleted as well, and "-f" with which the deletion of files (even if they are write protected) is forced without any prompt to the user. These options should be used carefully—note that for example the command "rm -rf /" deletes all the files and directories in the entire file system without prompting the user for confirmation.

The content of a file can be viewed with various different commands, including **cat**, **more** or **less**. The syntax of the latter (which is the most powerful of these commands) is

    less [filename]

If the command "less" is used on a short file, the content of the whole file is displayed. If the file is too long to fit on the screen, only the beginning of the file is displayed, and the user can display the next part of the file by pressing the "space" key. There are numerous other keyboard commands that can be used within the command—for example, the user can scroll up and down in the file with the up and down keys, respectively. Pressing "q" will close the file and return to the command prompt. Typing the forward slash followed by some string such as "/test" highlights all the occurrences of the string "test" in the file.

## 2.3 Linux

More details on this and other Linux commands can be found by either just executing the command without any options or arguments, which will typically create an output of the main syntax of the command, or by running commands with the option "–help", which will display detailed information on the command and all its options. The official manual page of a command can also be displayed with **man**. The command

    man [command]

displays the manual page of the given command.

Another powerful command to search within a file is **grep**. The syntax of the command is

    grep [options] pattern [files]

For example, to display all the lines of the file "names.txt" in which the string "Smith" occurs, the command "grep Smith names.txt" can be used. Common options include "-i" which makes the search case insensitive (so in this example, lines with "smith" and "SMITH" would also be displayed), and the option "-c", which simply returns the number of occurrences of the pattern in the file rather than the individual lines.

Linux offers numerous editors to change or create text files. A very basic text editor that is available on just about any UNIX based system is **vi**. However, the commands in this editor are not very intuitive. For example, to change from editing to command mode, the "Esc" key has to pressed, followed by a colon (":"), a letter indicting the command and the "Enter" key. For example, to exit the program, the key sequence "Esc" $\Rightarrow$ ":" $\Rightarrow$ "q" $\Rightarrow$ "Enter" is used.

A much more user friendly editor is **nano**. This editor has available keyboard commands listed at the bottom of the screen. For example, pressing "Ctrl-x" ends the program. If there are unsaved changed to the file, it asks the user whether the changes should be saved before exiting. It should be noted that a common technique to create new text based files such as configuration files first involves the command **touch**. When this command is invoked with a file name, it will change the timestamp of that file to the current time if it already exists. If the file does not exist, it creates a new empty file and the current timestamp. For example, to create and edit the file "local.conf", the command "touch local.conf" could be followed by "nano local.conf".

Files in Linux have a set of permissions associated with them. In particular, these permissions are whether the file can be read, written and executed. These three types of permissions apply to the owner of the file, users in the same group and everyone else.

For example, assume the command "ls -l test.txt" has the following output:
" $-rw-r-----$ 1 mary sales 225 Feb 11 11:35 test.txt"
This signifies that the file is owned by user "mary" who has read and write permissions on the file (but no permissions to execute the file as indicated by the "-" between the first "w" and the second "r"). Users in the group "sales" have read but no write or execute permissions (indicated by the following "$r--$"), while all other users have no permissions on the file.

Two important commands can be used to modify file access permissions and ownership. The command **chmod** changes access permissions of the file. The syntax of the command is

   chmod [options] mode files

A common option is "-R", which changes permissions recursively in subdirectories. The argument "mode" can be specified in different ways. One common approach is to specify "u", "g" or "o" to indicate who is affected by the change (the user=owner, group or other users), followed by a "+" or "-" to indicate whether a certain permission is granted or revoked, and "r", "w" or "x" to indicate the type of permission affected (read, write or execute). For example, to grant read permissions for all other users to the file "test.txt" shown above, the command "chmod o+r test.txt" could be used.

To change the ownership of a file to a different user, the command **chown** can be used. The syntax of the command is

   chown user[:group] files

For instance, to make the user "www" and the group "www" the owner of the file "test.txt", the command "chmod www:www test.txt" can be used.

It is quite common to download open source programs or other files to use. This can be done on the command line as well. To download a file from a web or ftp server, the command **wget** with the following syntax can be used

   wget url

The command simply downloads the file specified by the url into the current directory. Files downloaded like this are often compressed archives. Depending on the type of archive commands like **unzip** or **tar** can be used to extract these archives.

Another common way to download for instance open source projects is to simply clone a public git repository. While the details of the command **git** go far beyond this brief introduction of commands, the command "git clone [url]" can be used to create a local copy of a public git repository specified by the url.

## 2.3 Linux

Often it is necessary to update installed linux programs or to install new ones. The command **apt** can be used for that. It has the following syntax:

apt commands [packages]

In general, the command apt has to be executed with administrative permissions. In many modern Linux systems the "root" user with administrative permissions is not used directly for security reasons. Instead, users with administrative privileges use personalized accounts that can be elevated to administrative permissions with the command **sudo**.

For example, to update the existing packages in a Linux system, the commands "sudo apt update" followed by "sudo apt upgrade" can be used. The first command updates the package database to determine what updates are available, while the second command actually installs the available updates. If a program such as the editor "nano" is not installed on a Linux system, it can be installed with the command "sudo apt-get install nano".

The linux operating system can run many processes concurrently. If a program is started on the command line, it is by default started in the foreground, which means that the terminal will not be usable until the program finishes. This can be illustrated with the command "sleep 10" which will pause for 10 seconds and then finish, allowing the user to enter the next command. Note that the **sleep** command itself is not particularly useful, but it can be very convenient when e.g. a command script needs to pause for a fixed time period before continuing. If any long running program has been started in the foreground by accident, pressing the key combination "Ctrl-z" will pause its execution. The program can then be put into the background with the simple command **bg**. This makes the terminal immediately available again while the "sleep" command continues to run in the background. Commands can also be directly be started as background processes by adding an ampersand ("&") to the end of the command—e.g. "sleep 10 &".

A list of all background processes started by the terminal can be viewed with the command **ps**. This lists the processes with the process ID (PID), which is a simple integer value such as "2464". To terminate a process before its normal conclusion the command **kill** can be used. For example, the command "kill 2464" immediately terminates the process with the process ID 2464. Another useful command to see more information about the processes running in the Linux system is **top**. It outputs information about used and available memory, CPU utilization and details about the processes that use the most CPU time and memory in real time.

There are many more useful Linux commands, but the commands discussed above should give users a good start. Two more useful features that are independent of specific commands should be discussed here. The first is input and output redirection and the use of pipes. Many Linux commands create output that is displayed on the terminal. Instead of displaying the output on the terminal, we can also redirect it to a file with the "greater than" symbol. For example, to store a list of files in the current directory in a new file "files.txt", the command "ls >files.txt" can be used. If the file "files.txt" already exists, it is overwritten. To append to an existing file instead, two "greater than" signs can be used: "ls »files.txt". Similarly, the input for a command can come from a file rather than from the terminal with the less than ("<") operator.

With this input and output redirection, multiple commands can be combined together. A slightly contrived but simple example would be to store the output of the command "ls" in a text file and to use this text file as the input for another command like "grep" to search for specific string patters in these file names. The same can be achieved without writing to a file by using pipes ("|"). For example, the command "ls | grep data" will hand the output of the command "ls" as input to the command "grep". This can be done for more than two commands as well.

Finally, in most Linux environments, users do not have to retype frequently used commands. With the command **history** a list of recently executed commands is displayed. Simply pressing the up and down keys can be used to directly cycle through recently executed commands, either to double check them or to execute them again.

## 2.4 Modern Data Centers

This section gives an overview of what cloud computing data centers look like, regardless whether they are operated by organizations that choose to operate their own private cloud, or by public cloud service providers. Google maintains a photo gallery showing exterior and interior views of several of their data centers here[10]

### *2.4.1 Data Center Design*

Designers of modern data centers as they are used in cloud computing have a range of important aspects to consider, including:

- **Physical security:** Physical security is the most basic level of IT security. Whatever other measures are taken, if an unauthorized person gains physical access to a data center, security (confidentiality and integrity of data as well as the availability of applications) can no longer be guaranteed. Consequently, data centers have strong physical security features, including significant video surveillance and other intrusion detection systems, strong access control restrictions (often using biometric identification to ensure that only authorized individuals gain access) etc.

---

[10] https://datacenters.google/discover-more/photo-gallery/.

2.4 Modern Data Centers

**Fig. 2.11** A raised floor creates a hidden void for the passage of cables

- **The potential use of raised floors:** Another commonly used feature in data centers is that of raised floors (see Fig. 2.11). Rather than putting server racks directly on the concrete floor, they are put on an elevated floor that is typically a few feet above the actual floor of the building. This has several advantages, including that cables connections can be run underneath the floor. Also, it can help with airflow for cooling the equipment, and it offers an additional line of defense against flooding events. Because water pools to the lowest point, servers on the elevated floor will typically stay dry, while the isolated cables underneath are not affected by water. Some modern data centers do not use raised floors, for example if the room is not high enough to support them, or because alternative approaches to manage the airflow are used. As a final point with regard to floors (whether raised or not), attention has to be paid to the rather significant weight of tightly packed server racks—especially in buildings that are not specifically constructed as data centers, the floor might not be designed to hold the required weight safely.
- **Power:** Ensuring an uninterrupted supply of power is another major concern for large data centers. If possible, at least two redundant sources of power should be used (e.g. two different electricity providers, or at least two separate cables to connect the data center to the grid), to prevent the risk of a single fallen tree (or accidentally dug up underground cable) cutting power to the data center. In addition to that, power generators (typically powered by diesel fuel) are used

in the event of power failures. Since it usually takes several minutes to start up such power generators to full power, the time until then is generally covered by uninterruptible power supplies, which are essentially big battery packs that have enough capacity to supply the connected equipment for a relatively short time period (e.g. 15 minutes).

- **Climate control:** Cooling a data center is another major concern. Most of the electricity used by servers and other components such as networking equipment is ultimately transformed into heat. Servers are usually tightly packed to reduce space requirements, which in larger data centers means at least tens of thousands of servers in a relatively small floor space. Since each server might create a few hundred Watts of heat, the total cooling requirement of a larger data center can easily be in the range of Megawatts. In most climates zones, this type of cooling requires significant air conditioning equipment, and careful planning of fan placement to optimize air flows. To increase heat transfer and efficiency, water cooling approaches can be used. In addition to cooling the data center, climate control also has to ensure an adequate level of humidity. If humidity is too high, metal contacts running electricity might corrode over time, while very low levels of humidity might lead to the build-up of electric charges on different components that, once they discharge, can also damage equipment.
- **Network connection:** Data centers, especially cloud data centers, clearly depend on high bandwidth network connectivity that is very reliable. For that end, similar to the supply of power, multiple providers with separate physical connections are generally desirable. Different approaches are possible—either normal operation uses more than one network provider, or it uses only one with alternatives available on standby in the event of outages.
- **Fire suppression systems:** Modern buildings generally have fire detection systems with sensors for smoke or heat that trigger sprinklers to extinguish fires with water before they get out of control. This is obviously not a good solution in a data center, because water spray is likely to damage computer equipment due to short circuits caused. Consequently, data centers are usually equipped with fire suppression systems that work by reducing the oxygen levels in the room by replacing it with other gases such as argon.
- **Server (and networking equipment) organization:** In order to maximize the utilization of space, modern data centers organize servers in rows of racks, each of which contains multiple servers stacked on top of each other. The exact organization, including aspects such as the placement of networking equipment (switches and routers), cabling and cooling equipment is a complex optimization problem for which different approaches exist. For example, cables can be run under a raised floor or above the equipment on the ceiling and power equipment such as uninterruptible power supplies can be more centralized or distributed.

## 2.4.2 Modern Server Design

In the past, servers often used different hardware architectures than contemporary desktop or laptop machines. While there are still some alternatives in the marketplace such as ARM-based servers, most servers today use CPUs by Intel or AMD based on the same x86-64 instruction set as current consumer computers.

Despite this, servers used in data centers of course have significant differences compared to for instance desktop PCs. To begin with, different form factors are usually used, which are optimized to allow efficient stacking of servers in server racks. Additionally, servers are of course usually rather powerful, with often multiple CPUs with multiple CPU cores per server, large amounts of memory, secondary storage and high performance networking capabilities.

Additionally, servers often have features that increase reliability and fault-tolerance. This typically includes redundant power supplies and hard disks (e.g. in RAID arrays) that are hot-swappable. In other words, if for instance the power supply of a server fails, the redundant secondary power supply takes over instantaneously, and an alarm is raised. This allows maintenance technicians to replace the faulty power supply without ever turning off the server. Another common feature is *Error-Correcting Code* (ECC) memory that can detect and correct random bit errors in main memory.

Finally, servers often come with advanced management features. Server mainboards usually contain a baseboard management controller that implements the *Intelligent Platform Management Interface* (IPMI). This interface allows remote access to servers, for example to install an operating system or to reboot a hanging server, independently from any installed operating system. While software with similar features exists that can be run under common server operating systems, such software depends on the server being responsive, while the IPMI still works even if the system is down or if no operating system has been installed yet.

## 2.4.3 Modern Storage Approaches

Data centers have used different approaches to organizing secondary storage over time. Traditionally, each server stored the data it used on local hard disks. To increase reliability and performance, these disks were typically organized in a *Redundant Array of Independent Disk* (RAID) array. A significant downside of this approach is that the exact storage capacity each individual server in a data center needs is hard to predict and might vary over time. To prevent running out of local storage, disk capacity would have to be assigned generously, resulting in relatively low average space utilization, i.e. significant amounts of unused disk space.

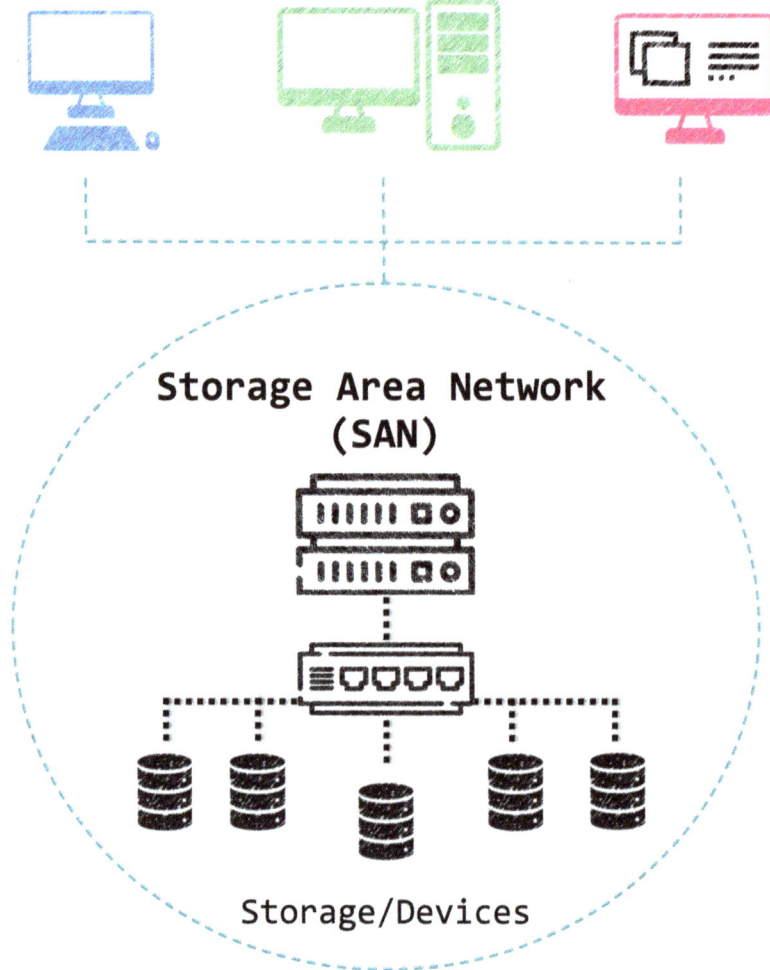

**Fig. 2.12** A storage area network

Consequently, secondary storage for a large number of servers was often consolidated in *Storage Area Networks* (SAN) (see Fig. 2.12). In a SAN setup, a large number of disks is combined in a centralized storage array. The servers are connected to the storage array through a high-speed network such as Fibre Channel that is separate from the regular local area network through which all other network traffic runs. From the perspective of the server, storage in the SAN can be accessed as if it was local disk storage. The big advantage of this setup is that storage can flexibly be assigned to servers, resulting in higher utilization and less unused storage capacity.

While SANs are still widely used in practice, a different approach that moves storage back to the individual servers is increasingly adopted. There are several reasons for this, including the fact that SANs tend to be expensive, and that regular

Local Area Networking (LAN) speeds have become fast enough to allow servers to efficiently share their local storage with other servers. In these new approaches that are often referred to as software defined storage, the disks installed locally at each server are combined into a large virtual pool of disks, the storage capacity of which is then flexibly assigned to individual servers. This general approach in which storage, networking and compute resources are no longer separated, but combined back into the individual servers making up the data center and virtualized is also referred to as Hyperconverged Infrastructure.

With regard to the actual storage devices used, flash memory based *Solid State Disks* (SSDs) that offer significantly lower access times and a much higher number of *input and output operations per second* (IOPS) than traditional magnetic hard disks are increasingly being used. While their cost is still higher, the difference has become small enough to make the use of SSDs for frequently accessed or performance critical data such as installed operating systems and programs, relational database systems etc. worthwhile. For other kinds of data, especially where access times are less important, hard disks are still used. For example, for large image or video files sustained data transfer rates are generally more important than access times, making magnetic hard disks the more economic choice. Even magnetic tapes (usually used in large tape libraries, in which automatically operated robot arms retrieve and insert the required tapes into one of several tape drives) are still used and economical for data that is kept for mostly archival purposes, and very rarely accessed, because the per-Gigabyte cost of tape storage is even lower than that of magnetic hard disks.

### 2.4.4 Cost and Other Considerations

Modern cloud data centers, especially those operated by public cloud providers, tend to be very large, often housing at least tens of thousands of servers. One of the main reasons for this is that many of the costs associated with running a data center scale much slower than linearly with the numbers of servers. Outside of volume discounts that cloud providers receive for their hardware purchases, the actual cost of purchased computing, storage and networking equipment is one of the few factors that scales relatively linearly. Many other costs—e.g. the cost for physical security and access control measures, technical measures such as redundant power systems, fire suppression systems etc. do increase with the size of the data center, but much slower than linearly. For example, if a handful of security guards can secure a small data center of one hundred servers around the clock, a few more personnel are likely required to secure a data center with a hundred times as many servers—but not nearly a hundred times as many.

In order to keep costs low, operators of large data centers place a very high value on the automation of processes. For example, if the installation of the software on new servers was done manually, the effort required would increase proportionally to the number of servers. If software installation (and other routine tasks) are automated through a set of scripts, the number of system administrators required to operate say a thousand servers is not much higher than the number needed to operate a hundred servers.

Another important consideration is the choice of location for data centers. While performance considerations (especially network latency) dictate that data centers are located relatively close to their intended end users, their precise placement depends on other factors, such as the risk of natural disasters at different locations. Proximity to active volcanoes, geological fault lines or even low lying locations with high flooding risk should generally be avoided. Furthermore, factors like climate (colder is generally better, to make cooling easier and cheaper) and the cost of electricity play a very important role.

Since disasters (natural and otherwise) can never be entirely prevented or mitigated, disaster recovery approaches are another important consideration. The fact that public cloud service providers operate a number of different data centers across the globe helps with that: If a data center experiences a significant outage, others can take over the load, and while that might result in some performance degradation for users, this is much preferable to a complete outage. Another related aspect is that backups of data should be synchronized between data centers in different locations to minimize the risk of data loss.

A final consideration is the use of proprietary vs. open source technology. This is not only relevant for software, but also for hardware (see e.g. the *Open Compute Project* (OCP)[11]). One of the reasons for the use of open source technology is potential cost savings, because licence costs typically are incurred for each individual machine on which e.g. a software package is used. In other words, while the cost of a $100 software package on an individual PC might not seem excessive, buying ten thousand licences for such a package to use on all the servers in a large data center costs a million dollars, making the in-house development of custom software an often attractive option. Such software might be made open source, to encourage other users to adopt it and to eventually contribute improvements from which the original developer can benefit as well, or be kept as in-house proprietary software if it is deemed to deliver the developing organization a competitive advantage that it does not want to share with others.

## 2.5 Summary

The large success of modern cloud computing has been made possible by relatively recent technical progress in key areas such as networking and virtualization. While cloud computing users generally do not need to understand the technical details of the underlying technologies, a basic understanding of them is crucial for anyone who wants to design secure, cost-effective and reliable applications in the cloud.

---

[11] https://www.opencompute.org/.

## 2.6 Key Terms

**LAN** A local area network (LAN) is a computer network connecting a number of devices in a small, localized area such a home, an office or a datacenter.

**WAN** A wide area network (WAN) is a computer network connecting devices and often entire LANs across a large geographic area.

**IPv4** The internet protocol in version 4 is the most widely used network protocol for computer networks. It specifies both a way to address individual hosts with 32 bit long addresses as well as a mechanism to send network packets between different hosts.

**IPv6** The IPv6 protocol is a more modern version of the IPv4 protocol. It uses 128 bit long addresses to overcome one of the main limitations of IPv4, a shortage of available IP addresses.

**TCP** The transmission control protocol is one of the most widely used transport protocols in computer networks, allowing for reliable communication in IP networks.

**Private IP Address** A private IP address is an IPv4 address that belongs to one of three specific ranges of IPv4 addresses that are not routed across network boundaries and can therefore be used by anybody.

**Subnet** Computer networks are often divided into smaller parts called subnets for reasons such as to separate users who need access to different resources on the network or to increase network performance.

**Switch** A switch is a networking device that connects multiple hosts in a computer network. It uses the MAC address of individual hosts to send data only to the intended destination rather than broadcasting it on the local network (like a hub would do).

**Router** Routers are used to connect multiple networks. They use internal routing tables to decide where to forward IP packets based on their destination IP address.

**DNS** The domain name system (DNS) is used to map human-friendly domain names such as douglas-college.ca into the IP addresses of the servers behind such domains, allowing users to use names rather than cryptic numbers to specify resources.

**Hypervisor** A hypervisor (also called virtual machine monitor or VMM ) is software that allows the creation and management of multiple virtual machines on a single host computer.

**RAID** The acronym RAID stands for redundant array of inexpensive[12] disks. It is usually used in servers to combine multiple physical disks (hard disks or solid state drives) in a larger virtual drive while also storing data redundantly. In most RAID configurations, the failure of a disk can be compensated because of this redundancy, meaning that it causes no server downtime.

---

[12] Or alternatively: independent.

**SAN** A storage area network (SAN) is a specialized high-speed network connecting a number of servers to a centralized array of storage devices.

**Hyperconverged Infrastructure** Hyperconverged infrastructure is a framework in which the compute, storage and network resources of a number of servers are combined into a unified virtual system, allowing for flexible resource allocation of resources independently of their physical location.

## 2.7 Review Questions

1. Describe how virtualization works and why it is important in cloud computing.
2. Explain the difference between a type 1 and type 2 hypervisor. Which type is used in cloud data centers, and why?
3. What are the main aspects to consider when designing a data center?
4. What are the main storage/devices used in modern data centers?
5. What is a SAN and how can it be useful in a data center?
6. How are servers used in data centers different from desktop or laptop PCs?
7. Assume you were in charge of deciding the location for the next data center of a large public cloud providers. What factors should you consider?

## 2.8 Exercises

The following laboratory exercises contain questions that require written responses and, in some instances, accompanying screenshots. If the exercises have been given as an assignment, please ensure that all answers and requested screenshots are compiled into a separate document for submission to the instructor, as specified by the instructor.

### 2.8.1 Install Ubuntu in Virtualbox

In this lab, we install Ubuntu Server in a new virtual machine. This virtual machine will be the basis for several other exercises. NOTE: This exercise assumes that you are using the Windows 11 operating systems. Many of the steps will work similarly if you use other systems such as Linux or MacOS, but some adjustments will be necessary.

2.8 Exercises 61

**Objectives**

1. Install Ubuntu Server in a new virtual machine
2. Update and clone the virtual machine

### A. Installing Ubuntu Server 24.04 LTS in a New Virtual Machine

1. In a web browser, go to https://www.virtualbox.org/wiki/Downloads and download the VirtualBox installation file for Windows hosts.
2. Install VirtualBox on your computer. You can use the default settings. Note that for our exercises the VirtualBox Python Support is not required, so you can choose to not install this feature for simplicity.
3. In a web browser, go to https://ubuntu.com/download/server and download Ubuntu Server 24.04LTS into your downloads folder.
4. Start VirtualBox
5. Click on "New" to create a new virtual machine
6. Enter UbuntuServer2404LTS as name. Next to "ISO Image", navigate to your downloads folder and select the iso file you just downloaded. Then click on "Open". Set the checkmark next to "Skip Unattended Installation".
7. Expand the section "Hardware". Change the Memory size to 4096 MB and allocate 2 CPUs.
8. Click on "Finish".
9. Start the new virtual machine by clicking on "Start".
10. In the following setup you will have to answer a number of questions. Note that the mouse does not work in the menus—use the Enter key to confirm a choice, up/down and tab keys to navigate between choices, and spacebar to select/unselect choices.
    (a) Hit Enter to Install Ubuntu Server
    (b) Use "English" as the preferred language
    (c) Accept the default keyboard configuration.
    (d) Select "Ubuntu Server"
    (e) Accept the default network configuration.
    (f) Hit "Enter" in the "configure proxy" screen.
    (g) Accept the default Ubuntu archive mirror.
    (h) Accept the default storage configuration (which should use the 25 GB virtual disk created earlier in Virtualbox). You will be prompted to "confirm destructive action"—this is ok, as it should only be this newly created disk.
    (i) Enter the following values in the profile setup screen:
        i. Your Name: Your full name
        ii. Your server's name: ubuntu
        iii. Pick a username: Your first (given) name
        iv. Choose a password: Use a password you can remember

(j) In the "Upgrade to Ubuntu Pro" screen choose "Skip for now". Make no changes in the "SSH configuration" screen—select "Done" and press "Enter".
(k) Do the same in the "Featured server snaps" screen.
(l) Once you reach the "Installation complete" screen, select "Reboot Now" and hit ENTER.
(m) If prompted to "Please remove the installation medium, then press ENTER", simply press "Enter". You might have to press "Enter" again for the system to actually reboot.

**B. Updating Linux**

1. Once the virtual machine has restarted, you should see a login prompt. Once again, you might have to press "Enter".
2. Log in with your username and password.
3. You should now see a welcome message, with information on the system, how many updates are available etc.
4. Insert a screenshot of this welcome message below:




5. On the command line, type `sudo apt-get update` to retrieve the list of available updates. When prompted, enter the password again.
6. What does the command `sudo` do? If you are not sure, use the command `man sudo` to look at the manual page for the command sudo. Why do we use the command sudo?

7. Use the command `sudo apt-get upgrade` to install the available updates

8. Type Y and hit enter to confirm and install the updates.

**C. Cloning the Virtual Machine**

1. Use the command sudo shutdown now to shut the virtual machine down (enter the password when prompted).
2. Once the virtual machine is powered off, right-click on "UntuntuServer2404LTS" and select "Clone". Enter UbuntuServer2404LTS Clone as name. Select "Full clone" and click on "Finish".
3. Once the clone operation is complete, start the new virtual machine UbuntuServer2404LTS Clone, and log in with your username and password.
4. Note that the clone of the virtual machine behaves identically to the original version.
5. Click on File ->Export Appliance.
6. Select "UbuntuServer2404LTS".
7. Expand "Format Settings".
8. Check the storage location and name of the .ova file in the field "File" and adjust the storage location if desired.
9. Check the checkbox next to "Include ISO image files".
10. Click on "Finished".
11. Once the export is completed, open a file explorer in the storage location of the .ova file and verify that a file with the ending. ova and a size of approximately 2 GBytes has been created.
12. Insert a screenshot showing the exported VM image and its size:

13. Note that you can import this .ova file on any computer with VirtualBox.

## 2.8.2 Basic Linux Commands

In this lab, we install Ubuntu Server in a new virtual machine. This virtual machine will be the basis for the next two labs. We will also familiarize ourselves with Ubuntu Server and the Linux command line.

**Objectives**

1. Get familiar with basic Linux commands

**A. Working with Files and Directories**

1. Open VirtualBox and start a clone of the virtual machine you created in the first hands-on exercise of Chapter 2.
2. Log in with the username and password you chose.
3. After logging in, you should be in your home directory. To confirm this, type the command: pwd
4. What is the output of the command?




5. To see the content of the current directory, type the command:

    ```
    ls
    ```

6. Note that the response is probably empty, as by default, hidden files and directories are not shown. For a more detailed output (all files, and also shown with file details), use the command:

    ```
    ls -la
    ```

7. Insert a screenshot of the output:

8. Now several hidden files and directories (beginning with a dot) should be displayed.
9. Next, create an empty text file with the command:

   ```
   touch test.txt
   ```

10. Note that if run the command ls again, this file should be displayed.
11. Create a directory with the name backup with he command:

    ```
    mkdir backup
    ```

12. To see the not-hidden content of the current directory with its details, run the command:

    ```
    ls -l
    ```

13. Insert a screenshot of the output:

14. Note that the line for backup begins with the letter "d", indicating that it is a directory, while the line for test.txt begins with a hyphen, indicating that it is a regular file. You can also see the file creating date and time and size among some other information.
15. To navigate into the subdirectory backup, use the command:

    ```
    cd backup
    ```

16. The prompt you can now see should show you that you are in the directory /backup, which means the subdirectory backup of your home directory.
17. To see the full path of your current directory, run the command:

    ```
    pwd
    ```

66                                                                                           2  Technical Foundations

18. What is the output of the command?

19. Practice moving around the directory structure. Where do each the following commands get you from here? (Note that you can always come back to this directory with the command cd ~/backup)

    cd /

    cd

    cd

    cd ..

20. Back in the directory backup, copy the file test.txt from the parent directory to the local directory with the command:

    cp ../test.txt .

21. Note that the cp command takes two arguments—the source (the file test.txt in the parent directory of the current directory, as indicated by the two dots) and the destination (the current directory as indicated by the single dot). Note also that we could have moved instead of copying the file with the command mv instead of cp.
22. Confirm with the command ls -l that there is a copy of the file test.txt in the current directory.
23. To go back to your home directory, use the command:

    cd ..

24. Try to remove the directory backup with the command:

    rmdir backup

25. What is the output?

26. To delete the directory, we first have to delete the file test.txt in it. You can do this with the command:

    `rm backup/test.txt`

27. Now, you should be able to delete the directory backup with the command:

    `rmdir backup`

28. Verify that the directory is gone with the `ls` command.

**B. File Content, Permissions and Wildcards**

1. To find out more details about how to use a linux command, you can use the command man. For example, to see the various options of the command ls, run the command:

    `man ls`

2. The manual page for the command ls should open. You can scroll up and down with the arrow keys or end the command by pressing the key q.
3. To create a file with some content that we can explore, you can redirect the output of the command man ls into a file with the command:

    `man ls > manual.txt`

4. Run the command `ls -l` to verify that the file `manual.txt` was created. What is its file size (the number between your username and the file creation date)?

5. There are several commands with which you can display the content of a file. Try the command:

    `cat manual.txt`

6. Note how you can only see the end of the file, because the file is too long to fit on the screen, and so simply scrolls through the file too fast to read. To read the content of the file one screen at a time, use the command:

    `less manual.txt`

7. Note that you can scroll up and down with the arrow keys and leave the command by pressing the key q.
8. The command less also has additional options. Run less manual.txt again, then type /file and hit the enter key. Describe what happens:



9. Press q again to leave the command.
10. Another way to search in a text file is the command grep. Type the command:

    grep file manual.txt

11. Insert a screenshot of the output:








12. To look at the access permission of the files in the current directory, run the command:

    ls -l

13. Note that for both files, it shows -rw-rw-r- at the beginning of the line. Note that the first hyphen shows that it is a file (and not for instance a directory or symbolic link). After that, there are three triples of characters, each time beginning with an r, indicating that the owner of the file (first triple), the group (second triple) and others else (third triple) can read the file. The second character, a w for owner and group but a hyphen instead of a w for everyone else indicates that the owner and group, but not everyone else, can write to the file. The third character (a hyphen in all three cases) means that nobody is allowed to execute the file, which makes sense, as it is not an executable file (e.g. a script file or program).

## 2.8 Exercises

14. Assume we want to modify the access permissions, for example by removing (with the minus sign) the permissions of everyone else (others) to read the file. We can achieve this with the following command:

    chmod o-r manual.txt

15. Run the command ls -l again and insert a screenshot to show that the file permissions were updated as expected:

16. To see the effect of wildcards, create four more files with the commands:
    touch test1.txt
    touch test2.txt
    touch test10.txt
    touch game.java

17. Also, create another directory with the command:

    mkdir archive

18. We can use wildcards to do operations on several files at once, rather than having to run a command for each file separately. For example, run the command:

    cp test?.txt archive

19. List the content of the directory archive with the command:

    ls -l archive

20. Which files are in the directory archive now?

21. Delete the content of the directory archive with the command:

    ```
    rm archive/*
    ```

22. Repeat steps 18 to 21 with the following three commands using wildcards, and write down which file were copied to the archive directory in each case:

    ```
    cp test*.txt
    ```

    ```
    cp *.txt
    ```

    ```
    cp *
    ```

## C. Some Other Useful Commands

1. Note that you can use the command history to see the history of all the commands you ran in this shell session. If you want to keep a copy of all the commands you used, you can simply write it to a file with the command like:

    ```
    history > commands.txt
    ```

2. Note that you can also cycle through previous commands with the up and down keys.
3. Another useful mechanism is that the shell with auto-complete things like file names for you. For example, if your current directory only contains one file beginning with the letter "m", and you begin typing a command like cp m, you can simply press the tab key, and the shell will complete the file name (such as manual.txt) for you.
4. Finally, we will explore handling multiple processes effectively. We will try this out with the command sleep, which simply waits for a specified number of seconds. Note that this can be useful e.g. in script files where you want a specific delay. Run the following command:

    ```
    sleep 5
    ```

5. Describe what happens:

2.8 Exercises                                                                  71

6. Now we will use the sleep command to illustrate how to handle a long running background process. For this, run the command:

    sleep 600

7. If you do now want to wait for the process to finish for ten minutes, you can simply press the key combination Ctrl-Z, followed by bg and the enter key.
8. The sleep process is now running in the background. To see all the processes running in the system, run the command:

    top

9. Note that you probably have to scroll down with the arrow keys to see the process sleep, because it does not use a lot of resources.
10. Press q to get back to the command prompt.
11. Run the following command to see all the processes started by the current shell:

    ps

12. Insert a screenshot of the output:

13. Note that you should see three processes—the current shell itself (called bash), the sleep process and the ps process. The first column (PID) shows the unique process ID of each process. To prematurely end the sleep process, you can use the command kill, followed by the process ID of the sleep process (e.g. 2113). In that case, the command would simply be:

    kill 2113

14. Verify with the ps command that the sleep process is now gone.

15. Note that rather than starting a long running process in the foreground and then putting it into the background as described above with Ctrl-Z followed by bg, you can simply start a process in the background with an appended ampersand. For example, try the command

    ```
    sleep 100 &
    ```

16. Using the commands ps and kill again end this new sleep process as well.
17. Feel free to explore other linux commands. When you are done, you can properly shut down the virtual machine with the command

    ```
    sudo shutdown -now
    ```

18. If prompted, enter the password again.

## 2.8.3 Networking

In this lab we explore basic networking in Linux and VirtualBox.

**Objectives**

1. Install basic networking tools and test network connectivity
2. Change network settings to make the virtual machine reachable from the outside

**A. Testing Basic Network Connectivity**

1. Open VirtualBox and start a clone of the virtual machine you created in the first hands-on exercise of this chapter.
2. Log in with the username and password you chose.
3. Install some basic networking tools with the command:

    ```
    sudo apt install net-tools
    ```

4. Enter your password if prompted.
5. To see the current network configuration, run the command:
6. ifconfig
7. Insert a screenshot of the output:
8. Note that your output should contain two sections—one beginning with the letters "lo" for loopback and an IP address 127.0.0.1, which is reserved to identify the local machine, and a different one with another IP address, typically either beginning with a 10 or a 192. Note that you might see different results

## 2.8 Exercises

based on the local network settings of your host computer. However, you should see two different IPv4 addresses, both in a line beginning with "inet", and then an IP address consisting of four numbers separated by three periods. For example, your IP address might be 10.0.2.15.

9. Write down your non-loopback IP address below:

10. On your host machine, enter a command prompt, and enter the command `ipconfig`.
11. What is the IP address of your host machine? Again, you are looking for an IPv4 address consisting of four numbers separated by dots, such as 192.168.56.1
12. Ping your host computer from your virtual machine with the command ping followed by the IP address of your host computer (e.g. ping 192.168.56.1).
13. The ping will by default be repeated continuously. Press Ctrl-C after a few seconds and insert a screenshot of the output:

14. You can also ping any other publicly reachable computer on the Internet. For example, to look up the IP address of www.google.ca, run the command:

    `nslookup www.google.ca`

15. Write down the IP address you get as a result:
16. Ping this IP address as well. After a few seconds, press Ctrl-C again. Compare the average time to reach the google web server compared to your local host machine. Which one takes longer, and by about how much on average?

17. Note that you could have also used the command `ping www.google.ca`.

**B. Connecting to the VM from the Outside**

1. In the command prompt of your host machine, try to ping the IP address of your virtual machine (which you determined with the ifconfig command above).
2. What is the output?



3. You cannot reach the virtual machine from the outside world because VirtualBox used Network Address Translation (NAT) by default. In other words, it creates a virtual switch that assigns a private IP address to the virtual machine. It can therefore not be reached from the outside world, only the replies to outgoing requests are returned back to the VM by the virtual switch.
4. In order to make the virtual machine reachable from the outside, we have to change its network settings. In the menu bar on the top of the virtual machine window, click on "Machine", then on "Settings".
5. Click on "Network"
6. Click on the combo box next to "Attached to" and change it from "NAT" to "Bridged Adapter". Then click on "Ok".
7. Wait for about a minute, then run the command ifconfig in the virtual machine again. What is the IP address of the virtual machine now?



8. Ping this IP address from the command prompt on you host machine. Insert a screenshot of the output:



9. Note that the IP address of your host machine and the virtual machine should now be in the same network (e.g. both begin with 10. ...), and that the ping should now be successful.

## 2.8 Exercises

10. In some networks it can happen that the virtual machine is not able to get an IP address from the DHCP server of the host network. In that case, you can use the setting "Host-Only Adapter" instead of "Bridged Adapter". VirtualBox will then create a private IP network connecting both host and virtual machine. The disadvantage compared to "Bridged Adapter" is that external IP addresses are no longer reachable from the virtual machine.
11. When you are done with this lab, shut the virtual machine down with the command:

    ```
    sudo shutdown now
    ```

12. Enter your password if prompted.

# Chapter 3
# Cloud Computing Platforms

In this chapter, we discuss common characteristics, features to compare and the architectures for both commercial and open source cloud platforms. The list of the cloud platforms available is changing day-by-day due to the dynamic nature of the field. Consequently, while we discuss the most active projects at the time of writing, this can have changed by the time this is read.

## 3.1 Introduction

Over the last few years, many different cloud platforms have been proposed both as commercial products and as open source projects. In Table 3.1, we list the most important cloud platforms at the time of writing. In the rest of this chapter, we illustrate the features to compare between the various platforms, the standard architecture and finally we describe in detail the most important cloud platforms.

## 3.2 Features to Compare

There are several features that must be considered when a company has to choose a cloud platform to run its business. Each of the platforms has different characteristics of the same feature, the same feature can be provided differently from one cloud platform to another or it can have different costs. For these reasons, the comparison between the various solutions could be a difficult task. In this section we list some of the main features to take into consideration when a company decides to adopt a cloud computing platform in order to improve its business.

| Name | Website | Note |
|---|---|---|
| Adobe | www.adobe.com/creativecloud | 20+ adobe apps in the cloud |
| Amazon Web Services | www.aws.amazon.com | Where everything starts |
| Dropbox | www.dropbox.com | The first popular cloud storage |
| Egnyte | www.egnyte.com | – |
| Google Cloud Platform | www.console.cloud.google.com | Focus on the PaaS |
| IBM Cloud | www.ibm.com/cloud | – |
| Kamatera | www.kamatera.com | 30 day free trial |
| Microsoft Azure | www.azure.microsoft.com | Microsoft office in the cloud |
| Navsite | www.navisite.com | Combine the best services from Azure, AWS and VMWare |
| OpenNebula | www.opennebula.io | Open source, multi tenancy |
| OpenStack | www.openstack.org | Open source |
| Oracle Cloud | www.oracle.com/cloud | – |
| phoenixNAP | www.phoenixnap.com | – |
| Rackspace | www.rackspace.com | OpenStack with professional support |
| Red Hat Cloud suite | cloud.redhat.com | As for Rackspace |
| Salesforce | www.salesforce.com | The first popular Customer Relationship Management (CRM) on the cloud |
| SAP | www.sap.com | – |
| Verizon Cloud | www.verizon.com/solutions-and-services/verizon-cloud | Cloud service and backup for your phone |
| VMware | www.vmware.com | From hypervisor to the cloud layer |

**Table 3.1** Some of the most active cloud platforms in alphabetic order

## 3.2.1 Application Programming Interface (API)

Most cloud platforms provide a web portal where users can interact with the offered services such as starting/shutting down virtual machines, managing storage, monitoring resource usage, configuring load balancers etc. However, some services provided by cloud platforms are not available via a web portal, so it is important that the cloud platform exposes the API to interact with all the features it provides. Moreover thanks to API support, a developer or a cloud manager can write routines to fully exploit the features available and at the same time automate procedures in order to improve the application performance or to prevent/recover from failures.

## 3.2.2 Availability Zones

At 12:47 AM PDT on April 21, 2011 an invalid traffic shift prior to a network upgrade caused some Amazon cloud services to lose connectivity in a wide area located in north-east USA.[1] The services were fully recovered only after 3 days, and the outage affected big name Amazon cloud customers, including popular Web sites like Foursquare, HootSuite, Quora and Reddit or applications like Twitter. For some of them, this outage meant significant financial losses that AWS reimburses with just a "10 day credit" of the services used by the company involved in the outage. In a note after the outage, AWS declared that it will work to make it easier for customers to take advantage of multiple Availability Zones.

The example above points out the importance of having different availability zones and of using them to improve both performance and reliability. In particular, by having different availability zones, the computation can be close to where the output data are necessary (this can improve the application performance) or more replicas of the same data/application can be spread in different locations so an outage in a specific area cannot prevent access to the data/applications.

### 3.2.3 Fault Tolerance and Failover

One of the informal definitions of cloud computing is: "Cloud computing simply increases the number of things that can go wrong. And go wrong they do." Applications provided by a cloud computing platform could fail in many ways due to hardware, software or network problems and they usually have to deal with a huge number of users. For these reasons it is necessary to have some fault tolerance or failover mechanisms. Some cloud platforms provide such mechanisms as part of the service available, so it is important to consider them as an essential feature.

### 3.2.4 Migration

Most of the applications in cloud platforms run inside a virtual machine. During its lifetime, it could be necessary to move the virtual machine from one physical machine to another, for example to another availability zone by considering the network traffic. Usually, cloud platforms provide two types of migration: the "hot" migration (also called live migration) where the service running inside the virtual machine is provided without any interruption or "cold migration" where the service has to be stopped for a while: the time necessary for another virtual machine to start the service and continue to provide it to the users connected to the previous virtual machine. This operation involves many sub tasks related to process management, session management and, of course, networking management so it is really important that this migration is fully supported by the cloud platform, so the developer can focus on the application and not on the migration procedure.

---

[1] https://aws.amazon.com/message/65648/.

## 3.2.5 Monitoring

Any cloud platform has some kind of monitoring tools to detect when a VM is ready, failed, booting, etc, but what is really interesting for a cloud user is what measures are available and with which granularity. The measures can be cpu usage (%), memory or disk occupancy (bytes), network traffic (bps) just to name a few, while the granularity is the frequency of the sample taken: for example, it could be one sample per second, one sample per minute or one sample per hour. Moreover, it is important to figure out if these measures are reachable by API so a developer can use these measures inside some routine. The monitoring capacities significantly differ from one platform to another in terms of both variety and granularity.

## 3.2.6 Cloud Federation and Open Virtualization Format

Despite the efforts from the *Open Cloud Computing Interface* (OCCI) open community, the *Open Cloud Consortium* (OCC) and the supporters of the *Open Virtualization Format* (OVF) standard, every cloud computing platform has selected its own protocol, its own API and its own command-line interface to interact with the platform itself. Concerning the command-line interface, Fig. 3.1 shows how to perform the same action (that is, starting up a virtual machine) in AWS (see Fig. 3.1a), in OpenStack (see Fig. 3.1b) and in GCP (see Fig. 3.1c). It is clear how the same action

```
$ aws ec2 run-instances \
    --image-id ami-1a2b3c4d \
    --count 1 \
    --instance-type c3.large \
    --key-name MyKeyPair \
    --security-groups MySecurityGroup
```
(a)

```
$ openstack server create --flavor 1 --image 397e713c-b95b-4186-ad46-6126863ea0a9 \
  --security-group default --key-name KeyPair01 --user-data cloudinit.file \
  myCirrosServer|
```
(b)

```
$ gcloud compute instances create "my-new-instance" \
    --zone="us-west1-b" \
    --image-family="tf-latest-cu92" \
    --image-project=deeplearning-platform-release \
    --maintenance-policy=TERMINATE \
    --accelerator="type=nvidia-tesla-v100,count=8" \
    --machine-type="n1-standard-8" \
    --boot-disk-size=120GB \
    --metadata="install-nvidia-driver=True"
```
(c)

**Fig. 3.1** How to run a new VM by using the command-line client software provided by (**a**) AWS, (**b**) OpenStack and (**c**) GCP respectively

can differ from one platform to another in terms of parameter names, sequence and cardinality. This situation is called "lock-in" (already discussed in Sect. 1.3.2): with the exception of a few attempts made by no longer active cloud platform projects like *Nimbus*,[2] all cloud platforms have defined their API/library/command-line interfaces and they avoid compatibility with other cloud platforms on purpose. This way, a user/developer who starts to get confidence with a cloud platform is discouraged from learning how to use a different platform. This is even more complicated if the developer works for a company that needs to have its services in the cloud as soon as possible. In the recent years, some software tools capable of interacting with different cloud platforms have been introduced. Some of these tools are discussed in Chapter 7.

## 3.2.7 Elasticity

One of the advantages of the cloud computing is elasticity, i.e. the ability to dynamically adapt the number and type of resources used depending on workload fluctuations. In order to realize this elasticity, it is necessary to predict the incoming workload and the reaction-time, i.e. how fast the system is able to start up/shut down the resources dedicated to a particular workload. Depending on how accurate the monitoring tool and on how reactive the system is, one cloud platform can perform much better than another in response to workload fluctuations.

## 3.2.8 User Management

A cloud platform can be used by various types of users and developers with different skills and different responsibilities. Therefore, it is important that a cloud platform can easily create different types of users with a different visibility of the whole platform. In particular, this means that a user should have a list of actions allowed, and all other actions should be forbidden. The permissions related to a user or to a group of users should not only be easy to set but also easily changeable at run time.

## 3.2.9 Services Provided

Nowadays cloud platforms are not only computational resource providers but also services providers. The services available in each cloud platform (in particular the commercial ones) are numerous and very different from each other. Concerning the quantity of services available, at the time of writing, AWS and Azure declare

---

[2] https://www.anl.gov/mcs/nimbus-cloud-computing-for-science.

more than 200 services, while GCP provides around 100 services, just to cite the three main cloud providers. The web consoles of the cloud providers divide these services into different categories, for example *Databases* (where the cloud user can exploit different solutions such as NoSQL databases, relational database services, in-memory cache service, just to name a few), *Machine learning* (where the cloud user can find services able to provide different deep learning models, time-series forecasting, natural language understating etc.) or *Containers* (where the cloud user can manage a Kubernetes installation very easily).

## 3.3 Architecture

As mentioned before, there are several cloud platforms with various features and/or services available. Despite these differences, the core components of each cloud platform are similar. In Fig. 3.2, we propose a general cloud platform architecture that, to the best of our knowledge, can fit any cloud computing platform mentioned in Sect. 3.1.

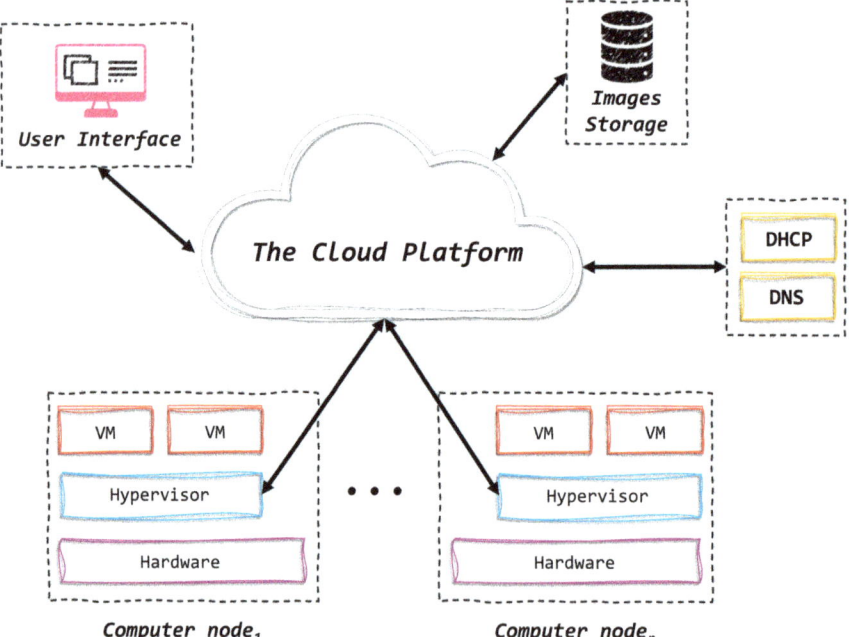

**Fig. 3.2** The common cloud platform architecture

The compute node is where the virtual machine (or containers) run to provide the services required. Inside a compute node, we can find the hardware, the operating system, the hypervisor and, finally, the virtual machines. Any of these components are necessary and any of them can be compatible or incompatible depending on the chosen cloud platform. In particular, if a system administrator plans to install a cloud platform, they for example have to verify which operating systems are compatible with the cloud solutions proposed.

DNS and DHCP are fundamental components of any cloud solution since any service provided by cloud computing is a network application. This means that it needs at least an IP address where the user can send their requests. Moreover the VM in a cloud environment can be started or shut down any time and with a high frequency. Therefore, these components must be able to assign an IP address to a VM and make it reachable from everywhere in the world in a fast and efficient manner.

The images used by virtual machines contain operating system files, libraries specific to a service and, in some cases, also user data. This means that an image can occupy several Gigabytes of disk space, and if hundreds or thousands of images are stored, image storage alone can become a challenge. As a matter of fact, any cloud platform has a specific component in charge of managing virtual machine images. These images not only have to be stored, but they also must be moved from the image repository to compute nodes. Even when they are not claimed by any service, they can be moved/replicated from an image repository to another for performance or fault tolerance purposes. For example, if a very important sport match (the Super Bowl or the UEFA championship final) will be seen by million of fans using a cloud service in a specific country, the cloud platform can decide to in advance move the image of the VM in charge of providing the streaming of the match into the availability zone closest to where the highest number of fans (and, in this case, also the highest number of users of the cloud service) is expected.

Last but not least, the user interface is really important. The major public cloud platforms provide several different interfaces: a web interface, a command-line interface and libraries for various programming languages.

## 3.4 Commercial and Open Source Cloud Platforms

This section presents the most important cloud platforms at the time of writing. As mentioned in Sect. 3.1 there are many different platforms and more will probably enter the market, but in the last few years the top four providers have been AWS, Microsoft Azure, Google Cloud and Alibaba Cloud as indicated by Canalys.[3]

---

[3] https://www.canalys.com.

## 3.4.1 Amazon Web Services (AWS)

The introduction by Amazon of its Elastic Compute Cloud (EC2) service in 2006 marked the true beginning of modern cloud computing. The roots for the idea of AWS go back to the 2000 timeframe when Amazon was a different company than it is today: a simple e-commerce company with a scalability issue. In order to face this problem, the company decided to build some solid internal systems to manage the hyper growth it was experiencing. At the beginning these core systems were used just to manage the e-commerce division of the company, and only a few years later Amazon started to plan how to make a business out of these systems.[4]

Moreover, in 2000, the company also wanted to help third-party merchants (such as Target, Marks & Spencer just to name a few) to build online shopping sites on the top of Amazon's e-commerce platform. This was the first step toward what would become AWS, since the developers at Amazon started to create well-documented APIs to make it easy for third parties to use the Amazon e-commerce engine to sell their products. In just three months, Amazon developers built the API, database, compute and storage components of the system with no thought to scale or reuse. The above components were used by different teams within Amazon, and developers started to think about these components as a set of common infrastructure services everyone could access. This is when Andy Jassy, who was Amazon CEO Jeff Bezos' chief of staff at the time, began to realize they might have something bigger. In 2003, three years before the launch of AWS, by providing infrastructure services (like compute, storage and database) to run what was becoming the biggest e-commerce website in the world, Jassy and the developer teams realized that they achieved high skills at running reliable, scalable and cost-effective data centers. During the fall of 2003, Jassy started to think about the Internet as an "operating system" on top of which the company could build their services, instead of building applications from scratch. In August 2006, Amazon launched "Amazon Elastic Compute Cloud" and surprisingly, for several years, no competitors responded. At the time of writing, AWS

- comprises well over 200 services besides the most famous ones like Elastic Compute Cloud (EC2) and Simple Storage Service (S3). Some services cannot directly be used by end users but are offered through APIs for developers for their applications;
- has distinct operations in 36 geographical "regions" world wide, and new regions are announced every year. Each region has multiple "Availability zones" that are one or more data centers;
- has come to play a crucial role at Amazon as its most reliable source of income. In the first quarter 2025, AWS contributed $11.5 billion in operating income, that is approximately 66% of Amazon's overall operating income;[5]
- has notable customers like NASA and Netflix.

---

[4] https://techcrunch.com/2016/07/02/andy-jassys-brief-history-of-the-genesis-of-aws/.

[5] Source:https://ir.aboutamazon.com/quarterly-results/default.aspx.

## 3.4 Commercial and Open Source Cloud Platforms

AWS is where cloud computing started in 2006, and it is still the leader in the market, as is illustrated in Fig. 3.3).

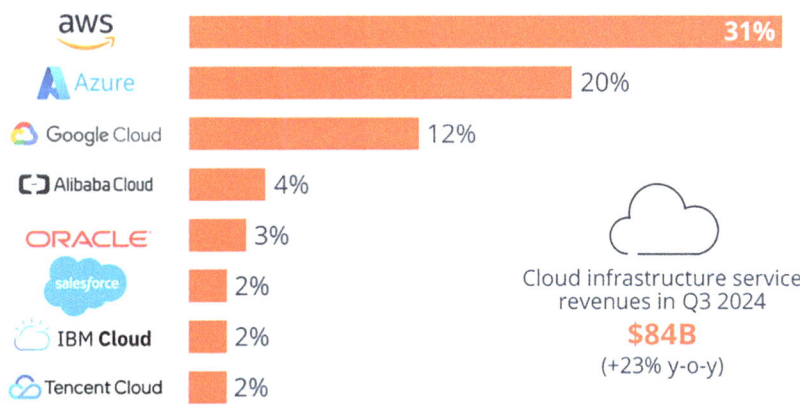

Fig. 3.3 Public cloud services market share trend[6]

### 3.4.2 Microsoft Azure

Microsoft's VM service was announced as Windows Azure in 2008 and became commercially available in February 2010. In 2014 it was rebranded as Microsoft Azure and is now the second largest public cloud platform in the world after AWS.

---

[6] Source: https://www.statista.com/chart/18819/worldwide-market-share-of-leading-cloud-infrastructure-service-providers/.

Microsoft lists over 200 Azure services related to areas like computation, identity, mobile, storage, messaging and many others. At the time of writing, Azure is available in over 60 regions around the world, and every year Microsoft announces new regions to be opened. From the developer's point of view, Azure provides an API built on REST, HTTP, and XML used to interact with the services mentioned above.

One of the main differences between Azure and other cloud platforms is the deployment models provided. Besides the "classic" deployment model where each resource—like VM, database, etc.—is managed individually, Azure in 2014 introduced the Azure Resource Manager where users can create closely coupled groups of resources that can be deployed, managed and monitored together. While AWS has grown by being the developer-friendly platform, Azure has grown thanks to large organizations already committed to Microsoft products deciding to start using Microsoft cloud services.

### 3.4.3 Google Cloud Platform (GCP)

Two years later than AWS, Google launched its computing service in 2008. The service was called "App Engine" and initially was just a developer tool that allowed users to run their web applications on Google infrastructure. At the beginning, App Engine was made available to 10,000 developers that could use the service with some restrictions: 500 MB of storage, 200 million megacycles of CPU per day and 10 GB of bandwidth per day. Only in November 2011, Google made App Engine a public service and now Google provides what is called "Google Cloud Platform" (GCP) with many different cloud services. Nowadays, several big companies have decided to use GCP to run their business (Airbnb, Zillow, Bloomberg and PayPal just to name a few).

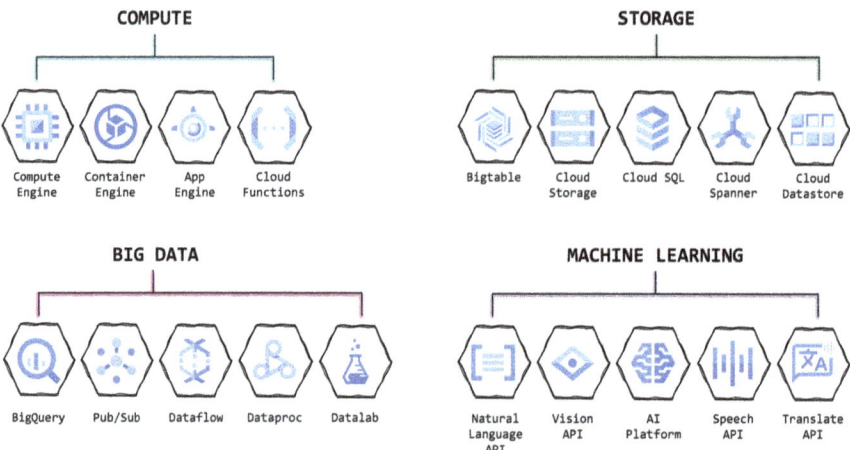

**Fig. 3.4** Google cloud platform services

3.4 Commercial and Open Source Cloud Platforms

Figure 3.4 illustrates a subset of the various GCP services (Google lists over 100 products under the Google Cloud brand). It is worth mentioning that some of the services provided are the same as everyday Google users use. For example, both the "Speech API" and "Natural Language API" are utilized every time we talk to our Android phone and Cloud Search is the service used anytime we perform a search in the Google search engine. At the time of writing, GCP is available in 40 regions and 120 zones.

### 3.4.4 Alibaba Cloud

Alibaba is the largest e-commerce company on earth with its three main e-commerce sites: Taobao, Tmall and Alibaba.com. At the time of writing, it has 674 million active users[7] and it continues to grow. As for Amazon, cloud computing initially was a platform to support its e-commerce websites for Alibaba. In September 2009, Alibaba Cloud was founded to provide cloud services to the public. In particular, Alibaba Cloud (also known as Aliyun) offers cloud services to online businesses such as Elastic Compute, Data Storage, Content Delivery Networks and so on. Currently, Alibaba Cloud operates in 29 regions and 87 availability zones.

### 3.4.5 OpenStack

The origin of OpenStack dates back to 2010 when two companies decided to work together to exploit their experiences and expertise. In particular, Rackspace wanted to rewrite the code related to its cloud infrastructure and, at the same time, Anso Labs (contracting for NASA) published the Python source code for its cloud computing fabric controller. The joint work of the developer teams formed the base for OpenStack which was officially announced at the Open Source Software Conference (OSCON) in Portland on July 21st, 2010.[8]

The OpenStack mission is "to produce a ubiquitous Open Source cloud computing platform that is easy to use, simple to implement, interoperable between deployments, works well at all scales, and meets the needs of users and operators of both public and private clouds".

While OpenStack is not the only open source software able to create a Cloud Platform, it is clearly the most important one. Other projects (e.g. Eucalyptus and Nimbus) were not able to keep their software up-to-date. One of the reasons for the success of OpenStack is the OpenStack Foundation: a non-profit corporation that promotes the project and its community. This foundation has been able to involve more than 500 companies like AT&T, Ericsson, Huawei, Intel and Red Hat, just to name a few.

---

[7] https://www.thestreet.com/world/history-of-alibaba-15145103.

[8] https://docs.openstack.org/project-team-guide/introduction.html.

Another reason for the success of OpenStack is related to its architecture and its project management. In particular, OpenStack is made up of various components (all of which play a role in managing the entire system). For each component, there is a developer team dedicated to the component, a mailing-list and a community. Like for the ISO/OSI stack, each component can improve its implementation independently from other components. The main components are illustrated in Fig. 3.5 (source: OpenStack website[9]).

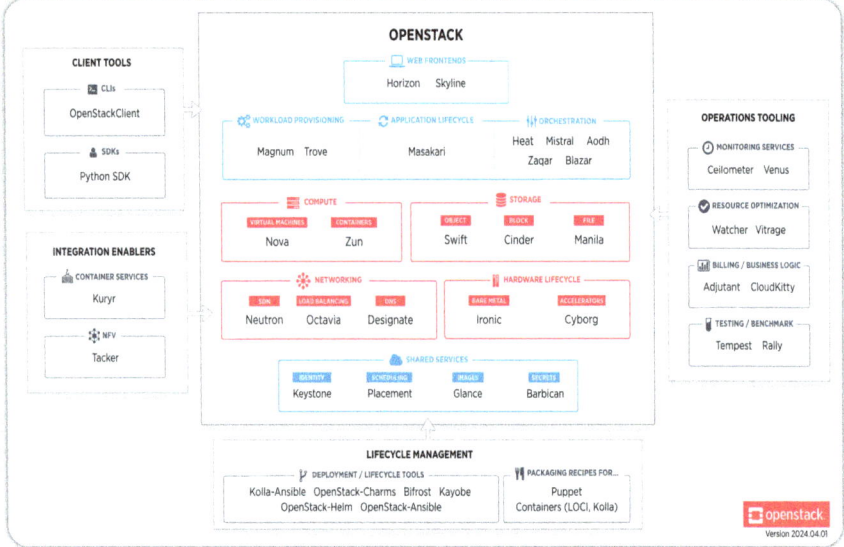

**Fig. 3.5** The main OpenStack components

Each component has a specific role:[10]

- **Horizon:** provides a single User Interface used for VM deployment, configuration and monitoring.
- **Nova:** compute service, controls compute resources and provides its telemetry.
- **Cinder:** block storage service, provides control over block storage resources (i.e. SSD).
- **Neutron:** networking service, provides control over networking (network abstraction layer).
- **Glance:** provides services and libraries to store and manage bootable disk images.
- **Swift:** object storage service, provides scalable object data storage.
- **Keystone:** authentication service, provides common authentication methods.

Since OpenStack is free, installations of this Cloud Platform that users can try out for free are available online. Some of the available websites are *Chameleon Project*[11] and *CloudLab*.[12]

---

[9] https://www.openstack.org/software/.

[10] https://www.tietoevry.com/en/blog/2020/07/openstack/.

[11] https://www.chameleoncloud.org/.

[12] https://www.cloudlab.us/.

## 3.4.6 OpenNebula

OpenNebula is an open source project that provides a cloud computing platform for managing heterogeneous distributed data center infrastructures.[13] OpenNebula started in 2005 as an internal research project of the University of Madrid and it is the only European open source platform to build an Infrastructure as a Service (IaaS) platform.

It has been designed to be a simple but feature-rich, production-ready, customizable solution to build and manage enterprise clouds. OpenNebula combines existing virtualization technologies with advanced features for multi-tenancy, automated provisioning and elasticity. In particular, OpenNebula supports Xen, KVM and VMware hypervisors, and the Linux distributions Ubuntu and Red Hat Enterprise have already integrated this cloud platform.

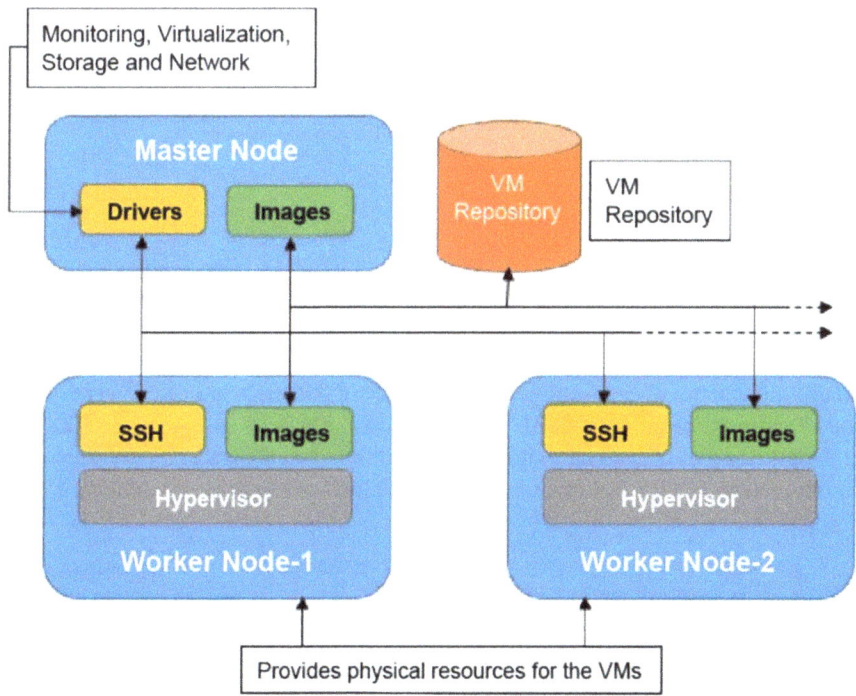

**Fig. 3.6** The OpenNebula architecture

As illustrated in Fig. 3.6, (source: OpenNebula forum[14]), the OpenNebula deployment is similar to a classic cluster architecture. In particular we have the following main components:

---

[13] https://opennebula.io.

[14] https://www.opensourceforu.com/2017/02/an-introduction-to-opennebula/.

- **Master node:** it is the front-end of the system, in charge of queuing, scheduling and submitting jobs to machines in the cluster. More specifically, it provides a user interface to create virtual machines and monitor their status.
- **Worker node:** these machines provide raw computing power for processing the jobs submitted to the cluster. More specifically, they deploy virtualisation supervisors, such as VMware, Xen or KVM.

The project includes features for integration, management, scalability, security and accounting and it also claims standardization, interoperability and portability, providing cloud users and administrators with a choice of several cloud interfaces such as Amazon EC2, OGF Open cloud computing Interface and vCloud. It can also accommodate multiple hardware and software combinations in a data center. The success of OpenNebula is owed to OpenNebula systems:[15] an international software company that develops and provides commercial support for this cloud platform. Thanks to this company, OpenNebula is widely used in a variety of industries including cloud providers, telecommunications, government, banking, gaming and research laboratories. Notable users from the telecommunications and internet industry include Akamai, Blackberry, Telefónica and INdigital.

## 3.5 Summary

Since cloud computing is dominated by a small number of large public cloud computing providers like AWS, Azure and the Google Cloud platform, it might seem that prospective cloud service users do not have a lot of choice when it comes to picking a cloud platform to use. This chapter has shown that this is not true. Not only is there a fairly diverse number of public cloud providers, but there are also several open source projects that allow users to create their own private cloud. Since the different providers and platform all have different strengths and weaknesses, it really depends on the specific needs of an organization which cloud platform is best suited for it.

## 3.6 Key Terms

**API** An application programming interface (API) is an interface through which user can interact with a service through function or method calls in source code rather than through manual interactions through a graphical user interface.

**Cloud Federation** is an approach that allows organizations to integrate applications that are deployed across multiple different cloud environments.

**AWS** Amazon Web Services (AWS) is the largest public cloud provider.

---

[15] https://en.wikipedia.org/wiki/OpenNebula_Systems.

**Azure** Microsoft Azure is the public cloud service offered by Microsoft.

**GCP** The Google Cloud Platform (GCP) is the public cloud service offered by Google.

**OpenStack** is the most widely used open source private cloud platform.

**OpenNebula** is another available open source private cloud platform.

## 3.7 Review Questions

1. In order to select a specific cloud platform to use, which are the feature to compare?
2. Describe the common cloud platform architecture.
3. Describe at least one commercial cloud platform.
4. Describe at least one open source cloud platform.
5. What are the main differences between commercial cloud platforms and open source cloud platforms?

## 3.8 Exercises

The following laboratory exercises contain questions that require written responses and, in some instances, accompanying screenshots. If the exercises have been given as an assignment, please ensure that all answers and requested screenshots are compiled into a separate document for submission to the instructor, as specified by the instructor.

### 3.8.1 Install and Use Nextcloud in Virtualbox

In this lab we try out Nextcloud, a simple private cloud solution that offers storage functionality similar to Dropbox, but can be installed locally.

**Objectives**

1. Installing Nextcloud server
2. Installing Nextcloud client
3. Testing the Nextcloud installation

**Installing Nextcloud**

1. Open VirtualBox and start a clone of the virtual machine you created in the first hands-on exercise of chapter 2.
2. Log on with your username and password
3. We first need to install the apache web server. To do this, enter the following commands:

    ```
    sudo apt update
    sudo apt install -y apache2 libapache2-mod-php bzip2
    ```

4. Then we install the required php modules with the following command:

    ```
    sudo apt install -y php-gd php-json php-mysql php-curl
    php-mbstring php-intl php-imagick php-xml php-zip
    php-sqlite3
    ```

5. Next we have to enable the rewrite module of apache:

    ```
    sudo a2enmod rewrite
    ```

6. Similarly, we have to enable four more modules:

    ```
    sudo a2enmod headers
    sudo a2enmod dir
    sudo a2enmod env
    sudo a2enmod mime
    ```

7. To apply all these changes, we restart apache:

    ```
    sudo systemctl restart apache2
    ```

8. To install the database, we use the following command:

    ```
    sudo apt install -y mariadb-server mariadb-client
    ```

9. Next, we log into the database with the following command. Note that we do not have to use a password for the root user because we are using sudo. Therefore, when prompted for a password, simply press enter:

    ```
    sudo mysql -u root -p
    ```

10. Now that we are logged into the database client, we first have to create a database for nextcloud:

    ```
    create database nextclouddb;
    ```

## 3.8 Exercises

11. Next, we grant the user nextclouduser permissions to access everything in nextclouddb, and assign a password to the user:
    ```
    grant all on nextclouddb.* to
    'nextclouduser'@'localhost' identified by 'Csis4270';
    ```

12. To exit the database client and go back to the Linux command line, we use the command:
    ```
    quit
    ```

13. Now we download:
    ```
    wget https://download.nextcloud.com/server/releases/latest.tar.bz2
    ```

14. Next, uncompress the downloaded archive:
    ```
    tar -jxvf latest.tar.bz2
    ```

15. Finally, we move it to the right place:
    ```
    sudo mv nextcloud /opt/
    ```

16. We change the ownership of the nextcloud directory so that apache can access it:
    ```
    sudo chown -R www-data:www-data /opt/nextcloud/
    ```

17. Now we have to create a configuration file for nextcloud:
    ```
    sudo nano /etc/apache2/sites-available/nextcloud.conf
    ```

18. Write the following into the configuration file:
    ```
    Alias /nextcloud "/opt/nextcloud/"

    <Directory /opt/nextcloud/>
    Require all granted
    AllowOverride All
    Options FollowSymLinks MultiViews

    <IfModule mod_dav.c>
            Dav off
    </IfModule>

    </Directory>
    ```

19. Close the editor nano and save the file: Press Ctrl-X, press Y when prompted if you want to save the file, and hit enter to confirm the file name.

20. Now we enable the new site:
    ```
    sudo a2ensite nextcloud
    ```

21. Finally, we restart apache:

    ```
    sudo systemctl restart apache2
    ```

**Configuring the Virtual Network Connection and Nextcloud**

1. We now have to activate bridged networking so that we can access our virtual machine from the outside. For this purpose, select the menu *Machine* on the top of the VirtualBox window of our NextCloud-lab3 virtual machine, click on *Settings*, and select *Network* on the left. Change the drop-down box next to "Attached to" from *NAT* to *Bridged Adapter* and click ok.
2. Back at the command prompt, we have to install basic networking tools so that we can find out the IP address of the virtual machine:

    ```
    sudo apt install net-tools
    ```

3. Use the following command to find out the network settings:

    ```
    ifconfig
    ```

4. You should now see two network adapters—Ethernet ("en...") and Local Loopback ("lo"). What is the IPv4 address in the section Ethernet with the name *inet*?
5. We are now ready to finish the configuration and installation of Nextcloud. In a web browser, go to the following address (but of course replace YourIPAddress with the value from the previous step): http://YourIPAddress/nextcloud
6. For username of the admin account enter *admin*, and for the password enter *Csis4270*.
7. **DO NOT hit ENTER or click on INSTALL yet!**
8. Click on Storage & database.
9. Select MySQL/MariaDB.
10. Enter the following values in the four text fields:

    ```
    nextclouduser
    Csis4270
    nextclouddb
    localhost
    ```

11. Click on "Install". Once the installation is complete after a few minutes, you might get an error because nextcloud tried to go to a non-existing page. Once again, point the browser to http://YourIPAddress/nextcloud
12. Close the "Nextcloud Hub" welcome screen.

3.8 Exercises

13. On the top left of the screen, click on "Files" icon. Insert a screenshot of the files and directories that are created by default:

**Using Nextcloud**

1. To try out Nextcloud, we install the desktop client under Windows. Download the desktop client for Windows 10/11 from nextcloud.com and install the program using the default options.
2. Once the installation is complete, start the Nextcloud desktop app. Do NOT reboot!
3. Click on "Log in".
4. As the server address, enter: http://IP-addr/nextcloud (once again, replacing IP-addr with your IP address from above), and click on "Next".
5. Click on "Log in". If necessary, enter username admin and password Csis4270 again to Log in.
6. Click on "Grant access".
7. Back in the Nextcloud Connection Wizard, select "Synchronize everything from server" and click on "Connect".
8. Open the Windows File Explorer and navigate to the Nextcloud folder (which should be in your user folder—so if your user name is "Michael", it would be *C:\Users\Michael\Nextcloud*). Note that you can see the same files and directories that you saw in the browser window above. Go into the folder Documents and create a new text document. As filename, use your first name.
9. Open the newly created file in notepad and enter the text "This is awesome!"
10. Save the file and close notepad.
11. Go back to the Nextcloud browser window and navigate to the Documents folder. You should now see the new text file.
12. Click on the text file and edit it in the browser by changing the text to "This is REALLY awesome!"
13. Close the file.

14. Wait for a few moments (so that the changes can synchronize) and open the file on your local hard drive with Notepad again. Can you see the updated version of the file?

15. In the Nextcloud browser window, right-click on your text file, and click on "Open details".
16. Click on "Versions". How many different versions of the file do you see?

17. Insert a screenshot showing the version history of the file.

## 3.8.2 Start a VM in OpenStack

In this lab we provide basic information about how to use the OpenStack web interface to create a VM.

**Objectives**

1. Managing Virtual Machine Instances
2. Associating a Floating IP Address and login

**A. Introduction**

In this lab, we suppose that the user is already able to log into the OpenStack Graphic User Interface called Horizon.

1. After a successful log in, you will see the Overview page as shown below. This page provides a summary of your current and recent usage and provides links to various other pages. Most of the tasks you will perform are done via the menu on the lower left and will be described below. One thing to note is that on the left, your current project is displayed. If you have multiple OpenStack projects, you can change which of them is your current project. All of the information displayed and actions that you take apply to your current project. So in the screen shot below, the quota and usage apply to the current project you have selected and no information about your other projects is shown.

3.8 Exercises

2. One of the main activities you will be performing in the GUI is management of virtual machines, or instances. Go to Project >Compute >Instances in the navigation sidebar. For instances that you have running, you can click on the name of the instance to get more information about it. The dropdown menu to the right of the instance lets you perform a variety of tasks such as suspending, terminating, or rebooting the instance.

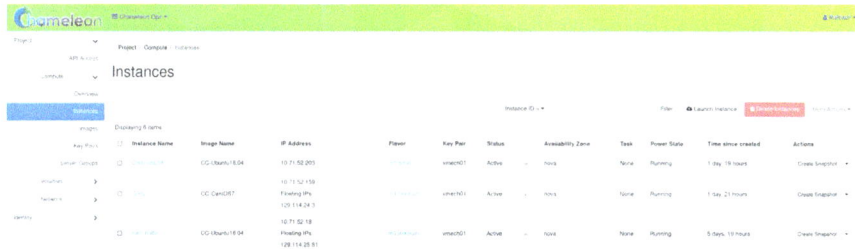

**B. Launching Instances**

1. To launch an Instance, click the Launch Instance button. This will open the Launch Instance dialog.
2. On the Details tab, provide a name for this instance (to help you identify instances that you are running).

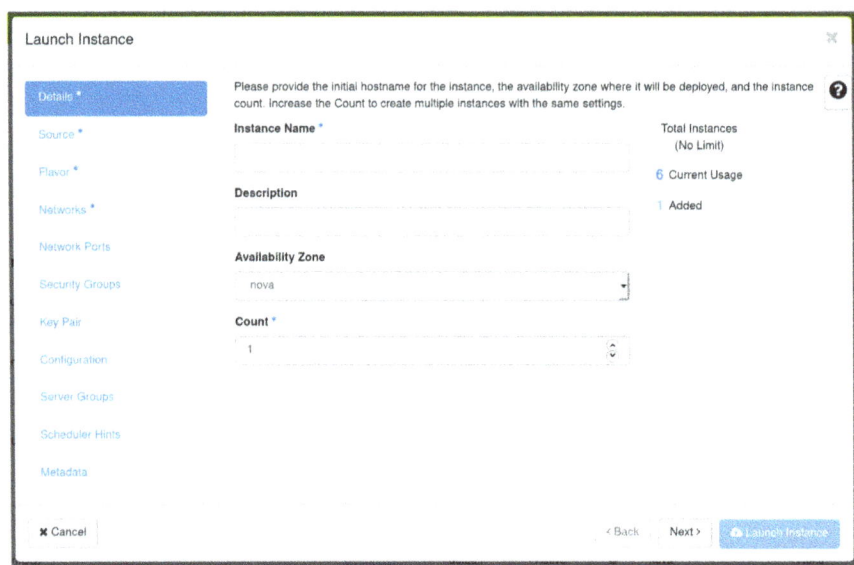

3. Next, go to the Source tab to select media to launch.

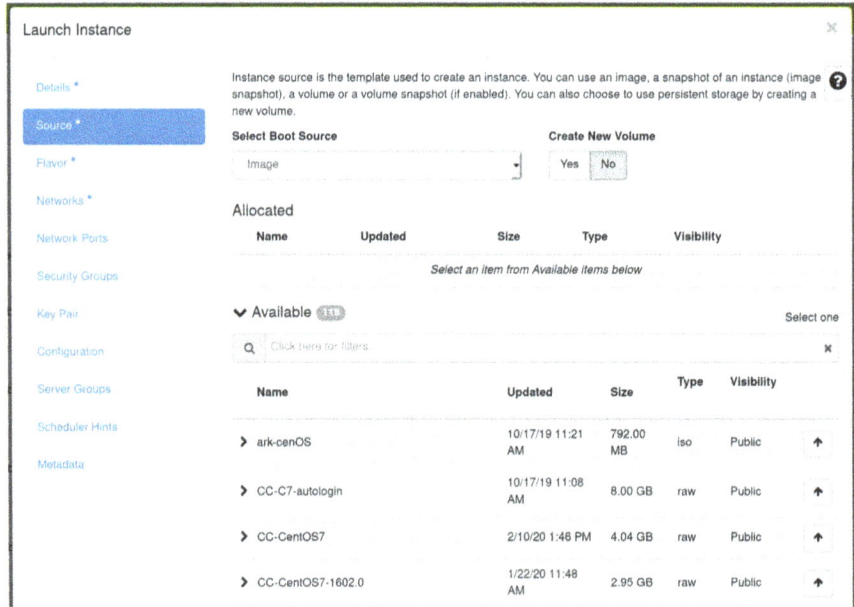

4. Select the Boot Source of the instance, which is either an Image, an Instance Snapshot (an image created from a running virtual machine), a Volume (a

## 3.8 Exercises

persistent virtual disk that can be attached to a virtual machine), or a "Volume Snapshot" . For this lab, select "Image" as the Boot Source, so the Image Name dropdown presents a list of virtual machine images. Pick up an image with operating system that is familiar to you.

5. Go to the Flavor Tab and select the amount of resources (Flavor) to allocate to the instance.

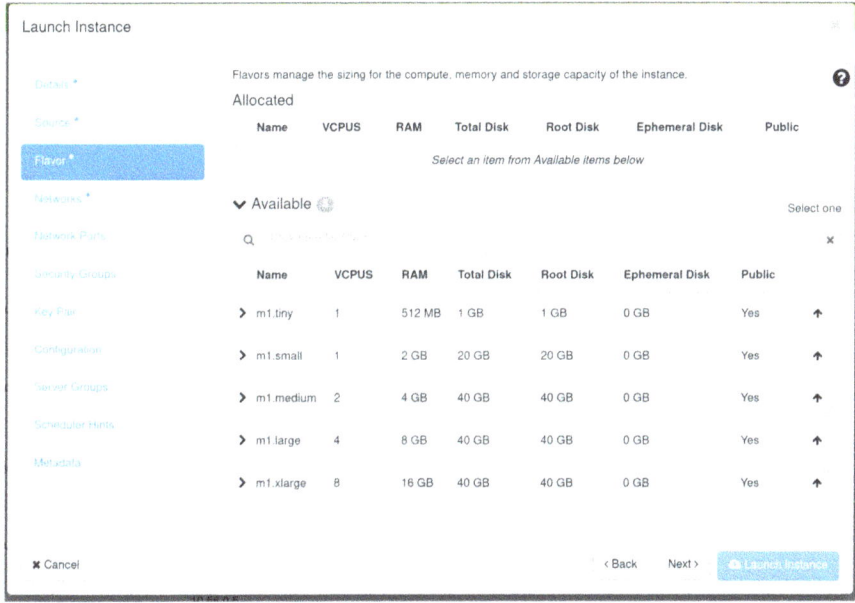

6. Flavors refer to the virtual machine's assigned memory and and disk size. Different images and snapshots may require a larger Flavor. For example, CentOS images require at least an m1.small flavor.
7. Now go to the Key Pair Tab:

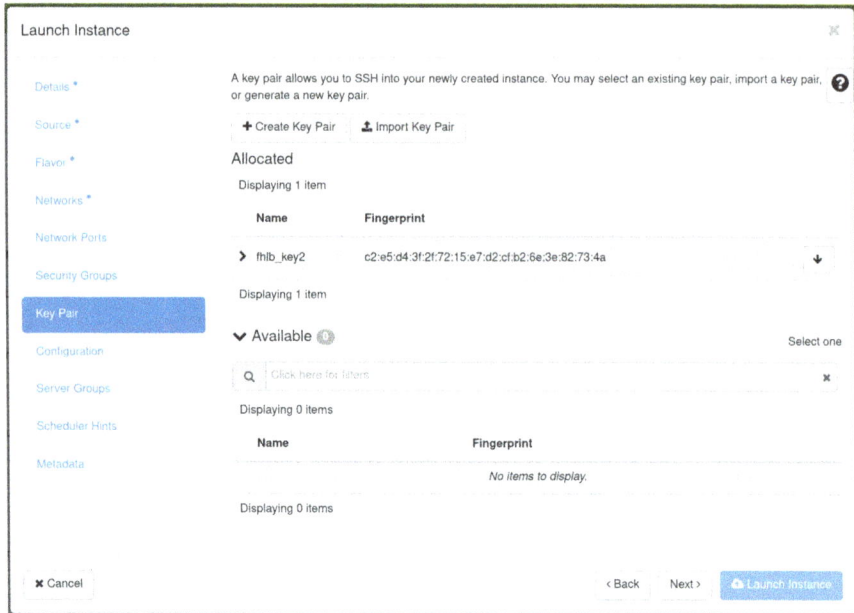

8. Select an SSH keypair that will be inserted into your virtual machine. You will need to select a keypair here to be able to access an instance created from one of the public images OpenStack provides. These images are not configured with a default root password and you will not be able to log in to them without configuring an SSH key.
9. Then, go to the Security Groups Tab.

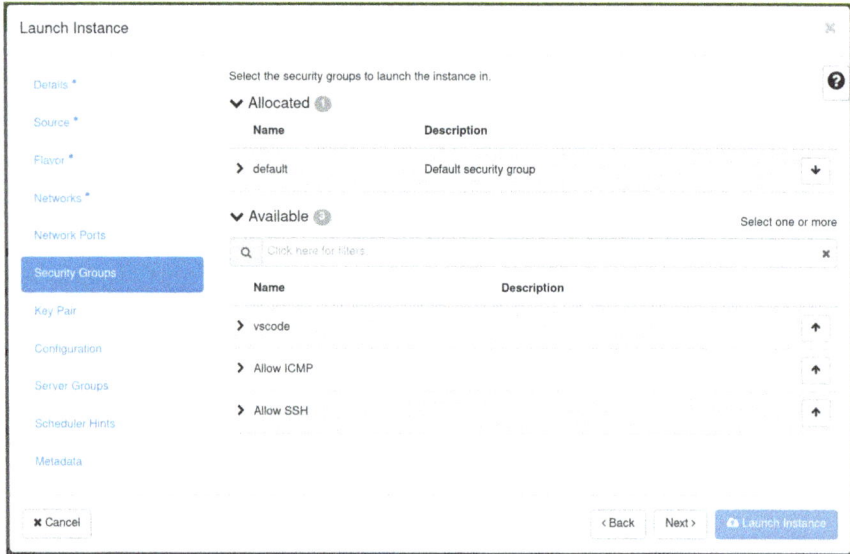

3.8 Exercises                                                                                              101

10. If you have previously defined Security Groups, you may select them here. Alternatively, you can configure them later.
11. Set up network using Network tab.

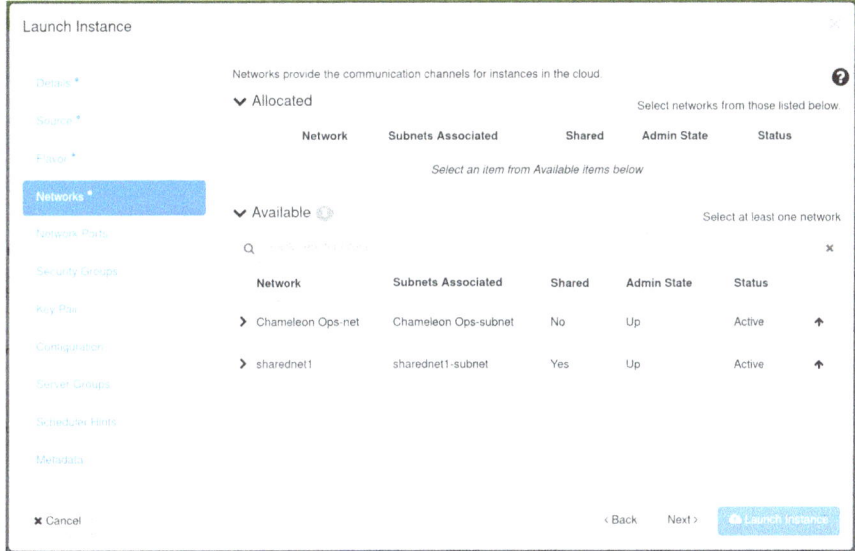

12. Select which network should be associated with the instance. Click the Up arrow next to your project's private network (PROJECT_NAME-net)
13. Now you can launch your instance by clicking on the Launch button and the Instances page will show progress as it starts.

## C. Associating Floating IP Address and Login

1. You may assign a Floating IP Address to your Instance by selecting Associate Floating IP in the dropdown menu next to your Instance on the Instances page.

2. Now you have an up and running instance with a public IP address. You just need to log in by using your favorite ssh client. If you use a Linux terminal you can use the following command:

    ssh -i <private_key> cc@<public_IP_address>

## 3.8.3 Elastic Block Store (EBS) in AWS

In this lab we will learn how to share a file between two instances in AWS by using EBS. This could be useful when an instance has to be shut down and the work must continue in another instance. If we suppose that the data to continue the work are stored in the volume, the passing of the volume from one instance to the other makes this possible.

**Objectives**

1. Create a EBS Volume
2. Attach a EBS Volume to an Instance
3. Make a EBS Volume available for use
4. Detach a EBS Volume to an Instance
5. Attach a EBS Volume to the other Instance
6. Delete a EBS Volume

**A. Preliminary Steps**

For this lab, you need to have two running instances, if you do not know how to launch an instance, you can refer to this tutorial: https://docs.aws.amazon.com/AWSEC2/latest/UserGuide/EC2_GetStarted.html

**B. Create a EBS Volume**

1. In the AWS console that you used to launch the two instances, on the left side menu select "Elastic Block Store", then click on the drop down menu and then click on the "Volume" item as illustrated in the figure below.

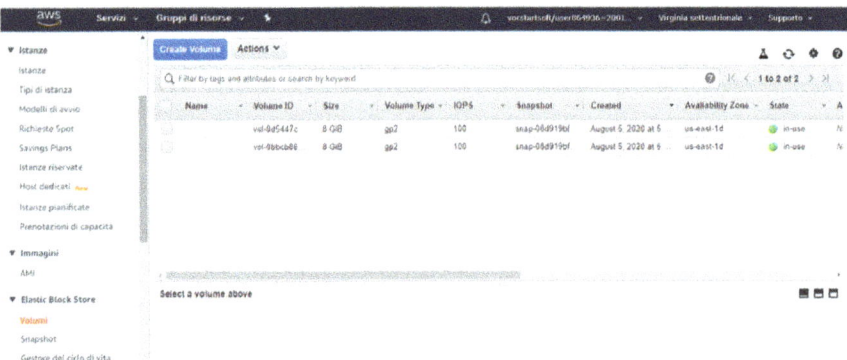

3.8 Exercises

2. Now, you can see that two volumes already exist: these volumes are the main volumes of the two running instances. Remember the availability zones for the next step. For this tutorial, we have to create a new volume by clicking on the "Create Volume" button; this creates a new window, as illustrated below.

3. In this lab, we create a volume with gp2 as type (where gp2 stays for general purpose, as mentioned before), 1 Gib as size and with the same availability zones of the instance volumes (see above). After that you can click on the blue button in order to create the volume. After a few seconds, you will see the new volume available.

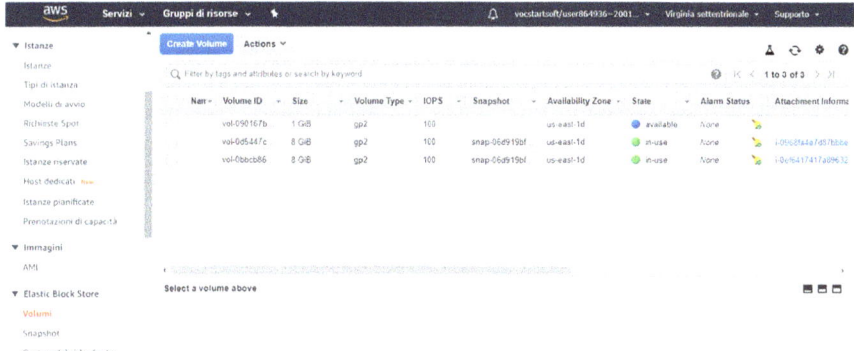

## C. Attach a EBS Volume to an Instance

1. The newly created volume is easily identifiable by the size of 1 GiB. In order to attach the volume to the first instance, you have to click on the "Actions" button and select the "Attach Volume" option.

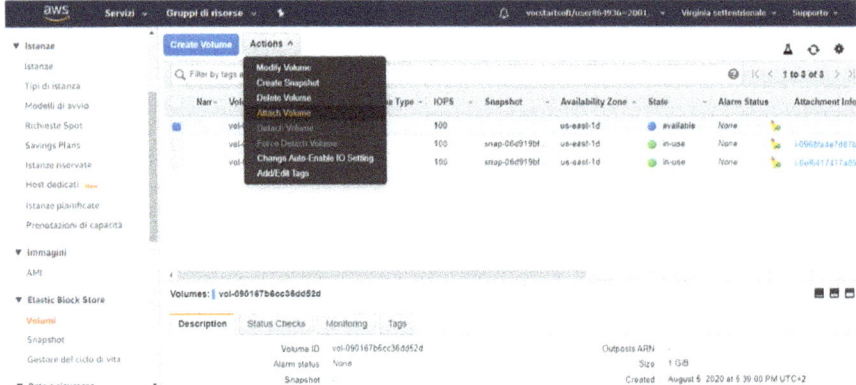

2. This generates a pop-up window where you can choose in which instance the volume will be attached.

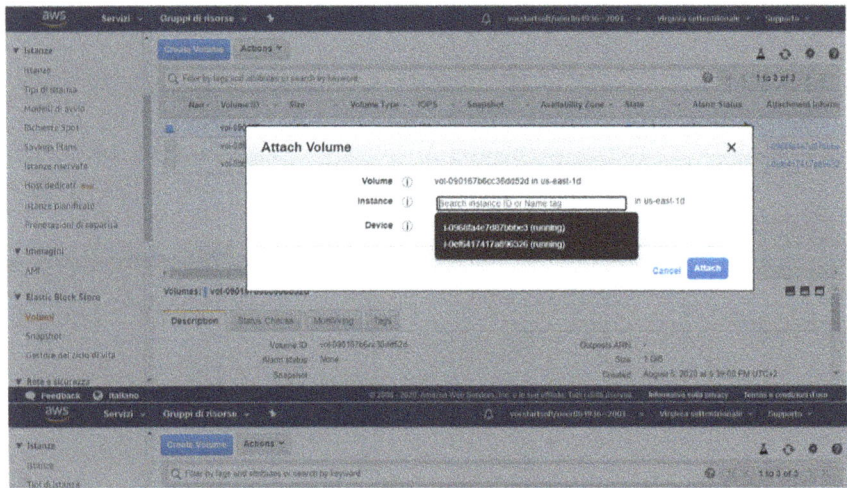

3. Once you have selected where to attach your volume, click on the "Attach" button.
4. In the new window you can see that "Attachment Information" is equal to the id of the instance selected in the previous step. Congratulations! You have attached a volume to an instance.

## 3.8 Exercises

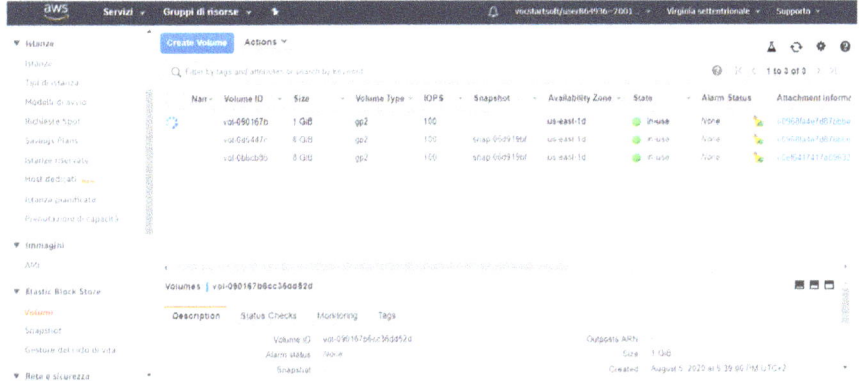

### D. Make a EBS Volume Available for Use

1. Now you have to access to your instance by using one of the methods specified here: https://docs.aws.amazon.com/AWSEC2/latest/UserGuide/AccessingInstances.html
2. Once you are logged in the first instance, you can run the `lsblk` command to verify which volumes are attached to the instance. As you can see from the screenshot below, the volume created in the previous step is located in the `/dev/xvdf` device.

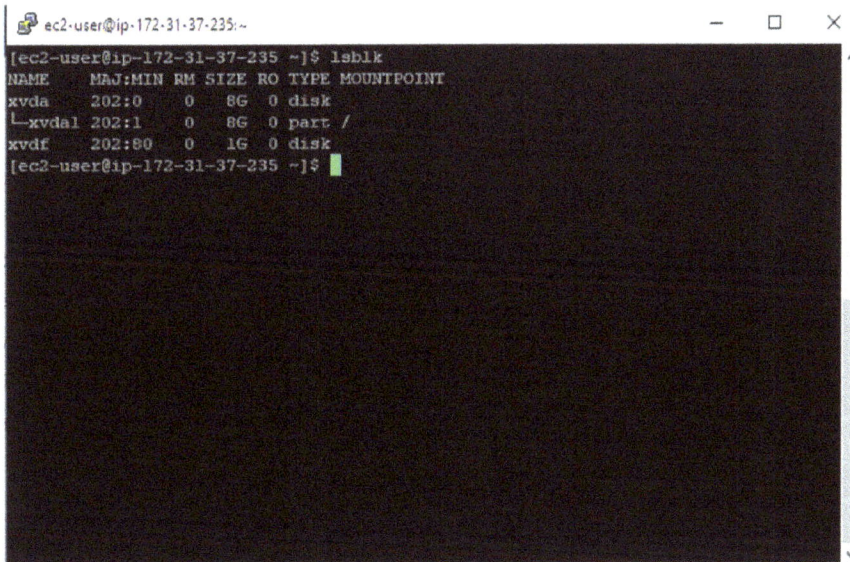

3. You can create a directory, where you will put all the files that your app needs by using the `mkdir` command.

4. Since the volume created does not have a file system, we can format the volume with XFS file system by running the following command:

    ```
    sudo mkfs -t xfs /dev/xvdf
    ```

5. Of course, by modifying the "-t" parameter, you can create a different file system into the volume. In the next screenshot, the output of the proposed commands (the file -s command is just to check which kind of file system is mounted: "data" means that the volume has to be formatted by specifying a file system)

    ```
    [ec2-user@ip-172-31-37-235 ~]$ lsblk
    NAME    MAJ:MIN RM SIZE RO TYPE MOUNTPOINT
    xvda    202:0    0   8G  0 disk
    └─xvda1 202:1    0   8G  0 part /
    xvdf    202:80   0   1G  0 disk
    [ec2-user@ip-172-31-37-235 ~]$ sudo mkdir data
    [ec2-user@ip-172-31-37-235 ~]$ ls
    data
    [ec2-user@ip-172-31-37-235 ~]$ sudo file -s /dev/xvdf
    /dev/xvdf: data
    [ec2-user@ip-172-31-37-235 ~]$ sudo mkfs -t xfs /dev/xvdf
    meta-data=/dev/xvdf          isize=512    agcount=4, agsize=65536 blks
             =                   sectsz=512   attr=2, projid32bit=1
             =                   crc=1        finobt=1, sparse=0
    data     =                   bsize=4096   blocks=262144, imaxpct=25
             =                   sunit=0      swidth=0 blks
    naming   =version 2          bsize=4096   ascii-ci=0 ftype=1
    log      =internal log       bsize=4096   blocks=2560, version=2
             =                   sectsz=512   sunit=0 blks, lazy-count=1
    realtime =none               extsz=4096   blocks=0, rtextents=0
    [ec2-user@ip-172-31-37-235 ~]$ sudo file -s /dev/xvdf
    /dev/xvdf: SGI XFS filesystem data (blksz 4096, inosz 512, v2 dirs)
    [ec2-user@ip-172-31-37-235 ~]$
    ```

6. Now it is possible to mount the new volume into the directory previously created:

    ```
    sudo mount /dev/xvdf data
    ```

7. Now we need to change the permissions of the data directory:

    ```
    sudo chmod a=rwx data
    ```

8. The output of the previous command should look like this:

    ```
    [ec2-user@ip-172-31-37-235 ~]$ ls -l
    total 0
    drwxr-xr-x 2 root root 6 Aug  5 15:45 data
    [ec2-user@ip-172-31-37-235 ~]$ sudo chmod a=rwx data
    [ec2-user@ip-172-31-37-235 ~]$ ls -l
    total 0
    drwxrwxrwx 2 root root 6 Aug  5 15:45 data
    [ec2-user@ip-172-31-37-235 ~]$
    ```

3.8 Exercises

9. Now you can use the `cat` command to create a file:

```
[ec2-user@ip-172-31-37-235 ~]$ cd data
[ec2-user@ip-172-31-37-235 data]$ cat > test.txt
Test file
[ec2-user@ip-172-31-37-235 data]$ cat test.txt
Test file
[ec2-user@ip-172-31-37-235 data]$ ls -l
total 4
-rw-rw-r-- 1 ec2-user ec2-user 10 Aug  5 15:54 test.txt
[ec2-user@ip-172-31-37-235 data]$
```

10. Congratulations! You have created the file inside a volume. This file and, more generally, the volume will be passed to the other instance but, before that, we have to detach the volume.

### E. Detach a EBS Volume from an Instance

In this section, we will detach the volume and repeat the operation to mount the volume on the other instance.

1. First of all, we need to unmount the volume by using the following command:

    ```
    sudo umount -d /dev/xvdf
    ```

2. With the `lsblk` command you can see the volume is no longer mounted:

```
[ec2-user@ip-172-31-37-235 ~]$ sudo umount -d /dev/xvdf
[ec2-user@ip-172-31-37-235 ~]$ lsblk
NAME    MAJ:MIN RM SIZE RO TYPE MOUNTPOINT
xvda    202:0    0   8G  0 disk
└─xvda1 202:1    0   8G  0 part /
[ec2-user@ip-172-31-37-235 ~]$
```

3. Then you have to go back to the Web Console and select the volume, finally just click on the "Actions" button. In the drop down menu, select the "Detach" option:

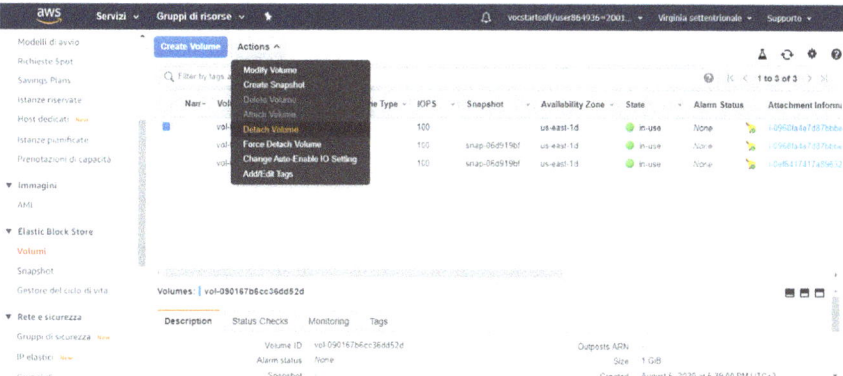

4. After this action, you can see that the "Attachment Information" of the selected volume has no information. Also the state of the volume is now "available" while before it was "in-use" :

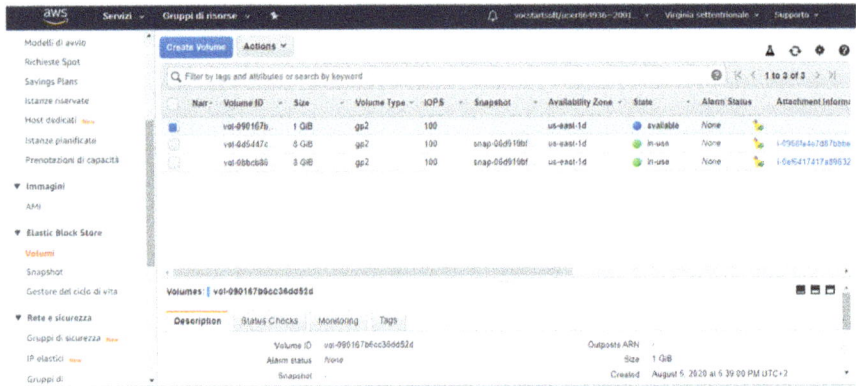

**Step F: Attach a EBS Volume to the Other Instance**

1. You have to repeat the operation of step C to attach the volume to the other instance. The volume contains the file that we have created, so after attaching it to the second instance, you do not have to repeat the operations of step D (the volume already has a file system) but you have only to mount the volume in a directory. You can run the following commands (note that `sudo file -s /dev/xvdf` and `ls -l` are optional: they just show you which kind of file system is used and the permission of the files/directories inside the volume):

```
lsblk
sudo file -s /dev/xvdf
mkdir data
sudo mount /dev/xvdf data
cd data
cat test.txt
```

2. The output of the above commands should look like this:

3.8 Exercises

```
python-libs.x86_64 0:2.7.18-1.amzn2.0.1
python2-rsa.noarch 0:3.4.1-1.amzn2.0.1
tzdata.noarch 0:2020a-1.amzn2
Complete!
[ec2-user@ip-172-31-42-134 ~]$ lsblk
NAME    MAJ:MIN RM SIZE RO TYPE MOUNTPOINT
xvda    202:0    0   8G  0 disk
└─xvda1 202:1    0   8G  0 part /
xvdf    202:80   0   1G  0 disk
[ec2-user@ip-172-31-42-134 ~]$ sudo file -s /dev/xvdf
/dev/xvdf: SGI XFS filesystem data (blksz 4096, inosz 512, v2 dirs)
[ec2-user@ip-172-31-42-134 ~]$ sudo mkdir data
[ec2-user@ip-172-31-42-134 ~]$ sudo mount /dev/xvdf data
[ec2-user@ip-172-31-42-134 ~]$ ls -l
total 0
drwxrwxrwx 2 root root 22 Aug  5 15:54 data
[ec2-user@ip-172-31-42-134 ~]$ cd data
[ec2-user@ip-172-31-42-134 data]$ ls -l
total 4
-rw-rw-r-- 1 ec2-user ec2-user 10 Aug  5 15:54 test.txt
[ec2-user@ip-172-31-42-134 data]$ cat test.txt
Test file
[ec2-user@ip-172-31-42-134 data]$
```

3. Congratulations! You have successfully completed the tutorial goal! Before you leave, just clean your working space by unmounting and detaching the volume. To unmount the volume, just run this command:

    sudo umount -d /dev/xvdf

4. Then detach the volume by following Step E proposed before.

**Step G: Delete a EBS Volume**

The last step is to delete the volume: this is important also because any volume created has a cost. As a general suggestion, any cloud resources that you do not need anymore, you should delete to avoid costs. Repeat the operation of Step 4 for detaching the volume from the instance, and then you have to select the volume and click on "Action". Finally, in the drop down menu just click on the "Delete Volume" option.

# 3 Cloud Computing Platforms

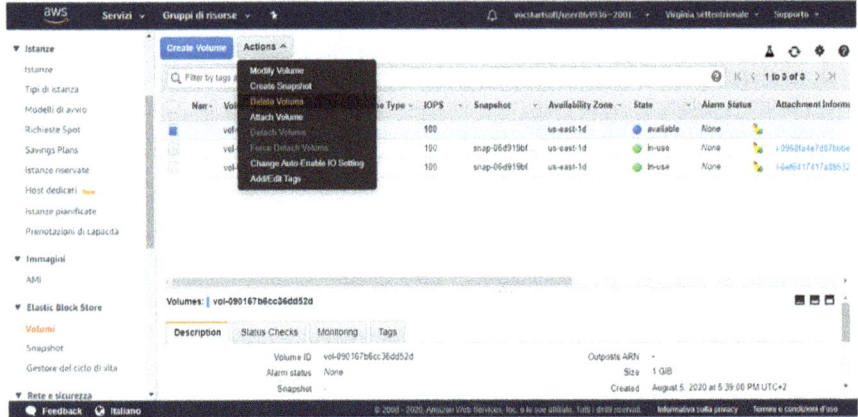

# Chapter 4
# Types of Cloud Services

This chapter describes the wide range of services that modern clouds offer to their users. These services can be categorized broadly into three levels of abstraction, which are described in Sect. 4.1. The rest of this chapter gives an overview of the types of cloud resources that are available in modern cloud systems, using the Google Cloud Platform as an example.

## 4.1 Levels of Abstractions

As described in the introduction, cloud services are typically categorized into three service models: Infrastructure as a Service (IaaS), Platform as a Service (PaaS) and Software as a Service (SaaS). To briefly recap, the cloud service provider offers bare (virtual) computing resources such as virtual machines or storage in IaaS, higher-level computing platforms in PaaS, and ready-to-use software applications in SaaS. An often used analogy to illustrate these different service models is shown in Fig. 4.1.

Someone who wants to eat pizza has four different ways to achieve this outcome:

- **Made at home:** In this scenario, the dining table (including chairs, cutlery, drinks etc.), the oven (including its power source), the pizza dough and all the toppings—in short, everything—is in the responsibility of the pizza eater. This is equivalent to the traditional on-premise hosting of IT, where everything (physical servers including power supply and cooling, operating systems and configurations, platform elements and the applications themselves) is in the responsibility of the user.
- **Take & Bake:** In this model, everything but the pizza itself remains in the responsibility of the user—i.e., they still need to have everything to actually bake and consume a ready-to-bake pizza. This can be compared to the IaaS model, where the majority of the responsibility still lies with the user (application software, platform software, operating system, configurations), but where the

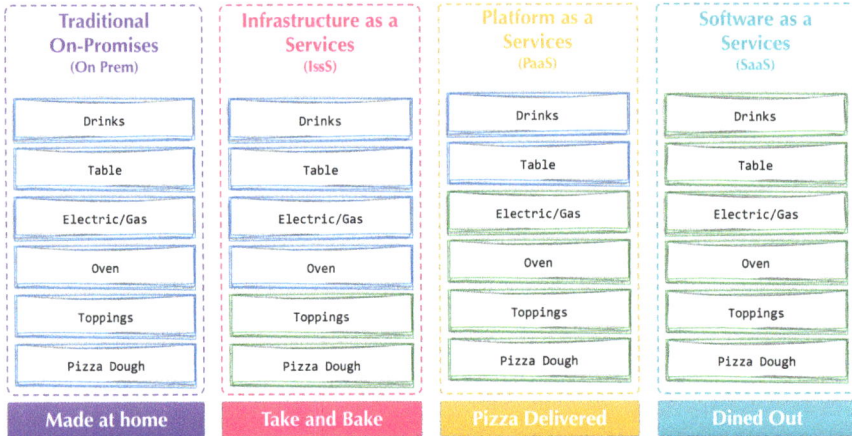

**Fig. 4.1** The Pizza-as-a-service metaphor

responsibility for maintaining the physical hardware rests with the cloud service provider.

- **Pizza Delivered:** Here, the user is only responsible for the eating environment, while the raw pizza and its baking (including everything that is needed for it) rests with the delivery service. The cloud analogy would be PaaS, where the user remains responsible for their software applications, but hands the physical hardware, its operating system and all required platform elements over to the cloud service provider.
- **Dining Out:** In this final model, the user simply has to consume the pizza—the responsibility for everything rests with the restaurant. The cloud equivalent is SaaS, where the cloud service provider offers a ready-to-use application, and takes care of everything that is required to run it.

How do you decide between these different models of pizza consumption? There is no best way to consume pizza—it depends on the circumstances and individual preferences. Broadly speaking, in the figure, both the price and the level of convenience increase from the left to the right. On the other hand, the level of control decreases from the left to the right: If you make and eat pizza at home, you can make whichever kind of pizza you want, and you can create the exact physical setting in which you want to consume the pizza. On the other side of the spectrum, if you eat pizza at a restaurant, you can only pick between all the restaurants offering pizza, and eat one of the pizzas they offer.

To be precise, the last two statements have to be slightly modified: At home, you can make whatever pizza you want only if you are able to, i.e. have the required knowledge, skills and ingredients. And at least in better (often more expensive) restaurants, within certain boundaries, you can actually get modifications to either the pizzas offered or the setting you consume them in, sometimes at an extra cost.

This analogy carries over fairly well to the computing world. For example, assume a company considers different alternatives to run its inventory management system.

## 4.1 Levels of Abstractions

Once again, generally speaking, the level of convenience increases from the left to the right (from traditional on-premise to SaaS), while the level of control decreases from the left from the right. Or more specifically, in the on-premise approach the company can create exactly the kind of inventory management system it wants, with whatever specific features are required, and operate it with the exact level of performance, scalability, fault tolerance etc. as desired. Just like above, this is limited by the capabilities of the company—from IT skills to necessary funds. On the other side of the spectrum, if the company chooses to use SaaS, then it is limited by what the vendors of SaaS solutions for inventory management offer. And again, just like in the pizza example, for an extra fee, the company might be able (within certain limits) to get its specific needs met by the provider.

One area of the analogy is particularly tricky—cost. Generally, it seems sensible to say that making a pizza at home is cheaper than eating a pizza at a restaurant: The ingredients and the required electricity cost significantly less than a restaurant meal. However, such a comparison makes assumptions. For example, it relies on the fact that the person owns an oven. Also, it assumes that the manual labor required to make the pizza is free. This translates quite well into the IT world—if a company already owns the necessary hardware to run an application, and if operating it creates no additional labor costs (e.g. because the IT department can handle the new application without additional personnel), then running the application on-premise is likely going to be cheaper than any of the cloud models. Of course, in practice, these assumptions do not usually hold. The hardware resources used to run applications create depreciation costs over time, and operating an extra application creates extra work that costs money. Consequently, it depends on each specific situation which approach is most cost effective, with a cloud computing model likely being cheapest in many cases due to the arguments discussed in Sect. 1.2.2.

In closing, it should be pointed out that cost is only one of many factors that influences whether cloud computing should be chosen, and if so, which cloud service model is most appropriate in a given situation. A more comprehensive analysis of different factors will be discussed in Sect. 8.3.2 on cloud migration. For illustrative purposes, we will look at one more factor here, the level of control that an organization has in the different approaches. For example, irrespective of how an application is run (in-house, or in the cloud with IaaS, PaaS or SaaS), it is likely to depend on a number of platform components. For example, a web application might run on the LAMP stack (Linux, Apache, MySQL and PHP). Any of these elements require regular updates to fix discovered security vulnerabilities. In the on-premise and IaaS models, updates to these elements are in the responsibility of the company that uses the application. In the PaaS and SaaS models, the updates are performed by the cloud provider.

A company that performs platform updates itself has more control over them. In particular, it can make sure to carefully test the updates with its applications to discover possible unintended side effects. On the flip side, it also has the responsibility to do the updates. Until tests are completed and the update performed, the application is vulnerable to security risks. So to decide between the different ways to operate the application, the company should consider carefully whether it has the resources to perform the necessary tests and updates in a timely manner. If so, this would be one argument towards on-premise or IaaS hosting, because only in these models application-specific compatibility tests of the platform updates are performed. If not, it might be better to utilize PaaS or SaaS, because the cloud service provider is likely able to perform a wide range of tests on the updates, and install the updates, in a timely manner. The tests of the provider (at least in PaaS) would not be specific to the application (which the cloud provider is not responsible for, after all), which would raise a small risk that potential issues are not discovered. However, this risk is probably preferable to the risk of either installing updates without any significant tests, or the longer exposure to the security vulnerability if the updates are delayed.

## 4.2 Types of Cloud Services

This section gives an overview of the range of cloud computing services that are available, using the Google Cloud Platform (GCP) as an example. Note that other cloud service providers such as AWS offer a very similar range of services (see e.g. here[1] for a comparison of AWS and Google Cloud Platform services).

The services can be categorized as follows:

- Computational Services
- Network Services
- Storage Services
- Big Data
- Machine Learning
- Management Services

When an organization uses the Google Cloud Platform, any individual resource (such as a virtual machine or a storage bucket) is associated with a single project. Projects are used to manage billing, access permissions, track use via budgets and quotas etc. Customers can simply use one or several separate projects for this purpose, or create an organizational node that can contain projects either directly and/or group them in a hierarchy of folders.

GCP resources are hosted in a specific region (e.g. us-west1). Regions contain multiple zones (e.g. us-west1 a,b,c) that are failure independent due to strict separation from each other. Therefore, a failure e.g. due to a fire or local flood in one zone should not affect the other zones in a region. This allows customers to place their cloud resources deliberately in multiple zones to increase fault tolerance and availability of their applications (see Fig. 4.2).

All cloud resources can be managed either through the web-based GCP console, on the command line via the GCP Cloud SDK (Software Development Kit) or the Cloud Shell, through REST-based APIs or (with limited functionality) in GCP mobile apps.

---

[1] https://cloud.google.com/docs/compare/aws.

4.2 Types of Cloud Services 115

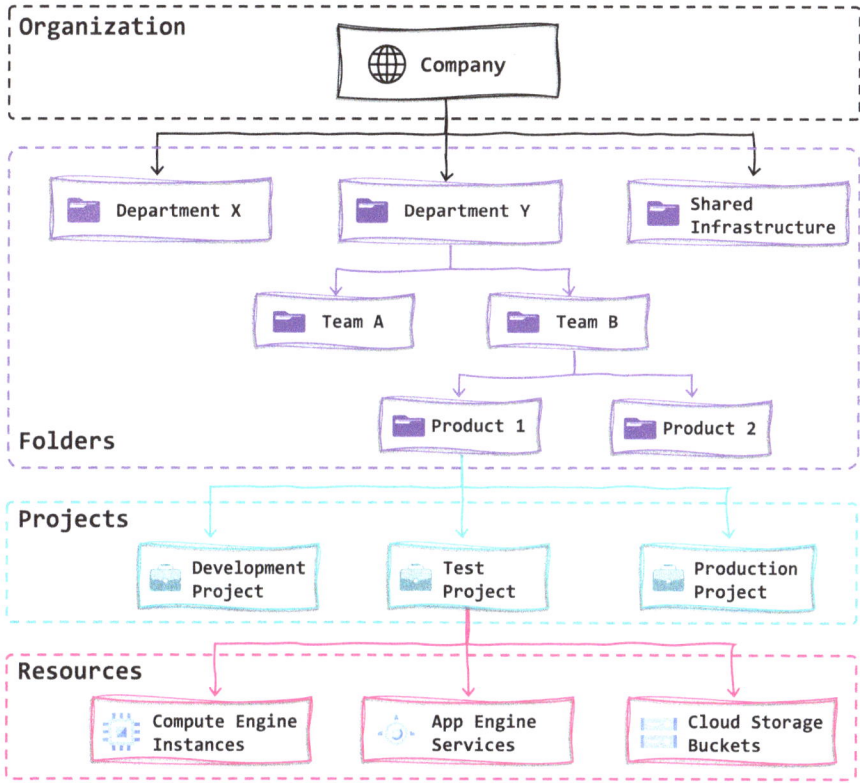

**Fig. 4.2** The Google cloud resource hierarchy

> **Early Days of Cloud Computing**
>
> While the major cloud providers today all offer a comparable and wide range of services, there were substantial differences between the services the different providers offered in the early days of cloud computing. As outlined in "Above the Clouds: A Berkeley View of Cloud Computing" (Armbrust, M. et al, 2009), providers typically focused on a smaller set of services that was often quite distinct from other providers. For example, in early 2009, with regard to compute resources, AWS offered mainly virtual machines while the Google Cloud Platform (GCP) focused on PaaS offerings in which customers deployed python code in a provider-managed environment. Both approaches had their advantages and disadvantages. AWS customers had more control over their compute resources but needed to implement automatic scaling for elastic workloads on their own. In contrast, GCP was much more restrictive about the kind of code that could be deployed but implemented automatic scaling of applications based on load for the customer.

## 4.2.1 Computational Services

Computational services allow cloud users to run applications in the cloud. In practice, this happens at one of the following four levels of abstraction: Infrastructure as a Service, Containers, Platform as a Service or Functions as a Service.

**Infrastructure as a Service (IaaS)**

Computing using IaaS means the use of virtual machines in the cloud. A wide variety of (virtual) hardware configurations are available, typically ranging from a single CPU core with less than 1 GByte of memory (costing less than a cent per hour) to more than a hundred CPU cores and several Terabytes of memory (costing around $20 per hour). Figure 4.3 shows the different machine type families available on GCP. Additionally, many different configurations with regard to storage (size, use of hard disks vs. solid state drives), GPUs etc. are possible. Virtual machines are available with a range of different (usually server) operating systems, including various Linux distributions and Windows Server. Of course, the user can also use their own operating system and configuration using pre-configured images. Virtual machines can be created very rapidly (often in less than a minute).

IaaS computing services usually offer features beyond bare virtual machines, including networking functionality such as firewalls. Another common feature would be automatic scaling. In GCP, users can define instance templates, which specify

| Series | Description | vCPUs | Memory | CPU Platfor |
|---|---|---|---|---|
| C4 | Consistently high performance | 2 - 192 | 4 - 1,488 GB | Intel Emerald |
| C4A | Arm-based consistently high performance | 1 - 72 | 2 - 576 GB | Google Axion |
| C4D | Preview Consistently high performance | 2 - 384 | 3 - 3,024 GB | AMD Turin |
| N4 | Flexible & cost-optimized | 2 - 80 | 4 - 640 GB | Intel Emerald |
| C3 | Consistently high performance | 4 - 192 | 8 - 1,536 GB | Intel Sapphire |
| C3D | Consistently high performance | 4 - 360 | 8 - 2,880 GB | AMD Genoa |
| E2 | Low cost, day-to-day computing | 0.25 - 32 | 1 - 128 GB | Intel Broadwe |
| N2 | Balanced price & performance | 2 - 128 | 2 - 864 GB | Intel Cascade |
| N2D | Balanced price & performance | 2 - 224 | 2 - 896 GB | AMD Milan |
| T2A | Scale-out workloads | 1 - 48 | 4 - 192 GB | Ampere Altra |
| T2D | Scale-out workloads | 1 - 60 | 4 - 240 GB | AMD Milan |
| N1 | Balanced price & performance | 0.25 - 96 | 0.6 - 624 GB | Intel Haswell |

**Fig. 4.3** Different families of machines types available on GCP

configuration details (e.g. using startup scripts) so that instances can be created automatically using the template. Using such an instance template, an instance group can be defined. Used in combination with auto-scaling load balancers (a networking feature in GCP), instance groups can be configured to e.g. automatically scale the number of web server instances serving a domain up and down based on load. Users can furthermore specify in which server center locations different virtual machine instances should be created. This allows users to make their applications extra resilient in the face of e.g. natural disasters, which typically only affect a single location. Even though IaaS-based computing is conceptually very similar to running virtual machines in an on-premise server center, these advanced features offer significant improvements in rapid scalability and reliability.

A final interesting feature is the availability of discounted virtual machine instances. The GCP offers spot instances (previously called preemptible instances). The price of these instances relative to standard instances changes over time, but is usually substantially lower, reflecting e.g. a 50–75% discount. The catch is that Google might shut these virtual machines down with minimal advance warning (a brief, orderly shutdown script can still be executed). While such instances are obviously out of the question for systems that cannot afford significant downtime, they are well suited for offline processing. For example, for scientific workloads evaluating massive amounts of data that run for days at a time, it might not matter very much if the results are available a few days earlier or later. However, the cost savings might make a huge difference.

Google offers these spot instances to increase the utilization of its computing resources. Since it cannot precisely predict how many virtual machine instances its customers will need, it has to keep a certain amount of spare capacity available so that it does not run out of resources. Rather than keep this spare capacity completely idle, Google sells some of it to customers in the form of spot instances. If a sudden spike in resource use occurs, Google can simply shut down a few spot instances to create free capacity. In the meantime these instances create at least some revenue.

Even if spot instances are not an option, users can get discounts either for "sustained use", i.e. if virtual machines are running for a significant portion of a month, or for committing to using virtual machines for a longer period of time upfront (e.g. for a whole year). While such options essentially eliminate the potential advantage of elasticity in cloud use, they can still be very appropriate for stable compute loads.

**Containers**

Containers (using the Docker[2] standard) are another way to deploy applications in the cloud. They are more "light-weight" than virtual machines, but still contain everything an application needs to run. In this section, we just discuss the GCP solutions to manage the containers, more details concerning what a container is can be found in Sect. 5.3.4.

---

[2] https://www.docker.com/.

The Google Cloud Platform uses the cloud orchestration system Kubernetes[3] to run and manage applications in its Container as a Service (CaaS) model. Kubernetes manages the deployment of applications in a declarative fashion—in other words, users specify what they want to achieve, rather than how to achieve it. For example, a user can specify that an application that consists of a number of containers is deployed redundantly (for fault tolerance purposes) on say two different nodes (i.e. underlying execution hardware). If one of the nodes on which that application is deployed fails (e.g. because of a network problem), Kubernetes will automatically deploy the application on another, reachable one. Similarly, it can be configured to scale the deployment up and down based on system load, to automatically roll out (and, in the case of errors, roll back) updates to the application on all the clusters on which it is deployed etc.

The Google Kubernetes Engine (GKE)[4] frees the user from having to manually deal with deployments and the underlying resources that support them.[5] Therefore, it can be considered to be at a higher level of abstraction than using bare IaaS, where the user is responsible for allocating required virtual machines and for deploying the application on them. Another significant advantage is that vendor lock-in is not a big concern since Kubernetes is an open-source system that can easily be migrated to other underlying platforms.

Google Cloud actually offers another way to run applications in containers—Google Cloud Run[6] In contrast to the GKE, Cloud Run offers users less influence over configuration and management of the underlying clusters, and instead manages these aspects for the user, which might make it a better choice for simple applications. As Fig. 4.4 showing the first step of the Cloud Run creation dialog illustrates, the Cloud Run service can not only be used to run containers, but also to directly deploy code from a repository or in the form a simple cloud function from an inline editor.

**Platform as a Service (PaaS)**

In the PaaS approach, the responsibility for the underlying infrastructure lies with the cloud provider, which frees the user from having to worry about it. The Google Cloud Platform's PaaS offering is the App Engine.

In the App Engine, users can deploy applications using a range of different programming languages, including Python, Java, PHP and Go. Each application consists of a number of services, which in turn can exist in several versions. Individual service versions are deployed in instances. The number of deployed instances can be configured manually, but automatic scaling based on load is also available.

---

[3] https://kubernetes.io/.

[4] https://cloud.google.com/kubernetes-engine.

[5] In fact, the Google Kubernetes Engine creates virtual machines in the Google Compute Engine to run the containers on. The advantage to using IaaS is that the user does not have to deal with these virtual machines directly at all.

[6] https://cloud.google.com/run.

## 4.2 Types of Cloud Services

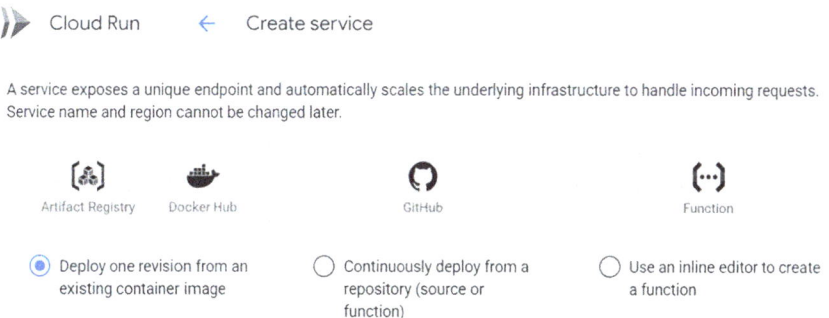

Fig. 4.4 Different cloud run options

The App Engine offers two different environments, the standard and the flexible environment. The standard environment is limited to specific supported programming languages in specific versions, and offers only limited configuration options. On the other hand, it is fully managed, and can scale down to zero, i.e. does not incur any costs if the application is not invoked at all. The flexible environment uses Docker containers, and is consequently not limited to a fixed list of programming languages and versions. It also offers more configuration options. However, while it can scale up and down, it incurs some costs even if idle, since at least one instance is always running, and it requires more configuration efforts from the user.

PaaS is a serverless approach. This term is technically incorrect—at the end of the day, deployed applications are still executed on servers (like any other type of application as well). The point is that in PaaS, the developers and operators of applications do not have to manage the servers themselves—this task is taken over by the cloud service provider. The App Engine is not the only serverless compute offering of the Google Cloud Platform. Cloud Functions (discussed below) are another option. The difference is that in the App Engine, the unit of deployment is usually an application that consists of multiple functions and that needs to maintain some context that survives beyond individual function calls. Typical examples for applications that are well suited for the App Engine include simple web applications or backends for mobile applications.

**Functions as a Service (FaaS)**

As discussed, FaaS is another serverless approach. Here, users write individual functions in languages like JavaScript (using the Node.js framework), Python, Go or Java. For each function, triggers are defined, such as http requests, specific cloud storage events, or other specific messaging or logging events. When a trigger event occurs, the corresponding cloud function is executed. Just like with PaaS, the user does not have to worry about provisioning the computing resources that execute Cloud Functions, and is only charged for the computing time that actual function invocations consume. Note how this is very different from e.g. the IaaS model, where the user allocates a number of virtual machines, and is charged for them (irrespective of whether they are busy or idle).

A typical example use of Cloud Functions could be a website or mobile app that allows end users to upload photos. Whenever a photo is uploaded, it has to be processed, e.g. optimized, smaller versions of the photo (including thumbnails) have to be created etc. Putting this functionality into a cloud a Cloud Function makes the application very scalable and cost effective. Cloud Functions can also be very useful to combine different cloud services—e.g. when changes in storage occur, processing steps can be triggered.

## 4.2.2 Network Services

The different types of cloud services described in this chapter are usually not used in isolation. For example, users of compute services often use storage services to store the data involved in their computations. Similarly, networking services are usually not used as a stand-alone services, but as an enabling feature that makes using just about any other cloud service type possible in the first place. To put this differently: Cloud network services are used to connect the other cloud services (such as compute or storage) with each other, with their end users and any in-house IT resources an organization might have (for example in a hybrid cloud scenario).

**Virtual Private Cloud (VPC)**

In the Google Cloud Platform, all cloud resources of an organization are by default placed into a Virtual Private Cloud (VPC). A VPC has global scope, i.e. can contain resources in any GCP data center in the world. VPCs offer managed networking functionality. In particular, this means that internal routing does not have to be configured manually. In fact, (virtual or physical) networking equipment such as routers or switches do not have to be provisioned or managed by cloud users at all.

By default, the network topology is managed automatically. For example, a subnet is created for each region, as subnets cannot span multiple regions. Organizations can also choose to define their network structure manually, which puts them in charge of defining appropriate subnets, IP ranges, firewall rules etc.

Cloud resources in a VPC have an internal IP address through which they communicate with other resources in the same VPC. For this purpose, private IP addresses (typically from the 10.*.*.* network) are used. To be accessible from the outside, they can also have an external IP address. External IP addresses can be ephemeral, i.e. assigned from a pool of addresses that are shared, and that consequently typically change if a resource such as a virtual machine is shut down and later restarted. Alternatively, for an extra charge, static IP addresses are available, which are reserved for a specific resource.

VPCs are protected by a distributed stateful firewall. Rather than having to manually create and manage virtual or physical firewalls between different cloud resources and other networks, firewall rules apply to the network as a whole, and allow or deny network traffic at the instance level. By default, all incoming data traffic (ingress) is denied, while all outgoing traffic (egress) is allowed. More specific firewall rules can be defined by users, specifying whether traffic is allowed or not based on its source or destination, protocol and port used. Firewall rules have a numeric priority attached to them, and are applied in priority order. The first applicable rule decides whether traffic is allowed or denied.

As mentioned above, resources in GCP are grouped into projects. VPCs can be shared by multiple projects in the same organization. Alternatively, multiple VPCs (containing projects from the same or different organizations) can use network peering to connect to each other, which allows for decentralized network administration.

**Load Balancing**

Load balancing (combined with the ability to scale computing resources up and down easily) is one of the core functionalities required in cloud computing. Load balancers enable the operation of applications with loads that exceed what a single server (even a powerful one) can handle. Such applications are very common—for example, any busy online store or other web site probably needs multiple web servers to handle incoming requests at peak loads. A load balancer distributes all incoming requests between whatever number of servers is necessary to handle the load.

The use of load balancers not only helps ensure adequate performance (e.g. low response time) of applications, it also increases their availability: Load balancers can detect malfunctioning servers, and forward incoming requests to any of the other servers. Of course, a poorly designed load balancer itself can become a "single point of failure". In other words, if the load balancer is implemented as an application on a single machine, a failure of that machine makes the whole application unreachable for all users, even if the actual servers behind the load balancer all work properly. Needless to say, the load balancers offered by GCP do not suffer from this problem, but are instead built with appropriate redundancy.

GCP offers different kinds of load balancers for different kinds of purposes. There are load balancers for HTTP(S), SSL and TCP traffic that are global in scale, meaning they can forward requests to servers in different regions based on proximity to the user. There are also network load balancers that work on a regional level and can handle any TCP or UDP traffic, both for internal only and for external traffic. Figure 4.5 shows some of the different options offered when a load balancer is created in GCP.

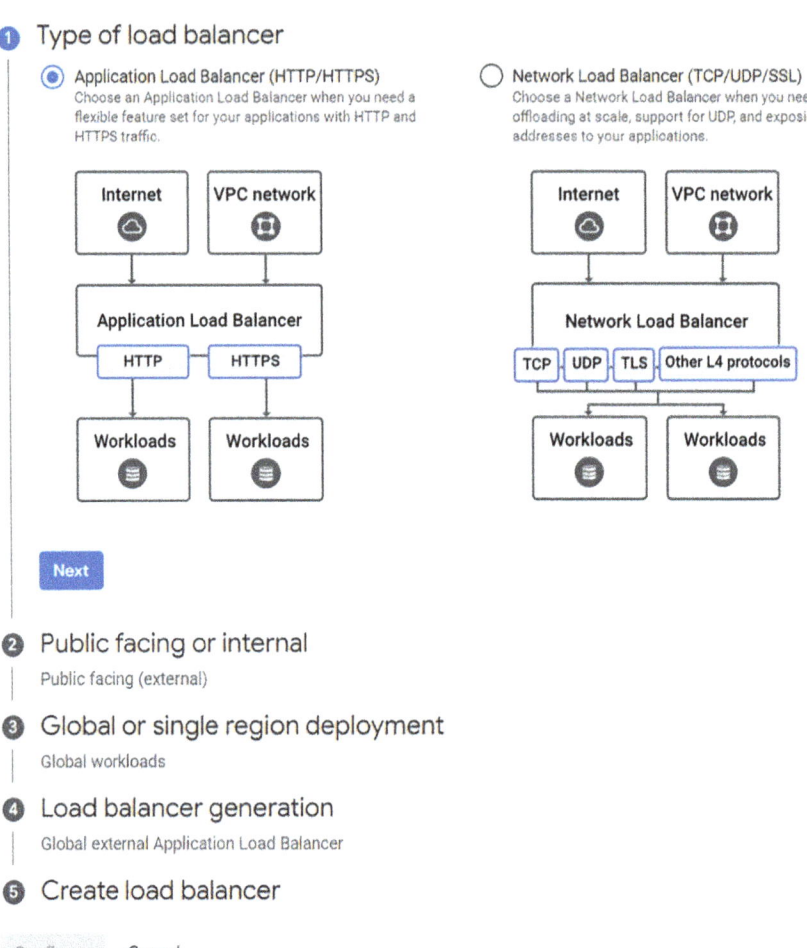

Fig. 4.5 Different load balancer options in GCP

**Other Networking Features**

GCP offers several other types of networking features. Cloud Interconnect allows organizations to connect their internal (on premise) networks to GCP VPC networks, either directly or through interconnect partners.

Especially for organizations that have users in many different locations, Cloud CDN (Content Delivery Network) allows to cache content closer to users, reducing end user latency and network traffic cost.

Cloud DNS is a scalable Domain Name Server that organizations can use to resolve domain names to IP addresses.

## 4.2 Types of Cloud Services

Finally, GCP offers a number of networking security features, including Cloud Armor, which helps mitigate potential DDoS (Distributed Denial of Service) attacks, as well as other common types of network based attacks such as cross-site scripting (XSS) and SQL injection attacks. Figure 4.6 shows the different levels of Cloud Armor protection available in GCP.

### 4.2.3 Storage Services

Just like networking, most cloud applications need storage services as well. Traditionally, storage meant file storage, and later storage in relational databases for structured data in table format. Today, a much more diverse range of storage options exists in the storage field in general, and this is reflected in storage cloud services as well.

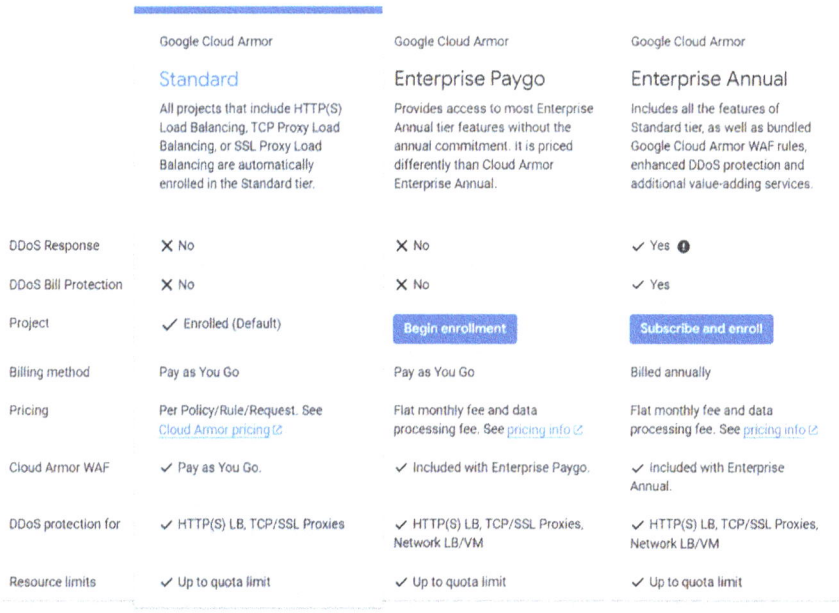

**Fig. 4.6** Different cloud armor protection levels offered in GCP

> **AWS S3**
>
> In the area of object storage, the Amazon Simple Storage Service, or short AWS S3, is the most widely used storage service and protocol. Just like in GCP Cloud Storage, AWS S3 organizes objects in storage buckets, offers a range of different storage classes and provides advanced options for object versioning, lifecycle rules for automatic data management (e.g. automatic deletion after a specific period of time) etc.
>
> Data in S3 can be accessed and manipulated via a RESTful API using HTTP requests. For example, a HTTP GET request with an object key retrieves the corresponding object, while a GET request with a bucket as argument lists the content of the storage bucket. HTTP PUT requests can be used to store objects, while HTTP DELETE requests remove objects from a bucket.
>
> First introduced by AWS in 2006, the S3 protocol has become a de facto standard to access object storage. Consequently, comparable storage services at other service providers like GCP typically offer S3 compatible APIs to allow for easier migration from or integration with AWS S3. Similarly, numerous open-source solution such as MinIO or Ceph support the S3 protocol.

**Cloud Storage**

GCP Cloud Storage allows organizations to store unstructured data in objects. This is used by Google itself for many of its other services—for example, Google Photos stores user photos and videos and Gmail stores email attachments using Cloud Storage.

Cloud Storage organizes data in buckets, which have a unique name, a location (in one or multiple regions), a storage class, access policies and object versioning and lifecycle management options.

There are four different storage classes:

- Standard Storage
- Nearline Storage
- Coldline Storage
- Archive Storage

Standard Storage is the default storage class for storing data that is accessed regularly. While it costs the most for storage (per GB per month), it features the lowest access costs. It also has no minimum storage duration. Nearline, Coldline and Archive Storage offer increasingly cheaper storage rates, but charge increasingly more for data accesses. They also feature minimum storage durations of 30, 90 and 365 days, respectively, which means that while storage buckets and their content in

4.2 Types of Cloud Services

these classes can be deleted at any time, the user is charged the minimum number of days as indicated.

All storage classes can be used within a single region, or in two or multiple regions. The latter offer slightly more reliability due to the extra redundancy, but also cost slightly more.

**Relational Databases**

Relational database systems are still the backbone of many business systems that deal with structured data. Therefore, it is not surprising that GCP offers relational databases in the cloud.

Cloud SQL offers users fully managed MySQL, PostgreSQL or SQL Server instances that handle replication, backups and automatic scaling for the user, supporting up to 64 CPU cores, 400 GByte of RAM, and 10TB of storage. Figure 4.7 shows the different options available in the CloudSQL service in GCP, with regard to both different database management systems as well as different deployments, ranging from small sandbox deployments for trial purposes to production ready deployments.

Users that need larger instances can instead use the Cloud Spanner service that, thanks to horizontal scalability, can be used for much larger applications.

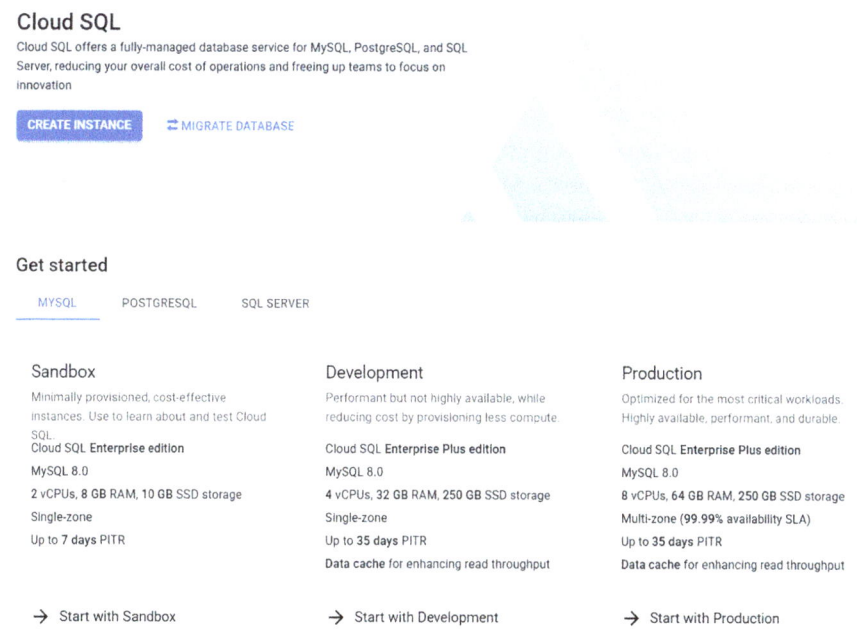

Fig. 4.7 Different CloudSQL options offered in GCP

**Non-Relational Databases**

Cloud Datastore is a NoSQL database. It doesn't require users to define a database schema, supports Atomic, Consistent, Isolated and Durable (ACID) transactions, and is fully managed, i.e. automatically taking care of scaling, replication etc. It supports SQL-like queries.

Compared to Cloud Datastore, Cloud Bigtable is meant for even larger amounts of data. It is another NoSQL database offering for large workloads. It can scale to billions of rows and thousands of columns of data. It is also fully managed, and integrated with open source big data tools like Hadoop.

**Data Warehousing**

BigQuery is another offering for very large amounts of data. In contrast to the non-relational databases from the previous section, the focus of BigQuery is on Online Analytical Processing (OLAP) type queries, rather than on Online Transactional Processing (OLTP) queries. In other words, it performs best if used in queries that summarize large amounts of data (e.g., how do the sales of products in category X in Q1 of last year compare to Q1 of current year?), rather than on large numbers of individual queries (e.g. inserting thousands of new sales transactions per hour).

**Block Storage**

Block storage is a technique where any data (like a file or database entry) is divided into blocks of equal sizes. Then, the block storage service decides where these blocks must be distributed in the cloud in order to optimize the access time. In particular, Block storage service is useful when application is latency sensitive and it requires high-performance. Comparing with file storage, Block storage architecture provides multiple paths to the data and this makes this solution more flexible and scalable with respect to file storage where only one path is provided to retrieve data.

**Solid-State Drives Vs Hard Disk Drives**

In some of the storage services discussed above, the user has to select between Solid-State Drivers (SSD) or Hard Disk Driver (HDD) when they provision a storage service (like Relational Databases). The option to prefer depends on how different factors: amount of data to store, data access frequency and performance requirements. In general, SSD storage is the most efficient and cost effective choice, while HDD storage is appropriate for large datasets (>10TB) where the latency is not important and the data requests frequency is low.

## 4.2.4 Big Data

With the three types of resources discussed above—compute, networking and storage—any kind of application can be built, and users take advantage of that to build and operate a wide variety of applications in the cloud. It has become apparent that cloud computing is often particularly beneficial for specific kinds of applications, and, consequently, modern cloud providers offer specialized features to support them.

One of these can be largely summarized as Big Data—or by related terms like Business Analytics, Data Mining, Business Intelligence, or whatever the most fashionable buzzword is right now. The essence of these kinds of applications is that they feature massive amounts of data—often in the range of Petabytes—that are to be analyzed to gain valuable insights from.

The idea behind Big Data is that most organizations have massive amounts of data from their normal operations. Consider an online retailer, who would not only have all the sales transactions, but probably also data about the click streams of visitors of their web site, whether the visit resulted in a sale of not, and of course a wide range of other relevant data that can easily be acquired, such as economic or even weather data (factors that would also influence online sales). Valuable insights for such an online retailer might be predictions of what kinds of products might be popular in the next season (so that enough inventory can be acquired), how to price items to maximize sales or profit or whatever else the goal is, etc.

One of the challenges of Big Data applicants is that they require very significant IT resources, not only with regard to storage, but also with regard to parallel processing and consequently networking, in order to be able to run analyses on massive amounts of data in a short period of time (such as minutes or hours, rather than days or weeks). Yet, in many cases, an organization would likely not be using these significant (and expensive) IT resources every day of the year, all day long, but probably only for a fraction of the time, when executives want analytical questions answered. This potential underutilization of expensive IT resources is an important argument why operating Big Data applications with a cloud service provider rather than on-premise is likely very cost effective.

The Google Cloud Platform offers three different services that support Big Data applications: BigQuery, Cloud Dataproc and Cloud Dataflow.

**BigQuery**

The observant reader might notice that BigQuery has already been discussed at the end of the last section about storage options in GCP. This is no accident—it fits in both areas. BigQuery can primarily be used to store large amounts of data, in which case it belongs in the storage category. On the other hand, if its query features are used extensively, it falls more into the category of Big Data. Figure 4.8 shows an example query in a BigQuery sample dataset.

As discussed above, BigQuery is a modern data warehouse solution, which means it is not so much meant to run transactions that support day-to-day business operations, but to perform larger analytical queries on relatively stable data. BigQuery is a fully managed service, meaning that storage management, backups, software updates, query optimization etc. are done by the platform. The user also does not have to provision resources such as storage capacity and clusters of virtual machines to process queries etc. Instead, resources are automatically provisioned as needed, and the user is only charged for the resources that are actually consumed.

**Cloud Dataproc**

Cloud Dataproc allows users to process large amounts of data with fully managed compute clusters using e.g. Apache Hadoop or Spark in the cloud. The basic idea of these tools is the map-reduce paradigm—to parallelize large computing tasks on massive amounts of data by breaking them into many smaller jobs that are processed in parallel, and to then collect the results and to combine them to the overall result in the end. The obvious advantage of this approach is that the processing is significantly sped up compared to serial processing on any individual machine, no matter how powerful that machine is.

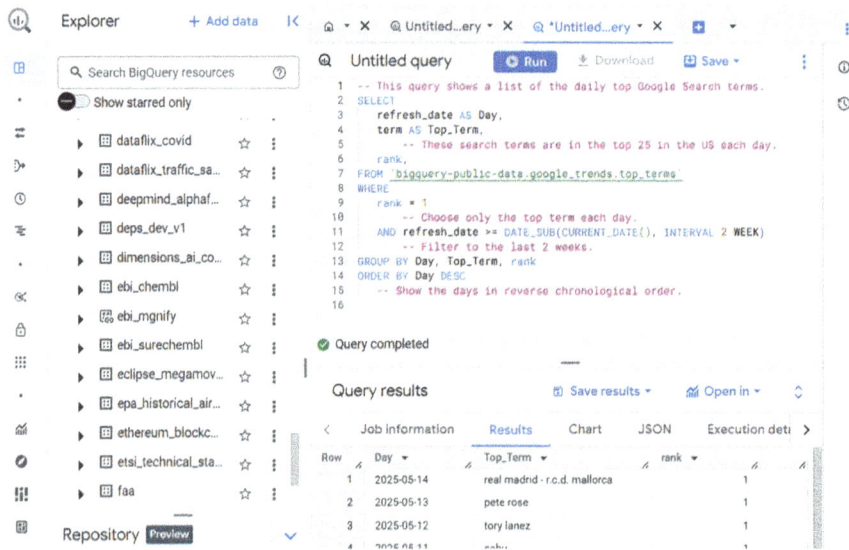

**Fig. 4.8** Example of a query in a sample data set in BigQuery

This general approach can be used for many different applications, from complex queries over batch processing to machine learning. Once again, cloud computing lends itself very well to this paradigm, because running e.g. fifty virtual machines

## 4.2 Types of Cloud Services

for an hour costs the same amount as running a single virtual machine for fifty hours. In other words, a task that can be parallelized well can be sped up massively compared to serial processing, at no significant increase in cost. Additionally, since users do not have to pay for idle resources, significant cost savings compared to operating similar clusters in-house can usually be realized, especially if tasks are not time critical and can be interrupted, in which case even cheaper spot instances can be used.

Figure 4.9 shows that Dataproc clusters can be created as clusters of virtual machines on the Compute Engine, or as clusters of containers on the Kubernetes Engine.

**Cloud Dataflow**

Cloud Dataflow is meant for processing streams of data in real time. This can be used in many different contexts, from ETL (extract, transform and load) tasks that move data between different data stores over batch processing of large amounts of data to processing of data that naturally arrives constantly over time such as sensor data. In Cloud Dataflow, users can define pipelines of operations on data that are processed in real time. These operations can include map/reduce steps. One of the big differences to Cloud Dataproc is that Cloud Dataflow is serverless. In other words, users do not have to allocate resources for their processing steps. Instead, the resources used for individual pipeline steps scale up and down automatically based on current demand.

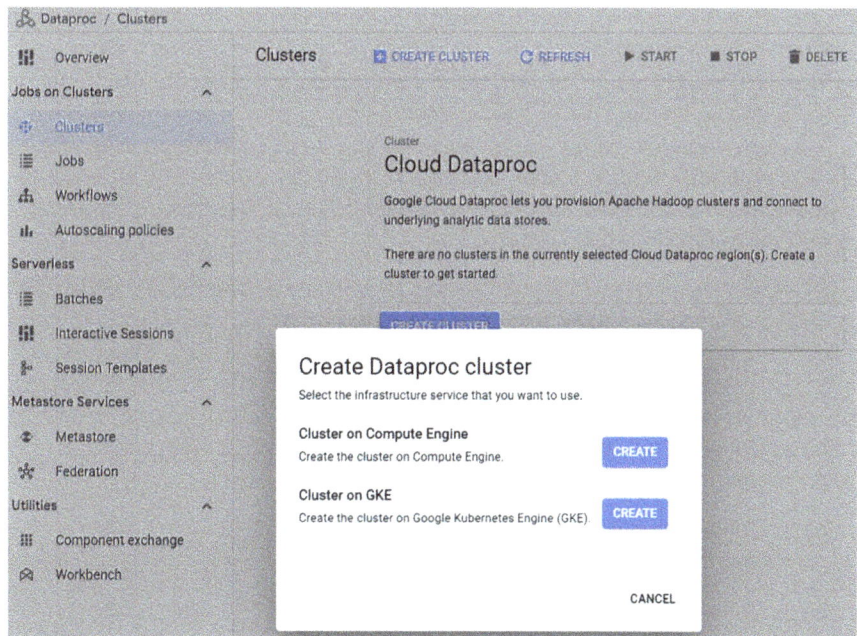

**Fig. 4.9** Different options when creating a Dataproc cluster in GCP

## 4.2.5 Machine Learning

Machine Learning is an Artificial Intelligence (AI) approach that uses neural networks (which mirror, in a simplified way, how the human brain works) to build models using training data to make "intelligent" predictions or decisions—e.g. about whether an email is spam, how to transcribe a spoken sentence into written language, or whether a person in a photo is smiling. These systems do not use explicit programming, which, in the third example, might look for say roughly u-shaped lips. Instead, the neural networks are fed with a large number of sample pictures of people. All the photos in this training data are sorted by human work into two groups—smiling or not smiling. The machine learning algorithms modify the detailed configuration of the neural network until it predicts with high accuracy whether a face in fact shows a smile or not.

Machine Learning requires large amounts of training data (often tens or hundreds of thousands of samples), and they require significant computing resources to train the models with the training data, and, to a lesser extent, to apply the resulting model to the actual data to be analyzed. These requirements make them excellent candidates for cloud computing.

The Google Cloud Platform features a range of Machine Learning offerings under the umbrella of Vertex AI[7] This is an area with rapid technological progress, so new features and offerings are released rapidly and often. The following are some of the main features:

- Vertex AI Model Garden allows users to find and try out a wide range existing machine learning models, to either use directly or adapt for a specific task.
- AutoML helps users with limited machine learning expertise to develop their own machine learning models
- VertexAI Workbench is an integrated development environment that supports users with their whole data science workflow
- Numerous tools like Vertex AI Pipelines and Vertex AI Model Monitoring support users with the whole machine learning life cycle, for example by enabling the automatic re-training of machine learning models when their precision declines with the availability of new data.

Two different types of machine learning models are generative AI models and predictive AI models. Generative AI can be used to create content, e.g. to autocomplete code, chat with a user, answer questions, create images based on user prompts, create short summaries of longer texts etc. Predictive AI models are used in a wide range of applications, such as predicting if a credit card transaction is likely fraudulent or not or whether a photograph of a person's skin displays signs of skin cancer or not.

---

[7] https://cloud.google.com/vertex-ai.

## 4.2 Types of Cloud Services

> **Artificial Intelligence, Machine Learning etc.**
>
> In recent years, the field of artificial intelligence (AI) has made major breakthroughs particularly in the area of generative AI, resulting in widely popular chatbots that users can interact with in natural language. In the buzz this generated, it is easy to lose track of the bigger picture of what the different fields and applications of AI are. This brief summary highlights the main concepts.
>
> **Artificial intelligence** is a decades-old field of computer science that focuses on building system ablet o perform tasks that would generally require human intelligence. For example, computer software that can play games such as chess falls into this broad category. For a long time, the majority of AI systems relied on predefined algorithms and rules to make decisions, making them not very flexible to solve problems beyond their original programming. An increasingly important field of AI is **machine learning**, in which a system is not programmed with specific application logic to make decisions but automatically learns patterns from training data. There are different forms in which this learning can take place, including supervised learning, in which the system learns from training data that has been labeled e.g. by human users, and unsupervised learning, in which the input is unlabeled, raw data.
>
> **Deep learning**, in turn, is a subcategory of machine learning, in which the machine learning model uses a multi-layered neural network that, at a very high level, mimics how the human brain works. The exact configuration of these neural network is fine-tuned with large amounts of training data.
>
> These machine learning models can serve different purposes. **Discriminative models** are used to distinguish between categories or predicting labels. For example, specialized models can be used to do image recognition, i.e. to be able to detect people, animals, and other objects in images, or for even more specialized tasks such as to determine whether a person is happy, sad or angry based on their facial expressions, or whether a specific skin mark is potentially malignant cancer or harmless.
>
> One of the most popular uses of machine learning models are **generative models**, which, fed with a prompt, generate an output. The popular **large language models (LLMs)** such as Chat-GPT, Gemini or LLaMA which users can ask questions and get natural language responses to fall into this category. Increasingly, multi-modal LLMs are becoming popular, which can use not just text, but also photos, sound, videos etc. as input prompt and generate output in these different formats.

**Pre-Trained ML Models**

In some cases, users need a Machine Learning solution for which GCP already offers ready-to-use pre-trained models that can be reached via ready-to-use application programming interfaces (APIs). These models include:

- The Vision API allows users to do standard tasks on images, such as detecting faces, judging facial expression, detecting famous landmarks, extracting text etc.
- The Speech-to-Text API converts speech to text and vice versa.
- The Cloud Translation API translates text between different languages.
- The Cloud Natural Language API helps users analyse e.g. the syntax, content or sentiment of unstructured text.
- The Video Intelligence API can be used to detect and label the content of videos.

## 4.2.6 Management Services

This final section describes cloud services that are not meant to be useful on their own, but to help manage the use of cloud services such as compute, storage, networking etc. The Cloud Infrastructure Manager supports users with managing their cloud infrastructure. Google Cloud Operations Suite is a collection of tools that allow users to monitor their applications, including more advanced features that can help with analyzing and debugging errors, identifying and solving performance issues etc.

**Cloud Infrastructure Manager**

Infrastructure as Code (IaC) refers to an approach that treats the structure of IT infrastructure like other software code. Only in the cloud is this fully possible, where resources are generally virtual, which allows them to be fully software defined. For example, an application might be designed to run on a dual-core machine with 8 GBytes of main memory, a 500 GByte solid state drive and a specific Linux version installed. If this application is operated on a physical machine on-premise, then only the details of the software installation can be defined in code (e.g. startup and shell scripts), while the physical hardware by necessity has to be installed "by hand"—including connecting the machine to a network etc. If the same application is run in the cloud, it could be deployed on a virtual machine. While the creation and configuration of the virtual machine can be done "by hand" through the GCP console (a web-based user interface), it is also possible to define it via code. This way, the whole application, including the virtual machine type, its software configuration, its network connectivity etc. can be defined in code.

Defining the infrastructure in code has significant advantages, especially if the code is treated like any other important source code and managed in a source control system with versioning etc. For example, it ensures consistency and repeatability

4.2 Types of Cloud Services 133

and reduces the amount of work necessary when infrastructure needs to be created. A typical operational system would not only be needed in a production environment, but also in separate (but ideally identical) environments for bug fixing purposes or for the development of new features. Creating these additional environments manually not only requires significant manual work for each new environment, it also increases the risk that errors or omissions happen, which would make the environments slightly different, resulting in possible problems when bug fixes or new features are deployed in production.

The GCP Cloud Infrastructure Manager allows users to manage infrastructure in the Google Cloud Platform via code. It is built on the IaC tool terraform which uses a declarative language to specify cloud infrastructure. In contrast to imperative languages which specify exactly how to achieve an outcome, a declarative language specifies the desired outcome, such as a virtual machine of a specific machine type in a specific region and connected to a specific network. Based on such a declarative configuration, the Cloud Infrastructure Manager figures out and executes the specific instructions required to create the desired state.

**Google Cloud Operations Suite**

The GCP Operations Suite (formerly known as Stackdriver) is an integrated monitoring solution for the Google Cloud Platform. Monitoring is an extremely important aspect of operating any productive IT system. Its purpose is generally to alert operators of any issues with an application, ranging from suspicious activities that might be a sign of a security problem over slow system response times to system failures resulting in a completely unavailable application. Rather than being alerted of any such issue by angry end users who eventually email somebody about problems they face, monitoring should ideally catch problems before they are noticeable to end users.

The GCP Operations Suite offers several different components with a wide range of features:

- **Monitoring** is used to track aspects such as whether systems are up or down, how high the load of systems and their components is and what kind of user response times applications have. Alerts can be defined that trigger if specific situations occur (e.g. if a server is not reachable or if the CPU utilization of a machine exceeds a certain threshold for a specified amount of time). These alerts can not only be displayed on administrative consoles, they can also be sent via email, text message etc. to alert on-call system administrators. Monitoring not only displays current values, it also keeps track of how values change over time, which is valuable information when potential issues are investigated.
- **Logging** integrates logs from all GCP resources. Needless to say, large-scale cloud deployments can generate massive amounts of log entries. Consequently, the logging component has to be and is highly scalable.
- **Error Reporting** provides instant notifications of application errors. While the number of errors should be significantly lower than the number of log entries, large

scale applications can still experience significant numbers of errors, so the error reporting component allows real-time aggregation of errors and other features that allow users to get an overview of all occurring errors, and to prioritize the most urgent or important ones.
- **Tracing** helps with the identification of performance bottlenecks. It can be used to break down the response latency of individual requests and to aggregate the information of many requests.
- The **Debugger** allows developers to debug the production system in real time. For example, snapshots of running applications showing the call stack, the contents of variables etc. can be taken. Needless to say, this can be very helpful for identifying and solving problems.
- The **Profiler** lets developers observe the performance of code in the production environment under production conditions. While performance tests that are performed before a system goes into production should give developers significant insights into how their application will behave in production, it is very hard to predict and simulate the exact request distribution, system load etc. that the system faces in real world use in a test environment. Therefore, insights gained from the profiler can be very valuable to improve code performance. Of course, collecting the necessary data for this in a running system creates some overhead. The Profiler minimizes this impact by very efficient instrumentation and through the use of statistical sampling.

## 4.3 Summary

Even though this chapter could only provide an overview, it hopefully successfully made the point that modern cloud computing offers a much wider range of cloud services than just virtual machines and file storage. These services include advanced networking features enabling enhanced scalability and security of applications, a range of flexible and high performance storage solutions and various other advanced services in areas such as Big Data and Machine Learning. While users can (at least theoretically) implement any of these services on their own on cloud-based virtual machines, using the available more advanced solutions is in most cases more efficient and effective. An analogy from the programming world would be that any application can be built with nothing but assembly language code, but that using higher-level programming languages and existing frameworks, libraries and tools usually saves a lot of time and effort and leads to a better outcome.

## 4.4 Key Terms

Note that most of the key terms in this section are specific to the Google Cloud Platform (GCP). While other cloud providers have similar concepts and products, they typically have different names and might work slightly differently.

## 4.4 Key Terms

**Region** A region is the geographic location in which cloud services are hosted. Examples for GCP regions are us-central1, europe-north1 or asia-east2.

**Zone** Each region contains several zones. For example, us-cental1 includes zones such as us-central1-a, us-central1-b and us-central1-c. The datacenters hosting the different zones in a region are in different physical locations.

**Project** Projects are used to control aspects such as billing and access control for resources. In particular, the costs for the resources in a project are paid from a designated billing account, and users often get certain access permission on all the resources of a project.

**Spot Instance** A spot instance is a heavily discounted virtual machine instance for which the provider reserves the right to shut it down without any significant prior notice if the resources are needed for other purposes.

**Container** Containers are often used light-weight virtual machines (VMs). They offer similar benefits to VMs such as the ability to package an application with all its dependencies in an easily distributable format. In contrast to VMs, containers do not include a full guest operating system and consequently create less overhead.

**Kubernetes** Kubernetes is a container orchestration tool. It allows users to declare how cloud applications should be deployed and then handles aspects such as fault tolerance, automatic scaling etc. automatically.

**App Engine** The app engine allows users to deploy applications without having to handle the underlying infrastructure (such as virtual machines etc.) It is a way to deploy applications using Platform as a Service (PaaS) in Google Cloud.

**Cloud Functions** allows users to deploy individual functions written in programming functions like Python or Java along with the specification of what should trigger their invocation.

**Virtual Private Cloud** The different resources a user created in the cloud are connected via a virtual private cloud (VPC), which is a virtual (software defined) computer network that is not visible to other cloud users.

**Load Balancer** A load balancer serves as a single point of entry for e.g. users of a web server, and distributes the incoming requests among a number of web server instances. Cloud load balancers can also be configured to react to changing load by scaling the number of virtual machines connected to it up and down as needed.

**Content Delivery Network** A content delivery network (CDN) allows organizations to deliver online content to users around the globe with lower latency by taking advantage of servers closer to the end user that cache (parts of) the requested content.

**Cloud Armor** is a network security feature in GCP that offers features such as intelligent detection and handling of distributed denial of service (DDoS) attacks.

**Cloud Storage** GCP Cloud Storage allows users to store files in so-called storage buckets, which provide a flat (not structured by directories) storage location.

**Storage Class** Storage buckets can be assigned to different storage classes—standard, nearline, coldline and archive. The main difference between these storage classes is the trade-off between the costs to store and access data—the former is highest in standard and lowest in archive, while the latter is free in standard and highest in archive.

**Cloud SQL** is a relational database operated as a service by Google Cloud. In contrast to self-hosting a relational database in a virtual machine, using Cloud SQL frees users from database administration activities such as backups, software updates etc.

**Datastore** is a NoSQL document database operated as a service in GCP.

**Bigtable** is a NoSQL column database operated as a service in GCP.

**BigQuery** is a data warehouse operated as a service in GCP.

**Dataproc** allows users to process large amounts of data in parallel in fully managed compute clusters using tools such as Apache Hadoop or Spark.

**Dataflow** is a fully managed service allowing users to process streams of data in real time with operations that are configured in a declarative fashion, without having to deal with the underlying infrastructure.

**Vertex AI** is Google Cloud's integrated platform for artificial intelligence (AI) tasks.

**Infrastructure as Code** describes the approach to build a cloud infrastructure with code rather than by manual interaction with the web-frontend of the cloud provider.

**Infrastructure Manager** is the IaC tool used by GCP to allow users to build their cloud infrastructure with code.

**Cloud Operations Suite** The GCP Cloud Operations Suite contains numerous abilities necessary to operate complex cloud deployments in production, ranging from monitoring and logging to debugging and error reporting.

## 4.5 Review Questions

1. What are the main different computational services offered by Google Cloud?
2. What is a container, and how is it similar to and different from a virtual machine?
3. Briefly explain some of the most important networking services offered by cloud providers.
4. Contrast some of the different services with which users can store data persistently in GCP.
5. Describe the importance of cloud management services, and the role that the Infrastructure Manager and the Cloud Operations Suite play in this context.

## 4.6 Exercises

The following laboratory exercises contain questions that require written responses and, in some instances, accompanying screenshots. If the exercises have been given as an assignment, please ensure that all answers and requested screenshots are compiled into a separate document for submission to the instructor, as specified by the instructor.

### *4.6.1 Using the Cloud Vision and Translation APIs*

In this lab, we explore two of the more advanced cloud APIs offered by Google.

**Objectives**

1. To use the Cloud Vision API
2. To use the Translation API
3. To look at Cloud Vision and Translation API pricing

**A. Enabling the APIs and Generating Credentials**

1. From the hamburger menu, click on "APIs & Services".
2. On the top of the screen, click on "Enable APIs and Services".
3. In the search box, enter "vision" and hit "enter".
4. Click on the result "Cloud Vision API".
5. Under "APIs & Services", click on "Library" to go back to the library of APIs.
6. In the search box, enter "translation" and hit "enter".
7. Click on the result "Cloud Translation API".
8. Click on "Enable".
9. Activate the Cloud Shell by clicking on the button ">_".
10. Under "APIs & Services", click on "Credentials".
11. Click on the button "Create credentials".
12. Click on "API key".
13. Copy the API key to the clipboard.
14. In the Cloud Shell, enter the following command (while replacing <YOUR_API_KEY> with the key you just copied):

    ```
    export API_KEY=<YOUR_API_KEY>
    ```

15. How many characters long is your API key?

**B. Using the Cloud Vision API**

1. We will use storage buckets to send images to the Cloud Vision API. To create a new storage bucket for this purpose, in the hamburger menu, click on "Cloud Storage" under the heading "Storage".
2. Click on "Create Bucket".
3. Give your storage bucket a unique name. Write down the name of your new bucket:




4. Keep the default settings and create the bucket.
5. Un-check the checkbox "Enforce public access prevention on this bucket" and click "Confirm".
6. In a separate browser window or tab, search for a photographic image of chocolate. Save the image in your downloads folder with a simple name like "chocolate.jpg". (For this and all the other photos in the lab, make sure you have fairly high-resolution photos of at least 1 million pixels).
7. In the Google Cloud Platform Window, click on "Upload" and upload the file you just saved to your bucket.
8. Repeat the last two steps for images of cats and of selfies in front of the Neuschwanstein Castle.
9. Make the bucket publicly accessible with the following steps:

    (a) Click on "Permissions", then click on "Grant Access".
    (b) In the "New principals" box, type allUsers
    (c) Under "Roles", select "Storage Object Viewer" (under Cloud Storage)
    (d) Click "Save" and confirm the warning dialog.
    (e) Refresh the page and click on "Objects". What does it say under "Public Access" for each of the three files?




10. From the top of the Cloud Shell window, launch the code editor (using the button " Open Editor").
11. Create a new file `request1.json` and save it in your home directory (/home/<YourUsername>)—you should not be in a further subdirectory. (If you accidentally create the file in a subdirectory of your home directory, you will just have to move it to your home directory.)
12. Click on "OK".

## 4.6 Exercises

13. Enter the following content, making sure to enter all the curly and square brackets and quotation marks correctly, and to replace my-bucket-name with the name of your bucket, and image.jpg with the name of your first image (e.g. chocolate.jpg):

```
{
    ''requests'': [
        {
            ''image'': {
                "source": {
                    "gcsImageUri": "gs://my-bucket-name/image.jpg"
                }
            },
            "features": [
                {
                    "type": "LABEL_DETECTION",
                    "maxResults": 10
                }
            ]
        }
    ]
}
```

14. Enter the following command in the Cloud Shell:

    ```
    curl -s -X POST -H "Content-Type: application/json" -data-binary @request1.json https://vision.googleapis.com/v1/images:annotate?key=${API_KEY}
    ```

15. In the output, you should see up to ten different annotations that the Vision API identified automatically. Insert the description of three of them:

16. Repeat steps 13–15 for the cat image (make sure to change the image name in the request1.json file and to save it). Insert the description of three of the annotations:

17. Repeat steps 13–15 for the selfie image (make sure to change the image name in the request1.json file and to save it). Insert the description of three of the annotations:

18. In the file request1.json, change the features section to the following:

```
"features": [
  {
    "type": "FACE_DETECTION"
  },
  {
    "type": "LANDMARK_DETECTION"
  }
]
```

19. Run the command from step 14 again.
20. Is the landmark detected and did the face recognition work? If not, try again with a different picture. Make sure it has a fairly high resolution and contains at least one person looking into the camera with the castle in the background.

21. Write down two different emotions, and how likely they are:

## C. Using the Translation API

1. In the Cloud Shell, enter the following:

    ```
    TEXT="Schokolade%20ist%20gesund"
    ```

2. Then enter the following command to Translate this text into English:

    ```
    curl "https://translation.googleapis.com/language/translate/v2?target=en&key=${API_KEY}&q=${TEXT}" -http1.1
    ```

3. What is the translated text?

## 4.6 Exercises

4. What is the source language?

5. In the Cloud Shell, enter the following:

    ```
    TEXT="food%20allergy"
    ```

6. Then enter the following command to Translate this text into German:

    ```
    curl "https://translation.googleapis.com/language/translate/v2?target=de&key=${API_KEY}&q=${TEXT}" -http1.1
    ```

7. What is the translated text in German?

8. Come up with another interesting or funny phrase and translate it from another language of your choosing into English (or the other way around). Write down the phrase and its translation below:

### D. Vision and Translation API Pricing

1. Find the google cloud price list.
2. How much do the first 1000 label detections per month in the Vision API cost?

3. How much would the next 1000 label detections cost?

4. Using the basic Cloud Translation API, how many characters per month can you translate for $20?

## 4.6.2 Deploying WordPress on a GCP VM

In this lab we will use a virtual machine to host WordPress in the cloud.

**Objectives**

1. Create a new VM and install the LAMP (linux, apache, mysql, php) stack
2. Install and use WordPress

**A. Create a New Virtual Machine**

1. In the Google cloud platform console, under Compute, click on "Compute Engine"
2. Click on the button "Create Instance" to create a new virtual machine
3. In the section "Name", change the name to "ubuntu"
4. In the section "Machine type", select "e2-small" (2 vCPU, 2 GB memory)
5. In the section "Boot disk", change the selection to "Ubuntu 24.04 LTS" (for x86/64, not arm64)
6. In the section "Firewall", allow both HTTP and HTTPS traffic
7. Then, click on the button "Create"
8. Click on the name of your virtual machine to see its details.
9. Under "Connect", select the dropdown box arrow next to "SSH" and select "Open in browser window"
10. This should open a console in a separate browser window
11. What does the command prompt look like (i.e. the line with the cursor in it)?



12. Which directory are you in right when the console opens?

## B. Installing and Testing the LAMP Stack

1. Update the package list:

    ```
    sudo apt-get update
    ```

2. Install any available updates:

    ```
    sudo apt-get upgrade
    ```

3. Install apache using the command:

    ```
    sudo apt-get install apache2
    ```

4. Enable apache to start automatically when the server boots:

    ```
    sudo systemctl enable apache2
    ```

5. Check that apache is running with the command:

    ```
    sudo service apache2 status
    ```

6. Insert a screenshot of the output:

7. In the Google Cloud Platform Console, in the details of your "ubuntu" virtual machine, look up the value of the field "External IP" in the section "Network interfaces".
8. What is the external IP address?

9. In a new browser tab, go to your external IP address. Make sure to use http, not https.
10. What is the headline of the page that now displays in the browser?

11. Back on the command prompt, install MySQL:

    ```
    sudo apt-get install mysql-server
    ```

12. Install PHP:
    ```
    sudo apt-get install php php-mysql libapache2-mod-php
    ```

13. Install phpMyAdmin
    (a) `sudo apt-get install phpmyadmin`
    (b) **With the space bar key**, select apache2 as web server to configure (use up/down and tab to move "cursor"). **Before you press >Ok< with the space bar key, there has to be an asterix * next to "apache2"**
    (c) When prompted to configure phpmyadmin, select yes.
    (d) Enter Csis4270 as database password when prompted (twice).

14. Current versions of MySQL do not allow remote logins with a password into the root user. To still be able to connect, we create a new super user for phpMyAdmin.

    (a) Log into the database as root:

    ```
    sudo mysql -p -u root
    ```

    (b) Hit enter when prompted to enter the password. Create a new user that is allowed to log in remotely by password:

    ```
    CREATE USER 'pmauser'@'localhost' IDENTIFIED WITH mysql_native_password BY 'Csis4270';
    ```

    (c) Grant super user privileges to the new user:

    ```
    GRANT ALL PRIVILEGES ON *.* TO 'pmauser'@'localhost';
    ```

    (d) Log out of the database:

    ```
    quit;
    ```

4.6 Exercises

15. Test phpMyAdmin:
    (a) Go to `http://<YourExternalIP>/phpmyadmin` in a web browser and log in with `pmauser` and `Csis4270`
    (b) In the browser window, you should see five boxes, two of which have the headlines "General settings" and "Appearance settings". Insert a screenshot of your browser window:

**C. Installing and Configuring Wordpress**

1. Downloading Wordpress
    (a) Go to /tmp folder and download wordpress there:

    ```
    cd /tmp
    wget http://wordpress.org/latest.tar.gz
    ```

    (b) Extract and move to apache directory document root:

    ```
    tar -xvzf latest.tar.gz
    sudo mv wordpress/* /var/www/html/
    ```

2. Configure WordPress database
    (a) Log into MySQL:

    ```
    sudo mysql -u root {p
    ```

    (b) Hit enter when prompted for a password

(c) Create database for wordpress:

    `CREATE DATABASE wpdb;`

(d) What is the output of the above command?

(e) Create database user:

    `CREATE USER wpuser@localhost IDENTIFIED BY 'Csis4270';`

(f) Grant the new user all privileges for the Wordpress database:

    `GRANT ALL ON wpdb.* to wpuser@localhost;`

(g) Make sure the new permissions are applied immediately:

    `FLUSH PRIVILEGES;`

(h) Log out of the database:

    `quit;`

3. Configure Wordpress to work with the new database
   (a) Create a settings file from the sample settings file:

       `sudo cp /var/www/html/wp-config-sample.php /var/www/html/wp-config.php`

   (b) Edit the file wp-config.php, e.g. using the command[8]

       `sudo nano /var/www/html/wp-config.php`

       i. Change the name of the database:

           `define('DB_NAME', 'wpdb');`

---

[8] In the event that nano is not installed, first use the command `sudo apt-get install nano`.

ii. Change the name of the database user:

   define('DB_USER', 'wpuser');

iii. Change the database user password:

   define('DB_PASSWORD', 'Csis4270');

(c) After you made the changes, press Ctrl-X to close nano. Press the Y key when asked whether you want to save the changes and Enter to confirm the file name.
(d) Give apache2 permissions to manage the directory;

   sudo chown -R www-data:www-data /var/www/html/

(e) Set the correct permissions for folders and files:

   sudo chmod -R 755 /var/www/html

(f) Restart apache2:

   sudo service apache2 restart

4. Remove index.html file from /var/www/html

   cd /var/www/html
   sudo mv index.html index.html.old

5. Configure Wordpress through its web interface

    (a) Open <ExternalIP>/wp-admin/index.php in a web browser
    (b) If prompted, select English as language and click Continue
    (c) Enter
       i. Site Title: CSIS 4270
       ii. Username: <Your given name>
       iii. Password: <A good password> (Make sure to write this password down!)
    (d) Enter an email address (this does not have to be your real email address)
    (e) Select "Discourage search engines from indexing this site"
    (f) Click on "Install WordPress"
    (g) Log into WordPress with your username and password

## D. Test Wordpress

1. Create at least two brief posts, at least one with a photo and one with a link. (Please make sure to respect copyright law and use only your own or public domain photos).
2. In a **separate incognito browser window**, look at what your site looks like to somebody who is not logged in by simply going to the external IP address of your VM.
3. Insert a screenshot of your blog posts:




4. Shut down your virtual machine in the GCP console (click on "Stop").
5. Once the virtual machine is down, note that your blog can no longer be reached.
6. In the GCP console, once your VM is stopped, wait three minutes, then start it again.
7. What is your new external IP? If it is different from the previous IP address, write it down here and skip the next step:



8. If the IP address is the same as before, click on the name of the VM (ubuntu) to open its details, then click on "Edit". Open up the section "Network interfaces". Expand the default network interface. Below "External IPv4 address", click on "Ephemeral", then click on "Reserve static external IP address" to create a new static IP address. Give the new IP address the name static-wordpress-IP and click on "Reserve". Click on "Save". Write down the new IP address below:

## 4.6 Exercises

9. Look at the google cloud platform documentation to answer the following questions: What is an ephemeral IP address?

   What other kind of external IP address is there?

   How much does each kind of external IP address cost per hour when it is used and unused on a standard VM instance?

10. Go to your new external IP address in a browser window (making sure again to use http, not https). What happens? Does your blog display correctly, including the photo?
11. Insert a screenshot of what your blog looks like now:

12. Go back to http://<YourExternalIP>/phpmyadmin and log in with pmauser and Csis4270
13. Navigate to the database wpdb, and the table wp_options
14. In the rows with the option_name siteurl and home, what is the value of the column option_value?

15. Using the link Edit in both rows, update the option_value to the correct, current value.
16. Open your current external IP address in a new incognito browser window (again, using the http protocol). What happens?
17. Insert a screenshot of what you blog looks like now:

18. If you previously changed the external IP address of the virtual machine to a static one, go back to the settings of the virtual machine and change the external IP address back to an ephemeral one. Click "Save" to accept the change.
19. If you used a static IP address, in the hamburger menu, select Networking->VPC network->IP addresses. Select the checkbox next to "static-wordpress-ip" and click on "Release Static Address". Then click on "Delete".
20. Shut your virtual machine down, either in the GCP console, or on the command line with:

    sudo shutdown now

21. **Always shut your virtual machines down when you are not using them— otherwise they incur hourly charges (even if they are just idle).**

4.6 Exercises 151

## 4.6.3 Cloud Storage

In this lab we explore storage buckets in more detail.

**Objectives**

1. Create storage bucket with advanced settings
2. Observe the behavior of storage buckets with advanced retention, versioning and settings

**A. Creating a Storage Bucket and Examining Detailed Bucket Settings**

1. Through the hamburger menu, navigate to Cloud Storage.
2. Create a new storage bucket with default settings. Write down the name you chose below:

3. Click on the name of your storage bucket to see it details.
4. Click on permissions. In "View by Principals", how many principals have permissions on the bucket?

5. What are the three primitive (or basic) roles that have permissions?

6. Select the tab "Protection".
7. What is the soft delete policy by default?

8. Click on "Object Versioning Off".
9. Insert a screenshot of the dialog box that opens.

10. Select "Add recommended lifecycle rules to manage version costs".
11. What are the default values for "Max. number of versions per object" and "Expire nonconcurrent versions after"?

12. Change the first value to 2 and click on "Confirm".
13. Click on "Set Retention Policy".
14. Set the retention period to 120 seconds and click on "Save".
15. Go back to the list of your storage buckets and click on the name of your storage bucket.
16. Create a file test.txt on your local hard disk with the content "Version 1".
17. Click on "Upload Files" and upload the file you just created to your bucket.
18. You will be prompted to confirm—insert a screenshot of the dialog box:

19. Click on "Confirm".

## B. Bucket Behavior with Advanced Bucket Settings

1. On your local computer, change the content of the file to "Version 2".
2. Upload the file to the bucket again (within 2 minutes of the original upload). Insert a screenshot of the dialog box that opens:

## 4.6 Exercises

3. Select "Overwrite object" and click on "Continue Uploading".
4. In the Cloud Shell, run the command

    ```
    gcloud storage buckets list
    ```

5. Insert a screenshot of the output:

6. Copy the file test.txt from the storage bucket to the local directory with the command (replacing <bucket-name> with the name of your bucket:

    ```
    gsutil cp gs://<bucket-name>/test.txt
    ```

7. Insert a screenshot of the output of the command:

    ```
    cat test.txt
    ```

8. Back in the details of the storage bucket, click on the file test.txt. Then click on "Version History". Insert a screenshot of the version history.

9. If the new version of the file is corrupted, we can now go back to the previous version. For that purpose, click on "Restore" next to the original version of the file. In the dialog "Restore this object version?" click on "Confirm".
10. Insert a screenshot of the version history now:

11. In the Cloud Shell, copy the file from the bucket to the local directory again, and display the content of the file again. What is it now?
12. Go back to the details of the bucket. Click on "Lifecycle".
13. Insert a screenshot of the current lifecycle rules:

14. Click on "Add a Rule". What are the five possible actions that can be set?

15. Select the first option and click on "Continue".
16. Under "Set Rule Scopes", select "Object name matches suffix" and enter ".txt".
17. Under "Set Conditions", select "Age" and enter "50".

## 4.6 Exercises

18. Click on "Continue", then on "Create".
19. Insert a screenshot of the rules that are defined now:

20. When you are done with this lab, you can delete the storage bucket we created. Note that you can also keep it if you like—the costs for the amount of data in the bucket should be negligible.

# Chapter 5
# Cloud Architecture

This chapter is about how to build applications in the cloud. It cannot cover this topic exhaustively. Not only is there a wide range of aspects involved, such as analysis, design, implementation, testing and operations, but there are also several different architectural approaches that can be used, each of which could easily fill not just a chapter, but a whole book. Therefore, the goal of this chapter is to give an overview of some of the most important architectural approaches, and to provide some guidance on their relative strengths and weaknesses. Additionally, several aspects that apply across these different approaches are covered.

## 5.1 Architecture Goals

Before specific architectural principles and approaches are discussed, this section briefly covers some of the most important goals that architectural decisions strive to achieve. While many of these goals are applicable for applications that do not run in the cloud as well, we analyze them specifically with a focus on cloud computing. The discussion illustrates that there are several potential conflicts between the goals, meaning that it is difficult to attain all of them simultaneously.

### 5.1.1 Performance

One of the most obvious goals of any application architecture is that it ensures adequate application performance. The vast majority of applications today is of an interactive nature (as opposed to being batch based). In such applications, a key aspect of performance is low response times. Additionally, performance under load is important, which means that the response times for individual users should remain consistent and low even if the number of concurrent users increases.

Performance is particularly important for many cloud-based applications, because they often have global reach and rather volatile usage rates. Thankfully, cloud providers offer many features that help ensure smooth performance, from the availability of multiple data centers across the globe (and consequently close to many customers) to performance enhancing features like content delivery networks and systems that automatically scale up and down with demand.

## 5.1.2 Reliability

Another important goal is reliability—that the system is available and working for its users at all times, or at least almost at all times. To achieve reliability, a system needs to be fault tolerant. Even in the cloud, individual components such as servers, networking components, or even software modules can and do occasionally fail. A good cloud architecture takes this into account and designs applications in such a way that the failure of individual components does not affect the overall availability of the system.

A good analogy for the desired behavior is the contrast between pets and cattle, as explained in a discussion of the cloud architecture used by Netflix:[1] The owners of pets know and care about their individual pets. If a pet dies, its owners are sad. A farmer who has a hundred cattle does not really know or particularly care about individual animals. If a cow dies, the milk production might go down by 1%, but that does not affect the overall output significantly, and can easily be rectified by buying another animal. To achieve a reliable system, individual servers must be like cattle, not pets, in other words, easy to replace. In order to ensure that this paradigm is strictly followed, Netflix uses the concept of the Chaos Monkey[2]—a system that randomly and unpredictably shuts down individual servers. A reliable cloud architecture should not have any individual components the failure of which would result in system outages, and should automatically replace any failing components.

## 5.1.3 Low Administrative Overhead

With the help of modern software development frameworks and libraries, applications can often be developed with surprisingly small amounts of code. In contrast, operating the infrastructure to run a modern web-based application can take significant amounts of effort. A technical report by the University of California at Berkeley[3] provides a good example for this: Imagine the backend for a smartphone application that wants to automatically create thumbnails of photos uploaded through the app

---

[1] Tilkov, S. "The Modern Cloud-Based Platform", IEEE Software, March/April 2015.

[2] More details here: https://netflix.github.io/chaosmonkey/.

[3] Jonas, E. et al. "Cloud Computing Simplified: A Berkeley View on Serverless Computing", Technical Report No. UCB/EECS-2019-3, February 10, 2019.

and place them on a website. While this functionality could probably be implemented in a few dozen lines of code, creating and managing an appropriate server infrastructure for such an application would take a lot more effort. For example, the server infrastructure would have to contain sufficient redundancy to ensure that individual failures could not take down the service. Appropriate measures would have to be taken so that the backend scales up and down with the load of user requests, appropriate monitoring and logging would have to take place to ensure the availability and security of the service, maintenance tasks such as security patches of all involved components would have to be performed regularly etc.

This example illustrates that a good architecture should minimize the necessary administrative work when possible. One approach to achieve this is the so-called serverless computing. The term is slightly misleading—no matter what architecture is chosen, computing tasks are ultimately executed on servers. Serverless computing refers to the approach that the user of a cloud service (which in the example above would be the developer of the smartphone application) can run the server side of their application on a cloud service that automatically manages the underlying servers and all their maintenance tasks without user interaction. In other words, if you use serverless computing, you do not have to worry about the servers that do your work—somebody else makes sure they work, receive security patches, are scaled up and down with the current load etc.

### 5.1.4 High Level of Control

Another important consideration of organizations using cloud computing services is the level of control that they retain over their cloud resources and applications. Sometimes this is driven by regulatory requirements. For example, organizations in sectors such as health care might be required by law to have full control over where their data is stored and how it is protected from unauthorized access by third parties. Specific regulations might prevent the use of storage services in countries that have lower privacy standards, or might dictate the use of certain encryption standards such as specific encryption algorithms and key lengths.

Another important consideration is that of vendor lock-in. Vendor lock-in describes the situation that users of a service might find it prohibitively difficult or expensive to switch to a different service provider. Since the use of public cloud services usually does not entail long-running contracts, it might seem that vendor lock-in might not be a big concern. However, the fact that most of the services of the major public cloud service providers are not standardized often makes the proposition to switch an application from one provider to another a very difficult one. The more control cloud users have over the services they run in a public cloud, the easier it should be to switch to a different provider. More details concerning vendor lock-in are discussed in Sect. 1.3.2, and tools able to reduce the problem are discussed in Chapter 7.

## 5.1.5 Support Modern Software Engineering Approaches

The architecture of cloud applications should also be compatible with modern software engineering approaches. For example, the incremental development often practiced in agile development approaches should be supported. This ideally includes the independent development and deployment of different parts of the application, along with automatic test suites etc.

Another important current software engineering paradigm is DevOps,[4] which attempts to better integrate development and operations of applications in order to increase agility, efficiency and quality. This requires architectures that allow applications and changes to them to easily be moved from development to test and production, and that already consider operational requirements and efficiency at the development stage, rather than treating them as an afterthought.

## 5.1.6 Cost Effectiveness

A final important goal is to have an architecture that allows for a cost-effective operation of the application. Since costs in cloud computing are directly related to the incremental use of computing resources, this means that the architecture should use resources efficiently. In the face of often highly variable application utilization over time, this means that the architecture should allow for smooth and efficient scaling up and down of resources based on demand. In addition to that, it should make resource use and consequently costs easy to monitor, manage and ideally even to predict.

## 5.1.7 Goal Conflicts

As indicated above, there are some clear conflicts between these goals. For example, using as few computing resources as possible improves cost effectiveness, while it tends to run counter to performance and to high reliability through redundancy. Similarly, low administrative overhead can be achieved by building an application on top of cloud services that are mostly managed by the cloud provider. However, such an approach reduces the amount of control that the cloud user has over the underlying infrastructure.

Since all the goals cannot fully be achieved at the same time, a good cloud architecture should strive to find a good balance between the goals, taking into account the specific priorities of the application under development.

---

[4] Zhu, L. et al. "DevOps and Its Practices", IEEE Software, May/June 2016.

> **Software Architecture**
>
> While the term architecture traditionally refers to the art and science of constructing buildings, its use has expanded to other areas outside of construction, to mean the structure and design of a system or product in more general terms (see https://en.wiktionary.org/wiki/architecture).
>
> In the field of computer science, the concept of architecture (both for software and hardware systems) has become more important over the decades as technological process in microchip manufacturing allowed increasingly complex system that could no longer be reliably developed in an unstructured ad-hoc way.
>
> Software architecture is a broad field with no generally accepted definition. Its scope has been ironically defined as "the important stuff—whatever that is" (https://en.wikipedia.org/wiki/Software_architecture). More practical accounts of what software architecture encompasses include the overall system structure, major design decisions and any aspects of a system that are hard to change. It should be noted that there is no generally accepted boundary between software architecture and related fields such as software design and requirements engineering.
>
> One key concept of software architecture is that of architecture or design patterns, i.e. reusable and proven solutions to specific kinds of problems that occur across multiple systems. The model-view-controller (MVC) pattern (see e.g. https://www.techtarget.com/whatis/definition/model-view-controller-MVC) is a good example of this. It deals with the difficulty of structuring a system with a user interface, application logic and state in such a way that these components can be mostly independent from each other. In this widely used pattern, the model stores the state of the system and implements the business logic, the view component implements the user interface and handles input and output while the controller links model and view by triggering model changes based on user input as well as generating output to the user based on model changes.

## 5.2 Architectural Principles

This section describes several architectural principles that many modern cloud applications use. They are about different aspects of cloud architecture, which means that they are not mutually exclusive choices. Instead, several principles can be combined in different ways to achieve the goals of a specific application in a given situation.

## 5.2.1 Infrastructure as Code

In traditional, non-cloud applications, there is a pretty strict boundary between software and the underlying physical infrastructure. Software includes a wide range of elements from source code, configuration settings, application specific data (e.g. product details, prices etc.), website layouts, images etc. The common aspect of all these elements is that they can be stored in files or version control systems, that they can be backed up and restored, or recreated in a different environment without any physical access or changes to physical hardware such as servers and networking equipment. The physical infrastructure is very different. For example, if an organization wants to clone the production environment into a separate environment, for example to help with debugging and bug fixing activities, this requires someone to set up an additional environment by physically installing a new set of servers, connecting them (mirroring the setup of the production environment) through network equipment such as switches and routers etc.

One of the key benefits of cloud computing is that the underlying infrastructure of cloud applications is typically[5] virtualized. In other words, rather than running directly on a set of physical machines, connected through a physical networking setup with switches, routers and network cables, cloud applications run in a virtualized environment, such as a set of virtual machines connected through a virtual network infrastructure. While these virtual resources of course ultimately still run on actual server and networking hardware, cloud computing users are not concerned with these physical resources. In other words, a cloud user can clone the environment in which an application runs in the cloud without touching any physical hardware (outside of the mouse and/or keyboard with which the cloning is requested).

In order to maximize the benefit of this virtualization, cloud users should treat their underlying infrastructure as code rather than just manually putting it together through the web interface of the cloud provider. This way, the infrastructure can be treated just like the software of an application—managed in a version control and configuration system, subjected to unit tests etc. This has multiple benefits such as the ability to rapidly set up or clone identical environments, to do so with minimal effort (e.g. by just running a script) and with perfect consistency of configurations.

In the Google Cloud Platform, the Cloud Infrastructure Manager[6] can be used to specify and create cloud resources using the IaC tool Terraform.[7] For example, the code to create a simple virtual machine test-vm with the machine type e2-small and a Ubuntu 24.04 boot disk connected to the default virtual network in the zone us-west1-b could look as follows:

---

[5] While most cloud applications run on virtual machines, either directly or through other cloud services that ultimately run on virtual machines, in specific niche cases it can make sense to run applications directly on physical hardware that is reserved for a specific customer. Consequently, cloud providers typically also offer what is called "bare metal" servers, e.g. https://cloud.google.com/bare-metal.

[6] https://cloud.google.com/infrastructure-manager/docs.

[7] https://developer.hashicorp.com/terraform.

## 5.2 Architectural Principles

```
resource "google_compute_instance" "default" {
  name         = "test-vm"
  machine_type = "e2-small"
  zone         = "us-west1-b"

  boot_disk {
    initialize_params {
      image = "ubuntu-os-cloud/ubuntu-2404-noble-amd64-
          v20241004"
    }
  }

  network_interface {
    network = "default"
  }
}
```

The code of the virtual infrastructure for a real cloud based application is obviously significantly larger, and includes many other resources such as database servers and load balancers, as well as more complex settings like several independent subnets with specific firewall rules. However, with the help of modern software tools and processes, such code can be handled easily and reliably.

### 5.2.2 Automation

Setting up the virtual infrastructure of an application using code as described in the previous section is only one of many different aspects that can be automated in a cloud setting. In order to understand the appeal and importance of automation, it is useful to look at an example. Imagine the online store of a retailer during the peak shopping season before Christmas. As customer traffic increases to multiple times the normal load, the infrastructure behind the web store might easily scale to dozens or more virtual machines running the necessary web and application servers. If for instance a security patch for a bug in the web server software becomes available, it should (after appropriate testing) be quickly installed on all the server instances. If this had to happen manually, it would not only take a fair amount of time to complete the task on all the servers, which would potentially leave the yet unpatched servers open to attacks, it would also take up a significant amount of work by the system administration team.

Automation tools can help in such situations. Ideally, an administrator should just need to specify which kind of change needs to happen on a set of machines, and the automation tool then performs these changes. In such a setting, the human effort required to implement a change would be fairly independent of the number of affected machines. To put this differently—in an automated environment, if an application running on a specific number of servers can be managed by a team of system administrators, the same team should still be able manage the application even if it scales up to a multiple of the original number of servers.

There are numerous automation tools, for example Puppet,[8] Chef[9] and SaltStack[10] We briefly look at yet another tool, Ansible,[11] as an example. The choice of Ansible should not be interpreted as an endorsement—it was chosen because it is conceptually quite simple, and because it supports the Google Cloud Platform well. However, other automation tools can be similarly effective.

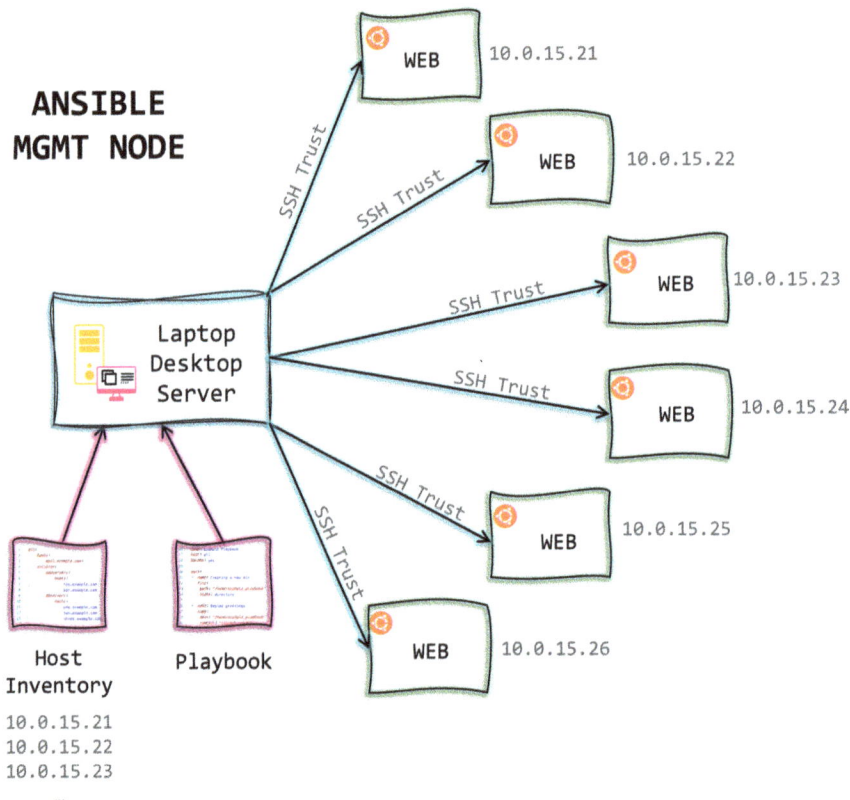

**Fig. 5.1** The Ansible architecture

Ansible (the architecture of which is illustrated in Fig. 5.1) is operated through the Ansible Management Node, a computer on which Ansible is installed, and through which system administrators manage the whole automation process. On this management node, the Host Inventory and the Playbook are kept.

---

[8] https://puppet.com/.
[9] https://www.chef.io/products/chef-infra.
[10] https://saltproject.io/.
[11] https://www.ansible.com/.

## 5.2 Architectural Principles

The Host Inventory is ultimately just a list of the machines (physical or virtual) that are managed by Ansible. In its simplest form, the Host Inventory could simply contain a list of DNS names or IP addresses. In practice, some additional features are typically used, such as organizing hosts into groups that make sense for the application (such as a group "web servers" and a group "database servers"), or storing additional information like connection types and user names to use with different hosts.

Ansible Playbooks contain different configurations that system administrators want to apply to systems. Playbooks are written in a YAML[12] based syntax, and describe in a declarative way a desired state of a resource. In other words, they do not directly contain code or commands to be executed, but allow system administrators to specify which result they would like to achieve on a managed system. For example, a playbook to ensure that Apache is updated to its latest version could look like the following:

```
tasks:
 - name: ensure apache is at the latest version
   yum:
     name: httpd
     state: latest
```

A system administrator could now simply apply this playbook on the group of machines that play the role of web servers. This would cause Ansible to connect to all the machines in that group via SSH, to check the installed version of Apache, and to update it if necessary (or do nothing if it already is the latest version). The fact that Ansible uses SSH to connect to target machines and to execute whatever actions are necessary means that Ansible does not require any special management software to be installed on the target machines, only a user account with sufficient permissions to connect to.

It should be clear that with a tool like Ansible, the effort required to manage servers does not scale linearly with their number. While increasing numbers of hosts might require a little extra effort in maintaining the host inventory, the work required to maintain and apply playbooks is ultimately the same whether ten or one hundred servers are administered.

Finally, Ansible directly supports several cloud environments such as AWS, Microsoft Azure, GCP and OpenStack by providing numerous plugins that can be used to include common tasks in the cloud in custom playbooks without any development effort.

### 5.2.3 Microservice Architectures

Another increasingly common architectural principle is to design applications as a collection of so-called microservices,[13] rather than in a monolithic fashion. Tradi-

---

[12] YAML is a recursive acronym for "YAML Ain't Markup Language".

tionally, applications are built in a monolithic way, i.e. they often consist of a single executable file. While such applications might internally consist of multiple fairly independent components, for instance to facilitate the development by several development teams, there is no mechanism to independently use only a subset of these components. The application is either deployed completely or not at all, and there is no simple way to replace parts of the application by other components.

Such a monolithic architecture has significant disadvantages. For example, if any part of the application needs to be changed, the entire application has to be recompiled and redeployed. While this is not a big concern for applications that are stable and rarely changed, it is not a very good fit for many cloud-based applications, which are often developed in a very agile fashion. These are often used in an environment in which frequent small changes—bug fixes or new features—are desirable, responding to business settings in which time-to-market is often of critical importance. Another problem of monolithic applications is that they often grow over time, and any initial separation into internal components deteriorates over time, which makes the applications harder and harder to maintain.

Microservice architectures do not suffer from many of these issues. In such architectures, applications are assembled from a number of independent components (microservices), each of which is only responsible for a small part of the overall functionality. This makes it possible to update or even replace individual microservices without impacting the entire system. As long as the interface of the microservice stays the same, the rest of the application should not be affected and does not have to be redeployed. This allows for agile development approaches in which different parts of the overall system can be developed and maintained by different teams of developers, and in which frequent changes to the application can be done with little overhead. The boundaries of responsibilities between the different components of the overall system are also explicit, which prevents their slow deterioration like in monolithic applications.

Despite their indisputable advantages, microservice architectures also introduce new challenges. To begin with, microservice applications have to be designed very carefully. In particular, the responsibilities of individual services and their interactions have to be well thought out, or the entire application becomes a complicated mess with countless unpredictable interdependencies between the different microservices. But even if the overall architecture is well designed, challenges remain. For example, microservices have to be able to locate instances of other microservices they communicate with. This communication should be secure, which might involve encryption. Microservices also need to be able to deal with the failure of other microservices—be it because the communication fails, or because actual system outages occur. Also, different microservices might have to deal with significantly different loads in service calls, often requiring scalable deployments with load balancing. Many of these issues are made even harder by the fact that especially in larger applications, microservices might well be deployed on numerous different servers,

---

[13] https://martinfowler.com/articles/microservices.html.

## 5.2 Architectural Principles

which makes unexpected and independent failures of parts of the application much more likely.

One approach to make many of these issues more manageable is to use a service mesh such as Istio.[14] The idea behind service meshes is to introduce an additional infrastructure layer that deals with aspects such as service discovery, message routing, security aspects such as encryption, load balancing, failure recovery and overall monitoring.

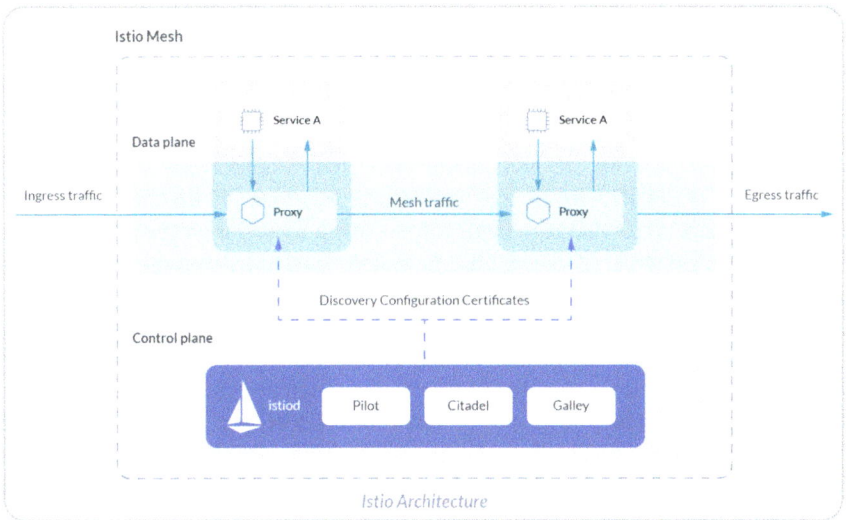

**Fig. 5.2** Istio service mesh architecture

Figure 5.2 (source: The Istio's website[15]) gives an overview of what a typical service mesh architecture looks like. Each service is connected to a proxy that takes care of the network traffic between different services. The services themselves and the proxies are both in the data plane in which the communication of the actual application happens. The separate control plane controls the proxies and implements higher-level infrastructure needs such failover support, load balancing, monitoring etc. The benefit of such an approach is that the actual service implementations do not have to deal with any of these issues, and instead can focus on the business logic of the application.

---

[14] https://istio.io/.
[15] https://istio.io/latest/docs/concepts/what-is-istio/.

## 5.2.4 Hybrid Cloud Architecture

As discussed in the first chapter of this book, the term hybrid cloud describes an approach in which an organization uses both a private cloud infrastructure and one or more public cloud providers. Reasons for doing this include the need to utilize existing hardware while still being able to rapidly scale resources beyond the available in-house capacity in the event of sudden surges of demand. Also, relying exclusively on a single public cloud provider puts an organization in significant dependency of that provider. For example, contract disputes could put such an organization at the brink of a complete interruption of their applications, which could easily put it out of business in a matter of days.

While organizations might well choose to operate their most critical applications in-house and to put everything else into public cloud, in the context of this chapter on cloud architecture we are particularly interested in approaches where a single application is distributed across a private and at least one public cloud. The most obvious approach to do this is to deploy the whole application in the private cloud, for example on a number of virtual machines. If the load requires more capacity than can be provided by the private cloud, the application is scaled into additional virtual machines with a public cloud provider. This approach is often called cloud bursting.

Another approach is to use a layered hybrid cloud architecture, for example as used by the electronics retailer BestBuy for its online store.[16] In this approach, parts of the application run only in the private cloud, while other parts run only in a public cloud. In the example of BestBuy, the frontend of their online store, i.e. the actual website with the catalogue of all the products and their details is run in a public cloud, while the backend, in particular the actual processing of customer purchases, is handled in their own data center.

The justification for this approach is twofold. Firstly, the frontend of the application is subject to significantly more load. Most visitors to the BestBuy website browse the products offered without actually ending up making purchases. This browsing can create significant load on the system, as customers use different ways of browsing and searching for products, invoking product comparisons etc. Given that customer demand is rather "peaky", i.e. volatile—for instance, busy in the Christmas shopping season, but not very busy at many other times, it makes a lot of sense to run this part of the application in a public cloud, where resources can be scaled up and down rapidly, and only actually consumed resources are charged. While the backend is of course also affected by the volatile nature of customer demand, the overall computational complexity of processing customer purchases once customers decide on the products they want to buy is relatively low. This means that a relatively small number of servers can handle the load, and the cost of keeping some spare capacity on these servers is limited.

Secondly, the frontend of the application is also much less critical to the business. For example, if an attacker managed to successfully break into the frontend servers in the public cloud, the main data they could steal would be the entire product

---

[16] Crabb, J. "The BestBuy.com Cloud Architecture", IEEE Software, March/April 2014, pp. 91–96.

catalog. However, this information could be gained without any attack by simply systematically going through the entire public website. The backend which processes actual customer purchases is obviously much more critical, as it has to store customer information such as credit card data and addresses, the loss or disclosure of which would be much more impactful. Hence, it makes sense to keep this part of the application in the internal data center, where the organization has full control over whatever security mechanisms are desired.

Irrespective of which hybrid architecture is used, the question remains how the combined use of private and public cloud infrastructure can be achieved in practice. One possible approach is to use in-house components provided by a public cloud provider. For example, Amazon's AWS offers so-called AWS Outposts, which essentially deploy parts of the AWS Infrastructure in the in-house data center of customers.[17] Similar functionality is available through Microsoft's Azure Stack[18] and Google's Anthos[19] platform. Another way to implement a hybrid cloud is to use an open source cloud platform such as OpenStack[20] in house, and to scale out into a public cloud provider that uses OpenStack as well.[21] A third possible approach that allows organizations to combine private and possibly even multiple public clouds together is to build applications on top of a platform that is supported across different clouds, such as the container orchestration platform Kubernetes[22] This platform will be explored in more detail in Sect. 5.3.4.

## 5.3 Architectural Building Blocks for Cloud Applications

Cloud applications can be built on top of different computational platforms. This choice has far-reaching implications for the whole application life cycle, as well as for the degree to which the different goals described in Sect. 5.1 can be attained.

### 5.3.1 Infrastructure as a Service

The most "traditional" way to use cloud services is to simply use the cloud as a virtualized data center, very much following the Infrastructure as a Service (IaaS) model. One of the main advantages of this approach is that it makes the migration of existing applications into the cloud very easy. Rather than redesigning the application with a different architecture, it can be moved to the cloud mostly as-is, by replacing

---

[17] https://aws.amazon.com/hybrid/.
[18] https://azure.microsoft.com/en-us/overview/azure-stack/.
[19] https://cloud.google.com/anthos.
[20] https://www.openstack.org/.
[21] https://www.openstack.org/marketplace/public-clouds/.
[22] https://kubernetes.io/.

the existing physical in-house server infrastructure running the application with a 1:1 copy of virtual machines in the cloud.

Such a move can yield many immediate benefits, such as increased system reliability (due to better fault-tolerance of the cloud infrastructure) and possibly cost savings due to the economics of scale by the cloud provider. However, several of the potential benefits of cloud computing cannot be fully achieved with such an approach. For example, consider an organization that runs its website in-house. A typical architecture for this would be to use a load balancer that distributes incoming requests between a fixed number of web servers. The scalability of such a setup is limited by the number of web server machines. The same will be true if the application is moved to the cloud by simply moving each individual server into a corresponding virtual machine. Hence, the ability of a public cloud to offer virtually unlimited automatic scalability is not realized.

In order to take full advantage of the possible benefits of cloud computing, a more cloud native approach than pure IaaS is needed. While there is no generally accepted definition of the term, its meaning is fairly well expressed by the following: "Cloud native infrastructure is infrastructure that is hidden behind useful abstractions, controlled by APIs, managed by software, and has the purpose of running applications".[23] In other words, to achieve the scalability that cloud computing can offer, traditional IaaS has to be supplemented by some higher-level abstractions offered by the cloud provider.

In the Google Cloud Platform, the cloud native abstractions of Instance Groups[24] and Load Balancers[25] can be used to achieve automatic scalability. While a detailed description of both concepts is beyond the scope of this book, we will provide an overview of how they can be used in the example of the company that is moving its web servers from in-house hosting into the cloud. The first step would be to define the web server instances through an Instance Template, which specifies the underlying virtual machine type and its resources, the boot disk image to be used, a startup script etc. An Instance Group is then configured to manage a number of instances based on the underlying Instance Template. Many detailed settings are available. Some of the most important ones include the minimum and maximum number of instances that should be maintained, the type of metric that should be used to determine load (such as requests per seconds or CPU load) and the thresholds above and below which the number of instances should be increased or decreased, the type of health check that should be performed to determine whether instances are still functioning (e.g. one ping per minute) etc. Finally, a Http(s) Load Balancer is attached to the Instance Group. Once again, a wide range of available settings can be used to specify how the Load Balancer should distribute incoming client requests between the different web server instances in the Instance Group.

Using an Instance Group and a Load Balancer, the system can relatively easily be configured so that a certain number of web server instances is maintained at all

---

[23] Justin Garrison, Kris Nova: Cloud Native Infrastructure, O'Reilly, 2017.

[24] https://cloud.google.com/compute/docs/instance-groups.

[25] https://cloud.google.com/load-balancing/docs/https.

5.3 Architectural Building Blocks for Cloud Applications            171

times (even during low load) to ensure reliability in the face of potential outages of individual instances. Similarly, it can rapidly and automatically respond to rising or falling numbers of client requests, ensuring low response times and cost effective operation.

While all the major cloud providers provide similar features, they are not standardized. In other words, using them makes switching between vendors a little harder than just sticking to pure IaaS would have. However, this disadvantage is in most cases be outweighed by the more powerful functionality. It should also be pointed out that while Load Balancers and Instance Groups clearly are "useful abstractions, controlled by APIs, managed by software [...]", i.e. can rightfully be considered cloud native features, building an application in such a way is still far from the most cloud native approaches possible. After all, the cloud user still bears the responsibility for the design of the underlying Instance Template, and is (through the configuration of the Instance Group) at least indirectly involved in the management of individual virtual machine instances. Some of the serverless approaches described in the sections below are more cloud native, as they reduce the administrative overhead and allow developers to focus more on the actual application and less on the infrastructure used to operate it.

### 5.3.2 Platform as a Service

All the major cloud providers offer a Platform as a Service (PaaS) product. For example, Amazon Web Services has AWS Elastic Beanstalk,[26] Microsoft offers Azure Cloud Services[27] and Google provides the GCP App Engine.[28] While these platforms are certainly comparable in overall features and functionality, there are many small differences, and the lack of standardization across the different platforms means that the choice of one provider makes switching to a different one more difficult than it would be if classic IaaS was used. On the other hand, using PaaS also reduces the administrative overhead compared to IaaS, because PaaS allows serverless operation. In other words, developers of an application deployed on PaaS do not need to worry about allocating sufficient compute resources to ensure scalability, reliability etc. PaaS could also be considered more cloud native than IaaS, because it offers more powerful and higher-level abstractions to developers.

In the following, we will briefly look at what an application deployed on the GCP App Engine could look like. An App Engine application consists of one or more services. The exact structure of a service depends on the programming language used. Supported languages include Java, Python, Go, Ruby and PHP. For example in Java, a service has to extend the HttpServlet class, and requests to the service invoke the doGet() method of the service class.

---

[26] https://aws.amazon.com/elasticbeanstalk/.
[27] https://azure.microsoft.com/en-us/services/cloud-services/.
[28] https://cloud.google.com/appengine.

Each service can have one or several versions. Different versions can represent different development stages of a service. Keeping old versions of a service around allows users to roll a service back to an earlier version if the most recent version causes problems. Multiple versions can also be used for testing purposes. For example, in a typical A/B testing[29] scenario some users are routed to version A of a service while others are presented with version B. By keeping track of the outcomes such as what percentage of users with each version end up performing desirable actions like making purchases later in the process, developers can determine which version of a service performs better.

Each version of a service can run one, several or no instances. A version without an instance would simply be an inactive version (which could still be reactivated by creating instances for it), while the number of instances for active services depends on the load of the application. By default, this scaling happens automatically. If necessary, developers can influence the scaling behaviour, for example by defining the metrics that determine scaling (e.g. request rate or response latency), by specifying the thresholds at which scaling should occur for these metrics, or by other configurations such as setting a minimum number of instances that should run at all times.

Figure 5.3 shows the overall structure of App Engine applications. Each applica-

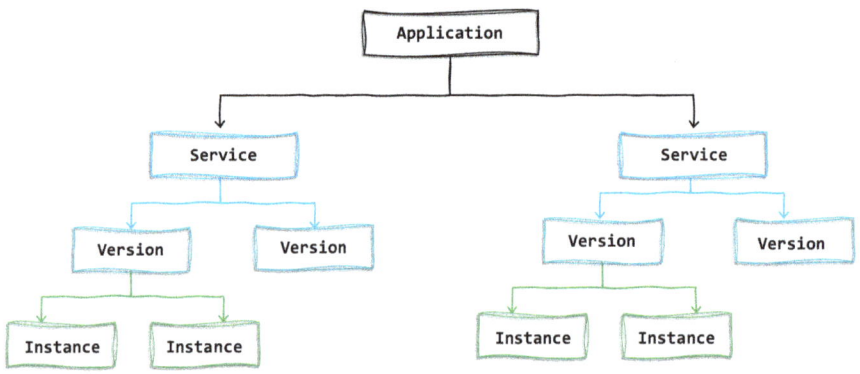

**Fig. 5.3** The structure of an App engine application

tion has at least one default service to which all incoming requests are routed. If the application has additional services, they can invoke each other using http requests. The URL of the request would include the identification of the requested service, and of the requested version of a service, if appropriate. User requests from outside of the application can be routed directly to the desired service either by including the correct service (and version) designation in the URL requested, or by creating a mapping based on patterns of the incoming URL to services in a dispatch configuration file. For example, all traffic from the mobile version of the application might

---

[29] https://en.wikipedia.org/wiki/A/B_testing.

5.3 Architectural Building Blocks for Cloud Applications

be routed to a specific mobile service, while all other traffic is forwarded to a default service.

It is also possible to create services that run periodically without being triggered by specific incoming requests. Just like cron jobs in Unix-based systems, such services can be used to run regularly needed tasks such as daily backups or weekly status reports. All services in the AppEngine can also easily access other GCP functionality such as Cloud SQL, Storage or Pub/Sub to store data persistently (either in a relational database or in flat files) or to integrate asynchronously through messaging systems with other cloud components.

### 5.3.3 Functions as a Service

Just like with Platform as a Service, all the major public cloud providers offer Functions as a Service (FaaS) products as well. For example, Amazon Web Services offers AWS Lambda,[30] Microsoft Azure features Azure Functions,[31] and the Google Cloud Platform provides Cloud Functions.[32] FaaS is similar to PaaS in many ways—it is a serverless platform that can be considered to be rather cloud native, with all the advantages and disadvantages discussed above that this entails.

In contrast to PaaS, in which entire applications that can consist of a number of collaborating services are deployed together, the focus in FaaS is on deploying individual functions to the cloud. These functions should be stateless, which means that each invocation of a cloud function should not depend on previous or have influence on future invocations. There are many use cases for which FaaS is an appropriate choice. As an example, consider an application in which automatic processing needs to be performed on newly created data, for instance if users of an app can upload photos into a public location. In such a scenario, it would be a sensible precaution to automatically analyse uploaded photos to detect offensive or otherwise problematic content. To achieve this, a function performing such checks could simply be automatically executed whenever a new photo arrives.

Just like the GCP App Engine, Google Cloud Functions support a number of different programming languages including Java, Python, Go and Ruby. If Java is used, a cloud function simply needs to implement the interface HttpFunction, which contains a single method called service with a HttpRequest and a HttpResponse object as arguments. Cloud functions are connected to so-called triggers, which specify that a specific cloud function should be invoked when a specific type of event occurs. In addition to direct HTTP requests, cloud functions can be invoked by relevant events from Google Cloud Storage, such as the creation or deletion of a

---

[30] https://aws.amazon.com/lambda/.

[31] https://azure.microsoft.com/en-ca/services/functions/.

[32] https://cloud.google.com/functions.

storage object, by the messaging service Pub/Sub, and by a few other services such as the mobile application development platform Firebase.[33]

GCP Cloud Functions can directly access a wide range of services on the Google Cloud Platform through API calls, ranging from different storage services to artificial intelligence based services such as the Cloud Translation or Vision APIs. Additionally, Cloud Functions scale automatically in response to the current load. For this purpose, the runtime automatically creates as many instances of the function as necessary to deal with all the incoming requests, and obviously scales the necessary underlying infrastructure accordingly. Different instances of the same Cloud Function, and different Cloud Functions are completely isolated from each other. All these features allow developers to focus on the intended functionality without having to worry about technical aspects such as managing and scaling the underlying infrastructure.

### 5.3.4 Containers

The idea behind containers in software architecture is similar to how containers work in the shipping industry. Prior to the invention and wide-spread adoption of containers, freight transported on ships or trucks was typically packaged in boxes or cases that were not standardized and differed widely between different kinds of goods. This made loading and unloading of transportation vessels rather time-intensive and at times difficult. The analogy in the software world is the difficulty of getting applications from the development environment deployed onto whatever target system they are intended to run on. This usually requires installation routines that are different for each application, and that have to ensure that the environment of the application, such as the required operating system, libraries, tools etc. all either exist or are created on a wide range of target machines.

Containers simplify commercial shipping significantly. A container ship can transport a certain number of containers, irrespective of their content, and loading and unloading can be done equally fast irrespective of what the different containers contain. In the software world, software that is packaged in a container can be deployed wherever containers are supported, and the container contains whatever environment the deployed software requires.

It should be pointed out that containers are not the only approach that simplifies packaging and deployment of software applications this way—the same can be achieved with virtual machines. Because virtual machines offer encapsulation, i.e. the entire state of a virtual machine is contained in a single file, applications can be moved from one machine to another through a virtual machine image. As long as the target machine for deployment runs the same virtualization software as the source system, the virtual machine running the application can simply be transferred as is. And since a single server can run multiple virtual machines simultaneously, different

---

[33] https://firebase.google.com/.

## 5.3 Architectural Building Blocks for Cloud Applications

applications can simply be executed on the same server in different virtual machines. Of course, it is possible to combine VMs and containers together as illustrated in Fig. 5.4: for example, a VM can run different containers.

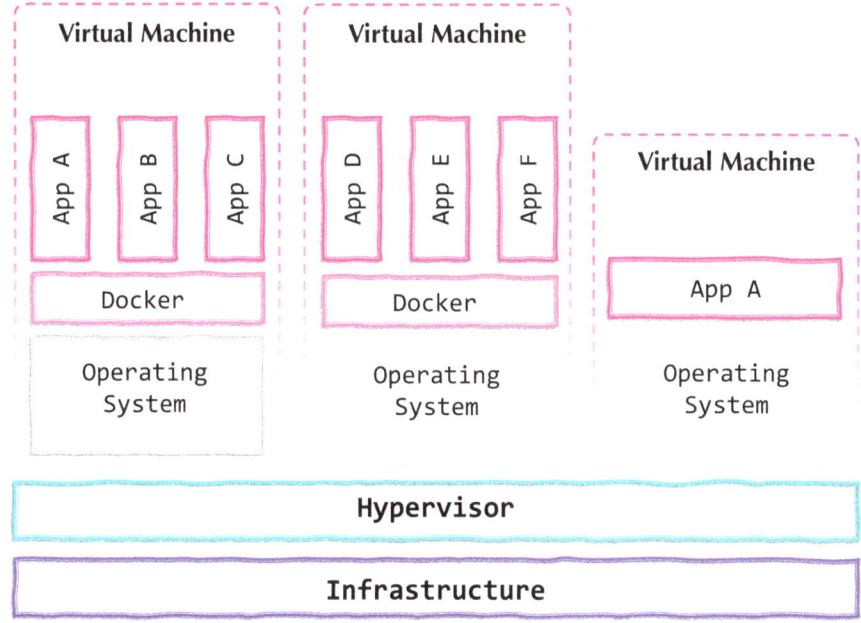

**Fig. 5.4** Containers and VMs can be combined together

One of the main downsides of this approach is that virtual machines are rather heavy-weight. In order for software to work in virtual machines just like they would directly on physical machines, a virtual machine has to contain the full (virtual) hardware of a complete computer, along with a complete operating system with full drivers etc. This contains a lot of overhead, because the vast majority of applications do not require all the components of a complete virtual computer. Containers are ultimately just light-weight virtual machines that contain everything that the applications deployed in them need.

While there are other container standards such as rkt[34] or LXD,[35] Docker[36] is by far the most widely adopted container standard. Figure 5.5 (source: the Docker's website[37]) shows the overall architecture of Docker. A server running docker containers runs the Docker daemon (dockerd), a background process that manages all running containers. It is controlled through a client program called docker with

---

[34] https://www.openshift.com/learn/topics/rkt.

[35] https://canonical.com/lxd.

[36] https://www.docker.com/.

[37] https://docs.docker.com/get-started/overview/.

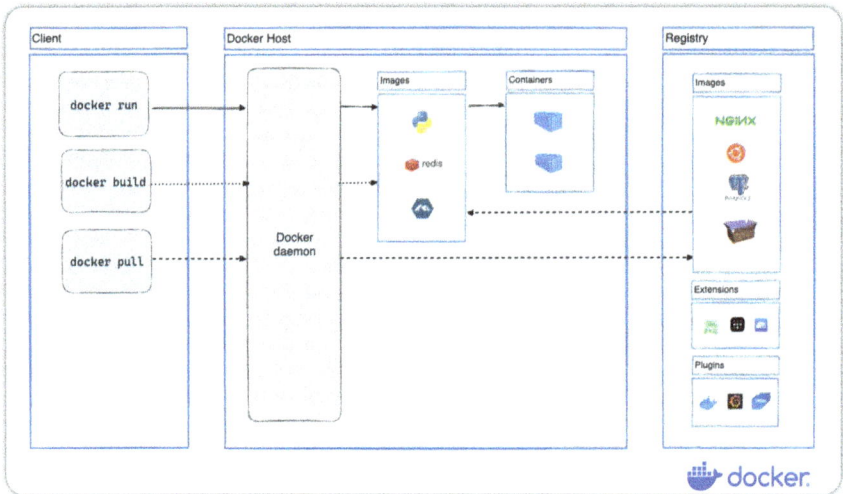

**Fig. 5.5** The docker architecture

which containers can be created and managed on the server. Docker containers are actually running instances of Docker images. In other words, a software developer who wants to distribute their applications creates a Docker image which can then be instantiated on any server running Docker. Docker registries are a convenient way of distributing or managing different Docker images, and can be either private to an organization or publicly accessible.

In practice, things often get more complicated than just deploying an application in a single instance of a container. For example, it is often desirable to deploy a single application in multiple containers, for instance to be able to scale the application in response to increasing load. Especially if this deployment of containers occurs across multiple physical servers, the deployed application becomes significantly more fault tolerant, increasing overall reliability. Additionally, even before fault tolerance or scalability are considered, it is often appropriate to deploy the different parts of a single application in multiple containers. There are many good reasons for this. For instance, if an application consisting of a web server and a database is deployed in two separate containers (one for each component), each of the two components can be developed, updated and deployed more independently, which is especially advantageous in agile environments with a lot of change. Similarly, it may well be that one of the two components—e.g. the web server—becomes the performance bottleneck of the application. If that is the case, deploying the database in a separate container makes it possible to scale the web server independently from the database by simply increasing the number of container instances for the web server container, but not for the database container.

While such multi-container deployments can be managed by Docker directly, it has become common to use container orchestration tools that automate container

## 5.3 Architectural Building Blocks for Cloud Applications

management tasks. The most popular such tool is Kubernetes.[38] It is beyond the scope of this chapter to discuss Kubernetes in detail, but we will look at some of its key concepts. They include nodes, clusters, pods and deployments:

- Node: A node is the basic abstraction of computing hardware that Kubernetes manages. In other words, nodes could be physical servers, virtual machines or a combination of the two on which Kubernetes can deploy containers. Users do not directly interact with or manipulate nodes.
- Cluster: A cluster is a combination of nodes managed together by Kubernetes. Nodes can dynamically be added or removed from a cluster. When that happens, Kubernetes can adjust how applications are deployed accordingly.
- Pod: A pod is the smallest deployable unit, and can contain either a single or multiple tightly coupled containers. All the containers in a pod are scaled up and down together.
- Deployment: Deployments are the high-level abstraction through which applications can be managed. For example, a deployment can specify that a certain number of replicas of a pod should be created on a cluster. This would mean that if a node in the cluster on which an instance of the pod was deployed failed (e.g. due to a hardware problem), Kubernetes would automatically create another instance of the pod on another node in the cluster to reach the specified number of replicas again.

Some of the key features of Kubernetes include:

- Automatic load balancing between pod instances.
- Automatic scaling by creating more instances in response to rising load, and by reducing their number when load decreases.
- Health checks of instances that can be used to automatically restart or replace non-responsive or failed instances.
- Automatic rollout and rollback of updates to the deployed containers to allow both for quick implementation of changes as well as the ability to go back to a previous version if an update causes problems.
- Support to securely configure infrastructure needs such as access to persistent storage, discovery of and communication between instances of services in other containers, and the management of secrets such as usernames and passwords used to access resources such as databases.

This rich set of features makes Kubernetes a compelling choice even in completely self-hosted, non-cloud applications that use a flexible and microservice style approach.

All the major public cloud providers offer Kubernetes deployments on their platforms—AWS provides the Amazon Elastic Kubernetes Service,[39] Microsoft Azure has the Azure Kubernetes Service[40] and the Google Cloud Platform the

---

[38] https://kubernetes.io/.
[39] https://aws.amazon.com/eks/.
[40] https://azure.microsoft.com/en-us/services/kubernetes-service/.

Google Kubernetes Engine.[41] Using Kubernetes in the cloud offers the additional advantages of not having to manage the underlying hardware and infrastructure running the platform, as well as the ability to scale applications in a practically unlimited way. Furthermore, since Kubernetes is supported across a wide range of cloud platforms, using it reduces the risk of vendor lock-in, especially compared to other cloud native approaches like Platform as a Service. The previous sentence says "reduces" rather than "prevents" because despite the fact that different providers offer Kubernetes, different implementation details still mean that moving applications between different Kubernetes environments entails at least careful testing, if not some adjustments. Finally, since Kubernetes itself can flexibly integrate nodes from different platforms, it is relatively easy to build hybrid or even multi-cloud applications in which some nodes are hosted in an in-house data center while others are based e.g. on virtual machines on two different cloud providers.

In addition to the Kubernetes Engine which has the full feature set of Kubernetes and gives users control over all the different aspects of container orchestration, the Google Cloud Platform also offers Cloud Run, which is another way to run containers serverlessly in the cloud. Cloud Run is more fully managed by Google, which means it gives users less control over the details of deployments, and offers fewer advanced features. However, for simple stateless applications it might be the better choice since it requires even less user involvement in the operation of deployed applications.

## 5.4 Summary

Throughout this chapter, it hopefully became clear that there is not a single best cloud application architecture, but that there are a wide range of choices, each of which has different strengths and weaknesses in different situations. There are a number of factors that should ultimately decide the best cloud architecture for a given application, from the specific business needs and their influence on the relative importance of the different architecture goals to the existing IT infrastructure and expertise in the organization (because cloud applications are usually not built entirely from scratch either).

It should also be repeated that this chapter barely scratched the surface of this topic area—the interested reader should easily be able to find entire books on many of the sections and topics covered, be it concepts such as microservice architectures or specific products such as Kubernetes. Additionally, for many applications it makes sense to not build all the technical aspects from scratch, but to use frameworks or toolsets like Google Firebase[42] which takes care of commonly needed technical services such as authentication, messaging, storage etc., and consequently save developers from having to "reinvent the wheel" for generic, not application specific tasks.

---

[41] https://cloud.google.com/kubernetes-engine.

[42] https://firebase.google.com/.

## 5.5 Key Terms

**Pet vs. Cattle Paradigm** Traditional IT infrastructures are often characterized by a small number of servers that are individually tended to (pets). In a modern cloud environment, infrastructure elements such as virtual machines should be dynamically allocated and de-allocated based on load, making individual instances less important (cattle).

**Chaos Monkey** The chaos monkey is a software component that randomly and unpredictably shuts down elements of the (cloud) infrastructure, thereby testing the fault tolerance of the overall system.

**Serverless Computing** is strictly speaking a misnomer, as all cloud services ultimately run on physical servers. However, a cloud service is called serverless if the underlying physical infrastructure is handled by the cloud provider (e.g. allocation, monitoring, patching etc.). For example, the GCP App Engine can be considered to be serverless.

**Agile Development** describes a family of software development methodologies that emphasize iterative development processes that can deal with change well, in contrast to more plan-driven approaches.

**DevOps** is a software development paradigm that emphasizes the need to integrate considerations about the operations of a software system with its development activities, rather than considering the two separate tasks.

**Terraform** is a widely used infrastructure as code tool that allows users to declaratively specify and provision their cloud resources.

**Ansible** is an open source tool that allows users to automate common IT infrastructure tasks. For exmaple, with Ansible it is possible to roll out a software update across multiple virtual machines with a single user interaction.

**Microservice Architecture** In a microservice architecture, applications are broken down into a number of small independent services that interact with each other. This has numerous benefits for application development and deployment, but also introduces additional complexity.

**Service Mesh** A service mesh can be used to handle most of the technical and infrastructure tasks of an application using a microservice architecture, such as service discovery, authentication and monitoring.

**Istio** is an open-source service mesh that is frequently used in microservice applications running in Kubernetes clusters.

**Control and Data Plane** An Istio service mesh consists of a data plane in which Istio proxies handle the secure and reliable communication between different services, and a control plane in which these proxies themselves are configured and managed.

**Hybrid Cloud** A hybrid cloud combines two different types of cloud, most commonly a private and a public cloud, in order to combine the benefits of both.

**Cloud Bursting** describes a common use of hybrid cloud infrastructure in which an application is fully deployed in a private cloud, but configured to use additional resources in a public cloud if the system load exceeds the capacity of the private cloud.

**Layered Hybrid Cloud** In a layered hybrid cloud, some layers of an application are deployed in a private cloud, while others are deployed in a public cloud. This can be an attractive alternative to a cloud bursting architecture in cases where an organization wants to use a hybrid cloud to allow for more elasticity of an application than their private cloud infrastructure alone would allow, but still wants to keep certain particularly sensitive parts of the application in house.

**Cloud Native** An application architecture that is specifically designed to leverage cloud APIs to take full advantage of advanced cloud features, in contrast to cloud applications that mirror an architecture as it would be used in a traditional, non-cloud deployment.

**Kubernetes** is a widely used open-source container orchestration system, with numerous features such as automatic scaling of applications, health checks that allow for automatic redeployment of failed components etc.

**Cluster** A Kubernetes cluster is a number of compute nodes that can be used to deploy container-based applications.

**Node** A node is one of the physical or virtual machines used in a Kubernetes cluster to run container-based applications.

**Pod** In Kubernetes, a pod is the smallest unit of computing that can be deployed independently. A pod can contain one or several containers.

## 5.6 Review Questions

1. What are some of the most important goals an organization might want to achieve with their cloud architecture?
2. What is "infrastructure as code", and what are some advantages of this approach?
3. Why is automation important in cloud computing, and how can it be implemented?
4. What are the main ideas behind microservice architectures?
5. What is a hybrid cloud architecture, and why is it important?
6. Briefly explain the concepts of cloud native and serverless computing.
7. Contrast the differences between using IaaS, PaaS, cloud functions and containers to implement cloud applications.
8. What is Kubernetes and why is it useful?

## 5.7 Exercises

The following laboratory exercises contain questions that require written responses and, in some instances, accompanying screenshots. If the exercises have been given as an assignment, please ensure that all answers and requested screenshots are compiled into a separate document for submission to the instructor, as specified by the instructor.

### 5.7.1 Infrastructure as Code with GCP Using Terraform

In this lab, we explore the IaC tool Terraform with the Google Cloud Platform.

**Objectives**

1. Setting up the infrastructure to use Terraform with GCP
2. Creating a simple VM
3. Deploying a simple Hello World application
4. Cleaning up

**A. Setting up the Infrastructure to Use Terraform with GCP**

1. Open the Google Cloud Shell.
2. Create a new directory for our terraform deployment:

    ```
    mkdir terraform
    ```

3. Change into the new directory:

    ```
    cd terraform
    ```

4. Create a service account for terraform to use:

    ```
    gcloud iam service-accounts create tf-lab
    ```

5. Attach a policy binding that allows full access to all compute engine resources in the project:

    ```
    gcloud projects add-iam-policy-binding ${GOOGLE_CLOUD_PROJECT} -member serviceAccount:tf-lab@${GOOGLE_CLOUD_PROJECT}.iam.gserviceaccount.com -role roles/compute.admin
    ```

6. Insert a screenshot of the output:
7. Finally, we create a service account key that terraform can use to access project resources, and store that key in the file tf-lab.json:

    ```
    gcloud iam service-accounts keys create tf-lab.json
    -iam-account tf-lab@${GOOGLE_CLOUD_PROJECT}
    .iam.gserviceaccount.com
    ```

**B. Creating a Simple Virtual Machine**

1. Now we create a terraform configuration file to specify the infrastructure that terraform should deploy:

    ```
    touch main.tf
    ```

2. In this terraform file, we first have to specify how terraform can access the Google Cloud Platform as deployment provider. Click on the "Open Editor" button, navigate to and open the file main.tf in the folder terraform and enter the following code:

    ```
    // Configure the GCP provider
    provider "google" {
        credentials = file("tf-lab.json")
        project     = "<REPLACE_ME>"
        region      = "us-west1"
    }
    ```

3. Change <REPLACE_ME> to your project ID, which you can find by clicking on the project name on the top left of the screen and copying the value of "ID" next to your project name.
4. Next, we enter the code to create a single virtual machine instance with a defined boot disk and a default network interface. Append the following code to the end of the file main.tf:

    ```
    // A single Compute Engine instance
    resource "google_compute_instance" "default" {
        name         = "tf-lab-vm"
        machine_type = "e2-small"
        zone         = "us-west1-b"

        boot_disk {
          initialize_params {
            image = "<REPLACE_ME>"
          }
        }
    ```

## 5.7 Exercises

```
    network_interface {
      network = "default"
    }
  }
```

5. We still have to replace the placeholder <REPLACE_ME> with an actual GCP image type. To find the correct image, open the terminal again and use the command

    ```
    gcloud compute images list -standard-images -filter name:ubuntu-2404*
    ```

6. We need to use the amd64 version of ubuntu with our E2 instance (not the arm64 version, which is for a different cpu architecture). From the image with amd64 in the name, take the values for PROJECT and NAME and put a forward slash / between them. Replace <REPLACE_ME> in main.tf with his value.
7. Insert a screenshot of your resulting main.tf file:
8. Before we can actually create the virtual machine, we have to first initialize terraform once. Back in the terminal:

    ```
    terraform init
    ```

9. Then we ask terraform to simulate the creation of the specified deployment. In this step, terraform works through the configuration file and outputs the changes it would make if we were to actually perform the deployment:

    ```
    terraform plan
    ```

10. Insert a screenshot of the output:
11. If the output above contains no errors and makes sense, we can now finally create the infrastructure by deploying the code:

    ```
    terraform apply
    ```

12. Through the hamburger menu, navigate to the compute engine and insert a screenshot of the virtual machines you currently have:

## C. Deploying a Hello World Application

1. We now want to modify the existing deployment by adding a web server running a simple hello world web page. For this, we have to first add an external IP address to the deployment.
2. Open the editor again and add a resource definition for a static IP address after the provider configuration and before the compute instance resource:

   ```
   // A single IPv4 address
   resource "google_compute_address" "static" {
     name = "ipv4-address"
   }
   ```

3. Now we have to edit the existing network_interface in the google_compute_instance to use this IP address. The resulting network_interface block should look as follows:

   ```
   network_interface {
     network = "default"
     access_config {
       nat_ip = google_compute_address.static.address
     }
   }
   ```

4. Next, we have to create a startup script that installs the webserver and puts a hello world site up on the webserver. For that, create a new file startupScript.sh with the following command in the cloud shell:

   ```
   touch startupScrip.sh
   ```

5. Open startupScript.sh with the editor and enter the following code:

   ```
   #! /bin/bash
   apt-get update
   apt-get install -y apache2
   cat <<EOF > /var/www/html/index.html
   <html><body><h1>Hello from Terraform! </h1>
   </body></html>
   EOF
   ```

6. Open main.tf in the editor again. Inside the google_compute_instance resource definition, add this script as the startup script with the following line of code:

   ```
   metadata_startup_script = "$file("startupScript.sh")"
   ```

7. Finally, we have to allow http traffic to reach our virtual machine. To do so, we simply add the tag "http-server" to the VM, because there is a

## 5.7 Exercises

default firewall rule with that tag that allows http traffic. So, again inside the google_compute_instance resource definition, add the following line of code:

```
tags = ["http-server"]
```

8. Insert a screenshot of your updated file main.tf below:
9. Now we are ready to deploy our hello world application. As before, we first simulate the changes terraform would make to ensure that what actually happens is what we intended by using the following command in the terminal:

```
terraform plan
```

10. Insert a screenshot of the output:
11. If the output looks ok (note that the existing VM will have to be destroyed and added again with its new specification), create the new configuration by again running the command:

```
terraform apply
```

12. Go back to the listing of your virtual machines in the compute engine. Insert a screenshot that shows the newly created VM with its external IP address:
13. Open the listed external IP address in a separate browser tab (making sure that you use http, not https), and insert a screenshot of its output (you might have to wait a couple of minutes):

### D. Cleanup

1. To clean up, we first ask terraform to delete the deployed resources with the command terraform destroy
2. Next we need to delete the service account key. In order to do this, we first display the file tf-lab.json with the command

```
cat tf-lab.json
```

3. In the output, locate the value of "private_key_id". Then run the following command, substituting the value you found for <KEY_ID>:

```
        gcloud iam service-accounts keys delete <KEY_ID>
-iam-account tf-lab@${GOOGLE_CLOUD_PROJECT}
.iam.gserviceaccount.com
```

4. Insert a screenshot of the command (including your private key id) and its output:

5. Now we remove the policy binding we added to the service account earlier:

   ```
                   gcloud projects remove-iam-policy-binding
   ${GOOGLE_CLOUD_PROJECT} -member serviceAccount:
   tf-lab@${GOOGLE_CLOUD_PROJECT}.iam.gserviceaccount.com -role
   roles/compute.admin
   ```

6. Finally, we delete the service account for terraform we created earlier:

   ```
       gcloud iam service-accounts delete
   tf-lab@${GOOGLE_CLOUD_PROJECT}.iam.gserviceaccount.com
   ```

7. Through the hamburger menu, go back to the compute engine and verify that the virtual machine tf-lab-vm is gone.

## 5.7.2 Auto-Scaling Load Balancer

In this lab, we will create an instance template for a simple web server. We will then create an instance group and a load balancer that scales automatically with the number of requests, and test the behavior of this configuration under artificially generated load.

**Objectives**

1. Create an instance template
2. Create a managed instance group and an HTTP load balancer
3. Test scaling and load balancing under load

**A. Creating an Instance Template**

1. From the hamburger menu, select "Compute Engine", and click on "Instance Templates".
2. Click on "Create instance template".
3. Change the name to "apache-template". Select the machine type "e2-micro". Check the box "allow HTTP traffic".
4. Expand the section "Advanced Options". Expand the section "Management". Below "Automation", write the following script code into the textbox "Startup script":

   ```
   #!/bin/bash
   apt-get update
   apt-get install -y apache2
   ```

5.7 Exercises

```
cat <<EOF > /var/www/html/index.html
<html><body><h1>Hello from $(hostname)</h1>
</body></html>
EOF
```

5. Click on "Create".

## B. Creating a Managed Instance Group

1. In the line "apache-template" click on the three dots below "Actions", then click on "Create Instance Group".
2. Make sure that "apache-template" is selected as instance template.
3. Set the location to "Multiple zones" in the region "us-central1".
4. Set "Minimum number of instances" to 2.
5. Set "Maximum number of instances" to 8.
6. Under "Autoscaling signals", click on the default metric (CPU utilization: 60%). Under Signal type, select "HTTP load balancing utilization".
7. Set "Target HTTP load balancing utilization" to 100% and click on "Done".
8. Click on "Create".
9. You should now get a warning message. Insert a screenshot of the warning message.
10. Click on Confirm to ignore the message for now—we will complete the configuration soon.
11. Once the instance group is created, click on it. Scroll to the bottom of the page to see the two instances that are currently part of the group. Insert a screenshot showing their names and external IP addresses.
12. In a separate Browser tab, open the external IP for both of the instances of your group. What is the output of each of the two instances?

## C. Creating an HTTP Load Balancer

1. From the hamburger menu, under "Networking", select "Network services", then "Load balancing". Then click on "Create load balancer".
2. Select "Application Load Balancer (HTTP/S)" and click on "Next".
3. Select "Public facing (external)" and click on "Next".
4. Select "Best for global workloads" and click on "Next".
5. Select "Classic Application Load Balancer" and click on "Next".
6. Click on "Configure".
7. Enter "apache-balancer" as Load Balancer name.
8. In the Frontend configuration, enter "apache-frontend" as Name and click on "Done".
9. Click on "Backend configuration".
10. Click on "Backend services & backend buckets", then on "Create a Backend Service".

11. Enter "apache-service" as name.
12. Under "Instance group", select "instance-group-1".
13. Under "Port numbers", enter 80.
14. Set "Balancing mode" to "Rate". Set "Maximum RPS" to 10 per instance. Set capacity to 20%.
15. Under "Health check", click on "Create a health check". Enter "apache-port80" as name. What are the default health criteria?

    a. Check Interval:
    b. Timeout:
    c. Healthy threshold:
    d. Unhealthy threshold:

16. Keep the default criteria and click on "Save".
17. Uncheck the option "Enable Cloud CDN".
18. Click on "Create".
19. Click on "OK".
20. Click on "Review and finalize" to review the settings, then click on "Create".

### D. Testing Scaling and Balancing under Load

1. Through the hamburger menu, go back to "Compute Engine", "Instance Groups".
2. Initially, you might still see a red exclamation mark with the message "There is no backend service attached to the instance group" next to "instance-group-1". After a few minutes, there should be a yellow/orange exclamation mark (you might have to reload the page.) Summarize the warning message that appears when you hover the mouse over the exclamation mark:
3. Through the hamburger menu, go back to "Networking", "Network Services", "Load Balancing". Click on the load balancer "apache-balancer".
4. In the section "Frontend", what is the IP address?
5. Go to this IP address in a separate browser tab or window. What is the output? If you get an error, wait a few minutes and try again.
6. Reload the page multiple times. What is the other output that is shown at some of the page reloads?
7. We will now test the autoscaler and load balancer under load. For that purpose, open the cloud shell by clicking on the icon ">_" in the blue bar on the top of the Google Cloud Platform window.
8. With the following command, we will use the tool hey to send requests to the load balancer. Replace <load-balancer-IP> with the IP address you wrote down above under D 4.

    ```
    hey -n 25000 -c 100 -q 1 http://<load-balancer-IP>
    ```

## 5.7 Exercises

9. Let this command run for a while.
10. Go back to "Compute Engine", "Instance Groups". Click on "instance-group-1" and scroll down. Wait until you can see more than 2 instances and look at the details for some of the instances by clicking on their name. What zones are the instance groups in?
11. Note how they belong to three different zones (nothing to write down here)—if one of these zones fails (e.g. due to a local natural disaster), the application is still reachable in the other two zones.
12. Click on "Monitoring" below the instance group and insert a screenshot of the diagrams shown:
13. When the hey command finishes in the cloud shell, look at the latency distribution of the 100,000 requests. What are the response times after which 50%, 90% and 99% of requests are completed?

    50%:

    90%:

    99%:

14. Wait for several minutes. How many instances are now in your instance group? (or, if you are too impatient to wait—what do you think will the number of instances in the instance group be if you wait long enough?)
15. To "clean up" after this lab (and to avoid incurring charges for resources created in this lab that are just sitting idle, please perform the following steps:

    (a) On the Load balancing page, select and delete the load balancer and its resources.
    (b) In the Backends tab, select and delete the backend (if it wasn't already deleted in the previous step)
    (c) On the Instance groups page, select and delete the instance group.
    (d) On the Instance templates page, select and delete the template.

---

### 5.7.3 Using Containers with Kubernetes

This lab demonstrates the use of containers to easily deploy applications, and the use of Kubernetes to manage clusters of containers for failover support.

**Objectives**

1. To package a simple java application as a Docker container
2. To create a Kubernetes cluster and to deploy a Docker container into it
3. To scale up the deployed service, and to roll out an update to it

**A. Package a Simple Java Application as a Container**

1. Open the google cloud shell using the ">_" button. Then enter the following command:

    ```
    git clone https://github.com/spring-guides/gs-spring-boot.git
    ```

2. Go to the directory gs-spring-boot/complete:

    ```
    cd gs-spring-boot/complete
    ```

3. List the content of the now current directory and show a screenshot of the files and directories you see:
4. Set the correct java version with the following command:

    ```
    export JAVA_HOME=/usr/lib/jvm/java-1.17.0-openjdk-amd64
    ```

5. To try out the simple java application, run the following command:

    ```
    ./mvnw -DskipTests spring-boot:run
    ```

6. Click the Web Preview Icon ( ), and then "Preview on port 8080" to run the application locally. What is the output?
7. Go back to the google cloud shell and press Ctrl-C to end the locally running application.
8. Next, we use a build tool called Maven (and its wrapper function mvnw) to package the application:

    ```
    ./mvnw -DskipTests package
    ```

9. Before we can actually push a Docker container image to the Container Registry, we have to enable the Google Artifact Registry API. To do this, from the main "hamburger menu", select "APIs & Services". Then click on "Enable APIs and Services", search for "artifact registry", and click on the search result "Artifact Registry API". Then click on the button "Enable".

## 5.7 Exercises

10. To create a new Docker repository, use the command:

    ```
    gcloud artifacts repositories create codelabrepo
    -repository-format=docker -location=us-central1
    ```

11. Now we create the container image and push it to the Artifact Registry:

    ```
    ./mvnw -DskipTests com.google.cloud.tools:
    jib-maven-plugin:build -Dimage=us-central1-docker.pkg.dev/
    $GOOGLE_CLOUD_PROJECT/codelabrepo/hello-java:v1
    ```

12. If prompted to Authorize the Cloud Shell, click "Authorize".
13. In the hamburger menu, go to CI/CD ->Container Registry. You should see a repository with the name "codelabrepo". Click on it to see the deployed image "hello-java" in its name. Insert a screenshot showing the image in the repository:
14. We can now test the Docker image locally with the following command:

    ```
    docker run -ti -rm -p 8080:8080
    us-central1-docker.pkg.dev/$GOOGLE_CLOUD_PROJECT/
    codelabrepo/hello-java:v1
    ```

15. Click the Web Preview Icon ( ), and then "Preview on port 8080" to run the Docker container image locally. What is the output?
16. Go back to the google cloud shell and press Ctrl-C to end the locally running application.

### B. Creating a Kubernetes Cluster and Deploying the Application

1. From the hamburger menu, open the menu item "Kubernetes Engine" (which is in the "Compute" section). If necessary, click on "Enable".
2. Once the Engine is finished getting ready (which might take a few minutes), click on "Clusters", then on "Create" to create a new cluster.
3. On the top right of the screen, click on "Switch to Standard Cluster.
4. In the pop-up that opens, click on "Switch to Standard Cluster" to confirm.
5. Click on "default-pool".
6. Change the field "Number of nodes" from 3 to 2.
7. In the menu on the left, click on "Nodes" and change the "Boot disk size (GB)" from 100 to 50.
8. Leave all other settings as they are.
9. Click on "Create" to create the cluster. Note that it will take several minutes to start the cluster.

10. Once the cluster is running (there is a green check mark next to its name), click on the "Actions" button (the one with the three dots) and click on "Connect". Then copy the command line shown ( "glcoud container clusters...") into your Cloud Shell and run it. If prompted, click on "Authorize".
11. Run the command

    ```
    kubectl version -output=yaml
    ```

12. Insert a screenshot of the output:
13. In the Cloud Shell, run the following command to deploy the application:

    ```
    kubectl create deployment hello-java
    -image=us-central1-docker.pkg.dev/$GOOGLE_CLOUD_PROJECT/
    codelabrepo/hello-java:v1
    ```

14. Run the following command to see whether the deployment was successful:

    ```
    kubectl get deployments
    ```

15. What is the output?
16. To view the application instances created by the deployment, run

    ```
    kubectl get pods
    ```

17. What is the output?
18. To allow outside access to our deployed application, run the following command:

    ```
    kubectl expose deployment hello-java
    -type=LoadBalancer -port 80  -target-port 8080
    ```

19. What is the output?
20. To find the publicly accessible IP address of the service, run the following command:

    ```
    kubectl get services
    ```

21. What is the external IP for hello-java? (You might have to wait for a couple of minutes and re-run the command for the <pending> to change to an actual IP address.)
22. In a separate browser window or tab, open this IP address. What is the output in the browser?

## C. Scaling up the Service and Rolling Out an Update

1. To scale up the service to three running instances, run the following command:

   ```
   kubectl scale deployment hello-java -replicas=3
   ```

2. To see the result, run this command

   ```
   kubectl get deployments
   ```

3. What is the output?
4. Now assume we want to update the deployed application (e.g. to add new features or to fix a bug). Open the code editor (click on the button " ![] Open Editor") and navigate to the file
   `gs-spring-boot/complete/src/main/java/com/example/springboot/HelloController.java`
5. Change the string in the return statement to "Greetings from Kubernetes!" and make sure to save the file.
6. Back in the Cloud Shell, rebuild the application with the following command (make sure you are still in the directory `gs-spring-boot/complete`):

   ```
   ./mvnw -DskipTests package
   ```

7. Build a new version of the container image and push it into the registry:

   ```
   ./mvnw -DskipTests package com.google.cloud.tools:jib-maven-plugin:build -Dimage=us-central1-docker.pkg.dev/$GOOGLE_CLOUD_PROJECT/codelabrepo/hello-java:v2
   ```

8. Deploy the new image to Kubernetes with the following command:

   ```
   kubectl set image deployment/hello-java hello-java=us-central1-docker.pkg.dev/$GOOGLE_CLOUD_PROJECT/codelabrepo/hello-java:v2
   ```

9. Open your external IP from above in a browser window again. What is the output? (Note that you might have to wait a couple of minutes for the update to take effect.)
10. When you are done testing the application, delete the Kubernetes cluster in the Google Cloud Platform. Otherwise, your GCP project will incur charges for the cluster, even if it just sits there idly.

# Chapter 6
# Cloud Security

For reasons that will be discussed in more detail below, security is one of the biggest concerns in cloud computing. Since cloud computing is built on "normal" IT resources such as servers, networking equipment, storage etc., traditional IT security concepts apply in cloud computing as well. The first part of this chapter briefly reviews IT security. The second part looks at how cloud computing can both help and hinder achieving IT security. The final part describes best practices on how to improve security in the cloud, both in general and specifically in the Google Cloud Platform.

## 6.1 A Brief Review of IT Security

IT Security is often broken down into three concepts: Confidentiality, integrity and availability:

- **Confidentiality** describes that data is only accessible to whoever is authorized to access it, and nobody else. The importance of confidentiality can be illustrated using countless examples. For example, if credit card information of a person is disclosed to somebody unauthorized, it might be misused to make unintended purchases. Medical information is generally considered to be even more sensitive—most people do not want their medical history to be disclosed, not only for privacy reasons, but also because such a disclosure might lead to harmful outcomes, for example being turned down when applying for different types of insurance, not being hired for jobs due to health concerns etc.
- **Integrity** means that data cannot be corrupted or otherwise changed by unauthorized users. For example, accounting records reflecting sales transactions are generally not allowed to be changed. If errors are discovered later, a correcting transaction should be recorded. Similarly, student grades should only be changed through a proper process if errors are discovered, and not because a student manages to break into the database and decides to improve their grades.

- **Availability** requires that data and/or applications that use data are actually accessible and working properly for their users. At first sight, it might seem that availability is not really related to security, or at least that it is less important. But two main points can be made to illustrate the importance of availability: Firstly, without the requirement of availability, confidentiality and integrity are trivially easy to achieve: If data is stored on a hard drive and locked up in a safe, nobody can steal or modify any of it. Secondly, and probably more importantly, computerized systems are often of critical importance for the organizations that use them. An online retailer with a website that cannot be accessed by its customers, a bank that cannot perform transactions, or an airline that cannot access its flight booking systems (either to check passengers into flights or to sell seats for future flights) incur such massive financial damage by the unavailability of their systems that the survival of the company may be at risk if an outage is not resolved in a matter of hours. Patient care in a hospital that cannot access patient data (such as diagnoses, laboratory results, treatment plans) could suffer to a point where the health or even life of patients are at risk.

There are of course many other categorizations of IT security such as the STRIDE[1] model used by Microsoft, which is an acronym of the terms Spoofing, Tampering, Repudiation, Information Disclosure, Denial of Service and Elevation of Privilege. Tampering is equivalent to violated integrity of data, information disclosure corresponds to a lack of confidentiality and denial of service is an attack on the availability of data or systems. The other elements of STRIDE describe more specific ways to attack systems to achieve one or several of these outcomes. The following sections review two more comprehensive categorizations of IT security risks.

## 6.1.1 Common IT Security Risks

IT systems face a wide range of risks and possible attacks that endanger one or several aspects of security (confidentiality, integrity and availability). A relatively simple classification scheme by Jouini et al.[2] distinguishes the following factors:

- Threat source: Either internal (e.g. an employee) or external (e.g. an outside attacker)
- Threat agents: Human actors, environmental factors or technological factors
- Threat motivation: Malicious or non-malicious
- Threat intention: Intentional or accidental
- Threat impact: Destruction of information, corruption of information, disclosure of information, denial of use etc.

---

[1] https://docs.microsoft.com/en-us/azure/security/develop/threat-modeling-tool-threats

[2] Jouini, M., Rabai, L.B.A., Aissa, A.B.: "Classification of security threats in information systems", 5th International Conference on Ambient Systems, Networks and Technologies, 2014.

## 6.1 A Brief Review of IT Security

Each real-world threat can be viewed as a combination of these five factors. For example, an internal human employee could non-maliciously and accidentally destroy data by accidentally deleting it with an incorrect shell command. Or, an external human hacker could maliciously and intentionally break into a system to steal personal information of customers of a company in order to later commit identity theft. Or, an external environmental factor (a massive rain storm) could accidentally flood a server center, making the applications and data hosted in it temporarily inaccessible. Clearly, many different combinations of the five factors are possible, indicating that there is a significant number of different threats to IT security. Herzog et al.[3] classify specific threats in a tree structure, with the distinction between active and passive attacks at the root.

It is beyond the scope of this book to discuss all these threats in detail. Instead, we only highlight some relevant examples:

- **Buffer overflow attacks:** If programmers do not carefully check user input, attackers can use unexpectedly long values in input fields to write data beyond the memory locations allocated for variables. If this attack is executed skillfully, attackers can write executable code into memory and trick the runtime to execute it, which enables them to take over control.
- **Cross Site Scripting:** Similarly, if user input to online forums or message boards is not checked carefully, attackers can insert malicious script code that is then executed in the browser of other users.
- **SQL Injection:** Yet another related attack, in which a database is tricked into executing malicious SQL code by specially prepared (and insufficiently checked) user input, typically in web forms.
- **Physical theft of hardware:** Attackers can steal end user devices (such as laptops or smartphones) or servers (or simply server hard drives) to get access to confidential data.
- **Phishing attacks:** Attackers trick users into revealing confidential data, such as their login name and password to an online banking site, by sending them emails that look like they come from their bank and lure them to a fake (but real looking) bank website.
- **Man in the middle attacks:** In this type of attack, users think that they interact with for example their online banking website, when in fact they are communicating with a website set up by an attacker that looks like the real website, and that forwards user requests to the real website and displays its results back to the end user in order to conceal the existence of the attacker.
- **Malicious code such as viruses:** A common type of virus is ransomware, which encrypts important data (documents, photos etc.) in the background, and then asks users to pay a ransom to get access to the decryption key, or lose all their data otherwise.
- **Distributed Denial of Service attack (DDoS):** In a DDoS attack, a large number of computers (often without knowledge of their owners, because they have been

---

[3] Herzog, A., Shahmehri, N., Duma, C.: "An Ontology of Information Security", International Journal of Information Security and Privacy, January 2007.

taken over by attackers) flood a service such as a website with so many fake requests that the website becomes completely overloaded and cannot respond to real user requests anymore.
- **Eavesdropping:** Attackers intercept network packets, e.g. in a Wifi network, for example to intercept user passwords for websites.
- **Vulnerability Scanner:** Attackers systematically scan open ports of a server for installed software to find known vulnerabilities (due to missing security updates) that can be exploited for other attacks.

## *6.1.2 General IT Security Measures*

When most of the IT technologies and standards that are still used today were developed, security was not a major concern. For example, many of the networking standards still in use today are from a time when only a small number of participants (typically researchers) who generally considered each other to be trustworthy, or at least not malicious, used them. Additionally, in the early days of what we call the Internet today, there was very little that a potential attacker could gain—no payments or purchases were made over the network, no medical or other sensitive data was stored on reachable servers etc.

As technology advanced and the Internet became used more and more for commercial purposes, the need for security increased, and an ever growing market for security software and services began to emerge. The marketing approach of many IT security vendors (such as Anti-Virus software companies) seems to be to try to convince their prospective customers that if they adopt their security product, security will be a solved problem. While this is a very comforting message, it is unfortunately very untrue. There is no single measure anybody can take to secure their IT systems. Instead, IT security is often pictured as a metal chain which is only as strong as its weakest link.

IT security includes (at least) the following aspects:

- Host security
- Network security
- Encryption
- Access control
- Human/organizational aspects

To illustrate the previous point, even if all the host machines and the network are very secure, everything is encrypted and access control uses strong credentials, all it takes for security to fail is a user who falls for a social engineering attack and gives out their username and password to an attacker. Or, if users are well trained to not fall for such attacks, and everything else is very secure, but an attacker pretending to be a technician can gain physical access to the server room, such an attacker can simply steal or destroy storage media with sensitive data right out of the servers, once again breaking security.

## 6.1 A Brief Review of IT Security

The following gives a very brief overview of different aspects of IT security:

- **Host security** involves securing the individual server and clients machines that are used. This begins with physical security, which means that devices cannot be stolen or otherwise accessed by unauthorized users. Also, hosts should be hardened against potential attacks, which involves disabling or uninstalling any unnecessary services to reduce the potential attack surface, to install all available security patches, and to include appropriate controls in all application software to e.g. prevent buffer overflow attacks. Finally, regular backups of important data should be performed, to ensure availability of data in case of successful attacks or simple hardware failures.
- **Network security** involves partitioning networks into subnets to separate hosts that are in different security domains. For example, servers that need to be reachable from outside of the organization should be in a different subnet than client machines that should be hidden from the outside world. Between the different network segments firewalls should be installed. These firewalls check all network traffic and only allow authorized traffic to pass through. In addition, intrusion detection and/or prevention systems (IDSs/IPSs) should be installed. Both IDSs and IPSs constantly monitor network traffic, and trigger an alarm (in the case of an IDS) or even block suspicious network traffic (in the case of an IPS) if unusual traffic occurs.
- **Encryption** is often considered a separate security measure different from host security and network security measures. Both moving data (i.e., network traffic) and resting data (stored data) should be encrypted for security purposes. This prevents attackers who might succeed in eavesdropping on network traffic or get physical access to storage media from actually getting access to confidential data. One of the challenges of encryption is the management of encryption and decryption keys- attackers must be prevented from getting access to these keys, because otherwise the whole exercise of encryption becomes pointless. On the other hand, keys can also not be lost, because otherwise the data becomes unusable even to authorized users.
- **Access Control** describes measures to ensure that users can only access whatever data or resources they are authorized to access. This usually involves authenticating users (i.e. enabling users to prove their identity to the system) and keeping track of what resources an individual user is actually authorized to access. The first part is usually still done with usernames and passwords, even though this approach has many problems, some of which can be mitigated by multi-factor authentication, where a user does not only have to know a password, but also has to be in possession of e.g. a specific hardware device to access the system. The second step, determining the permissions of an authenticated user, is often done with constructs such as roles, which group users that share the same permissions together.
- **Human/organizational aspects** must be considered since IT security is not a purely technical problem, and consequently cannot be achieved by only technological solutions. In particular, as IT systems are used by individual users in organizations, appropriate security policies and procedures have to be in place.

For example, the best encryption, the strongest passwords etc. can be defeated if an attacker can convince a user to share their password with them. Similarly, if a user copies important data onto a USB drive so that they can take it home to continue working there, simple loss or theft of that drive can break the confidentiality of that data. Therefore, organizations need to reduce the likelihood of such occurrences by appropriate policies, procedures and constant security training and awareness measures.

## 6.1.3 IT Security Limitations and Tradeoffs

As the brief overview of IT security risks and security measures above has probably made clear, IT security is a highly complex issue. One of the consequences of that is that achieving complete security is practically impossible.

IT security involves several tradeoffs. In particular, security can generally be increased by spending more money and effort. This relationship is not surprising—spending money on additional security products, hiring more security experts etc. is generally going to increase security. Another important tradeoff is between security and user friendliness—the higher the level of security required, the less user friendly systems tend to be. Access control is a good example—security enhancing requirements like long and complex passwords, frequent changes of passwords, multi-factor authentication etc. make life harder for users.

It follows from these tradeoffs that complete security is not only impossible, but often also not even desirable. Instead, each organization needs to assess its risks and security needs and consequently balance its security measures accordingly. For example, for a hospital processing personal health data about its patients, any unauthorized disclosures of that data, or even temporary unavailability of that data could have very severe consequences, in extreme cases up to the death of patients. Accordingly, such an organization should strive to achieve a high level of IT security, even if it comes at the expense of significant cost and reduced comfort for its users. On the other hand, an amateur softball league might run a website on which upcoming matches and past results are posted. While a temporary unavailability of such a website or the manipulation of its data might be annoying, it would clearly have significantly milder consequences compared to the hospital example. Therefore, it does not make a lot of sense for the softball league to heavily invest in IT security because of the additional cost, which ultimately has to be paid for by league members who would gain little in exchange for the expense.

There is a fairly popular joke that can be found on T-shirts aimed at tourists in many places in Canada: "You don't have to outrun the bear, you only have to outrun the person with whom you are walking in the wilderness". Applied to IT security this means that an organization (or individual) only has to strive to make their IT more secure than many of their peers. If that is achieved, many kinds of security risks are significantly reduced, because attackers are likely to "go for the low hanging fruit". For example, a criminal organization with the business model to infect people's

## 6.1 A Brief Review of IT Security

computers with ransomware generally goes for the least well defended victims. A common attack vector is to scan the systems of potential victims for known security vulnerabilities that can be exploited to infect them. As long as a significant percentage of users do not regularly update their operating systems, browsers, browser-plug-ins etc., those who do are not necessarily safe from a ransomware attack, but probably have a much reduced risk.

Of course, this approach is not sufficient for larger organizations or organizations that handle particularly valuable data, because in such cases attackers might be willing to spend the extra effort necessary for a successful attack due to the expected higher return. Therefore, even if such organizations "do their homework" and implement basic IT security measures, they can still be attacked successfully. In the absence of gaping security holes, successful attacks typically involve multiple stages, which might include social engineering attacks on employees to get a first foothold in the organization e.g. by taking over the computer of an employee. The attackers then progress step by step towards the actual goal of the attack (e.g. by attaining local administrative rights, then gaining access to important servers, taking over networking equipment to open a channel to transfer data out etc.).

Two commonly used frameworks break down typical steps in cyber attacks. Lockheed Martin's Cyber Kill Chain[4] contains the following seven steps:

1. Reconnaissance: Figuring out the IT resources of an organization and their possible weaknesses
2. Weaponization: Preparing to apply an exploitable vulnerability in the organization with a customized payload
3. Delivery: Delivering the attack to the vulnerable system
4. Exploitation: Taking over the vulnerable system with he exploit
5. Installation: Installing malware on the vulnerable system
6. Command and Control: Establishing a channel to continue the attack from a remote system
7. Actions on Objectives: Achieving the ultimate objective, which might me copying sensitive information, disabling sytems etc.

The Mitre Attack Framework[5] breaks attacks down even more into 14 different steps, some of which (partially) overlap with the steps of the Cyber Kill Chain described above. Some notable additions include:

- Persistence: Making sure that the attacker maintains control over a successfully attacked system even after the system reboots
- Privilege Escalation: Expanding permissions e.g. from an initially compromised user account to administrative permissions
- Lateral Movement: Moving from an successfully compromised system onto other systems e.g. in the same network
- Exfiltration: Successfully transferring data from the attacked system to the attacker, bypassing defenses such as network firewalls

---

[4] https://www.lockheedmartin.com/en-us/capabilities/cyber/cyber-kill-chain.html
[5] https://attack.mitre.org/

These multi-stage attacks typically take several days or even weeks to succeed. The concept of Mean Time To Breach (MTTB) is used to indicate how long a successful attack takes on average. While it is impossible to determine the exact value for MTTB in an organization, the analysis of past attacks, or "read team" approaches where a team of outside security consultants is paid to attempt to break into IT systems can be used to get an approximate value. A second important security concept is that of Detection Coverage, which expresses the percentage of hacking activities that is discovered by the intrusion detection systems of an organization. The goal is to detect attacks before they achieve their final goal. Consequently, the lower the MTTB is, the more effort an organization should put into achieving a high Detection Coverage, to increase the chance that an attack can be discovered and ultimately foiled.

## 6.2 Impact of Cloud Computing on IT Security

If cloud computing is used, the responsibilities for the various IT security measures are split between the cloud service provider and the cloud service user. How exactly they are split depends heavily on what type of deployment model and service model is used. For example, an organization that uses Infrastructure as a Service in a private or hybrid cloud model has to spend a lot more effort on in-house IT security than an organization that uses Software as a Service with a public cloud service provider. In the latter case, the provider takes care of most of the host and network security measures, while the cloud service user is mostly concerned with human and organizational security measures.

Irrespective of the deployment and service models used, a common question is whether cloud computing is secure. This question is addressed brilliantly in a paper entitled "Is Chocolate Good for You—or, Is the Cloud Secure?".[6] The authors make the point that the first question can only be answered by "it depends"—on what is meant by "good for you" (health, well-being, happiness, etc.), on exactly what kind of chocolate is consumed in what quantity and frequency, by characteristics of the individual consuming the chocolate etc.[7] In analogy, cloud computing is neither secure nor insecure in general—it depends on what type of cloud services are used, what the cloud deployment and service models are, what security needs the organization has, what specific security measures are taken etc. It is generally accepted that cloud computing introduces or increases certain risks, especially if not only in-house private cloud computing is used. However, cloud computing also offers

---

[6] Netkachova, K., Bloomfield, R. "Is Chocolate Good for You - or, Is the Cloud Secure?", IEEE Computer, August 2017, pp. 74–78.

[7] The author feels he would be amiss if he did not express his unscientific (yet strongly held) opinion that the regular consumption of a reasonable amount of quality chocolate is in fact good for most people.

## 6.2.1 Cloud Security Risks

This section describes risks that might be introduced or worsened by the use of cloud computing.

### System Complexity

Cloud computing environments are generally very complex. Workloads usually do not run directly on hardware, but on top of a virtualization layer. Similarly, storage and network resources are also typically virtualized on top of physical hardware. The cloud service provider has to operate complex management systems to allocate resources efficiently, to bill customers in a very fine-grained way, to implement automatic scalability and failover, to allow the geographic distribution of resources etc.

This complexity not only increases the attack surface compared to systems that are run directly on physical hardware, it also makes accidental configuration errors that can be exploited for attacks more likely. On top of that, the incentive for attackers to find security holes in a cloud service provider is very high, because they represent a very attractive target: A successful attack on a public cloud service provider might give access to data from multiple customer companies.

### Multi-Tenant Environment

Public cloud providers usually utilize multi-tenancy, i.e. physical hardware is shared by multiple different customers. For example, virtual machines of multiple customer companies can be placed on the same physical server. The obvious benefit of this approach is that the cloud service provider can utilize its hardware resources more efficiently, which reduces costs. In theory, the different tenants on the same physical hardware are strictly isolated from each other. In practice, this isolation can break down due to bugs in software such as virtualization software or even hardware such as modern CPUs. The most famous example for the latter are the Meltdown and Spectre vulnerabilities[10] that affect many server CPUs.

---

[8] Dekker, M.A.C., Liveri, D.: "Cloud Security Guide for SMEs", European Union Agency for Network and Information Security, April 2015.

[9] Jansen, W., France, T.: "Guidelines on Security and Privacy in Public Cloud Computing", National Institute of Standards and Technology, special publication 800-144, December 2011.

[10] https://meltdownattack.com/

Multi-tenancy not only introduces the risk that confidential data might be accessed by unauthorized parties, it also might affect availability of resources. Even though modern virtualization platforms offer performance isolation features that (once again, in theory) guarantee that resources such as CPU time, memory or network capacity cannot be monopolized by one of the virtual machines running on a physical server, these guarantees might break down in the face of implementation errors or extreme situations such as distributed denial of service attacks.

## System Management is Internet-Facing

In applications that are hosted in a traditional in-house data center setting, there is a strict separation between the customer-facing functionality that is accessible from the Internet, and the system management functionality that is only accessible from the internal network and shielded from the outside Internet through firewalls, often in a *demilitarized zone* (DMZ) configuration. If a public cloud service provider is used, this separation is not possible, since the management interfaces of the cloud platform are also accessed through the Internet. This significantly increases the potential attack surface.

## Vendor Lock-in

Vendor lock-in is a particularly important issue in cloud computing because the majority of services offered by the different providers are proprietary, despite being similar in functionality. This is a security issue because it potentially puts the availability of services that are hosted by a public cloud provider at risk, for example if the provider goes out of business or if there are significant contractual disagreements with the provider. To mitigate the risks of vendor lock-in, multi-cloud systems have been implemented as discussed in Chapter 7.

## Legal Issues

Legal risks with cloud computing are often caused by a combination of other risks, such as multi-tenancy and vendor lock-in. For example, legal problems of other customers who happen to share the same physical hardware might result in court-ordered actions such as confiscation of hardware that could affect uninvolved parties. Another significant issue is that due to the global nature of large cloud service providers, foreign laws might apply to applications that are hosted in different geographic locations. For example, content that is allowed by free speech laws in one country might be illegal due to anti-defamation, youth protection or public decency legislation in other countries, potentially exposing companies who host their application across different jurisdictions to legal challenges that could affect their availability. Another common problem is that different jurisdictions (such as the European Union, but also Canada) have stricter privacy laws than other jurisdictions (such as the USA), potentially putting organizations that transfer data into countries with lower standards into trouble with government regulators.

### 6.2.2 Cloud Security Opportunities

The appropriate use of cloud computing can also increase IT security. This section briefly introduces some of the reason for that.

### Elasticity

The elasticity offered by the large cloud service providers greatly increases the availability of an application that is hosted on it. A simple example could be the website of a small online store. Before cloud computing was widely adopted, it was not uncommon that unexpected spikes in users (e.g. because the site was mentioned on a popular website or even TV show) effectively crashed the website, because the server could not keep up with the increase in requests. An even more serious scenario is a distributed denial of service attack, in which an attacker uses a large number of (typically hijacked) computers to flood a server with so many requests that it becomes unresponsive to real users. It is very difficult for an organization that hosts its applications on its own servers to defend itself against such attacks. In contrast to that, the use of cloud computing allows organizations to set up their systems in such a way that any spike in demand (whether caused by legitimate users or a DDoS attack) is met by an automatic and near-instantaneous scaling up of capacity.

### Geographic Spread

Public cloud service providers operate data centers in multiple geographic locations. While this has other benefits such as lower latency for end users, it can also be used to increase the availability of an application. Even though modern data centers (such as the ones operated by cloud service providers) go to great lengths to protect against service outages, they can never eliminate all risks. For example, data centers typically have at least two redundant Internet connections and emergency power generators in case of power failures, in addition to significant physical protections. However, for instance sufficiently severe natural disasters such as earthquakes can still render such a data center inoperable. Therefore, an organization that hosts its applications across multiple geographically spread-out data centers of a cloud service provider can virtually ensure the availability of its applications in the face of natural disasters, as long as they are not of a global nature. This benefit not only applies to applications, but also to backups of data, which, unless stored in multiple geographic locations, are also at risk of destruction in severe disasters such as large-scale fires.

## *Economics of Scale of Cloud Service Providers*

The sheer size of the large public cloud service providers is an additional factor that can increase security significantly. For example, data centers operated by cloud service providers are likely significantly better protected from physical intrusion than self-hosted servers at most organizations. Economics of scale of cloud data centers (which typically contain at least tens of thousands of physical servers) allow providers to split expenses for physical security over thousands of customers. Therefore, they can afford to spend significantly more on physical security, which results in not just higher availability, but also higher integrity and confidentiality of customer data and applications.

Essentially the same argument applies in other areas that are relevant for security. Cloud service providers are likely able to have more, more specialized and better security exports than any customer organization could employ on its own. Consequently, they are likely able to respond quicker and more effectively to security incidents, and can more extensively test and more quickly install available security patches and updates, again increasing all aspects of security.

## *Server-Side Storage*

Cloud-based applications typically store data not on client machines, but in the cloud. The contrast can easily be illustrated with an office application suite containing a word processor, spreadsheet, presentation and database applications. Traditionally, such application suites were installed on end-user machines, and kept user data (documents, spreadsheets etc.) there as well. If such an application suite is hosted as a SaaS offering in the cloud, then both the applications and all user data are stored in the cloud, while client machines only need a web browser and an Internet connection. An example for this would be the so-called Chromebooks, which are laptops powered by Google's Chrome OS and which primarily rely on software and user data in the cloud. A significant security advantage of the cloud approach is that the loss or theft of end user devices such as laptops or tablets puts the confidentiality of data much less at risk, as long as user authentication is sufficiently robust.

## Certification and Compliance

A final security-related point is related to regulatory requirements. Governments require companies operating in certain sectors (such as health care, financial services etc.) to demonstrate that they are complying with very specific regulatory requirements, some of which are about IT security. The reason behind these requirements is that for instance IT outages at organizations like credit card companies do not just affect those companies themselves, but just about any other company (and countless consumers) who use credit cards. To help protect the broader economy from significant damage due to negligence of for example credit card companies, they are required to take specific and significant steps to protect their systems.

In order for companies that have to fulfill such compliance requirements to be able to use public cloud service providers, providers typically implement a wide range of compliance requirements themselves. This gives anybody else who uses public cloud services additional assurances about their security. It is also very efficient, since it allows countless customer companies to rely on the certified compliance of cloud resources they use, rather than having to audit compliance of in-house operations themselves.

It should be noted that the cloud security opportunities discussed here are exactly that—opportunities. Incompetent use of cloud services can easily negate these potential benefits. For example, a severe thunderstorm caused power outages that took down a large AWS data center in Virginia, USA for well over an hour.[11] Several popular websites, including Netflix, Instagram and Pinterest experienced service outages for many of their users, because they apparently hosted most or all of their servers in this one AWS data center, rather than taking advantage of the availability of multiple geographically distributed data centers by the provider.

## 6.3 Cloud Security Best Practices

This section describes best practices for cloud security in a number of different areas, including access control, encryption, network security and monitoring and logging.

### 6.3.1 General Considerations

Before the best practices in these areas are covered, some general considerations about cloud security measures are presented.

---

[11] https://venturebeat.com/2012/06/29/amazon-outage-netflix-instagram-pinterest/.

## *Follow General IT Security Best Practices*

The first best practice to achieve security in cloud computing is to follow general IT security best practices. Since the cloud is made up of "normal" IT resources (servers, networking equipment, storage etc.), a first important step towards securing the cloud is to secure the individual resources as discussed above, by installing all available patches and security updates, reducing the attack surface by only installing what is needed, ensuring physical security from intruders who might try to directly access or steal hardware etc. It depends on the cloud deployment and service models chosen to which degrees this falls into the responsibility of the cloud service provider and the cloud service user, respectively.

## *Choose Appropriate Deployment and Service Models*

Related to this point, another important consideration is to choose appropriate deployment and service models. These choices depend highly on the situation. In one extreme, for particularly security critical applications, cloud computing might not be an appropriate choice at all—for example, the control systems of a nuclear power plant should probably not be reachable over any network at all. In slightly less extreme cases, where particularly sensitive data is handled, and where government regulations might be very restrictive, private cloud use might be the only practical solution.

While the choice of service model depends on other factors as well, security considerations should play a big role. Given that on the spectrum from Infrastructure as a Service over Platform as a Service to Software as a Service the percentage of the security responsibilities increasingly shift from the cloud service user to the cloud service provider, users considering models further on the left (such as IaaS) should make sure that they are able to keep up with the necessary security tasks. To illustrate this with a simple example—an organization could host their website using IaaS on a cluster of virtual machines that run a system such as Wordpress on top of the LAMP (Linux, Apache, MySQL and PHP) stack, or they could use Wordpress as a SaaS solution offered by some provider. The former approach would give the organization more control over the infrastructure, but it would also make them responsible for keeping the whole platform—the Linux operating system, all the necessary packages including the web server, database, and Wordpress itself—up to date with security patches. This in turn requires personnel that is aware of security updates and carefully tests and installs them on short notice. Because employees sometimes go on vacation or get sick, this typically requires at least a small team of system administrators. Consequently, small organizations might not be able to guarantee timely installation of patches, or it might simply not be economical to keep the necessary in-house IT experts to do so, in which case a different service model like SaaS might be more appropriate from a security perspective.

## *Mitigate Cloud Security Risks*

The next piece of general advice is to mitigate the security risks introduced or worsened by cloud computing as much as possible. In public cloud computing, dealing with the high degree of system complexity is mostly the responsibility of the cloud service provider. However, if private or hybrid cloud computing is used, extra care should be taken to not inadvertently open security holes by careless configuration errors.

Similarly, mitigation of risks caused by multi-tenancy is also mostly the responsibility of the cloud service provider. Even so, users can take extra measures with particularly sensitive data, including the use of modern in-memory encryption approaches.

To reduce the impact of the fact that the system management interfaces are accessed through the Internet, extra care should be taken with how cloud administrators connect to the provider. This can include the use of Virtual Private Network (VPN) connections between the administrator's system and the cloud.

Finally, vendor lock-in and legal risks can be addressed by making sure that sufficient in-house IT expertise remains to not be completely dependent on the cloud service provider. The details depend very much on the situation, but organizations should always have an understanding of how they can export important data back from the cloud service provider, and how they could move to an alternative way to run their core applications, be it in house, or with a different service provider. Depending on the risk assessment, it might be worthwhile to follow a multi-cloud strategy, in which more than one provider is used, which greatly reduces the dependency on any single provider. Specifically with regard to potential legal problems, legal experts (either in-house or by external service providers) should be involved when cloud computing strategies are developed or changed.

## *Take Advantage of Cloud Security Opportunities*

As discussed above, the security opportunities that cloud computing offers have to be deliberately exploited in order to be fully realized. While cloud computing promises practically unlimited scalability, this elasticity is only the result of appropriate application design and/or configuration. For example, if an application is deployed using IaaS, a properly configured auto-scaling load balancer can be used to ensure that the application smoothly scales up and down with system load.

Similarly, the geographic spread of available data centers by the large public cloud service providers has to be utilized in order to yield the increased resiliency against system outages caused by natural disasters. This can be realized by making sure that the application is deployed redundantly across multiple data centers.

Taking advantage of server-side storage, and leveraging the resulting reduced security impact of lost or stolen end-user devices requires applications that in fact do not store significant amounts of data on client machines, that ideally encrypt any data stored there, and that take appropriate steps to make sure that stolen devices cannot easily be used to access data on servers.

The security opportunities created by the economics of scale of the cloud-service providers and the ability to leverage certification and compliance steps taken by cloud service providers generally do not require specific actions by cloud service users to apply.

## 6.3.2 Access Control

Managing access control properly is a crucial component of IT security. It is especially relevant in a cloud computing context, because irrespective of the cloud deployment and service models chosen, making sure that the right users have the right permissions is a key task that has to be managed (at least in part) by cloud service users.

Access control is generally done with user accounts that have specific sets of permissions to access specific resources (such as servers, applications or storage). User accounts are not just given to real persons, but are also used for technical resources. For example, a program such as a web server typically runs with a specific user account on the operating system level that has specific permissions attached to it, such as the permission to read from and/or write to specific folders in a file system.

### General Access Control Principles

All users should be authenticated using strong credentials. As far as human users are concerned, this should preferably require 2-factor authentication, especially for users who have administrative rights.

The principle of least privilege means that each user (whether a human user or a technical user) should have exactly the required permissions, and nothing more. For example, in a simple example where two virtual machines are used to run a web server and a database server, respectively, and in which the database server is accessed by the web server to generate dynamic web pages, using just one technical account to run both virtual machines would violate this principle. The web server might only need direct read access to the document root directory, write access to some logging directories and the permissions to send specific queries to the database. The database might only need read and write access to the storage locations of the database and write access to the same logging directories. Consequently, both processes should be run using separate accounts with exactly these permissions. This increases security in multiple ways. For example, if an attacker successfully takes over the database server, they cannot directly access static data stored on the web server, increasing confidentiality and integrity of that data. Similarly, programming errors in one process could not accidentally harm the data of the other process, increasing overall availability.

Another important principle is that of the separation of duties. In general, the idea is that no single user should be able to complete critical functions alone. A common example from the business world is that performing and recording transactions should be done by separate entities. For example, in a retail store, if the only record of sales transactions are recordings manually made by cashiers, then it becomes very easy for cashiers to simply not record a sale and to pocket the cash that the customer gave them, pretending that the sale did not happen. When the resulting discrepancy of inventory is eventually discovered, it could not be tracked back to the individual cashier in any way. To prevent this, retail stores have cash registers that automatically record sales transactions. Whenever appropriate, separation of duties should also be enforced in cloud computing. For example, separate technical user accounts should be used to create, archive, delete, and analyze log entries.

A final general principle is that roles (which specify a set of permissions) should not be assigned to individual users, but to groups. Individual users should then be assigned to the groups. While it is equally possible to assign exactly the same set of permissions to a number of users directly or with the use of intermediate groups, the latter is clearly preferable because it simplifies the management of permissions, and likely is less error prone due to the reduced complexity. In practice, this means that individuals that have the same job function and therefore require the same permissions should be placed in a group which is given the necessary roles (and consequently permissions) for this job function.

## *Google Cloud Identity and Access Management*

On the Google Cloud Platform, access control is handled by Google Cloud Identity and Access Management (IAM). Its main functionality can be broken down into three parts:

1. Who...
2. Can do what...
3. On which resources?

The first aspect, "who", can be either accounts held by people or technical accounts. Accounts held by people, in turn, can for example be normal Google accounts, Google groups accounts or Cloud Identity accounts (i.e. accounts that are managed using Google's Identity as a Service (IDaaS) offering). Technical accounts used to give specific roles and permissions to google cloud resources are called service accounts. For example, when a new virtual machine is created in the GCP Compute Engine, by default it is run with the permissions of a default service account that is associated with the project that the virtual machine is attached to.

Default service accounts are very useful in the prototype phase of new applications, because they allow users to create resources without having to worry about assigning fine-tuned access permissions. However, the use of default service accounts is not recommended in a production environment, as it would likely violate the principle of least privilege. Instead, custom service accounts which grant exactly the required permissions (but nothing else) should be used.

Before we discuss the "can do what" aspect, it is easier to first look at the "on which resources" part. As explained earlier, resources on the Google Cloud Platform are organized in a hierarchy. At the top of the hierarchy is an (optional) organization node, which in turn contains (again optionally) a hierarchy of folders. Folders eventually contain projects, which in turn contain resources. Only the last two elements—projects and resources—are required: Any resource in GCP must be contained in a project, which, among other things, is used for billing purposes. Coming back to the "on which resources" question, permissions can be granted on individual resources, at the level of projects (in which case the permissions apply to all resources in the project), or at the level of folders or the whole organization, in which case once again the permission apply to everything contained in the folder or organization. Permissions are inherited from higher levels—in other words, the permissions an account has on a resource are the union of the permission this account has been granted on the resource itself, the project containing the resource, any folders that contain the project, and the organization node (if any) containing the folders.

The final part of the puzzle, the "can do what part", is defined by roles, which contain the actual permissions that users receive. There are three types of roles in GCP IAM: Basic (formerly called primitive), predefined and custom roles.

There are three basic roles—reader, writer and admin. The reader role allows read-only access to existing resources or data. The writer role contains the permissions of the reader role and additionally allows actions that modify state, such as changing existing resources. Finally, the admin role contains the permissions of the writer role and additionally allows managing roles, permissions and billing. The three basic roles can be applied at the level of projects or individual resources, and are basically a very coarse-grained legacy mechanism to manage permissions.

Predefined roles offer much more fine-grained management of permissions. They offer very specific permissions on different types of GCP resources. For example, the role storage.objectViewer grants read only access to the content of storage buckets, while the role storage.objectUser additionally allows the creation, deletion and updating of storage objects. Consequently, storage.objectViewer only has the storage object permissions storage.objects.get and storage.objects.list, while storage.objectUser additionally has storage.objects.create, storage.objects.delete, storage.objects.move, storage.objects.restore and storage.objects.update. Predefined roles are designed to contain everything a specific job function (or technical functionality) typically requires. At the time of writing, GCP offers just over 2000 different predefined roles, allowing users to grant permissions in a fairly fine-tuned way.

Custom roles allow users to custom-tailor the exact set of permissions they want to grant to a specific role. In situations where the available predefined roles offer too many permissions, custom roles are necessary to fully apply the principle of least privilege. While they offer full control, custom roles have their disadvantages.

## 6.3 Cloud Security Best Practices

In particular, since custom roles are completely managed by the user, great care must be taken to not accidentally grant too many or insufficient permissions in them. Otherwise, the principle of least privilege is violated, or applications might not function properly due to insufficient permissions. An additional argument for the use of predefined roles is that since they are managed by Google, they are also updated in the face of new GCP features. If custom roles are used, the roles have to be manually updated to allow their users access to new functionality. Therefore, in most instances, predefined roles should probably be used, and custom roles should only be considered if the existing predefined roles match up poorly with requirements.

> **Encryption**
>
> The basic idea behind encryption is to scramble confidential data into a cyphertext that can only be decrypted (converted back to its readable representation) with a decryption key. By restricting the distribution of the decryption key, confidentiality of the data can be ensured.
>
> Encryption algorithms can be categorized into symmetric and asymmetric approaches. In symmetric key schemes, the same key that is used to encrypt data can also decrypt it. This works well in some situations, for instance when a user wants to protect data stored on a laptop computer from being accessed by a thief who steals the laptop—without the key, the data would be in accessible.
>
> However, for secure network communications, symmetric key algorithms are problematic. For example, if a user wants to transfer sensitive data from and to an online banking website (such as account balances), they need to have a secure way to exchange the key before such communications. Simply sending the key over the network does not work, because attacks could intercept the key and consequently get access to the confidential information. While the key could be exchanged via a secure second channel (e.g. by postal mail), this is inconvenient, slow and expensive.
>
> In such situations, asymmetric (or public-key) encryption schemes are used. They work as follows: Each user generates a key pair of a private and a public key. A message that is encrypted with the public key of a user can only be decrypted with the corresponding private key. Consequently, each user makes their public keys publicly available and keeps their private keys secret, allowing communication partners to retrieve their public key, encrypting messages to them with it, and sending it over the network. Even if the messages are intercepted by an attacker, they cannot decrypt the cyphertext without the private key, which is only in the possession of the recipient and never has to be shared with anybody.
>
> Such asymmetric encryption is used whenever the https protocol is used in a web browser. Two practical challenges remain. Firstly, the sender must be sure to use the correct public key. If an attacker can trick the sender to use their public key (rather than they public key of the recipient) to encrypt

the communication, then the attacker intercepting the message (and not the intended recipient) can decrypt the cyphertext with their private key. Consequently, the authenticity of public keys is ensured by certificates that prove that a specific public key in fact belongs to the intended recipient. These certificates themselves are validated through a public key infrastructure by certificate authorities such as "Let's Enrypt" (https://letsencrypt.org/). The second issue with asymmetric encryption is that it tends to be computationally complex, meaning that it does not perform well for larger messages. To address this, asymmetric encryption is often used to safely exchange a single symmetric key between sender and receiver, which can then be used to efficiently encrypt and decrypt larger amounts of data.

A crucial aspect of asymmetric encryption is that there is no way to calculate the correct private key for a given public key. Using today's computers, this can only be done using so-called brute force attacks in which all possible keys are systematically tried out. This makes such attacks impractical for sufficiently long keys. However, the currently used asymmetric encryption algorithms all depend on specific mathematical problems being extremely hard to solve. Unfortunately, it has been shown that sufficiently advanced quantum computers could in fact solve these problems rapidly, rending the existing algorithms completely insecure. While it is unclear when (if ever) such quantum computers will become available, significant work has started on devising and implementing algorithms that would not be vulnerable to attacks with quantum computers. This field of work is called post-quantum cryptography.

### 6.3.3 Encryption

Encryption is a useful mechanism to secure IT systems in general. The facts that cloud computing is generally accessed over the Internet, and that public cloud computing features multi-tenancy, make encryption particularly relevant in cloud computing

**General Encryption Principles**

Data in the cloud should be encrypted, both data "in transit" (i.e. data that is transferred over a network) and data "at rest" (i.e. data that is stored in secondary storage). The need to encrypt data that is being transferred does not need a lot of justification—since cloud computing is generally accessed over the Internet, it would otherwise be a relatively easy target for attackers. It might be less obvious that data stored on hard disks or other secondary storage devices should also be encrypted. There are multiple reasons for this requirement. Firstly, it protects data from unauthorized access if an attacker gains access to a server that can access the storage (e.g. due to a failure of virtual machine isolation). Secondly, it provides an additional layer of protection if an attacker manages to get physical access to the hard drive (e.g. by gaining unauthorized access to a data center). Finally, it reduces the risk that data is accidentally disclosed when secondary storage devices are discarded, e.g. because they failed or are replaced by newer models. Encrypted data on a hard drive is inaccessible if the encryption key is not available. This actually provides a very quick and convenient way to erase data—if the decryption key is destroyed, the data is effectively inaccessible, just as if it was safely erased.[12]

For additional security in situations with particularly sensitive data, cloud service providers are starting to offer encryption not only of data in transit and at rest, but also while it is being processed. For example, the Google Cloud Platform offers so-called Confidential Virtual Machines, which use specialized features of current server CPUs to use in-memory encryption with encryption keys generated and stored by specialized hardware within the CPU. This provides a significant additional level of protection against attacks that manage to overcome VM Isolation, effectively eliminating many risks caused by multitenancy.

## *Encryption in the Google Cloud Platform*

This section focuses on the encryption of data in rest. By default, the Google Cloud Platform encrypts all data that it stores, without any user interaction required. The mechanism encrypts chunks of data with so-called Data Encryption Keys (DEK), and encrypts these DEKs with so-called Key Encryption Keys (KEK). Keys are regularly changed (typically approximately every 90 days), and stored redundantly. The final point is very important: Since strong encryption methods are used, if the encryption keys were lost, so would be the data.

GCP users have three choices with regard to encryption: They can either rely on this default encryption mechanism, they can choose to use customer managed encryption keys, or they can use customer supplied encryption keys instead.

In the customer managed encryption approach, users still let GCP handle key creation, storage etc., but they take control of aspects such as the key rotation schedule. In other words, they control how often and when keys are changed. Using customer supplied encryption keys goes one step further—here encryption keys are provided by the user. This puts full responsibility for the creation, redundant storage, life cycle management etc. of the encryption keys into the hands of the user. This

---

[12] Note that for extra security in case of particularly sensitive data, the deletion of a decryption key might not be considered sufficient by regulatory requirements, because the encryption could (at least theoretically) be cracked. In such cases, it is not uncommon to additionally physically destroy hard disks in an industrial shredder.

means that a potential attacker would have to gain access to both the encrypted data (in GCP) and the keys (managed by the customer), which can increase security if done well, and might be a necessary approach in areas with particularly strong regulatory requirements. The big disadvantage is that the organization has to take great care to not lose its encryption keys e.g. due storage media failures or ransomware attacks, because they would then also lose their data stored in the Google Cloud Platform.

### 6.3.4 Network Security

The importance of network security in a cloud computing should be self-explanatory given that cloud computing is accessed through computer networks.

#### General Network Security Principles

General network security principles in a cloud setting are essentially the same as in a non-cloud setting. Just like with access control, the principle of least privilege should be observed. In particular, firewalls should be configured in such a way that only the exactly needed traffic is allowed, but any other traffic (e.g. to ports or from sources or to destinations that are not necessary) should be blocked. This reduces the attack surface. Furthermore, all network communication should be encrypted. Encryption can happen at different levels, such as at the internet layer or application layer of the TCP/IP model with the use of IPsec or https, respectively. Depending on security requirements, it might be advisable to encrypt traffic independently at multiple layers. Finally, since attacks are often not immediately obvious, network traffic should be monitored carefully, for example by intrusion detection and/or intrusion prevention systems.

In cloud computing, some of the traditional pre-cloud network security approaches can no longer be applied. In particular, with in-house only IT, it is customary to partition computer networks into different segments, and to trust all requests that come from a "secure" segment. A common design uses three areas, the internal (safe) network, a so-called DMZ hosting servers that need to be accessible from both the internal network and the Internet, and the Internet (see Fig. 6.1). Between the internal network and the DMZ, and between the DMZ and the Internet firewalls are placed that only let authorized traffic through. In particular, the DMZ can be accessed from both directions, while the internal network cannot be reached from the outside (unless in response to a prior outgoing request).

## 6.3 Cloud Security Best Practices

If public cloud computing is used, no strict network separation between the different segments exists—machines in all three areas can be in the cloud. Consequently, a zero trust security model[13] is typically much more appropriate, where requests are no longer categorized as "safe" simply because they come from a trusted network, but where all requests are by default not trusted, unless they can be shown to be safe (e.g. by appropriate authentication and authorization mechanisms).

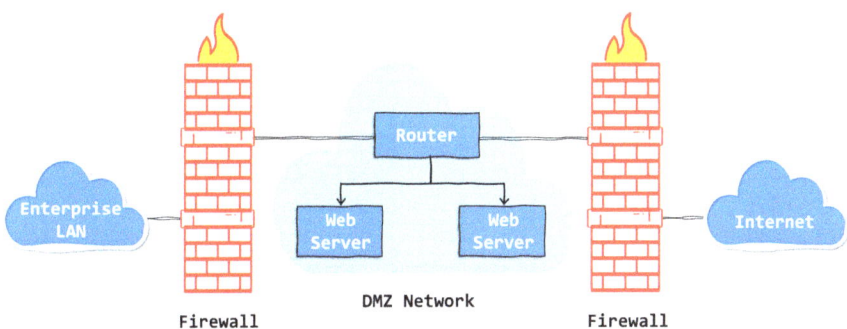

**Fig. 6.1** A network DMZ sits between two firewalls, creating a semi-safe buffer zone between the Internet and the enterprise LAN

## Network Security in the Google Cloud Platform

Resources in the Google Cloud platform such as virtual machines or Kubernetes clusters are by default connected through a Virtual Private Cloud (VPC) network. VPCs are global in scale, i.e. they can contain resources in any GCP data center, irrespective of its location, and consist of a number of regional virtual subnets. From the perspective of cloud resources, a VPN behaves like an exclusive physical network, even though it of course is routed through shared network connections. However, VPCs of different customers are strictly isolated from each other.

A new GCP project is created with a default VPC network using the class A private IPv4 address range of 10.*.*.*. This class A network is broken into subnets for each GCP region, alphabetically ranging from africa-south1 to us-west4, using the first 20 bits of the IPv4 address to specify the network ID and the remaining 12 bits to identify individual hosts in each network. Figure 6.2 shows some of the default subnets created in the default VPC.

---

[13] https://en.wikipedia.org/wiki/Zero_trust_security_model

| Name ↓ | Region | Stack Type | Primary IPv4 range | Gateway | Flow logs |
|---|---|---|---|---|---|
| default | africa-south1 | IPv4 (single-stack) | 10.218.0.0/20 | 10.218.0.1 | Off |
| default | asia-east1 | IPv4 (single-stack) | 10.140.0.0/20 | 10.140.0.1 | Off |
| default | asia-east2 | IPv4 (single-stack) | 10.170.0.0/20 | 10.170.0.1 | Off |
| default | asia-northeast1 | IPv4 (single-stack) | 10.146.0.0/20 | 10.146.0.1 | Off |
| default | asia-northeast2 | IPv4 (single-stack) | 10.174.0.0/20 | 10.174.0.1 | Off |
| default | asia-northeast3 | IPv4 (single-stack) | 10.178.0.0/20 | 10.178.0.1 | Off |
| default | asia-south1 | IPv4 (single-stack) | 10.160.0.0/20 | 10.160.0.1 | Off |
| default | asia-south2 | IPv4 (single-stack) | 10.190.0.0/20 | 10.190.0.1 | Off |
| default | asia-southeast1 | IPv4 (single-stack) | 10.148.0.0/20 | 10.148.0.1 | Off |
| default | asia-southeast2 | IPv4 (single-stack) | 10.184.0.0/20 | 10.184.0.1 | Off |
| default | australia-southeast1 | IPv4 (single-stack) | 10.152.0.0/20 | 10.152.0.1 | Off |
| default | australia-southeast2 | IPv4 (single-stack) | 10.192.0.0/20 | 10.192.0.1 | Off |
| default | europe-central2 | IPv4 (single-stack) | 10.186.0.0/20 | 10.186.0.1 | Off |

**Fig. 6.2** Default subnets created in the default VPC

VPCs are secured by a distributed firewall. While the firewall rules are defined at the network level, connections are denied or allowed on an instance level. What this means is that just like users do not have to manually configure (virtual or physical) switches and routers to connect their GCP resources, they also do not have to worry about placing (virtual or physical) firewalls at the appropriate locations in and between networks and subnets. Instead, rules that specify how network connections are to be treated at any point in the network are defined globally.

Firewall rules can be applied globally across the whole network, or limited to apply to tags that are attached to specific target resources. For example, a rule could specify that connections to port 443 are allowed on all resources (e.g. virtual machines) with the tag "webserver". The firewall is stateful. In other words, if for instance outbound traffic is allowed, return traffic (within a timeout window of ten minutes) is also allowed.

Firewall rules have the following parameters:

- **Target:** Which instances does the firewall rule apply to—this can be either specified via tags as described above, or via service accounts.
- **Direction:** Ingress or egress (i.e. inbound or outbound traffic).
- **Source (for ingress) or destination (for egress):** Individual IP addresses or address ranges for which the rule applies.
- **Protocol** (e.g. TCP, UDP or ICMP) **and port.**
- **Action to be taken**, either allow or deny.
- **Priority of the rule:** an integer between 0 and 65,535, with 0 being the highest priority, and 65,535 the lowest. Firewall rules are applied in order of priority, and the highest priority rule that matches a specific situation decides the action taken.

## 6.3 Cloud Security Best Practices

There are two implicit default rules with the lowest priority, allowing all outgoing traffic, and denying all inbound traffic. Additional explicit default rules with the second lowest priority allow all VPC internal inbound traffic, and by default allow all ssh, rdp and icmp traffic. Figure 6.3 shows the explicit default firewall rules.

| | Name | Type | Targets | Protocols / ports | Action | Priority | Network ↑ | Logs |
|---|---|---|---|---|---|---|---|---|
| ☐ | default-allow-icmp | Ingress | Apply to all | icmp | Allow | 65534 | default | Off |
| ☐ | default-allow-internal | Ingress | Apply to all | tcp:0-65535 udp:0-65535 icmp | Allow | 65534 | default | Off |
| ☐ | default-allow-rdp | Ingress | Apply to all | tcp:3389 | Allow | 65534 | default | Off |
| ☐ | default-allow-ssh | Ingress | Apply to all | tcp:22 | Allow | 65534 | default | Off |

**Fig. 6.3** Explicit default firewall rules

Obviously, these default rules should generally be changed or overridden by additional (more detailed) rules with higher priority.[14] The principle of least privilege dictates that only required network traffic is allowed. This is clearly violated by a default rule allowing all outbound traffic. In practice, only the ports that are actually used should be opened. This for instance makes it harder for an attacker who takes over a server to transfer data out of the network. It is also generally considered good practice to have rules with low priority that block all network traffic (in-and outbound) that is not explicitly allowed by rules with a higher priority. This way, a configuration error leads to traffic by default being blocked rather than allowed, which is better from a security perspective.

Furthermore, it is generally recommended to specify the target of rules via service accounts rather than via tags. The reason is that fewer permissions are necessary to attach tags to servers than to change the service account they run with. In other words, users with relatively limited permissions (such as administrative rights on individual virtual machines) could either inadvertently or with malicious intent attach tags to their virtual machine that allow more network traffic than should be permitted.

Also, since real-world firewall configuration can get complicated quickly due to the necessary number of rules, a good naming convention in which the name of firewall rules clearly reflects their meaning is also strongly recommended, to avoid potentially security relevant configuration errors due to misunderstandings.

Finally, in many cases (e.g. in hybrid cloud scenarios) it might be necessary to connect an on-premise network to a VPC. This can be achieved in different ways. If there are no particularly high performance requirements, a simple VPN using the IPsec protocol can be used. Cloud Interconnect is a different approach to connect directly (rather than through the public Internet) to the VPC using either a dedicated

---
[14] In fact, in production environments, the default VPC network should be deleted, and a custom VPC representing only the regions actually used should be created, along with custom firewall rules.

interconnect or a partner provider. These kinds of connections generally offer lower latency and higher reliability and scalability, but they are also significantly more expensive than a VPN connection.

### 6.3.5 Security Monitoring and Logging

The final area discussed in this chapter is the role monitoring and logging play in cloud security.

#### *Monitoring and Logging for IT Security*

Monitoring and logging are obviously done for reasons other than security as well, such as to keep track of resource use to ensure low response times and to keep costs under control. One of the main reasons why monitoring and logging are crucial for cloud security is that the occurrence of an attack is often not obvious at all—routine analysis of monitoring data or logs might in many cases be the best way to detect an ongoing attack and to prevent and minimize resulting damage. Similarly, once an attack has been detected, monitoring and logging data can be very helpful to determine the scope of the attack and to figure out which weaknesses allowed the attack to succeed in the first place, and consequently should be mitigated to prevent future attacks from succeeding.

#### *Monitoring and Logging in the Google Cloud Platform*

The Google Cloud Platform offers comprehensive monitoring and logging features. The monitoring functionality includes collecting a wide range of metrics, such as uptime and response times of services, utilization rates of resources such as CPUs, networks etc., many of which can be useful indicators to detect for instance denial-of-service attacks or other factors that influence for example the availability of services. Monitoring data can be visualized in custom dashboards that make it easy to compare current to historic data, and it can be used in alerting policies that trigger notifications if certain conditions occur or are violated (e.g., if a service does not respond). While they are not conclusive, significant deviations of monitored metrics from normal values can often be a sign of an attack.

The logging functionality allows centralized access to and management of logs that would otherwise be spread out through the whole application and all its resources. Of particular interest from a security perspective are admin activity logs and data access logs. The former logs creation, deletion and other changes of resources. Admin activity logs cannot be disabled and are by default kept for 400 days.

## 6.3 Cloud Security Best Practices

Data access logs keep track of which users access data in GCP. Depending on the applications and its data use, these logs can get very large, which is why they are turned off by default, and why the default storage duration if turned on is only 30 days. Still, especially if data is sensitive, data access logs can play a key role in keeping data secure.

Figure 6.4 shows a simple example of the GCP Logs Explorer, using filter conditions to display all the log entries on a specific virtual machine in the last hour that had at least the severity "Warning".

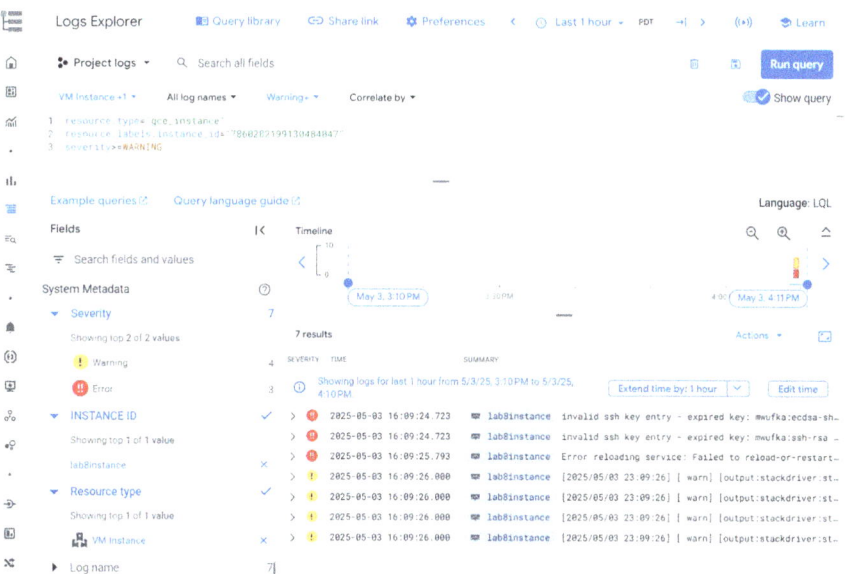

**Fig. 6.4** Example of the GCP logs explorer

Because logs can grow very large, a life cycle should be defined for them, i.e. there should be clear rules about how long logs are kept before they are deleted, or at least archived (e.g. for auditing or compliance reasons) to cheaper, longer term storage such as coldline storage buckets. The size of log files is not only a potential issue with regard to storage costs—it can also make it hard to extract useful information for security purposes from them—the analogy of searching for a needle in a haystack comes to mind. To make this task easier, log management in GCP offers powerful features to aggregate, filter or even statistically sample log data from multiple resources or even projects, and to write the resulting consolidated log data to cloud storage (e.g. as simple text files) for long time archiving, to BigQuery to allow for SQL queries against the log data to analyze it in more detail, or to PubSub to export it to other tools.

## 6.4 Summary

In summary, securing applications in the cloud is a complex undertaking that can be achieved by no single product or technology. Instead, a defense-in-depth approach should be used, in which multiple lines of defense are used to make it as hard as possible for attackers, and to increase the chance of the discovery of attacks before they achieve their ultimate targets. The additional risks incurred by using (especially public) cloud providers can, if done correctly, be overcome by taking advantage of the increased level of security cloud service providers can offer in their area of responsibility due to their size and experience. However, it is critical to realize that the security of the cloud (i.e the infrastructure operated by the cloud provider) needs to be complemented by the security in the cloud (i.e. of the applications deployed in the cloud) to achieve an acceptable level of overall security.

## 6.5 Key terms

**Confidentiality** is one of three critical aspects of IT security, indicating that information is not shared with unauthorized parties.

**Integrity** is one of three critical aspects of IT security, indicating that information cannot be deleted or corrupted by accident or unauthorized parties.

**Availability** is one of three critical aspects of IT security, indicating that systems and data are accessible to authorized users.

**Distributed Denial of Service Attack:** In a distributed denial of service (DDoS) attack, an attacker simultaneously floods a target system with fake requests, typically from a number of compromised computers, with the intention of making the target system unavailable to its real users, typically in order to inflict economic harm on the owner of the target system or with the goal to extort a ransom in exchange for stopping the attack.

**Defense in Depth** is an important principle of IT security that states that IT systems should be redundantly defended with a number of separate security mechanisms, to still protect the system if one or even several of the security mechanisms fail and are overcome by an attacker.

**Least Privilege** is an important principle of IT security that states that systems and users should only have the level of access and permissions they require to fulfill their task, and nothing more. The benefit is that an attacker who successfully takes over a system or an account only gains access to a minimal amount of resources.

**Separation of Duties** is an important principle of IT security that states that no individual user or system has full control over an important process. For example, separate accounts should be used by processes that write log entries and by systems that manage the log life cycle (e.g. by archiving and ultimately deleting log entries).

## 6.5 Key terms

**Mean Time To Breach (MTTB)** describes the average time it takes an attacker from the start of an attack to achieving their ultimate objective. The goal of security principles like defense in depth, least privilege and separation of duties is to increase the MTTB, giving defenders more time to detect the attack before it succeeds.

**Detection Coverage** is a measure of the level to which IT security monitoring systems can detect steps taken by attackers. The higher the detection coverage is, the higher are the chances of defenders of detecting and foiling an attacker before they reach their ultimate objective.

**Role-Based Access Control:** The main idea behind role-based access control is that decisions about granting access permissions to resources are not made for individual users, but based on roles. For example, roles such as "accounts payable clerk" are defined along with their required access permissions, and then assigned to all users who hold these roles.

**Service Account:** In the Google Cloud Platform (GCP), service accounts are used to specify the permissions that a system such as a virtual machine has at runtime. For example, a specific virtual machine might need the ability to read files from a storage bucket, in which case a custom service account with a role such as "storage object viewer" would be used.

**Default Service Account:** The GCP Compute Engine and App Engine both feature default service accounts with fairly far reaching permissions (by default with editor level permissions on the whole project). The default service account is great for the prototyping stage of applications, as it frees developers from having to worry about granting sufficient permissions to their virtual machines and applications. However, systems used in production should use more restrictive custom service accounts to respect the principle of least privilege.

**Basic Role:** GCP has three different basic roles: Reader, writer and admin. As the names indicate, the reader role has read-only access to all resources in a project, the writer role can additionally modify the state of resources, and the admin role can additionally grant or revoke permissions on resources to other roles, set up billing etc. While these basic roles are very simple to understand and use, they typically violate the principle of least privilege and should therefore in most cases not be used in production.

**Predefined Role:** There are approximately 2000 predefined roles in GCP, each of which gives a set of specific permissions on a specific set of resources. While an individual predefined roles might contain a small number of permissions that an application does not in fact need, carefully selecting predefined roles will typically result in permissions that are quite close to following the principle of least privilege. Therefore, predefined roles are in many cases the best choice for production use.

**Custom Role:** GCP custom roles allow users to fully specify the individual permissions of a role, allowing full implementation of the principle of least privilege. While custom roles might therefore be the correct choice in situations with particularly stringent security requirements, they come with disadvantages. In particular, role maintenance of custom roles is up to the user, and the complexity of specifying exactly the correct permissions can easily lead to security problems, making predefined roles the better choice in many situations.

**Demilitarized Zone:** In computer networks, a demilitarized zone (DMZ) is a network segment that is separated from a trusted internal network and an untrusted external network (typically the Internet) by firewalls. Resources such as web servers that need to be accessible from the external network are typically placed in the DMZ, where they can receive some protection from unauthorized accesses, while resources in the trusted internal network are usually not reachable from the untrusted network.

**Virtual Private Cloud:** In GCP, a virtual private cloud (VPC) is a private virtual network that is automatically created to connect all the cloud resources a user creates in a project, regardless of which region they reside in. It by default contains a subnet for each region in GCP, abstracting away the complexity of the underlying physical network infrastructure from the user.

**Firewall:** A firewall is a network security system that filters network traffic on the basis of defined firewall rules that specify which traffic should be allowed or blocked based on criteria such as direction, source/destination and port/protocol of the network traffic.

**Admin Log:** In GCP, admin logs contain all the administrative actions that modify the configuration or metadata of cloud resources. Admin logs cannot be disabled or deleted, so that attackers who modify cloud resources (e.g. by granting additional permissions or relaxing firewall rules) cannot delete all traces of their actions.

**Data Access Log:** In GCP, data access logs record all API calls that affect user data stored in cloud resources. In many systems, data access by users occurs much more frequently than admin activities, which makes full data access logs much larger than admin logs. Therefore, users can configure the level to which user access of data is logged.

## 6.6 Review Questions

1. How is IT security typically defined?
2. What are some common IT security risks?
3. Describe some common IT security measures.
4. Is complete IT security achievable, and why or why not?
5. Briefly describe how real-world cyber attacks typically proceed.
6. What is MTTB, and what does it have to do with detection coverage?
7. What impact does cloud computing have on IT security? Describe some cloud security opportunities and threats.
8. Name some common IT security best practices.
9. What are some cloud security best practices?
10. Briefly describe how access control works in GCP.

11. Briefly describe the role encryption plays in cloud security.
12. Briefly describe how network security works in GCP.
13. Briefly describe how access control works in GCP.
14. Briefly describe the role of monitoring and logging in cloud security.

## 6.7 Exercises

The following laboratory exercises contain questions that require written responses and, in some instances, accompanying screenshots. If the exercises have been given as an assignment, please ensure that all answers and requested screenshots are compiled into a separate document for submission to the instructor, as specified by the instructor.

### 6.7.1 Encryption in GCP—Key Management

In this lab, we illustrate the use of the Google Cloud Key Management Service.

*Objectives*

1. Enable the Cloud KMS Service
2. Create encryption keys
3. Encrypt a file

*Procedure*

1. Enable the Cloud KMS Service with the following command (replacing Project_ID with your actual project ID):

    ```
    gcloud services enable cloudkms.googleapis.com -project Project_ID
    ```

2. If prompted, click on "Authorize".
3. Next we create a KMS key ring, which is a logical collection of cryptographic keys:

    ```
    gcloud kms keyrings create "my-keyring" -location "global"
    ```

4. Now we create an encryption key named my-symmetric-key inside the key ring we just created.

   ```
   gcloud kms keys create "my-symmetric-key"
   -location "global"
   -keyring "my-keyring"
   -purpose "encryption"
   ```

5. Consult the documentation of the gcloud command kms. List three other commands that you can perform on keys other than create:




6. Create a file to encrypt (feel free to use a different file content):

   ```
   echo "Chocolate is delicious." > ./data.txt
   ```

7. Encrypt the file using the glcoud tool:

   ```
   gcloud kms encrypt
   -location "global"
   -keyring "my-keyring"
   -key "my-symmetric-key"
   -plaintext-file ./data.txt
   -ciphertext-file ./data.txt.enc
   ```

8. Display the content of the encrypted file:

   ```
   cat data.txt.enc
   ```

9. Insert a screenshot of the content of the file:

## 6.7 Exercises

10. Repeat steps 7 and 8 to encrypt the file data.txt again, this time storing the encrypted version under a different name, e.g. data1.txt.enc. Insert a screenshot of the second encrypted version of the file:

11. Note that the two encrypted versions of the file should be different—this is called non-convergent encryption. Why do you think this is a useful feature to have?

12. Decrypt the encrypted file again using the following command:

    ```
    gcloud kms decrypt \
    --location "global" \
    --keyring "my-keyring" \
    --key "my-symmetric-key" \
    --plaintext-file ./decrypted.txt \
    --ciphertext-file ./data.txt.enc
    ```

13. Is the result the original text? Display decrypted.txt and insert a screenshot.

14. Encryption keys should be (and automatically are) rotated regularly. Rotation means that the key to encrypt files is regularly changed. Files that have been encrypted with older keys can still be decrypted using the old key. To rotate a key manually, we create a new crypto key and set it as the primary version:

    ```
    gcloud kms keys versions create \
    -location "global" \
    -keyring "my-keyring" \
    -key "my-symmetric-key" \
    -primary
    ```

15. What message is displayed?
16. To display the different versions of the crypto key in the keyring, use the following command:

    ```
    gcloud kms keys versions list
    -location "global"
    -keyring "my-keyring"
    -key "my-symmetric-key"
    ```

17. What is its output?

18. Older versions of crypto keys can be temporarily disabled or destroyed, making the decryption of files that were encrypted using these keys temporarily or permanently impossible. To try this out, disable the original version of the key:

    ```
    gcloud kms keys versions disable "1"
    -location "global"
    -keyring "my-keyring"
    -key "my-symmetric-key"
    ```

19. What is the output?

20. Display the different versions of the key again (using the command from step 16). What is the output?

## 6.7 Exercises

21. Try to decrypt the file again:
    ```
    gcloud kms decrypt
    -location "global"
    -keyring "my-keyring"
    -key "my-symmetric-key"
    -plaintext-file ./decrypted1.txt
    -ciphertext-file ./data.txt.enc
    ```
22. What is the output?

23. We recommend checking your credits regularly.

### 6.7.2 Access Control

In this lab, we will use a custom service account to access a Storage bucket from a virtual machine.

#### Objectives

1. Creating a Storage Bucket
2. Creating a Custom Service Account
3. Creating and Running the Python Application

#### A. Creating a Storage Bucket

1. First, we create a storage bucket with the file to access. In the hamburger menu, go to "Cloud Storage", then click on "Create Bucket".
2. Give the bucket a unique name- write down the name you chose.
3. Click "Continue". Keep the default settings for the bucket and click on "Create".
4. Click on "Confirm" in the warning message.
5. On your local machine, create a file hello.txt with the content "Hello World!".
6. Click on the Storage bucket you just created. Click on "Upload", then "Upload Files", select the file you just created and upload it to the bucket.

## B. Creating a Custom Service Account

1. In the hamburger menu, click on "IAM & Admin".
2. On the left, click on "Service Accounts".
3. Click on "Create Service Account".
4. In the field "Service account name" enter "bucket-access", then click on "Create and Continue".
5. Click on "Select a role", scroll down to "Cloud Storage" on the left, and select "Storage Object Viewer" on the right.
6. Click on "Continue", then on "Done".
7. Find the just created service account in the list of service accounts and click on the "..." button in the column "Actions" on the right. Click on "Manage Keys".
8. Click on "Add Key", then on "Create New Key".
9. Select "JSON" as Key type and click on "Create".
10. Save the key file on your local computer.
11. What does the warning message popping up say?



12. Click on "Close" to close the warning message.

## C. Creating and Setting Up the Virtual Machine

1. In the hamburger menu, click on "Compute Engine".
2. Click on "Create Instance".
3. As "Name", enter "lab4vm".
4. As machine type, select "e2-small".
5. Click on "OS and Storage" on the left and change the operating system to "Ubuntu", with version "Ubuntu 24.04 LTS".
6. Click on "Security" on the left. Click on the "Service Account" combo box and change the default value "Compute Engine default service account" to the service account we just created.
7. Click on "Create" to create the virtual machine.
8. Once the VM is running, click on "SSH" to open a terminal on the VM.
9. In the VM terminal, enter the command

```
sudo apt update
```

## 6.7 Exercises

10. Then install the following python packages:

    sudo apt install python3 python3-dev python3-venv python3-pip

11. Verify that pip is installed:

    pip3 -version

12. What is the output?




13. Create a virtual environment:

    python3 -m venv env

14. Activate the virtual environment:

    source env/bin/activate

15. Install the google cloud storage python library:

    pip install google-cloud-storage

16. Click on "Upload File" at the top of the SSH window.
17. Click on "Choose Files" and select the JSON file you downloaded to the local PC earlier.
18. Click on "Upload Files"
19. Use the command ls to confirm that the key file is on the VM. Show the output below:




20. Use the command pwd to see the current directory. Show the output below:
21. We finally have to set up the environment variable for GCP credentials. Edit the following command to reflect the name and path to your json file, then run it.

    export GOOGLE_APPLICATION_CREDENTIALS=/path/to/your-service-account-key.json

22. To verify this worked, run the command

    ```
    echo $GOOGLE_APPLICATION_CREDENTIALS
    ```

23. What is its output?

## D. Creating and Running the Python Application

1. To open an editor to create our python application, run the command

    ```
    nano bucket_reader.py
    ```

2. Paste or type the following code:

    ```python
    from google.cloud import storage

    # Set your bucket name
    bucket_name = 'YOUR_BUCKET_NAME'

    # Create a storage client
    client = storage.Client()

    # List all files in the bucket
    blobs = client.list_blobs(bucket_name)
    print("Files in bucket:")
    for blob in blobs:
        print(blob.name)
        with blob.open("r") as f:
            print(f.read())
    ```

3. Change YOUR_BUCKET_NAME the name of your bucket. Then press Ctrl-X followed by "Y" and "Enter" to save the file and close the editor.
4. To run the application, use the command

    ```
    python3 bucket_reader.py
    ```

## 6.7 Exercises

5. If the python application runs successfully, insert a screenshot of the output. If not, it is time for troubleshooting!

6. Now we want to try to write to the bucket. For that, create a copy of the python file with the following command:

   ```
   cp bucket_reader.py bucket_writer.py
   ```

7. Open the new file bucket_writer.py in nano and change the last two lines in the file to

   ```
   with blob.open("w") as f:
       f.write("Hello only known planet with chocolate!")
   ```

8. To run our new application, use the command:

   ```
   python3 bucket_writer.py
   ```

9. Insert a screenshot of the output:

10. Why do you think writing to the bucket failed?

## E. Giving Write Permissions

1. In the hamburger menu, go back to "IAM & Admin", and click on "IAM".
2. Click on the pencil button (the tooltip should say "Edit Principal") next to the "bucket-access" service account.
3. Click in the combo box below "Role" and change it from "Storage Object Viewer" to "Storage Object User" (once again in the Cloud Storage section).
4. Click "Save".
5. Back in the SSH window of the VM, run the bucket writer application again. Insert a screenshot of the output. Note that you might have to wait for a few minutes for the changed service account to take effect.
6. If the change takes too long to take effect, you can also create a new service account with the "Storage Object User" role, save the json file locally, upload it to the VM and change the GOOGLE_APPLICATION_CREDENTIALS environment variable accordingly. Then run the bucket writer application again and insert a screenshot of the output. If the bucket writer application already ran successfully in the previous step, simple skip this one.
7. In the hamburger menu go to "Cloud Storage". Click on "Buckets", then on the bucket you created earlier. Download the file hello.txt. What is its content now?

## F. Cleanup

1. Make sure to shut down the VM (e.g. with sudo shutdown now). This should stop most of the charges for the resources of this lab.
2. To fully clean up the lab, you can also
   a. Delete the virtual machine
   b. Delete the storage bucket
   c. Delete the service accounts created

### 6.7.3 Network Security and Firewall Configuration

In this lab we will examine the use of firewall rules in a custom VPC network to implement least privilege from a network perspective.

### Objectives

1. Creating a Custom VPC Network with two VMs
2. Configure Firewall Rules
3. Installing Database and Testing Connectivity

### A. Creating a Custom VPC Network with two VMs

1. In the hamburger menu, select "VPC Networks".
2. Click on "Create VPC Network".
3. As name, enter secure-network. Make sure the "subnet creation mode" is "custom". Leave the default values for the remaining settings (including IPv4 single stack etc.). Delete the empty subnet if there is one—we will create subnets in the next step. Click on "Create"
4. Click on the name of the new VPC network to go to its details.
5. Click on the tab "Subnets".
6. Click on "Add Subnet".
7. First, we create a subnet for our web server. As name, enter web-subnet. As region, select us-central1. For IPv4 range, enter 10.10.1.0/24. Click on "Add".
8. Next, we create a subnet for our database server. As name, enter database-subnet. As region, select us-central1. For IPv4 range, enter 10.10.2.0/24. Click on "Add".
9. Once they are both created, insert a screenshot showing your two subnets:

10. In the hamburger menu, select "Compute Engine".

11. First, we create a VM as our web server. Click on "Create Instance".
12. As name, enter web-vm. As region, select us-central1. As machine type, select e2-micro.
13. Click on "OS and storage". Change the operating system to Ubuntu 24.04 LTS.
14. Click on "Networking".
15. Allow HTTP and HTTPS traffic.
16. As network tags, enter web-server.
17. Below "Network Interfaces", expand the drop down that says "default".
18. As network, select secure-network.
19. As subnetwork, select web-subnet.
20. For "External IPv4 address" keep the default value (ephemeral). What are the other two choices for external IP address?

21. Click on "Security" on the left.
22. Leave the default values for service account (the compute engine default service account) and for access scopes (allow default access).
23. Answer the following questions (feel free to google): What is an access scope in GCP, and what is the default access scope for VMs?

24. Click on "Create".
25. Next, we create a database VM. Click on "Create Instance" again.
26. As name, enter database-vm. As region, select us-central1. As machine type, select e2-micro.
27. Click on "OS and storage". Change the operating system to Ubuntu 24.04 LTS.
28. Click on "Networking".
29. Do NOT allow HTTP and HTTPS traffic—the database server should not be accessible via these protocols.
30. As network tags, enter database-server.
31. Below "Network Interfaces", expand the drop down that says "default".
32. As network, select secure-network.
33. As subnetwork, select database-subnet.
34. For "External IPv4 address" keep the default value (ephemeral).
35. Click on "Security" on the left.
36. Leave the default values for service account (the compute engine default service account) and for access scopes (allow default access).

6.7 Exercises

37. Click on "Create". Once both VMs are created, insert a screenshot showing them, including their internal and external IP addresses:
38. Try to connect to either of the two VMs by clicking on the SSH button. What happens, and why?

## B. Configure Firewall Rules

1. Through the hamburger menu, navigate to VPC Network ->Firewall.
2. How many firewall rules do you see?

3. To display on the firewall rules that apply to our new secure-network, create a filter to only see firewall rules affecting our network: Click next to "Filter", select "Network", type secure-network and hit Enter.
4. Now you should see only two firewall rules. This raises the questions how network traffic is treated in GCP in the absence of an applying allow or deny rule. To understand the behaviour, google "GCP implied firewall rules". What are the two default implied firewall rules for IPv4, and how does this explain that we cannot connect to the database VM via SSH?

5. Now we create the firewall rules we need for our application.
6. Click on "Create Firewall Rule".
7. Create the following firewall rules, one at a time, with the following settings:

    a. To allow HTTP/HTTPS traffic:

        i. Name: allow-web-http-https
        ii. Network: secure-network
        iii. Priority: 1000
        iv. Direction of traffic: Ingress
        v. Action on match: Allow
        vi. Target tags: web-server
        vii. Source/Destination IP ranges: 0.0.0.0/0
        viii. Protocols and ports: TCP, ports 80, 443

    b. To allow ssh traffic:

        i. Name: allow-ssh

ii. Network: secure-network
iii. Priority: 1000
iv. Direction of traffic: Ingress
v. Action on match: Allow
vi. Target tags: web-server, database-server
vii. Source/Destination IP ranges: 0.0.0.0/0
viii. Protocols and ports: TCP, ports 22

c. Deny traffic from database subnet to web subnet:

   i. Name: deny-web-from-database
   ii. Network: secure-network
   iii. Priority: 900
   iv. Direction of traffic: Ingress
   v. Action on match: Deny
   vi. Target tags: web-server
   vii. Source/Destination IP ranges: 10.10.2.0/24
   viii. Protocols and ports: Deny all

d. To allow database traffic from the web to the database subnet:

   i. Name: allow-database-from-web
   ii. Network: secure-network
   iii. Priority: 800
   iv. Direction of traffic: Ingress
   v. Action on match: Allow
   vi. Target tags: database-server
   vii. Source/Destination IP ranges: 10.10.1.0/24
   viii. Protocols and ports: TCP, ports 3306

e. Deny all other ingress traffic to the database subnet:

   i. Name: deny-all-other-database-ingress
   ii. Network: secure-network
   iii. Priority: 1200
   iv. Direction of traffic: Ingress
   v. Action on match: Deny
   vi. Target tags: database-server
   vii. Source/Destination IP ranges: 0.0.0.0/0
   viii. Protocols and ports: Deny all

f. Deny all other egress traffic from the database subnet:

   i. Name: deny-all-other-database-egress
   ii. Network: secure-network
   iii. Priority: 1200
   iv. Direction of traffic: Egress
   v. Action on match: Deny
   vi. Target tags: database-server

6.7 Exercises 239

    vii. Source/Destination IP ranges: 0.0.0.0/0
    viii. Protocols and ports: Deny all

8. With the filter for secure-network in place, you should now see eight firewall rules. Insert a screenshot showing them:

9. To be able to install MariaDB on the database VM, we temporarily disable the rule deny-all-other-database-egress. Click on the rule, click on Edit, expand "Disable rule", click on "Disabled" and click on "Save". You can turn this firewall rule on again after finishing Part C.

## C. Installing Database and Testing Connectivity

1. We now install MariaDB on the database VM, so that we can test the network connectivity.
2. Go back to Compute Engine -> VM instances
3. Click on "SSH" next to "database-vm" to connect to the database VM.
4. In the database VM terminal, run the command

    ```
    sudo apt-get update
    ```

5. Install MariaDB with the following command:

    ```
    sudo apt-get install mariadb-server
    ```

6. To allow remote connections to MariaDB, open its configuration file with the command

    ```
    sudo nano /etc/mysql/mariadb.conf.d/50-server.cnf
    ```

7. Change the value for "bind-address" from the default of 127.0.0.1 to 0.0.0.0
8. Press Ctrl-X, then Y, then Enter to save the changes and close nano.
9. Restart MariaDB to make apply the changed configuration:

    ```
    sudo systemctl restart mariadb
    ```

10. Check that MariaDB is running with the command:

    ```
    sudo systemctl status mariadb
    ```

11. Insert a screenshot of the output, then press "q" to get back to the command line:

12. Finally, we create a database, a database user, and give the database user permission on the database.
13. To log into the database run the following command and simply hit Enter when prompted for a password (since we are calling this with sudo):

    ```
    sudo mysql -u root -p
    ```

14. In the MariaDB prompt, create a new database with:

    ```
    CREATE DATABASE sampledb;
    ```

15. Next we create a new user:

    ```
    CREATE USER 'demo'@'%' IDENTIFIED BY 'Csis4460';
    ```

16. Then we give the new user access to the new database:

    ```
    GRANT ALL PRIVILEGES ON sampledb.* TO 'demo'@'%';
    ```

17. Finally, we ensure that the newly granted privileges are applied right away:

    ```
    FLUSH PRIVILEGES;
    ```

18. Exit the database with the command:

    ```
    quit;
    ```

19. Go back to the list of VMs in GCP and connect to the VM "web-vm" by clicking on "SSH".

20. First we install the database client. Run the following two commands:

    ```
        sudo apt-get update
    sudo apt-get install mariadb-client
    ```

21. In the list of VM instances, look up the internal IP address of "database-vm" and write it down here:

22. Now we connect to the database from web-vm with the command (adjusting the IP address to the actual IP address):

    ```
        mysql -h 10.10.2.2 -P 3306 -u demo -p
    ```

23. Enter the password Csis4460. Insert a screenshot of the successful connection:

## D. Reflections

1. Can you think of other tests we should do to test the security of the system as intended and the firewall rules as defined? Note that we should test that all allowed connections in fact work, and that forbidden connections should in fact be blocked by the firewall.

2. Can you think of ways how the security of the configuration could be improved? Hint: Think about stricter firewall rules (but other suggestions are welcome too).

3. When you are done with this lab, make sure to shut down both VMs. Please do not delete them yet—we might use them again in next week's lab. When the VMs are not running you should be charged very minimal amounts for the resources (storage of the VM hard disks, network configurations etc.)

# Chapter 7
# Multi-Cloud Systems

According to ISO/IEC 22123-1: "multi-cloud is a cloud deployment model in which a customer uses public cloud services provided by two or more cloud service providers".[1] There are cloud infrastructures which implement this deployment model in order to make it simple for a user/company to exploit different cloud providers at the same time. Thanks to these infrastructures the user can switch from a cloud provider to another in order to save money or exploit specific services that are available only in a specific cloud provider. Unfortunately, keeping these multi-cloud systems up and running requires more effort since cloud providers can change their services anytime and often the API documentation to interact with new/updated services is missing.

In the rest of this chapter, we provide an overview of multi-cloud systems, defining them as the use of services from multiple cloud providers and highlighting motivations such as cost saving and access to specific features. It distinguishes multi-cloud from federated and hybrid cloud models based on provider collaboration and user interaction. The text then examines various academic and commercial multi-cloud toolkits, outlining their features and limitations regarding interoperability, platform independence, resource provisioning and ease of use. Finally, it discusses current trends in multi-cloud adoption and the emergence of multi-cloud native applications, alongside challenges related to portability, security, and the need for standardised solutions.

## 7.1 Approaches to Use Different Clouds

First of all, it is necessary to clarify the distinction between the various models that include the interaction between different cloud systems. In particular, the core architectural distinctions between federated, multi-cloud, and hybrid cloud models

---

[1] "ISO/IEC 22123-1:2023(E)—Information technology—Cloud computing—Part 1: Vocabulary". International Organization for Standardization: 2.

are primarily based on the degree of collaboration between cloud providers, the user's awareness and interaction with multiple clouds, and the purpose and architecture of the cloud deployment.

A *Federated Cloud* model is characterized by an agreement between different Cloud providers to share their resources. This collaboration is often of a voluntary type and the user interacts with one Cloud and is not aware that the resources or services being consumed might originate from another Cloud. The complexity of resource sharing is abstracted away from the user. The main driver for Cloud providers to adopt a Federated Cloud is often the need to acquire new resources due to limitations of their own. Other reasons include geographical location restrictions or cost reduction policies. Federated clouds aim to increase interoperability and portability of applications between participating clouds. Data can be migrated more easily due to underlying Service Level Agreements (SLAs) between providers. Cloud brokers often play a role in federated clouds, potentially as part of a centralised entity, to manage the relationships and resource sharing between providers.

A Hybrid Cloud (already discussed in Sect. 5.2.4) is defined as a specific type of multi-cloud that involves two or more Clouds, typically a Private and a Public Cloud. It represents a subset of multi-cloud networks where private cloud deployment methods are combined with one or more public ones. Hybrid Clouds are often used for specific purposes like *Cloud Busting* (using Public Cloud for peak loads in a Private Cloud) or for scenarios where an organization aims to share some data across various user types while keeping certain elements confidential. For instance, it is being explored in healthcare for managing big data securely. A key characteristic is that the different deployment models (private and public) remain separate entities but are unified by an underlying technology that allows for data and application portability between them. This distinguishes it from a pure multi-cloud where the combined clouds might be entirely unique systems. While multi-clouds can handle a variety of tasks using distinct clouds, hybrid clouds are often more unified in their framework and may be used to handle a specific task in a secure fashion, such as storing and distributing sensitive data. The usage of Hybrid Clouds was an initial approach to using services from multiple clouds, but concerns about the trustfulness of public clouds have led to further discussions

In contrast to Federated Clouds, a Multi-Cloud model involves the usage of multiple and independent Clouds by a client or a service, with no agreement between the different Cloud providers to share their resources. In this model, the user is aware of the different Clouds and is responsible, or a third party is responsible, for dealing with the provisioning of the services or resources. The user actively manages and integrates services from different providers. The multi-cloud application interface aims to hide the underlying system complexities. The primary motivation for Cloud clients to use a Multi-Cloud model is often the need to identify the appropriate service or resource for a concrete application or new service, potentially relying on their own or third-party capacity. However, any reason from avoiding vendor lock-in (already discussed in Sect. 1.3.2) to optimising costs and improving Quality of Service (QoS) can motivate its use. The main challenge in Multi-Cloud environments is the portability of applications between Clouds. Multi-Clouds can be service-based (offering brokerage between clouds) or library-based (facilitating uniform access to multiple services). Multi-cloud systems simply use more than one Cloud Service Provider (CSP) simultaneously for different roles or applications. For example, a company might use different clouds for data storage, document sharing, and data analysis. Multi-cloud architectures can offer enhanced security through techniques like application imitation, layer-wise partitioning, application segmentation across clouds, and distribution of data chunks across different clouds.

In summary, the key architectural distinctions lie in the intentional collaboration and resource sharing in federated clouds, the independent and parallel usage of multiple distinct clouds in multi-cloud environments (with the user managing the integration), and the specific combination of private and public clouds with a focus on unified portability in hybrid cloud models. In the rest of this chapter, we focus our attention on Multi-Cloud systems since it is the most promising and challenging approach with respect to hybrid and federated clouds.

## 7.2 Introduction of Multi-Cloud Systems

As discussed in this[2] paper, in the last few years, cloud computing has become a very popular and effective solution for enterprises to provide their services on a "pay-per-use" basis. In particular, with the Infrastructure-as-a-Service model, users can rent virtualized resources, hosted by remote data centers, where they run their services inside isolated execution environments like Virtual Machine instances and containers.

Cloud companies such as Amazon, Google and Microsoft have developed their own platforms featuring proprietary web, command-line, and programming interfaces, by means of which customers can manage their VMs and analyze the performance of their applications.

Unfortunately, the lack of standard interfaces to access these platforms makes it difficult for customers to switch between different providers. This can limit their cloud experience in many ways. For example, it makes it hard to

- figure out which one of the cloud platforms provides the best solution that fits with their needs or to combine services of multiple providers to get the best from each of them.
- use private and public cloud together (e.g. to use already existing in-house hardware, to be not fully dependent on external providers etc.)
- use multiple cloud providers to avoid being fully dependent on a single cloud provider in case of contractual disputes, the provider going out of business, increasing prices, the discontinuation of a specific product/service used etc.

---

[2] Cosimo Anglano, Massimo Canonico and Marco Guazzone. EasyCloud: Multi-clouds made easy. IEEE Computers, Software, and Applications Conference (COMPSAC ), 2021.

- realize the extra reliability of using multiple cloud providers (e.g. in case of a single provider screwing up their internal provisioning, networking, authentication or other systems).

As mentioned before, this situation often leads to so-called vendor lock-in, whereby users are effectively locked into specific providers, and where new cloud providers cannot easily enter the market.

To overcome these limitations, Multi-cloud Systems (MS),[3] i.e. cloud infrastructures composed of resources drawn from different cloud platforms, are increasingly often used as a way to combine services or resources of different cloud platforms by means of a unified interface. That way, customer organizations can exploit the advantages of different cloud providers (e.g., in terms of service cost, quality of service, and performance) without being locked into a single one. To create a MS, a suitable toolkit, providing the necessary "glue" between different cloud infrastructures and the appropriate level of abstraction, is required. In particular, such a toolkit should provide the following features:

- **Interoperability**, i.e. the ability to support multiple cloud platforms, so as to avoid vendor lock-in;
- **Platform independence**, i.e. the provision of a unified, platform-agnostic user interface that hides the API heterogeneity of these platforms;
- **Effective resource provisioning**, i.e. the ability to ensure that the VMs delivering a given cloud service will be sufficiently resourced in a timely manner as load increases, so as to achieve desired levels of performance, efficiency, and availability;
- **Ease of use**, i.e. the provision of suitable mechanisms enabling users to interact with ease and effectiveness with the MS.

Various toolkits have been developed from both academia and commercial providers to allow smooth cloud interoperability and to harness multi-cloud heterogeneous resources. Unfortunately, they provide only a subset of the features mentioned above, so we can assert that an efficient and complete MS is still missing at the time of writing. The rest of this section briefly discusses the main characteristics of some of the most important MS toolkits.

## 7.3 MS from Academia

- **Apache JClouds**[4] is an open source multi-cloud toolkit for the Java platform that facilitates developing applications for a wide range of cloud platforms. JClouds supports about 30 cloud providers and cloud software stacks, including AmazonAWS, Microsoft Azure, OpenStack and Google Cloud, just to name a few.

---

[3] A. N. Toosi, R. N. Calheiros, and R. Buyya, "Interconnected cloud computing environments: Challenges, taxonomy, and survey,"ÏACMComput. Surv., vol. 47, no. 1, 2014.

[4] E. Toews and D. Advocate, "Introduction to apache jclouds," Apr, vol. 7,p. 23, 2014.

Moreover, it offers several API abstractions as Java and Clojure libraries. Despite its many features, JClouds does not provide any effective resource provisioning mechanisms (for instance, it is not possible to check the health of the VMs), and provides ease of use to a limited extent, since it requires Java programming skills to be used.

- **Apache LibCloud**[5] is an MS toolkit, provided in the form of a library, written in Python and allowing interactions with several popular cloud service providers. In particular, LibCloud provides a unified API able to hide the differences between the APIs of different cloud providers. As JClouds, Libcloud does not provide any effective resource provisioning mechanisms (monitoring and performance measurements are not provided), and provides ease of use to a limited extent, since it requires Python programming skills to be used.
- **Cloudmesh**[6] is another MS toolkit able to provide access to various cloud platforms such as AWS, Azure, Google Cloud and OpenStack. It has a variety of repositories that add features to Cloudmesh based on needs by the user. Compared to JClouds and Libcloud, Cloudmesh is easier to use, but it also does not provide any effective resource provisioning mechanism.
- **Occopus**[7] is a MS toolkit supporting various cloud platforms that is focused on resource orchestration and management. In particular, it allows describing virtual infrastructures and node definitions in a cloud agnostic way, and can automatically deploy and maintain the specified virtual infrastructures in the target clouds. Occopus provides only some of the mechanisms needed to achieve desired levels of performance, efficiency and availability (for example, it provides the health monitoring of the VMs). In particular, Occopus needs to exploit external tools like Prometheus to provide auto-scaling mechanisms. For this reason, Occopus provides only partially effective resource provisioning features.
- **EasyCloud**[8] is a MS toolkit able to effectively support the creation and use of MSs by providing interoperability and platform-independence by means of an extensible cloud interfacing subsystem. EasyCloud also provides effective resource provisioning by coupling two separate mechanisms, namely:
  - VM metrics collection and dispatching that collects in (near) real-time user-defined metrics data (e.g., CPU and memory load) from VMs and dispatches them to multiple "sinks" for storage as well as for further analysis and processing, thus enabling users to analyze and understand how their applications and services are performing;

---

[5] Apache Software Foundation. (2021, Jan.) Libcloud. [Online]. Available: https://libcloud.apache.org

[6] G. Von Laszewski, F. Wang, H. Lee, H. Chen, and G. C. Fox, "Accessing multiple clouds with cloudmesh," in Proceedings of the 2014 ACM international workshop on Software-defined ecosystems, 2014, pp. 21–28.

[7] J. Kovács and P. Kacsuk, "Occopus: a multi-cloud orchestrator to deploy and manage complex scientific infrastructures," Journal of Grid Computing, vol. 16, no. 1, pp. 19–37, 2018.

[8] C. Anglano, M. Canonico and M. Guazzone. An educational toolkit for teaching cloud computing. In ACM SIGCOMM Computer Communication Review, 51(4), 2021.

- VM monitoring and provisioning that exploits collected metric data to monitor the performance of VMs in realtime and to trigger management actions according to user-defined policies (e.g., to implement load balancing and autoscaling).

Finally, EasyCloud provides ease of use by means of a unifiedAPI that frees users from learning the different proprietaryAPIs exposed by the various cloud platforms it supports, and by an interactive and intuitive user interface that allows even inexperienced users to easily manage their VMs. The main problem of EasyCloud is similar to other MS: delayed updates of the tool in response to modifications of the API of the supported cloud platforms. EasyCloud is managed by faculty staff members (mainly assistant professors and associate professors) that are not always involved in the software development in their duties. This means that when, for example, OpenStack decided to change the API of the monitoring component, EasyCloud took almost three months to update its code in order to work with the new component of OpenStack.

## 7.4 Commercial MS

In this section we propose a subset of the most relevant commercial multi-cloud systems available at the time of writing. Due to the dynamicity of cloud computing, the list of most relevant products could change very quickly. From our point of view, it is still important to present what these solutions claim to provide to their users. Most of them offer a free trial period, so the interested reader can evaluate the actual features provided by each system.

- **CloudHealth**[9] is a product provided by the company VMWare which claims to provide the following main features:[10] data collection, performance reporting and analysis, cost management (that is, compute which user/department is spending most) and user management (authorization and role-base access control).
- **Morpheus**[11] is a Linux package which claims to be able to manage both on-premises private clouds from existing hypervisors (like VMWare and Nautilus) and public clouds (like AWS, Azure, GCP, etc.).
- **OpenShift**[12] is developed by Red Hat and it claims to be designed to allow applications and data centers to scale up/down quickly by exploiting containers both in on-premises and multi-cloud environments.

Finally, there are tools that cannot be considered as MS but they can help with integrating multi-cloud systems:

---

[9] https://www.cloudhealthtech.com/
[10] https://searchcloudcomputing.techtarget.com/definition/CloudHealth-Technologies
[11] https://morpheusdata.com/
[12] https://www.openshift.com/

- **Terraform**[13] is an open source tool which claims to be focused on the software delivery process through code instead of interacting with console or command line interfaces (this approach is called *Infrastructure as Code* (IaC)).
- **TOSCA**[14] is an acronym for Topology and Orchestration Specification for Cloud Applications and it proposes an XML-based modeling language to address three problems: (1) automated application deployment and management, (2) portability of applications and their management, and (3) interoperability and reusability of components.

The projects mentioned in this section are just a subset of all multi-cloud solutions provided by the scientific community and by commercial vendors.

## 7.5 MS Current and Future Trends

According to the 2025 State of the Cloud Report by Flexera,[15] multi-cloud adoption has continued to rise in 2024. Enterprises increasingly silo applications into specific clouds and select best-fit services. Key use cases include data analysis in separate clouds and cross-cloud disaster recovery.

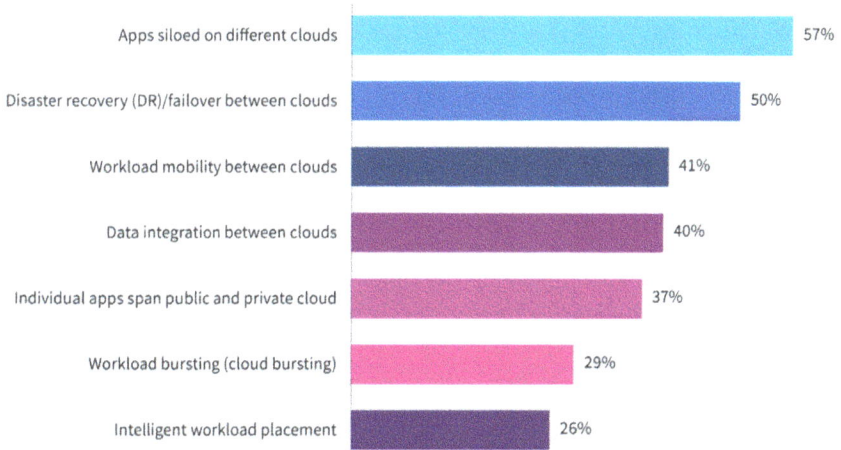

**Fig. 7.1** Use of multi-cloud architectures by all organizations. Source: Flexera 2025 state of the Cloud Report

In particular, from the report, it seems that organizations have found their steady state, that is, the mix of clouds that meets their current needs (see Fig. 7.1). Large

---

[13] https://www.terraform.io

[14] Binz et al., "TOSCA: Portable Automated Deployment and Management of Cloud Applications", Advanced Web Services, 2014.

[15] https://info.flexera.com/CM-REPORT-State-of-the-Cloud-2025-Thanks

enterprises make use of multi-cloud tools more than do smaller organizations, regardless of the tool type. Security tools see the greatest use in large enterprises (59%), which is an ongoing trend (see Fig. 7.2).

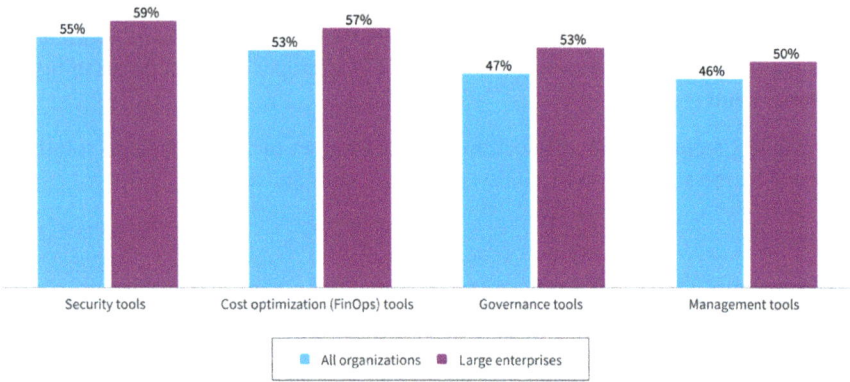

**Fig. 7.2** Use of multi-cloud tools. Source: Flexera 2025 state of the Cloud Report

Another interesting trend is related to **multi-cloud native applications**,[16] that is applications that try to fully exploit the access to different cloud platform to increase efficiency or saving money. These applications can be classified in two categories: a) *replicated multi-cloud applications* where applications are replicated as a whole across different cloud services and b) *distributed multi-cloud applications* where applications with subcomponents simultaneously deployed on different resources from different providers, relying on the combined use of multiple independent cloud services for benefits like high availability and cost reduction. Unfortunately, in order to adopt multi-cloud native applications several unsolved issues must be considered. In particular, there is a need for specific architectural patterns for multi-cloud native applications that go beyond general cloud native principles. Current design application patterns for multi-cloud native applications are underdeveloped. Future research should focus on technology and Cloud Service Provider (CSP) agnostic patterns, as well as patterns addressing the architectural aspects rather than just deployment and portability.

Another aspect to be faced is related to the portability of data and stateful components. Moving these at runtime across different cloud providers remains a significant hurdle due to vendor lock-in, lack of standards, and open interoperability mechanisms. Solutions for data portability, stateful component migration, and ensuring data integrity and confidentiality during migration are needed.

---

[16] Alonso et al., Understanding the challenges and novel architectural models of multi-cloud native applications—a systematic literature review, Journal of Cloud Computing (2023) 12:6 https://doi.org/10.1186/s13677-022-00367-6

Last but not least, there are security problems in multi-cloud systems that have not yet been fully addressed and resolved like ensuring adequate transparency and security awareness in multi-cloud environments, considering the shared-responsibility model. Moreover, increased security concerns due to wider attack surfaces and potential policy conflicts necessitate the development of novel security-by-design methodologies and frameworks for multi-cloud applications. In other words, there is a need for policy-related and standard-based solutions to assure the trustworthiness of cloud services in complex multi-cloud environments.

## 7.6 Summary

In this chapter we discuss various multi-cloud systems by explaining pros and cons for each of them. Due to the dynamicity of the different cloud platforms these considerations could become obsolete very quickly, but it is worth mentioning that the lack of standardization in the way cloud services are operating, portability of cloud services and cloud security can potentially slow down the innovation process in cloud environments. Finally, as mentioned before, we report what the various multi-cloud systems claim in their documentation: the actual pros and cons of the solutions in the context of the specific requirements of a given user must be tested. To the best of our knowledge, an objective and complete study comparing the various multi-cloud systems is still missing.

## 7.7 Key Terms

**Hybrid Cloud:** A hybrid cloud deployment is a multi-cloud deployment that uses different types of cloud deployment models, typically a public and a private cloud.

**Federated Cloud:** A federated cloud is characterized by multiple cloud providers collaborating and sharing physical resources between themselves. This is typically transparent to cloud service users, i.e. they would not be aware that their cloud resources are not hosted by a single cloud provider, but by a federation of two or more providers.

**Multi-Cloud System:** A multi-cloud system (MS) is a software system or service that has the goal of helping users of multi- or hybrid cloud deployments integrate and manage their cloud deployments efficiently and effectively.

**Multi-Cloud Native Application:** A multi-cloud native application is an application that is intentionally designed to run on multiple cloud providers to optimize costs, maximize efficiency etc.

**Replicated Multi-Cloud Applications:** In a replicated multi-cloud application, the application as a whole is deployed across different cloud services, typically to increase redundancy or performance.

**Distributed Multi-Cloud Applications:** In a distributed multi-cloud application, different components of the overall application are deployed with different cloud providers, for instance to take advantage of cloud specific features or to optimize cost efficiency.

## 7.8 Review Questions

1. Why do many organizations adopt multi-cloud deployments, rather than just using a single cloud provider?
2. Briefly explain the differences between multi-cloud, hybrid cloud and federated cloud deployments.
3. Briefly name some of the challenges of using more than one cloud provider that multi-cloud systems (MS)s try to overcome. What are their mean features?
4. Describe at least two multi-cloud systems from academia.
5. Describe at least two commercial multi-cloud systems.
6. Briefly describe the difference between replicated and distributed multi-cloud applications.

## 7.9 Exercises

The following laboratory exercises contain questions that require written responses and, in some instances, accompanying screenshots. If the exercises have been given as an assignment, please ensure that all answers and requested screenshots are compiled into a separate document for submission to the instructor, as specified by the instructor.

### 7.9.1 Deploy a New VM on AWS Using Apache Libcloud

In this lab, we illustrate how to start a VM by exploiting libcloud: a python library for interacting with many of the popular cloud service providers using a unified API.

#### Objectives

1. Install the python libcloud library
2. Setup AWS console
3. Start a VM

## A. Installation and Configuration of the Environment

1. Install the libcloud library by running

   ```
   pip install -user apache-libcloud
   ```

2. Create a file with all variables concerning the settings related to the VM that we are going to create:

   ```
   # Configurations
   instance_name = 'my-instance'
   security_name = 'my-security'
   key_name = 'my-key'
   image_id = 'ami-06c68f701d8090592'
   size_id = 't2.micro'

   ACCESS_ID = '<YOUR_ACCESS_ID>'
   SECRET_KEY = '<YOUR_SECRET_KEY>'
   ```

   Where the parameters above are:

   - **instance_name:** the name of the VM's instance you want to create.
   - **security_name:** the name assigned to the security group shown in the AWS Security Group step.
   - **key_name:** the name assigned to the key-pair shown in the AWS Key-Pairs step.
   - **mage_id:** this variable has the id of one of the AMI (Amazon Machine Images) that AWS leaves available for use. In this case I used the Amazon Linux image, but you can change it to another one of your liking. You can find a list of all the possible AMI under EC2 > AMI Catalog. **Note:** when you select an AMI, the default user for each machine may vary; for example using Amazon Linux you will have ec2-user as the user, but in the case of Ubuntu you will have ubuntu as user.
   - **size_id:** this variable indicates what type of instance we are going to create, or rather how many resources we are going to assign to our VM. These are given by AWS, so we can only choose one of the various pre-assigned combinations.
   - **ACCESS_ID:** this is the id we took in the AWS Credentials step.
   - **SECRET_KEY:** this is the key we took in the AWS Credentials step.

3. Next we need to create a driver to interface with the AWS EC2 service by typing the following command on the terminal:

   ```
   from libcloud.compute.types import Provider
   from libcloud.compute.providers import import
       get_driver

   Driver = get_driver(Provider.EC2)
   ```

```
driver = Driver(ACCESS_ID, SECRET_KEY)
```

where the first two lines are the libraries to import and while the other two load the AWS EC2 API via the get_driver() by using the access keys related to the user account.

## B. Set All Parameters and Start a VM

1. Now we need to manage the security group by setting the group variable as describe here

```
# Creation or retrieval of the Security group
try:
    group = driver.ex_get_security_groups(group_names
        =[security_name])
except:
    group_id = driver.ex_create_security_group(
        security_name, 'ssh')
    group_id = group_id['group_id']
    cidr_ips = ['0.0.0.0/0']
    driver.ex_authorize_security_group_ingress(
        group_id, 22, 22, cidr_ips)
    group = driver.ex_get_security_groups(group_ids=[
        group_id])
group = group[0]
print(f"Selected group: {group}")
```

In the `try` section we use the call to get the groups and if it does not find them it throws an exception. In the except block, we create a new security group with the assigned name and the description set as 'ssh' (which can be changed at will). The next line just indicates that we are going to get the id of the newly created group. The variable cidr_ips is a list with all the IP addresses that can connect to the VM; in our case the value 0.0.0.0/0 means that ALL IPs have the permission to connect. The ex_authorize_security_group_ingress function allows to add an inbound rule authorizing from port 22 to 22 with the specified addresses. The last statement of the except block retrieves the newly created group from the previously saved id.

2. Now we need to manage the key pair for accessing the VM. As for the security group by using the following code:

```
# Import or retrieval of the SSH key
try:
    key_pair = driver.get_key_pair(key_name)
except:
    from pathlib import Path
```

## 7.9 Exercises

```
        key_file = str(Path.home()) + '/.ssh/id_rsa.
            pub'
        key_pair = driver.import_key_pair_from_file(
            key_name, key_file)
    print(f"Selected key: {key_pair}")
```

In the code, we check that if the key exists (see the try block); otherwise if the key pair does not exist then we enter in the except block, we want to import or create the key. In the code proposed how, we import the id_rsa public key (i.e. the one used by default by the ssh command) on AWS EC2. Then we use the driver to send the file, assigning it the name previously entered. Otherwise, if we want to create a key from scratch, that is used specifically to connect to the VM, then we can modify the except block using the create_key_pairs driver method as shown below:

```
except:
    import os
    from pathlib import Path

    key_pair = driver.create_key_pair(key_name)
    key_file = str(Path.home()) + '/.ssh/' +
        key_name

    # Saving the private key to .ssh
    opener = lambda path, flags: os.open(path,
        flags, 0o600)
    with open(key_file, 'w', opener=opener) as
        file:
            file.write(key_pair.private_key)
```

In this case, we need to save the private key locally, the path can be chosen as desired (in code we decide to save it in the .ssh folder located in the user's HOME). **Note:** the opener variable, which contains the lambda, is used to create the file directly with permissions of 600, so that only the user can access the key. This is because it is critical information and the ssh command would not accept a private key that others can read.

3. Check if the image selected by its id is the right one:

```
# Check the AMI
image = driver.get_image(image_id)
print(f"Selected AMI: {image.name}")
```

4. Check the instance size by running the following code lines:

```
# Searching the instance type
size = [x for x in driver.list_sizes() if x.id ==
    size_id][0]
print(f"Selected size: {size.name}")
```

This code recovers the entire list of sizes and filters it by taking only those that have the value indicated in size_id variable; if it does not find the type, it returns an exception and blocks the script.

5. Finally we are ready to start a VM and get a public IP address by running the following code:

```
# Instance creation
node = driver.create_node(instance_name,
                          size,
                          image,
                          ex_keyname=key_pair.name,
                          ex_securitygroup=group.name
                          )
print(f'VM created, waiting until running...')


node, ips = driver.wait_until_running([node])[0]
print(f'VM running: {node.name} {node.id}')
print(f'VM IP: {ips[0]}')
```

The code proposed takes the variables we created previously and inserts them into the create_node method. The first three parameters (instance_name, size, and image) are mandatory, while the other ones (ex_keyname and ex_securitygroup) are extra parameters specific to AWS EC2. After creating the VM we wait for it to be ready before returning control to the user via the wait_until_running method. At the end of the method you see a [0]; this indicates that we take the first value of the returned list since in input we can put more nodes to wait for.

## *The Complete Script*

In this section we propose the whole script. By coping and pasting all the lines into, for example, startVM.py file, you can run it by typing:

```
python3 startVM.py
```
and you will get something similar to this output from the terminal:

```
Selected group: <EC2SecurityGroup: id=..., name=my-security>
Selected key: <KeyPair name=my-ssh fingerprint=... driver=Amazon EC2>
Selected AMI: al2023-ami-2023.5.20240701.0-kernel-6.1-x86_64
Selected size: t2.micro
VM created, waiting until running...
VM running: my-instance i-017cc25a7da1d652c
```

## 7.9 Exercises

VM IP: 54.87.135.159

The whole script is available below.

```python
from libcloud.compute.types import Provider
from libcloud.compute.providers import get_driver

# Configurations
instance_name = 'my-instance'
security_name = 'my-security'
key_name = 'my-ssh'
image_id = 'ami-06c68f701d8090592'
size_id = 't2.micro'

ACCESS_ID = '<YOUR_ACCESS_ID>'
SECRET_KEY = '<YOUR_SECRET_KEY>'

# EC2 driver initialization.
Driver = get_driver(Provider.EC2)
driver = Driver(ACCESS_ID, SECRET_KEY)

# Creation or retrieval of the Security group
try:
    group = driver.ex_get_security_groups(group_names=[
        security_name])
except:
    group_id = driver.ex_create_security_group(
        security_name, 'ssh')
    group_id = group_id['group_id']
    cidr_ips = ['0.0.0.0/0']
    driver.ex_authorize_security_group_ingress(group_id
        , 22, 22, cidr_ips)
    group = driver.ex_get_security_groups(group_ids=[
        group_id])
group = group[0]
print(f"Selected group: {group}")


# Creation or retrieval of the SSH key
try:
    key_pair = driver.get_key_pair(key_name)
except:
    from pathlib import Path
    key_file = str(Path.home()) + '/.ssh/id_rsa.pub'
    key_pair = driver.import_key_pair_from_file(
        key_name, key_file)
```

```python
print(f"Selected key: {key_pair}")

# Check the AMI
image = driver.get_image(image_id)
print(f"Selected AMI: {image.name}")

# Searching the instance type
size = [x for x in driver.list_sizes() if x.id ==
    size_id][0]
print(f"Selected size: {size.name}")

# Instance creation
node = driver.create_node(instance_name,
                         size, image, ex_keyname=
                            key_pair.name,\\
                         ex_securitygroup=group.name)
print(f'VM created, waiting until running...')

node, ips = driver.wait_until_running([node])[0]
print(f'VM running: {node.name} {node.id}')
print(f'VM IP: {ips[0]}')
```

### 7.9.2 Deploy a New VM on OpenStack Using JCloud

In this lab, we illustrate how to start a VM by exploiting JCloud: an open-source multi-cloud toolkit for the Java platform. It allows to build applications that can run on different cloud providers (like AWS, Google Cloud, Azure, etc.) with a unified interface. In this lab, we will learn how to use the jclouds Compute API to launch a VM instance on the OpenStack Cloud platform.

### *Objectives*

1. Create a project with jclouds dependencies
2. Setup a ComputerService client
3. Start a VM

## 7.9 Exercises

### A. Create a Project with jclouds Dependencies

1. The first step is getting jclouds. Create a directory:

   ```
   mkdir jcloud
   ```

   ```
   cd jcloud
   ```

2. Make a local copy of the pom.xml file below in the jclouds directory:

   ```xml
   <?xml version="1.0" encoding="UTF-8"?>
   <project xmlns="http://maven.apache.org/POM/4.0.0"
       xmlns:xsi="http://www.w3.org/2001/XMLSchema-instance"
       xsi:schemaLocation="http://maven.apache.org/POM/4.0.0
       http://maven.apache.org/xsd/maven-4.0.0.xsd">
     <modelVersion>4.0.0</modelVersion>
     <properties>
       <jclouds.version>2.5.0</jclouds.version>
     </properties>
     <groupId>com.yourcompany.app</groupId>
     <artifactId>app-name</artifactId>
     <version>1.0</version>
     <dependencies>
       <!-- jclouds dependencies -->
       <dependency>
         <groupId>org.apache.jclouds.driver</groupId>
         <artifactId>jclouds-slf4j</artifactId>
         <version>{{${jclouds.version}</version>
       </dependency>
       <dependency>
         <groupId>org.apache.jclouds.driver</groupId>
         <artifactId>jclouds-sshj</artifactId>
         <version>$}}{jclouds.version}</version>
       </dependency>
       <!-- jclouds OpenStack dependencies -->
       <dependency>
         <groupId>org.apache.jclouds.api</groupId>
         <artifactId>openstack-nova</artifactId>
         <version>{{{${jclouds.version}</version>
   ```

```xml
      </dependency>
      <!-- 3rd party dependencies -->
      <dependency>
        <groupId>ch.qos.logback</groupId>
        <artifactId>logback-classic</artifactId>
        <version>1.0.13</version>
      </dependency>
      <dependency>
        <groupId>mysql</groupId>
        <artifactId>mysql-connector-java</artifactId>
        <version>5.1.25</version>
      </dependency>
    </dependencies>
</project>
```

This pom.xml file specifies all of the dependencies needed to create a VM using OpenStack.

3. Then execute:

   ```
   mvn dependency:copy-dependencies "-DoutputDirectory=./lib"
   ```

   You should now have a directory with the following structure:

   ```
   jclouds/
       pom.xml
       lib/
           *.jar
   ```

   Now that you have all the dependencies you will need, proceed to create the rest of your project. You should have a directory with a structure like this:

   ```
   jclouds/
       pom.xml
       src/
           main/
               java/
                   com/yourcompany/app
                       YourMainClass.java
       lib/
           *.jar
   ```

4. To compile your code, execute the following command in the jclouds directory:

   ```
   mvn package
   ```

5. And to run the code, you can use:

7.9 Exercises

```
            java -cp target/<artifactId>-1.0.jar:lib/*
com.yourcompany.app.YourMainClass
```

## *B. Get an Authorization Token Using the Chameleon CLI*

1. To get the authorization token you need to download the OpenStack RC file: log into your OpenStack Dashboard and go to API Access, then click on Download OpenStack RC file and select the OpenStack RC file option from the menu: The

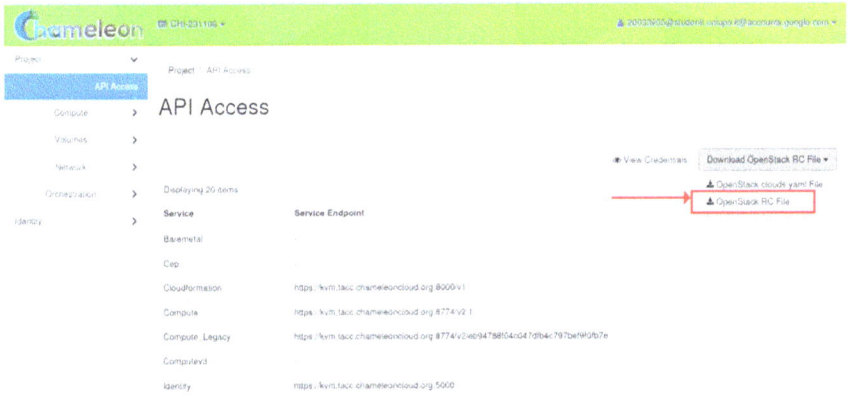

OpenStack RC file contains the credentials necessary for you to authenticate through jclouds and allows you to obtain the authorization token through the Chameleon CLI, which is based on the Openstack CLI.

2. On a Unix machine, you can use the following command in a shell to install the Openstack CLI:

    ```
    pip install -user python-openstackclient
    ```

3. Additionally, if you have not already do it, you should create a CLI password using the Authentication Portal.
4. Next, open a shell in the directory where your Openstack RC file is located, run the command below and input your CLI password when asked:

    ```
    source CHI-<id>-openrc.sh
    ```

5. Then obtain a token by running the following command:

    ```
    openstack token issue
    ```

save the value of the token id. Remember to request a new token when the old one expires.

## C. Set up Properties

1. In your Java class, define the following variables and replace the missing values with the values in your OpenStackRC file:

    ```
    String provider = "openstack-nova";
    String username = "<yourUsername>";
    String projectName = "<projectName>";
    String authEndpoint = "<yourAuthEndpoint>";
    String region = "<regionName>";  //e.g. '
    KVM@TACC'
    ```

2. To use Keystone v3 (scoped) for authentication, you must also set these variables:

    ```
    String identity = "chameleon:" + username;  // domainName:userName
    String scope = "project:" + projectName;    // project:projectName
    ```

3. Then replace <token> below with the token you obtained in Step 2:

    ```
    String token = "<token>";
    ```

    Let's configure the properties to create a ComputeServiceContext instance next. Include in your file the imports below:

    ```
    import java.util.Properties;
    import org.jclouds.location.reference.LocationConstants;
    import org.jclouds.openstack.keystone.auth.config.CredentialTypes;
    import org.jclouds.openstack.keystone.config.KeystoneProperties;
    ```

4. Then create a new Properties object using the variables you just set up:

    ```
    final Properties overrides = new Properties();
    overrides.put(KeystoneProperties.KEYSTONE_VERSION, "3");
    overrides.put(LocationConstants.PROPERTY_REGIONS, region);
    overrides.put(KeystoneProperties.SCOPE, scope);
    overrides.put(KeystoneProperties.CREDENTIAL_TYPE, CredentialTypes.TOKEN_CREDENTIALS);
    ```

## D. Get ComputeService Client

1. For this step you will need the following imports:

    ```
    import org.jclouds.ContextBuilder;
    import org.jclouds.compute.ComputeServiceContext;
    import com.google.common.collect.ImmutableSet;
    import org.jclouds.compute.ComputeService;
    ```

2. To get a ComputeService client, first create a ComputeServiceContext instance using the variables and properties that you configured in the previous step:

    ```
    ComputeServiceContext context = ContextBuilder
                    .newBuilder(provider)
                    .endpoint(authEndpoint)
                    .credentials(identity, token
                    )
                    .overrides(overrides)
                    .modules(
                ImmutableSet.of(new
                    SLF4JLoggingModule()))
                    .buildView(
                        ComputeServiceContext.
                        class);
    ```

    You can enable logging by specifying the use of the SLF4JLoggingModule as above, but it's optional.

3. Then you can obtain a ComputeService instance using the context:

    ```
    ComputeService client = context.getComputeService
        ();
    ```

## E. Create a Template

1. Set up the variables required for the creation of the VM:

    a. Choose a name for your VM (optional) and specify a groupName, which is used by jclouds to group servers internally:

    ```
    String nodeName = "<nodeName>";
    String groupName = "<groupName>";
    ```

    b. Choose an image and flavor for your VM:

    ```
    String imageId = "<imageId>";
    String flavorId = "<flavorId>";
    ```

c. To choose the image and flavor IDs, you could also list all available values for them through jclouds and ask the user to input their choice. For example:

```
Scanner scanner = new Scanner(System.in);

System.out.println("Images:   id | name ");
for (Image image : client.listImages()) {
    System.out.println(image.getId().split("/")[1] + " | " + image.getName());
}

System.out.print("\nEnter the image ID : ");
String imageId = scanner.nextLine();

System.out.println("\nFlavors: id | name");
for (Hardware flavor : client.listHardwareProfiles()) {
    System.out.println(flavor.getId().split("/")[1] + " | " + flavor.getName());
}

System.out.print("\nEnter the flavor ID: ");
String flavorId = scanner.nextLine();
```

d. The keyPairName and the securityGroup name are optional. You might want to set these variables if you're interested in accessing your VM using ssh and/or you need to open ports other than port 22, which is opened by default when creating the VM through jclouds.

```
String keyPairName = "<yourKeyPairName>";
String securityGroup = "<securityGroupName>";
```

e. To choose the key pair and the security group names, you could also list all available values for them through jclouds and ask the user to input their choice. For example:

```
NovaApi novaApi = context.unwrapApi(NovaApi.class);
```

7.9 Exercises

```
System.out.println("\nKeypair names:");
FluentIterable<KeyPair> keyPairs = novaApi
    .getKeyPairApi(region).get().list();
for (KeyPair keypair : keyPairs) {
    System.out.println(keypair.getName());
}

System.out.print("\nEnter the name of the
    keypair: ");
String keyPairName = scanner.nextLine();

System.out.println("\nSecurity groups:");
FluentIterable<SecurityGroup>
    securityGroups =         novaApi.
    getSecurityGroupApi(region).get().list
    ();
for (SecurityGroup secGroup :
    securityGroups) {
    System.out.println(secGroup.getName())
        ;
}

System.out.print("\nEnter the name of the
    security group: ");
String securityGroup = scanner.nextLine();

scanner.close();
```

2. Next, build a TemplateOptions object with the keyPairName, nodeName and securityGroup variables that you just defined.

If you want to be able to access the VM through ssh you'll also need to associate a FloatingIP address to the instance after its creation: setting autoAssignFloatingIp in TemplateOptions to true means jclouds will automatically allocate a FloatingIP address to the node when it's created.

If you're not interested in any of the settings included in these options you can skip this part and proceed to the creation of a Template without the options. If you wish to proceed with configuring the options, however, you'll need the following imports:

```
import org.jclouds.compute.options.
    TemplateOptions;
import org.jclouds.openstack.nova.v2_0.
    compute.options.NovaTemplateOptions;
import java.util.Arrays;
```

3. Then, to build the template options:

```
TemplateOptions templateOptions =
    NovaTemplateOptions.Builder
                .autoAssignFloatingIp(true)
                .keyPairName(keyPairName)
                .nodeNames(Arrays.asList(
                    nodeName))
                .securityGroups(Arrays.
                    asList(securityGroup));
```

4. Next, let's create a Template:

```
import org.jclouds.compute.domain.Template;

Template template = client.templateBuilder()
    .imageId(region + "/" + imageId)
    .hardwareId(region + "/" + flavorId)
    .options(templateOptions).build();
```

## F. Launch the VM Instance

1. Start the VM in the following way:

```
import org.jclouds.compute.domain.NodeMetadata;
import static com.google.common.collect.Iterables
    .getOnlyElement;


NodeMetadata node = getOnlyElement(client
    .createNodesInGroup(groupName, 1,
        template));
```

If everything has been configured correctly, your VM will be created successfully in a short time, and you will also be able to verify its creation through your Chameleon dashboard: go to Compute → Instances to visualize the list of all the instances, which will include the newly created one. This tutorial covers how to launch a single VM, but the method createNodesInGroup allows to create multiple ones: the second parameter indicates the number of VMs to be created. In this particular case its value is set to 1, but it can be easily modified. Note: the above method could also cause an exception of type RunNodesException: make sure to handle it properly (e.g. by surrounding it with a try/catch clause).

## G. Monitor VM Status and Close the Context

Once you've launched the VM successfully you can check its status and print out detailed information about it, such as its ID or its IP addresses.

1. For the status:

    ```
    System.out.println("Status: " + node.getStatus());
    ```

2. To print the ID and the IP addresses:

    ```
    import static com.google.common.collect.Iterables.concat;

    System.out.printf("<< node %s: %s%n", node.getId(), concat(
        node.getPrivateAddresses(), node.getPublicAddresses()));
    ```

3. Finally, remember to close the context:

    ```
    context.close();
    ```

## H. Source Code

Here the source code use in this lab.

```
package com.upo.app;

import java.util.Arrays;
import java.util.Properties;
import java.util.Scanner;

import org.jclouds.location.reference.LocationConstants;
import org.jclouds.openstack.keystone.auth.config.CredentialTypes;
import org.jclouds.openstack.keystone.config.KeystoneProperties;
import org.jclouds.openstack.nova.v2_0.NovaApi;
import org.jclouds.openstack.nova.v2_0.compute.options.NovaTemplateOptions;
import org.jclouds.openstack.nova.v2_0.domain.KeyPair;
import org.jclouds.openstack.nova.v2_0.domain.SecurityGroup;
```

```java
import org.jclouds.ContextBuilder;
import org.jclouds.compute.ComputeService;
import org.jclouds.compute.ComputeServiceContext;
import org.jclouds.compute.RunNodesException;
import org.jclouds.compute.domain.Hardware;
import org.jclouds.compute.domain.Image;
import org.jclouds.compute.domain.NodeMetadata;
import org.jclouds.compute.domain.Template;
import org.jclouds.compute.options.TemplateOptions;

import com.google.common.collect.FluentIterable;
import static com.google.common.collect.Iterables.getOnlyElement;
import static com.google.common.collect.Iterables.concat;

public class Main {
    public static void main(String[] args) {
        String provider = "openstack-nova";
        String username = "<yourUsername>";
        String identity = "chameleon:" + username;
        String projectName = "<projectName>";
        String authEndpoint = "<yourAuthEndpoint"; //e.g. 'https://kvm.tacc.chameleoncloud.org:5000/v3'
        String region = "<regionName>"; //e.g. 'KVM@TACC'
        String scope = "project:" + projectName; // project:projectName
        String token = "token";

        final Properties overrides = new Properties();
        overrides.put(KeystoneProperties.KEYSTONE_VERSION, "3");
        overrides.put(LocationConstants.PROPERTY_REGIONS, region);
        overrides.put(KeystoneProperties.SCOPE, scope);
        overrides.put(KeystoneProperties.CREDENTIAL_TYPE, CredentialTypes.TOKEN_CREDENTIALS);
```

## 7.9 Exercises

```
ComputeServiceContext context =
    ContextBuilder
        .newBuilder(provider)
        .endpoint(authEndpoint)
        .credentials(identity, token)
        .overrides(overrides)
        //.modules(ImmutableSet.of(
            new SLF4JLoggingModule())
        )
        .buildView(
            ComputeServiceContext.
            class);


ComputeService client = context.
    getComputeService();

String nodeName = "<nodeName>";
String groupName = "<groupName>";

/* Without using the interactive code:

String imageId = "<yourImageId>"; // e.g
    c2a51044-f3fd-4eac-8e69-f58fa4f90109 (CC
    -Ubuntu 22.04)
String flavorId = "<flavorId>"; // e.g. 2 (
    m1.small)

String keyPairName = "<yourKeyPairName>";
String securityGroup = "<securityGroupName
    "; e.g. default

*/

//using the interactive code to ask the
    user to input the ids and the names
Scanner scanner = new Scanner(System.in);

System.out.println("Images:  id | name");
for (Image image : client.listImages()) {
    System.out.println(image.getId().split("/")
        [1] + " | " + image.getName());
}
```

```
System.out.print("\nEnter the image ID: ");
String imageId = scanner.nextLine();

System.out.println("\nFlavors: id | name");
for (Hardware flavor : client.
   listHardwareProfiles()) {
     System.out.println(flavor.getId().split
        ("/")[1] + " | " + flavor.getName());
}

System.out.print("\nEnter the flavor ID: ");
String flavorId = scanner.nextLine();


NovaApi novaApi = context.unwrapApi(NovaApi.
   class);

System.out.println("\nKeypair names:");
FluentIterable<KeyPair> keyPairs = novaApi.
   getKeyPairApi(region).get().list();
for (KeyPair keypair : keyPairs) {
    System.out.println(keypair.getName());
}

System.out.print("\nEnter the name of the
   keypair: ");
String keyPairName = scanner.nextLine();

System.out.println("\nSecurity groups:");
FluentIterable<SecurityGroup> securityGroups =
   novaApi.getSecurityGroupApi(region).get().
   list();
for (SecurityGroup secGroup : securityGroups) {
    System.out.println(secGroup.getName());
}

System.out.print("\nEnter the name of the
   security group: ");
String securityGroup = scanner.nextLine();

   scanner.close();

   TemplateOptions templateOptions =
      NovaTemplateOptions.Builder
              .autoAssignFloatingIp(true)
```

## 7.9 Exercises

```
                                .keyPairName(
                                    keyPairName)
                                .nodeNames(Arrays.
                                    asList(nodeName))
                                .securityGroups(Arrays.
                                    asList(securityGroup
                                    ));

                Template template = client.templateBuilder
                    ()
                                .imageId(region + "/" + imageId
                                    )
                            .hardwareId(region + "/" + flavorId
                                )
                            .options(templateOptions).build();

                try {
                                NodeMetadata node =
                                    getOnlyElement(client.
                                    createNodesInGroup(groupName
                                    , 1,template));

                                System.out.println("Status: " +
                                    node.getStatus());

                                System.out.printf("Node %s: %s%
                                    n", node.getId(), concat(
                                    node.getPrivateAddresses
                                    (), node.
                                    getPublicAddresses()))
                                    ;

                    } catch (RunNodesException e) {
                                e.printStackTrace();
                    }

                context.close();
        }
}
```

## 7.9.3 Deploy a Basic Flask Web Server by Using Terraform

In this lab, you learn how to get started with Terraform by using Terraform to create a basic web server on Compute Engine.

### Objectives

1. Use Terraform to create a VM in Google Cloud
2. Start a basic Python Flask server

### A. Preliminary Steps

1. In the Google Cloud console, go to the project selector page (https://console.cloud.google.com/projectselector2/home/dashboard) and select or create a Google Cloud project.
2. Make sure that you have the necessary Compute Engine permissions on your user account (https://console.cloud.google.com/iam-admin/iam):
    - compute.instances.*
    - compute.firewalls.*
3. Enable the Compute Engine API (https://console.cloud.google.com/flows/enableapi?apiid=compute.googleapis.com)
4. Start Cloud Shell (https://cloud.google.com/shell/docs/using-cloud-shell). Cloud Shell is a Compute Engine virtual machine. The service credentials associated with this virtual machine are automatic, so there is no need to set up or download a service account key. Terraform is integrated with Cloud Shell, and Cloud Shell automatically authenticates Terraform, letting you get started with less setup.

### B. Create the Compute Engine VM

First, you define the VM's settings in a Terraform configuration file. Then, you run Terraform commands to create the VM in your project.

1. Create a new directory.

    ```
    mkdir tf-tutorial && cd tf-tutorial
    ```

2. In your new directory, create a main.tf file for the Terraform configuration. The contents of this file describe all of the Google Cloud resources to be created in

## 7.9 Exercises

the project.

```
nano main.tf
```

3. Create the Virtual Private Cloud network and subnet by addind the following code to the main.tf file:

```
resource "google_compute_network" "vpc_network" {
    name                    = "my-custom-mode-network"
    auto_create_subnetworks = false
    mtu                     = 1460
}

resource "google_compute_subnetwork" "default" {
    name          = "my-custom-subnet"
    ip_cidr_range = "10.0.1.0/24"
    region        = "us-west1"
    network       = google_compute_network.vpc_network.id
}
```

4. Create the Compute Engine VM resource running Debian by adding the following google_compute_instance Terraform resource to the main.tf file:

```
# Create a single Compute Engine instance
resource "google_compute_instance" "default" {
    name         = "flask-vm"
    machine_type = "f1-micro"
    zone         = "us-west1-a"
    tags         = ["ssh"]

    boot_disk {
        initialize_params {
            image = "debian-cloud/debian-11"
        }
    }

    # Install Flask
    metadata_startup_script = "sudo apt-get update;
        sudo apt-get install -yq build-essential
        python3-pip rsync; pip install flask"

    network_interface {
        subnetwork = google_compute_subnetwork.default.id
```

```
        access_config {
          # Include this section to give the VM an
              external IP address
        }
      }
    }
```

5. Initialize Terraform to add the necessary plugins and build the .terraform directory:

    ```
    terraform init
    ```

6. Validate the Terraform configuration:

    ```
    terraform plan
    ```

7. If everything is ok, the output will look like this:

    ```
    ...

    Plan: 1 to add, 0 to change, 0 to destroy.

    Note: You didn't use the -out option to save this
        plan, so Terraform can't
    guarantee to take exactly these actions if you
        run "terraform apply" now.
    ```

8. Apply the configuration to create a VM:

    ```
    terraform apply
    ```

9. When prompted, enter yes.

## C. Run a Web Server on Google Cloud

Your next steps are getting a web application created, deploying it to the VM, and creating a firewall rule to allow client requests to the web application.

1. Add a custom SSH firewall rule.

    - This is necessary if and only if you want use your own custom firewall rule (by default the SSH port is open), by modify the main.tf file as follows:

        ```
        resource "google_compute_firewall" "ssh" {
            name = "allow-ssh"
            allow {
        ```

## 7.9 Exercises

```
            ports     = ["22"]
            protocol  = "tcp"
        }
        direction    = "INGRESS"
        network      = google_compute_network.
            vpc_network.id
        priority     = 1000
        source_ranges = ["0.0.0.0/0"]
        target_tags  = ["ssh"]
    }
```

- Apply the firewall rule by running:

    ```
    terraform apply
    ```

2. Validate that everything is set up correctly at this point by connecting to the VM with SSH.

    a. Go to the VM Instances page (https://console.cloud.google.com/compute/instances).
    b. Find the VM with the name *flask-vm*.
    c. In Connect column, click SSH and a SSH-in-browser terminal window opens for the running VM.

3. Now you can build a Python Flask App by creating a single file describing your web server and test endpoints.

    a. In the SSH-in-browser terminal, create a file called app.py:

    ```
    nano app.py
    ```

    b. Add the following to the app.py file:

    ```
    from flask import Flask
    app = Flask(__name__)

    @app.route('/')
    def hello_cloud():
        return 'Hello Cloud!'

    app.run(host='0.0.0.0')
    ```

    c. Run app.py:

    ```
    python3 app.py
    ```

d. Open a second SSH connection by going to VM instances page (https://console.cloud.google.com/compute/instances) and find the VM named flask-vm and click SSH.
e. In the second SSH connection, run curl to confirm that the greeting that you configured in app.py is returned:

```
curl http://0.0.0.0:5000
```

f. Report here the output of the previous command:




4. To connect to the web server from your local computer, the VM must have port 5000 open.
    a. Google Cloud lets you open ports to traffic by using firewall rules by adding the following google_compute_firewall Terraform resource at the end of your main.tf file:

```
resource "google_compute_firewall" "flask" {
    name    = "flask-app-firewall"
    network = google_compute_network.vpc_network.id

    allow {
        protocol = "tcp"
        ports    = ["5000"]
    }
    source_ranges = ["0.0.0.0/0"]
}
```

    b. Now you have to create the firewall rule by run this command:

```
terraform apply
```

5. Add an output variable for the web server URL
    a. At the end of main.tf, add a Terraform output variable to output the web server URL:

```
// A variable for extracting the external IP
    address of the VM
output "Web-server-URL" {
```

## 7.9 Exercises

```
    value = join("",["http://",google_compute_instance
        .default.network_interface.0.access_config.0.
        nat_ip,":5000"])
}
```

b. Run the following command:

   `terraform apply`

c. When prompted, enter yes and report here the output produced:

d. At any time, you can run terraform output to return this output:

   `terraform output`

e. Click the URL from the previous step, and see the "Hello Cloud!" message: this means that your server is running.

6. After completing the tutorial, you can delete everything that you created so that you do not incur any further costs:

   `terraform destroy`

   and enter `yes` to allow Terraform to delete your resources.

# Chapter 8
# Cloud Operations

The previous chapters are mostly concerned with technical aspects of and design decisions related to the use of cloud computing—including topics such as the best choice of deployment and service models, different architectures for cloud applications and how to design secure systems in the cloud. Once all these decisions have been made, another important area is to make sure that cloud applications can be operated efficiently and effectively.

Operations is of course not a completely separate issue. For example, when the security measures of an application are designed, the way it will be operated has to be considered carefully, including how users and their access to the application are managed operationally. In general, as is discussed briefly in the chapter on Cloud Architecture, modern software engineering approaches usually contain the concept of DevOps, which strives to better integrate development and operations of an application.

Still, there are a few areas of cloud operations that deserve to be covered in more detail in this chapter. We begin by looking at a number of different areas of managing cloud operations, followed by an overview of cloud monitoring and migration. A brief review of challenges and limitations of cloud computing and of some potential ethical issues complete the chapter.

## 8.1 Cloud Management

One of the key reasons why managing an application in the cloud is different from managing a non-cloud application is that a number of responsibilities for the application are split between the cloud service provider and the cloud service user. While the details depend on multiple factors, including the cloud service and deployment models chosen, several areas require specific management attention irrespective of the choices in a given situation. They are described in this section.

## 8.1.1 Service Level Agreements (SLA)

One key management tool to handle split responsibilities between a service provider and a service user is the Service Level Agreement (SLA). SLAs specify a number of issues such as

- The percentage of uptime for a service (e.g. 99%, 99.9% or 99.99%)
- Guaranteed network bandwidth and performance and/or capacity of other resources
- The consequences if these guarantees are not met (typically (partial) refunds)
- Planned maintenance windows of resources
- Maximum help desk response times, escalation levels etc.

An SLA is typically a legally binding contract that allows the organization using cloud services to assess to what degree the guaranteed service levels are sufficient for them. For example, while a 99.9% uptime might sound like a lot, the allowed downtime per year is still almost nine hours, which, if they were to occur at a bad time (e.g. for an online retailer on a major shopping day such as Black Friday) might still be very damaging. Additionally, if the guaranteed uptime was violated, and the contractual consequence (e.g. a partial refund of the monthly service fees) was triggered, the damage caused by the lost business due to the outage might significantly exceed the applicable refund. Consequently, based on such an SLA, an organization with high reliability needs would probably take extra steps to design its application more fault tolerant, e.g. by using cloud resources in multiple different data centers, possibly even by multiple cloud service providers, to achieve the required reliability.

SLAs are not only helpful to organizations using public cloud providers. Even in private cloud settings they are often used as formal contracts between different organizational units, e.g. the IT department operating the cloud resources, and different business units using them for their applications.

## 8.1.2 Organizational Measures

Just like software development differs significantly between e.g. a student writing a small program for a class assignment and a team of dozens of developers writing a large business application, managing cloud applications or cloud infrastructure for complex, real-world cloud deployments requires significantly more organizational measures than doing a small assignment in a cloud computing class in order to be successful. In a modern real-world cloud deployment, automation allows users to perform changes to large numbers of systems with often a single command. While this is generally a good thing—it allows a small number of administrators to manage a large cloud deployment—it also means that small errors can have large effects.

For instance, AWS experienced an outage on March 2, 2017 that affected significant parts of the Internet for several hours. This outage was the result of an error by an operator who tried to take a small number of servers offline for planned maintenance, but entered one of the inputs to the executed command incorrectly, resulting in a much larger number of servers being taken offline than intended.[1] While this is just one example of a small error resulting in significant damage at a public cloud provider (and its customers), it is clear that similar issues could happen at any organization operating or using cloud resources at a large scale. Consequently, the management of cloud resources, irrespective of whether the organization is a cloud service provider, user, or both, requires particularly careful organizational measures to reduce errors and their consequences as much as possible.[2]

Two commonly used organizational measures are policies and procedures. Policies are rules that an organization sets itself, while procedures describe the steps that need to be taken to achieve certain tasks. In an organization that operates applications in a public cloud, a policy could specify who in the organization has the authority to approve different types of changes to applications. A related procedure implementing such a policy could list the specific steps that need to be taken, such as required sign-offs by development leads, test managers etc. Both policies and procedures standardize processes and can, if used appropriately, reduce errors and resulting problems.

This section barely scratches the surface of possible organizational measures. There are several frameworks related to IT operations in general that also apply in a cloud computing context, including ITIL[3] and COBIT.[4]

## 8.1.3 Risk Management

A particularly important aspect of cloud management that is often strongly embedded within the organizational measures taken by organizations is risk management. As already discussed in the cloud security chapter, complete security (i.e., confidentiality, integrity and availability) can never realistically be achieved. Consequently, handling the risks a cloud deployment faces effectively is a crucial aspect of cloud management.

Risk management is a complex topic on which entire books are available. There are numerous risk management standards such as ISO 31000[5] that organizations either choose to follow or are required to follow by government regulations if they operate in specific industries. This section only aims at providing a basic introduction to some of the key concepts of risk management in the context of cloud computing.

---

[1] https://www.geekwire.com/2017/amazon-explains-massive-aws-outage-says-employee-error-took-servers-offline-promises-changes/

[2] Clearly, as a leading public cloud provider, AWS is aware of this, and is surely taking significant organizational measures. The fact that such problems can still occur further illustrates the need to build cloud applications with multiple levels of fault tolerance.

[3] https://www.axelos.com/best-practice-solutions/itil

[4] https://www.isaca.org/resources/cobit

[5] https://www.iso.org/standard/65694.html

The first step to dealing with risks effectively is to identify the most important risks an organization faces. While many organizations might face similar risks (e.g. becoming the victim of a ransomware attack), the likelihood and impact of each risk can differ substantially between different organizations. For example, a large and profitable online retailer is probably more likely to become the victim of targeted spear-phishing attacks than a small non-profit organization.

Once risks and their likelihood and impact are identified, the next step is to make informed decisions about how each risk is handled. Four of the most common responses to risks are:

- **Mitigation:** One of the most common responses to risk is to mitigate the risk by reducing either the likelihood of it occurring or the impact if it does. For example, training employees about social engineering attacks could reduce the likelihood that a ransomware attack using phishing emails as the attack vector succeeds, while ensuring that comprehensive and current backups of all important data exist reduces the impact of a successful ransomware attack.
- **Transfer:** Another possible reaction is to transfer a risk to another party. For example, many organizations choose to purchase insurance policies that cover the costs to recover after a successful cyber attack.
- **Avoidance:** Risks that are particularly likely or impactful are sometimes best met with risk avoidance. For example, an organization worried about the confidentiality of extremely sensitive data in a public cloud might choose to avoid this risk by storing the data in a specially secured internal system.
- **Acceptance:** In many cases, the most rational response to low or medium impact risks is simply risk acceptance. For example, errors by a cloud provider might cause an outage of a service hosted in a public cloud. If a temporary outage of that service does not endanger the survival of the organization, it might be the right decision to simply accept this as a low likelihood risk, as other risk responses are limited because the operations of the cloud provider are not under the control of the client organization.

A significant part of risk management is preparedness for the occasion that given risks materialize despite the measures taken to minimize them. Such preparedness includes contingency plans to recover critical systems for instance after successful cyber attacks or outages caused by natural disasters. Many of the cloud architecture techniques discussed in this book such as automation and infrastructure as code can make system recovery much easier and faster in a modern cloud deployment compared to traditional in-house IT.

> **Important Risk Management Standards**
>
> While it is in the self-interest of organizations to protect themselves from IT outages and other problems disrupting their operations, in most countries, there are substantial levels of government regulations that set out legal requirements in this area. This is especially true for industries in which

disruptions in one organization typically affect numerous other companies or the general public, or where the health or even life of people is at stake. For example, if payment service providers such as banks or credit card companies have system outages, it can become impossible for retail stores to process electronic payments, which has massive economic impacts and creates significant challenges for individuals who might just try to buy their lunch, pay for a train ticket etc. Similarly, an IT outage in a hospital might put people's lives at risk if diagnostic data, treatment plans etc. become unavailable.

An additional argument for government regulations is that they "level the playing field". Expenses for IT security and resilience provide no immediately observable benefit. Immediate financial results such as profits can be negatively affected by long-term investments in reliable IT systems. Since investors often have short-term time horizons when judging corporate performance, executives might be tempted to avoid spending money on measures that increase IT resilience in the long term, and do not pay off immediately. But if government regulations require all companies in a specific sector to take the same steps to secure their systems, nobody is put at a short-term disadvantage for doing so.

Specific government regulations are different in each jurisdiction. However, there are some standards that are used internationally, and even standards that might only be a requirement in a specific country like the United States are typically reflected in similar standards in other jurisdictions. Below are a few important examples of risk management standards that affect the IT of organizations:

- ISO/IEC 27001: An international IT security standard that focuses on the establishment of an information security management system, to help coordinate IT security measures taken in an organization.
- NIST Risk Management Framework (NIST SP 800-37): A guideline published by the US federal government on how organizations should manage and control risks to their IT systems.
- COBIT (Control Objectives for Information and Related Technologies): A framework created by ISACA (Information Systems Audit and Control Association) for the management and governance of IT resources.
- SOX (Sarbanes-Oxley Act): A US law that mandates practices and strict rules for financial record keeping and reporting of corporations, typically enforced with the use of IT controls.
- PCI DSS (Payment Card Industry Data Security Standard): An international standard that regulates IT security measures for credit card companies and other related organizations in the financial sector.

- HIPAA (Health Insurance Portability and Accountability Act) and ISO 27799: US and international standards on how to secure confidential medical data such as patient records.

## 8.1.4 Workload Management

One of the key advantages of cloud computing that is discussed in multiple contexts in this book is that in a cloud setting, applications can dynamically allocate and deallocate resources. In contrast to this, the traditional way to deploy applications on dedicated physical servers gives applications a fixed set of resources that can only be changed slowly by up- or downgrading the hardware that they are deployed on. For individual applications, this flexibility is great—if they are designed to scale automatically, there is no need to accurately predict usage patterns such as peak time loads to prevent overloaded or underutilized servers.

Of course the need to make sure that there are sufficient computing resources available at all times does not disappear in cloud computing—the responsibility is simply shifted to the cloud provider. The fact that cloud applications get resources from a pool of available virtual resources means that resources deallocated dynamically from one application become available for other applications. Therefore, cloud providers try to host a wide range of different applications with peaks and troughs that do not occur simultaneously, in order to maximize resource utilization and reduce the risk of resource shortages.

Another tool cloud providers use are discounted non-guaranteed instances. For example, AWS, Azure and Google offer so called Spot Instances[6,7,8]. Spot instances behave like normal virtual machine instances, except that they are significantly discounted (for example by 75%), and that the cloud provider reserves the right to shut them down on very short notice (just sufficient to have a proper shutdown of the deployed applications) if they need the resources for other users. In effect, spot instances serve as a buffer, significantly reducing the risk that the cloud provider runs out of instances when too many applications deployed on regular virtual machines attempt to allocate more resources at once.

In addition to this, cloud providers need to carefully monitor the utilization of their resources, and model future resource needs based on past utilization patterns. Given the still strongly growing market for cloud computing services, the question is ultimately not if additional computing resources will be needed in the future, but

---

[6] https://aws.amazon.com/ec2/spot/

[7] https://docs.microsoft.com/en-us/azure/virtual-machines/spot-vms

[8] https://cloud.google.com/spot-vms

at which rate they need to be added to keep up with demand. Still, if unexpected general peaks in demand occur, cloud providers can shut down spot instances, or even increase the discount given to spot instances to encourage even more users to use them and to consequently increase the available resource buffer.

The problem of ensuring sufficient capacity to satisfy occurring workloads is typically more difficult for organizations that use a private cloud, because the set of applications in the cloud is given by the IT needs of the organization, and could well be rather homogeneous with co-occurring peaks and troughs of demand. This, of course, is often a key motivation for the use of a hybrid rather than purely private cloud, so that additional public cloud resources can be used during peak workloads.

### 8.1.5 Mobile Device Management

Mobile Device Management might seem like an odd section in a book on cloud computing, where applications are deployed in large data centers and not on mobile devices. However, the shift to cloud computing has generally made it much easier to access applications from a wide range of devices, including devices with limited computational resources. In contrast, when applications were operated following more traditional client-server paradigms, they could only be used on devices with client-side software installed. Modern applications deployed on the cloud usually require only network connectivity and a web browser, requirements which are fulfilled by a wide range of devices including tablets and smartphones.

As already briefly discussed in the chapter on security, the fact that applications and their data reside in a centralized location in the cloud (and are not distributed across a large number of end user client devices) is a security opportunity of cloud computing. In contrast, in more distributed client-server architectures or completely client side applications, the loss or theft of a client device (such as a laptop or smartphone) potentially puts all the data of the application into the hands of the finder or thief. One of the chief purposes of mobile device management is to ensure that the cloud application and its data remain safe from attackers when mobile devices fall into the wrong hands.

In order to achieve this, mobile device management systems have a wide range of features. For example, they can typically enforce security settings on the devices. For example, if an employee wants to access a cloud application with sensitive data from their phone, the phone has to have at least a five digit PIN which has to be entered to unlock the screen. Additionally, the device has to lock after five unsuccessful attempts to enter the PIN, and the screen has to lock automatically after the device has not been used for more than a few seconds. Additional common features include the ability to manage phones remotely, including the ability to remotely lock or wipe phones that have been reported lost or stolen, to locate missing devices, or to have separate environments on the phone for company use and personal use (e.g. separate address books etc.). There are many other mobile device management features such as the ability to automatically manage VPN connections, to make sure that security updates are installed when available and to collect usage data and device diagnostics.

Properly used mobile device management can significantly increase the security of a cloud application while at the same time allowing users the flexibility to use their personal mobile devices to access company applications.

## 8.2 Cloud Monitoring

Any significant IT system or infrastructure is subject to a wide range of issues that can negatively affect its users, such as power or network outages, other physical hardware failures, software bugs, security breaches as a result of outside attacks etc. The main purpose of monitoring systems is to detect any such issues as early as possible, ideally before they impact end users negatively, and to support operators in fixing the underlying causes as quickly as possible. This is equally true for cloud systems as it is for non-cloud systems. The following two sections compare monitoring in the cloud to general monitoring, and illustrate some of the monitoring features offered by the Google Cloud Platform.

### 8.2.1 Introduction

There are two main aspects of how monitoring in cloud deployments differs from monitoring of non-cloud IT systems. The first one is that monitoring (just like many other aspects such as security) is a split responsibility between cloud service provider and cloud service user. In general, cloud service users are not responsible for and consequently do not have to monitor the underlying physical and network infrastructure. The exact boundaries of which parts are monitored by the provider as opposed to the cloud service user depend on the service model chosen. While there is some overlap, monitoring systems used by cloud service providers and cloud service users focus on different aspects. Cloud service providers are more interested in monitoring system usage levels carefully to support their workload and capacity planning as well as general data center management. Cloud service users care more about monitoring their application on higher levels of the cloud stack, often with application specific aspects such as login errors or end-user response times being of particular interest. Monitoring of some areas such as SLA compliance and billing would be equally relevant for both.

The second difference is that monitoring of (at least modern) cloud applications has a different focus. This can be best explained with the pet vs. cattle[9] paradigm shift in cloud computing, according to which traditional administrators manually managed (and consequently monitored) individual servers, while cloud deployments are made

---

[9] Tilkov, S. "The Modern Cloud-Based Platform", IEEE Software, March/April 2015.

up of a large number of easily (often automatically) replaceable systems that are administered (and consequently monitored) as a collective. To illustrate this point, a traditional non-cloud web server might have been deployed on four physical servers, the health, load and performance of each of which a system administrators would have carefully monitored. In a modern cloud deployment, the same web server might run on an automatically scaling instance group of virtual machines or a Kubernetes cluster with multiple nodes. In such cloud deployments, the health of each individual virtual machine or node is less interesting, because they are automatically restarted or replaced in the event of failures. Instead, the focus of monitoring shifts more towards the application and deployment as a whole.

Cloud monitoring systems for cloud service users typically have a centralized user interface that displays data from all the cloud resources used. This data can either be collected by installing small programs called agents on all the systems that are monitored, or simply by having a centralized monitoring application automatically connect to the systems regularly e.g. via ssh and collect data about e.g. disk, memory or CPU usage using standard operating system commands. While agents increase the overhead a little because they first have to be installed, and because they take up some memory and CPU time on the monitored system itself, they tend to offer richer and more real-time data than agentless systems can.

### 8.2.2 Monitoring in GCP

The monitoring component integrated in the Google Cloud Platform uses agents to collect monitoring and logging data on monitored machines. For customer managed cloud resources like virtual machines, the cloud service user can install these agents to enable detailed monitoring.

One of the key monitoring features in GCP are alerting policies. Alerting policies are based on conditions, which in turn define that certain metrics exceed a specified threshold for a defined minimum time period. For example, a metric could be the mean CPU utilization on a virtual machine, a threshold could be 80%, and the minimum duration could be one minute. In this case, the alerting policy would trigger if the CPUs of a virtual machine have a load of 80% or more for at least one minute. A very wide range of metrics can be used, covering all kinds of cloud resources. For example, virtual machines or containers can be monitored just as well as cloud databases or flat cloud storage, or network traffic and service and other user accounts. A special type of condition is an uptime check, which simply regularly attempts to connect to a server (e.g. by sending an HTTP(S) request in the case of a web server) from multiple different locations in the world, and records responses and response times.

Once an alerting policy is triggered, an incident is raised. Initially the incident is in the state "open". An administrator can change the state to "acknowledged" to indicate that the incident is under investigation, and finally to "closed" once it is resolved. Incidents can also be configured to trigger notifications through a number of different notification channels such as emails or text messages. This is very useful especially for smaller organizations which may not have system administrators monitoring their cloud applications 24/7, but that can now put an administrator on call to be alerted automatically if serious problems occur. Another important monitoring feature is dashboards. Dashboards allow administrators to combine all the important monitoring information of a number of systems in one display. GCP comes with a number of default dashboards that provide generally useful summary information about different types of cloud resources such as storage, firewalls or VM instances. Users can create their own custom dashboards to display whatever data is most important and organize them in the way that serves their individual needs best. On dashboards, data is often represented in graphs, because humans tend to be much quicker at gaining useful information from data that is represented graphically as opposed to in textual form. The graphs often show how important metrics change over time, which is another important feature, because for many metrics, an absolute number is hard to interpret. For example, if the learning management system of a mid-size college has forty failed login attempts in an hour, is that a potential sign of an attack, or simply the normal volume of students forgetting their passwords? Being able to (visually) compare current with historic data (e.g., how many failed login attempts did we have in the same hour yesterday, or last week, or last term?) makes it much easier to interpret.

In GCP, monitoring is now only one aspect under the umbrella of the more comprehensive concept of observability. Other aspects of observability include tracing and logging of applications. While tracing can be used to identify perormance bottlenecks in applications, the logging component allows easy and centralized access to log data. Real-world cloud applications are often deployed on a significant number of systems (e.g. virtual machines), and might consist of different types of components for different purposes—for instance, web and application servers, relational databases, non-relational databases, connectors to messaging systems etc. All these underlying machines, and all the different framework elements, applications etc. tend to write their own separate log files. Manually retrieving and analyzing the logs on multiple machines, for example to analyze a bug report by end users, would be a rather labor intensive task. Therefore, the GCP logging agent collects all the relevant log files, and the logging component provides users with a centralized log explorer. In the log explorer, queries can be defined to retrieve information of interest from the logs. Even here, graphical representations are used to help users make sense of the data. For example, users can generate histograms of log files which show how the number and relative frequency of log entries of the different severities (e.g. warning, error, critical) changed over time.

## 8.3 Cloud Migration Strategies

When organizations adopt cloud computing, they can either do that for newly created applications, or they can move applications that were previously operated on

8.3 Cloud Migration Strategies 289

in-house servers. It certainly happens that completely new applications are created in the cloud—due to the minimal up-front costs for physical hardware and infrastructure and the inherent elasticity of especially public cloud providers, this is certainly an attractive option for startup companies, which tend to have completely new applications. However, the majority of new cloud deployments are likely of previously existing non-cloud applications. This raises a number of questions about how to perform such migrations into the cloud.

## 8.3.1 Perspectives to Consider

When an organization decides to migrate an application into the cloud, there are a wide range of perspectives to consider. The most obvious one is the technical perspective, which primarily focuses on how the application can be implemented on the cloud computing platform. This includes aspects such as which compute service to use (e.g. virtual machines, containers, or some PaaS offering), how data should be stored (in a relational database, in a noSQL database...) etc.

Another important perspective is operations. Getting the application to run in the cloud is one thing, but it also has to be operated, which includes a wide range of ongoing routine tasks such as end user support, bug fixing, the installation of updates, monitoring, backups etc. A lot of these tasks change significantly when an application is moved from an in-house deployment to a cloud service provider. For example, some tasks that previously used to be completely under the control of in-house IT become split responsibilities between the cloud service provider and the organization using cloud services: Depending on the Service Model chosen, e.g. different parts of monitoring and of the installation of updates become the responsibilities of the provider. While the cloud provider is only in charge of the physical hardware and the networking infrastructure in Infrastructure as a Service, it takes on additional responsibilities for installed operating systems and other platform elements if Platform or Software as a Service is used. Similarly, while cloud users likely retain some responsibilities for backups, the actual process of scheduling and performing backup and restore operations is likely quite different in a cloud deployment. Consequently, existing operations handbooks, policies and procedures need to be completely rewritten when an application is migrated into the cloud.

Security is another key aspect. It affects both the implementation of the application in the cloud and its operations. Once again, compared to an application that is hosted in-house, parts of the security responsibilities such as physical security of the underlying hardware are taken on by the cloud provider. Different components of a security architecture likely need to be adjusted when an application is migrated to the cloud, for example firewall rules and other parts of network security or user authentication mechanisms.

Another key consideration should be the impact on people in the organization. Some tasks such as taking care of the physical IT infrastructure will either be eliminated or significantly reduced by the migration. This can lead to justified fears about job security, and result in resistance to the changes that come with a migration into the cloud. Even employees whose jobs are not at risk might see their responsibilities significantly changed, and likely will have to learn a number of new skills to still be successful in their roles. This is likely true for most IT personnel, ranging from developers and architects over testers to operators, all of whom need to be trained in cloud technologies.

All the perspectives discussed so far are directly related to technology. However, other business functions and the business overall also need to be considered. For example, Human Resources departments likely have extra work to change the roles of employees and to possibly hire and lay off other employees. Similarly, Finance and Accounting departments have to adjust to much more volatile costs (as cloud applications scale up and down based on load), and different levels of management have to deal with significant migration projects, often with the temporary addition of external consultants and other service providers. In order to achieve the full benefits of a migration to the cloud, even departments that are not directly affected need to embrace the changes that come with cloud computing. For example, in order to take full advantage of the increased technical agility that comes with cloud computing, such as the ability to scale, change and update applications more rapidly than before, a higher level of organizational agility is necessary, so that new capabilities are actively exploited when business opportunities to do so arise.

In summary, in order to successfully migrate (parts of) an organization's IT into the cloud, significantly more aspects than just the technical implementation need to be considered.

## *8.3.2 Migration Assessments and Prioritization*

When an organization begins considering moving parts of its IT into the cloud, a number of detailed assessments should be performed to determine whether a migration to the cloud is in fact beneficial overall, and for which specific applications in particular. These assessments partially relate to key factors that determine whether there is a good business case for migration into the cloud, including:

- Reduced costs, both bound capital in the form of physical IT resources, as well as ongoing costs in the form of rent, electricity, payroll etc. to operate IT resources
- Operational resilience, a higher level of which can typically be achieved more easily and more cost effectively with a cloud provider, due to the wide geographic distribution of available data centers (resulting in reduced vulnerability to local outages caused e.g. by natural disasters), the practically unlimited scalability offered by cloud providers etc.
- Increased agility and productivity due to the ability to rapidly scale cloud resources up and down, to provision additional test environments, to roll out new versions of applications etc.

A comprehensive business case also has to include costs and other disadvantages of a cloud migration. An example of an (at least temporary) negative effect of a cloud migration is the cost incurred by the migration itself, which, considering the wide range of perspectives that have to be appropriately considered as discussed in the previous section, typically is a sizable change project with corresponding costs.

The following are some of the key assessments that should be performed:

- **Financial Assessment:** A detailed financial assessment is often done in the form of a Total Cost of Ownership (TCO) analysis, which compares all costs over the whole (typically multi-year or even multi-decade) lifecycle of an application, both in a cloud and a non-cloud scenario. Such an analysis has to include factors like the cost to maintain or retire existing IT resources such as servers and networking equipment, but also software licenses and long-term support contracts, as well as short-term costs for potential cloud migration projects. Such a detailed analysis heavily depends on assumptions about factors such as the future growth and volatility of the processing load of the application. For example, with a relatively stable and predictable load, in-house IT resources can achieve consistently high utilization and consequently be fairly cost effective. In contrast, if the load fluctuates strongly, in-house IT resources would have a low average utilization rate and therefore not be cost competitive compared to a public cloud in which only actually used resources have to be paid for.

- **Security and Compliance Assessment:** Another important assessment revolves around the security and compliance requirements of the application. As discussed in the chapter on cloud security, the use of cloud computing brings both cloud security risks and opportunities, the importance of each of which has to be analyzed in the given situation. Typical factors to consider are how sensitive the data that an application uses is, what security threats the application might face, and to what degree these threats can be mitigated by security measures offered by different cloud providers. In addition to these considerations, organizations in many industries have to comply with government imposed security and privacy regulations. This can especially be problematic when data crosses regulatory boundaries. To just give a simple example, educational institutions in countries such as Canada have to follow strict standards to protect personal data about their students. This often prevents them from storing such data in public cloud data centers in countries like the USA which have lower privacy standards. Another example is that financial institutions are typically required to maintain specific certifications in order to reduce the risk of failures of their IT systems, because such failures would have wide-ranging impacts on many other companies. Such requirements do not necessarily prevent the use of public cloud computing. However, they typically require that a public cloud provider which itself carries the required certifications has to be chosen. For example, the Google Cloud Platform supports a number of compliance requirements from a wide range of industries in all major regions of the world.[10]

---

[10] Compliance information for the GCP can be found at https://cloud.google.com/security/compliance

- **Technical Assessment:** The third kind of assessment revolves around technical aspects of the application. A critical issue in this area especially for legacy systems is whether cloud platforms under consideration support the platforms, protocols and tools required by the application. Older, mainframe based legacy applications might require operating systems or networking protocols that are not directly supported by the virtualization layer of the cloud provider. Similarly, an organization that uses old, uncommon or custom development tools such as version and configuration management tools might find it challenging to integrate them with a modern public cloud provider. Another aspect are performance requirements of the application. For instance, applications that transfer significant amounts of data or require very short response times might find network bandwidth or latency limiting factors that could make the use of public cloud providers either impractical or uneconomical.

These assessments are quite interdependent- for example, security requirements or technical challenges can result in (or be resolved by) additional measures that cause additional costs, and thereby affect the financial assessment. It should also be noted that the assessments typically do not result in a binary yes-or-no answer. While it might occasionally happen that a specific assessment shows that the migration to the cloud is infeasible for a specific application, the more likely outcome is a possible, but more or less challenging migration.

In practice, most established organizations have significantly more existing applications than they can realistically migrate into the cloud at once, for example because of limited personnel and financial resources. In such a situation, the various assessments can form a solid basis on which prioritization decisions can be made. The ultimate decision on which applications should be migrated to the cloud first often takes additional factors into account. While it might be tempting to begin with whatever application would benefit most from a move into the cloud, for example because it is highly elastic and could consequently lead to significant cost savings, many organizations also consider the relative importance of the different candidates for the organizations. Especially if there is little in-house expertise with cloud computing and migration projects, it might be best to begin with less important applications (even if they do not promise the highest migration return), simply to reduce risk by building expertise when less critical applications are migrated first. This argument ultimately returns to the point made earlier that cloud migrations are not purely based on technical considerations, but that they should be made with the impact on the whole business in mind.

### 8.3.3 Migration Strategies

Once the decision about the migration of a specific application into the cloud is made, there are six common migration strategies, often referred to as "the 6 R's:[11] Re-host, Re-platform, Re-factor, Re-purchase, Retire or Retain. In particular:

---

[11] AWS Migration Whitepaper: https://pages.awscloud.com/rs/112-TZM-766/images/aws-migration-whitepaper-2018.pdf

## 8.3 Cloud Migration Strategies

- **Re-host:** In this strategy, which is also referred to as "lift and shift", applications are moved without changes from physical in-house servers onto equivalent virtual machines in the cloud. This is obviously a relatively straightforward approach that can be done pretty quickly. One of the disadvantages is that it tends to miss out on many of the advantages that more cloud native deployment approaches can bring, such as reduced manual maintenance effort, higher agility etc.
- **Re-platform:** Also called "lift, tinker and shift", the re-platform approach leaves the overall architecture of the application unchanged. However, in contrast to the re-host approach, some of the underlying platform elements are changed. For example, rather than operating a relational database management system in a customer managed virtual machine, a cloud-provider managed relational database system (such as GCP Cloud SQL) could be used. While such a change likely requires some more development and testing effort than a simple re-hosting, it can lead to additional benefits such as reduced costs (e.g. for software licenses) and reduced ongoing operations effort.
- **Re-factor:** In the re-factor or re-architect approach, the architecture of the application (which is often monolithic to begin with) is changed into a more cloud native architecture, such as a microservice architecture deployed in a Kubernetes cluster. This migration strategy costs the most time and effort. However, once the migration is complete, all the benefits of modern cloud architectures can be realized, including reduced ongoing costs (both for cloud resources and system operations), a highly flexible and easily changeable application, and maximum performance and fault tolerance.
- **Re-purchase:** In this approach, an application that could either be a custom or off-the-shelf software system that was previously operated in-house is replaced by a Software as a Service (SaaS) offering. This only works if there is a SaaS application that matches the needs of the organization well. Even then, it might still be necessary to adjust some business process to the software (rather than the other way around). The big benefit is that the cloud provider takes care of almost all aspects of running the application, which means that in-house IT at most needs to deal with a few aspects such as managing user accounts.
- **Retire:** The remaining two approaches are not strictly migration strategies, because they do not actually result in the application being migrated into the cloud. One possible outcome is that the careful analysis of all existing in-house applications in the course of a cloud migration assessment reveals that an application can actually be retired. This might sound surprising to readers who have no first-hand experience with the often vast IT landscapes of especially larger organizations. However, especially in older organizations, or organizations that are the result of a number of mergers and acquisitions, it is very common to find that some applications are for instance no longer used at all, or only used by users who are not aware that a different, newer application fulfills the same purpose even better. Retiring such legacy applications reduces costs and the complexity of the overall IT in the organization.
- **Retain:** The second migration strategy that does not result in the actual migration of an application into the cloud is to retain the application as it is. There are

multiple reasons why this might be the best choice at least for the time being—of course, this decision can be revisited in the future, and the application can be migrated into the cloud then. A common reason to retain an application is that the expected benefits of migrating it into the cloud are less than those of other applications, which consequently, in the face of limited resources, get moved first. Another reason might be that an application is very critical for an organization, and that a move at this point in time (possibly with limited cloud experience) is deemed too risky.

No matter what migration strategy is chosen, moving an application into the cloud consists of multiple stages. Following the Systems Development Life Cycle (SDLC)[12] model, these stages typically include planning, analysis, design, implementation, testing and maintenance stages. They are not usually performed in a single, linear way. Instead, the various stages often overlap, and might be performed multiple times in an iterative fashion, depending on the specific project management and software development methods chosen.

Discussing these stages in detail is beyond the scope of this chapter and book. However, we briefly cover two aspects that are often of particular interest in cloud migration projects, namely the migration of application data and the cutover strategy chosen.

Migrating the existing data of an application into the cloud deserves specific attention already in the analysis phase. As mentioned above, the analysis phase needs to pay specific attention to regulatory and other privacy and security requirements. A common scenario is that both the migration of data into the cloud and its storage there needs to be more protected e.g. by encryption than is necessary when data is kept in-house. Applications with large volumes of data can create additional challenges, because even if the organization has a high-bandwidth upload connection to the cloud provider, transferring Terabytes or even Petabytes of data can take impractically long. If this is the case, the data can be transferred by shipping storage media. For example, AWS allows customers to order special storage devices that can hold up to 210 TB of data each.[13]

Cutover strategies describe how the switch from the in-house to the cloud-based application is performed. The simplest, but also riskiest strategy is a direct cutover, in which at a specific point in time the in-house application is turned off and all traffic is switched over to the new cloud-based application. The main disadvantage of this approach is that it is rather risky. Any problems missed in testing can potentially affect all users of the application at the same time, which might be more than the support can handle. Therefore, some sort of parallel operation between the old in-house system and the new cloud based system is often chosen instead. A common approach is to have a pilot phase in which the cloud based system is initially only used by a small percentage of users, which is increased to all users over a period of days or weeks, depending on how many problems occur. Alternatively, if the architecture of the application permits it, only parts of the application might be

---

[12] https://en.wikipedia.org/wiki/Systems_development_life_cycle

[13] https://aws.amazon.com/snowball/

moved to the cloud at first, and the remaining parts are migrated step-by step until the whole application runs in the cloud, once again at a speed determined by how long it takes to fix whatever problems are found at each stage.

## 8.4 A Critical View of Cloud Computing

At this point in the book, readers might have the impression that the authors generally believe cloud computing is an important and useful technology. If so, they would be correct. However, just like any other innovation or technology, cloud computing has its potential dark sides as well. We look at some of them in the following section.

### 8.4.1 Common Cloud Computing Challenges

A number of common issues that organizations face when they begin adopting cloud computing has already been discussed in the first chapter. They include:

- Security and privacy concerns—because applications, especially on a public cloud, tend to be more exposed to potential attackers.
- Vendor lock-in—because many cloud computing features are proprietary, it can be difficult to move applications from one cloud provider to another.
- Cost and cost management—while elasticity is a great feature to scale applications based on demand, costs for cloud resources scale with them, which can result in significant and potentially unexpectedly high costs.
- Lack of expertise—because wide-spread adoption of cloud computing is still a relatively recent phenomenon, demand for employees who are trained in and experienced with cloud computing typically outstrips supply.
- Organizational issues—to fully leverage the potential of cloud computing, significant organizational changes are necessary, which often face resistance by employees.

These and similar issues are commonly encountered by organizations, irrespective of factors like the industry the organization operates in or the kinds of applications that are migrated into the cloud. A number of ways to address these issues have already been covered in other parts of the book—e.g. ways to secure cloud applications in the chapter on cloud security, ways to reduce vendor lock-in risks like using multi-cloud deployments in the chapter on multi-cloud systems, and several of the other issues raised in the chapter on cloud migration.

## 8.4.2 Cloud Computing Limitations

While the issues covered in the previous section apply in most situations, there are specific types of organizations and applications that face additional challenges in a cloud computing setting. In some cases, these challenges can effectively make the use of cloud computing, especially public cloud computing, infeasible.

Organizations that operate in industries with particularly heavy regulatory burdens or security requirements might find adopting cloud computing either undesirable or impossible. For example, government organizations such as police, military or intelligence agencies that are potential targets of highly skilled foreign adversaries are likely to find the security risks of deploying applications especially in a public cloud too high. Similarly, organizations that either handle particularly sensitive information such as patient data in the case of hospitals, or organizations that operate critical infrastructures such as water, energy and telecommunications often face very stringent security requirements that might be hard to fulfill in a cloud setting. These types of regulations often include requirements to only use certified hardware and software products, to have specially trained employees, and to be in full control of where critical data is stored. While some of these requirements can be fulfilled even by public cloud providers, there are often practical limitations.

Industry lobby groups tend to paint government regulations as unnecessary burdens that obstruct businesses unduly, and might not even be effective at reaching their goals. Some populist politicians build on such sentiments when they promise to "cut unnecessary red tape".[14] While there are certainly instances where this is true, recent incidents like the successful ransomware attack on an oil pipeline operator in the USA[15] that resulted in gasoline shortages in significant parts of the country certainly illustrate that a lack of effective and enforced regulations can lead to organizations neglecting sufficient protection of critical infrastructures e.g. in order to save costs. This in turn can cause widespread harm to other organizations and individuals.

Applications that either transfer very large amounts of data, that require particularly low latencies or have especially stringent requirements for guaranteed response times are also often hard or impossible to implement in the cloud. For example, imagine a manufacturing company that uses a large number of sensors, including visual sensors such as video cameras, to supervise and control its automated production processes. In such a scenario, it might be inefficient or impossible to upload all the real-time data to the cloud to process it there, because the necessary upload capacity is either too expensive or simply not available. And even if all the data can be uploaded, for time critical applications like automatic discovery of e.g. a robot arm that is about to injure an employee due to an erroneous movement it might take too long to do so and to wait for the return transmission of the results.

---

[14] See e.g. https://en.wikipedia.org/wiki/Red_tape
[15] https://www.cpomagazine.com/cyber-security/colonial-fuel-pipeline-ransomware-attack-that-caused-gas-shortages-in-eastern-u-s-may-be-the-work-of-amateurs/

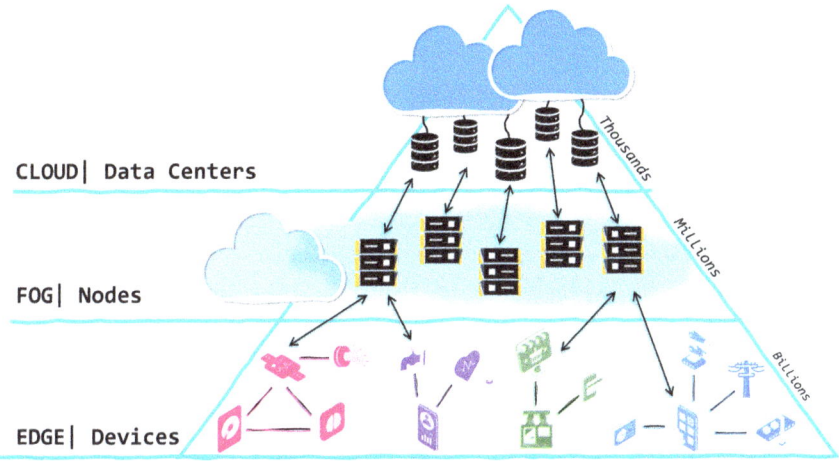

**Fig. 8.1** Fog, cloud and edge computing

For these types of applications, local extensions of cloud computing can often be beneficial. Two commonly used terms in this context are Fog and Edge computing (see Fig. 8.1).

Like the term implies, fog computing refers to having cloud-like computing resources (e.g. mini data centers) much closer to the end user. In our example, the manufacturing company might do most of the processing in a small in-house data center that is co-located with its factory, to minimize latencies and to utilize the high bandwidth of local area networks. Edge computing even goes one step further, where (at least some of) the processing happens on the actual devices that create or use the data. In our example, the safety cameras might have sufficient processing power to analyze the live video streams in real time themselves, and might only transfer results (e.g. "danger" or "no danger") to centralized fog or cloud computing resources. Fog and edge computing are discussed in more detail in Chapter 9.

## 8.5 Ethical Issues in Cloud Computing

This final section looks into situations in which the use of cloud computing could be beneficial for an organization, but might create other, often non-monetary harm to other stakeholders.

## 8.5.1 Introduction to Ethics in Computing

The concept of ethics can be defined as the "moral principles that govern a person's behaviour or the conducting of an activity" or the "branch of knowledge that deals with moral principles."[16]

A minimum threshold for ethical behaviour is often that laws are followed—or to put this differently, behaviour that breaks laws (e.g. stealing) is usually also unethical. However, not all legal behaviour is also ethical. For example, in many contexts, lying would be considered unethical. However, while there are situations in which lying is actually illegal (e.g. when testifying under oath), there is generally now law prohibiting telling falsehoods.

The fact that just following the law is not sufficient for ethical behaviour is particularly true in connection with technical innovations. The following anecdote can illustrate this. When electricity first became commercially available, some people started to secretly hook up their machines to wires transporting electricity from power plants to paying customers, without paying themselves. When they were caught, attempts to convict them of the crime of theft apparently failed, because the crime of theft is in most jurisdictions defined as something along the lines of the act of taking a physical thing from its rightful owner without permission. However, these "electricity thieves" did not take any physical object from anybody. More recent examples of similar cases where laws were slow to follow technology are areas like copyright and computer security, where early copiers of commercial software or hackers gaining access to computers without authorization might in many jurisdictions not actually have been breaking any laws.

There are some frameworks for deciding what ethical behaviour in computing in general could be. Maybe most notably, the Association for Computing Machinery (ACM) adopted the "ACM Code of Ethics and Professional Conduct"[17] in 1992. It defines a number of general principles that computing professionals should follow, such as respecting privacy, honoring confidentiality, knowing and following applicable laws and regulations.

While such guidelines apply to cloud computing and cloud computing professionals as well, there are several specific areas in cloud computing in which new ethical questions arise. Some of them are briefly discussed in the following sections.

## 8.5.2 Amplification of Existing Negative Effects of Technology

Many of the applications operated in the cloud could also be operated in non-cloud, on premise data centers. They are often run in the cloud because doing so reduces costs (especially for very elastic applications), increases performance or reliability. Consequently, if such applications cause ethical issues when they are operated in-

---

[16] Definition from Oxford Languages (https://www.google.com/search?q=ethics).

[17] https://www.acm.org/code-of-ethics

## 8.5 Ethical Issues in Cloud Computing

house, these issues are typically amplified when they are migrated to the cloud, because it becomes economical for more organizations to use them to a greater extent.

An example of this effect is the use of applications using Artificial Intelligence (AI) in the cloud, for example to automatically recognize the content of images and to tag them accordingly. It turns out that such image recognition services are often biased, for example with regard to gender. For example, when presented with images of men and women with the same position (e.g. members of the US senate), men are more likely tagged with labels regarding their role (e.g. business person or official), while women are more likely tagged with superficial aspects of their appearance (e.g. hairstyle or beauty).[18] While this specific example might not create direct harm to anybody, AI algorithms used e.g. for decisions such as whether to grant a loan to or hire a person based on available data can create very tangible harm for minorities that might be discriminated against because the algorithm relies on biased data.

### 8.5.3 Privacy Risks

Privacy risks are in some ways just a special example of the previous point, because privacy can of course also be endangered by bad applications operated in-house. But once again, the widespread and inexpensive availability of cloud computing significantly amplifies the issue.

The concept of online or data privacy can be best understood by looking at the concept of "Informational Self-Determination" that exists in Germany.[19] This right essentially means that individuals should be able to decide which information about themselves they reveal to others (e.g. to corporations), and for what purposes this information is used. This kind of self-determination does de facto not exist for users of online services. One of many examples is that social network providers and companies involved in placing advertisements on websites can typically track users across different websites. This is highly profitable, because it allows the creation of detailed profiles about individuals, which in turn allows targeted placement of advertisements, which pays a lot more than ads placed on websites randomly. As mentioned above, such privacy risks do not entirely depend on the use of cloud computing. However, the use of cloud computing makes it a lot more feasible (e.g. easier and cheaper) to collect and combine data about individuals from multiple sources, and to run advanced analyses on the data, for example for targeted marketing purposes.

A frequently made argument is that such privacy intrusions are not truly harmful. In fact, they can be beneficial to individuals, because they for example allow for more targeted (and consequently, relevant or interesting) ads, or because it is a reasonable tradeoff for individuals to give up some of their privacy in exchange for online

---

[18] https://www.wired.com/story/ai-sees-man-thinks-official-woman-smile/

[19] https://medium.com/golden-data/history-of-informational-self-determination-1abe03f98dc1

services they do not have to pay for, such as the use of social media platforms. To make this argument in its probably bluntest form: If you are doing nothing illegal, you have nothing to worry about.

Unfortunately, this is not always true. A fairly unusual example showing that even the use of anonymized data can have unexpected consequences is when a fitness tracker app released global maps showing where users of its app were exercising.[20] Even though the released maps contained no data through which individual users could be identified, the mere knowledge that some users were exercising in specific locations created significant security risks. Frequently used jogging routes near an American military base in Afghanistan showed up in the map—since these were almost certainly used by American soldiers, knowledge of these specific routes put them at risk of terrorist attacks.

Another point that could be made is that most people in fact do break the law regularly, mostly by minor offenses, such as driving slightly above the speed limit, by dropping passengers off in a non-stopping zone, or by not coming to a complete halt at every stop sign. These kinds of very minor offenses are usually not prosecuted, because it would require massive police resources and not be in the best public interest. However, the more data is collected about people online (e.g. by dash cams that upload recordings into the cloud), the easier it becomes to actually punish such offenses. This bears significant potential for abuse by law enforcement authorities, who could still only enforce punishment for such minor offenses very selectively due to limited resources, and might well end up deciding who to prosecute on a discriminatory basis e.g. against racial minorities.

Furthermore, many people have secrets that they want to keep to themselves, for example about their health, religious or political views or sexual orientation. Imagine users of a fitness tracker who want to use features such as automatic tracking of their heart rate, amounts of exercise and sleep in order to keep track of and improve their health. If all the data stays on a local device under the control of the user, rather than being uploaded into the cloud, they might (justifiably) have more trust in the expectation that this data stays private and is not shared with advertisers or other outside parties, either intentionally or accidentally. Finally, it needs to be considered that cloud technology is available globally, which means that countries with authoritarian regimes that suppress any opposition can also use it. This is especially worth considering in debates about whether encryption mechanisms should be legally required to have back doors so that law enforcement can decrypt messages if authorized by a judge. While this sort of mechanism might sound like a good idea, and could in some instances allow the conviction of a criminal who would have otherwise not been caught, it also needs to be considered that such backdoors will ultimately also be available to totalitarian regimes or criminal organizations, putting legitimate users such as supporters of political opposition movements at risk.

---

[20] https://www.theguardian.com/world/2018/jan/28/fitness-tracking-app-gives-away-location-of-secret-us-army-bases

> **Privacy Regulations**
>
> Privacy has widely been recognized as in important value that is under significant threat with the widespread use of personal data by organisations such as online retailers, email and cell phone service providers, social media platforms etc. In response to this, in many jurisdictions, legislation with the goal to protect the privacy of individuals has been passed.
>
> One of the most well-known and impactful pieces of legislation in this area is the European General Data Protection Regulation (GDPR) that applies to all organizations that process personal data of citizens of EU countries, and therefore also to most companies that offer online services that are accessible globally. It has many important provisions, including:
>
> - The requirement that organizations are transparent about what data they store and process, and what that data is used for
> - Various rights for individuals, including the rights to object to their data being processed, to have their personal data deleted upon request or corrected in the case of errors
> - Various requirements for organizations processing personal data to take strong measures to protect such data from accidental disclosure and to report any data breaches to the responsible authorities as well as inform affected individuals quickly
> - Significant sanctions and penalties if any of these provisions are violated.
>
> Since the GDPR came into effect in 2018, numerous fines for violations have been handed out by European regulators, some of which are in the range of hundreds of millions of Euros.
>
> Another example for privacy regulations in the Canadian Personal Information Protection and Electronic Documents Act (PIPEDA) act, applying to private-sector organizations in Canada that process personal data. It has similar requirements as the GDPR. For example, companies need to be transparent about the purposes they use data for, they must get the consent from the affected individuals to process their data, take reasonable steps to protect data etc.

## *8.5.4 Environmental Impacts*

A completely different ethical concern is the environmental impact of cloud computing. While this contains other aspects like pollution created by mining to retrieve the raw materials required for all the physical infrastructure in data centers, the energy consumption to operate cloud data centers often gets particular attention, especially due to the increasingly commonly accepted risks of climate change.

According to a study from 2020,[21] data centers annually consume about 200 terawatt hours of electricity, or approximately 1% of the overall global consumption of electricity. While this might seem like a relatively low percentage, it could be argued that a lot of the cloud applications used are not strictly necessary, and that the high growth rates of cloud computing means that the amount of electricity used has already significantly increased since then and it likely to climb further.

An important counter argument is that the environmental impact of cloud computing should reasonably be compared to alternative ways to achieve the same results. For example, while online video streaming services like Netflix clearly consume a significant amount of electricity, which, depending on how the electricity is generated, could result in a significant amount of emissions, the prior approach—people driving to video rental stores to pick up and drop off movies—might well have had even higher emissions. Similarly, it could be argued that large public cloud data centers likely operate more energy efficiently than cloud service users could when they run their own, smaller, and often more under-utilized in-house data centers.

Still, the fact that cloud computing makes computational resources easier and often cheaper to use could well lead to so much more consumption that the overall environmental impact is larger, which does raise ethical questions, such as whether excessive use of computing resources should be curbed e.g. by higher taxes on electricity consumption or emissions.

### 8.5.5 Market Concentration Risks

Another potential ethical issue is that cloud computing seems to lead to significant market concentration. Due to the effect of economies of scale, large public cloud providers can operate more efficiently than smaller providers, or than organizations can operate their own IT resources in-house. This leads to increasing consolidation of computing in a small number of very large public cloud providers.

Economic pressures can practically force organizations to operate their critical IT systems with public cloud providers. At the same time, especially since most cloud services are not standardized and contain proprietary offerings, moving between different cloud providers or moving systems back in-house becomes increasingly challenging. This gives cloud providers significant power over their users. For example, if in the case of a dispute, a cloud provider threatened to shut down an organization's systems on short notice, this would leave many customer organizations little choice but to concede whatever demands the provider has, because an outage of their systems would often endanger the survival of the organization. While the affected organization could of course use the courts to rectify the situation, this would almost certainly take too long.

Another aspect of the same one-sided dependency on a small number or large public cloud providers is that the three largest cloud providers (AWS, Azure and

---

[21] https://www.datacenterknowledge.com/sustainability

Google Cloud) are all American companies that are subject to interference by the US government. Especially the often aggressive forein policy approach taken by the recent Trump administration created significant concerns in other countries that the US government could force the large cloud providers to stop providing services to companies or government agencies of specific countries as a powerful weapon in trade or other disagreements. In the European Union, this has led to the realization that digital sovereignty, i.e. the ability to be in control over one's own data, is an important goal. Consequently, in recent years, significant resources and effort has to be put into the GAIA-X[22] initiative which aims to create a European infrastructure for cloud services that is independent and safe from potential foreign interference.

## 8.6 Summary

This chapter discussed a number of different issues around operating applications in the cloud, beginning with cloud management, monitoring and migration, and ending with a critical view of cloud computing challenges, limitations and ethical concerns. A unified theme of all these topics is that cloud computing is much more than a purely technical solution. In order to use cloud computing efficiently, effectively and in an ethical way, appropriate organizational measures need to be taken as well.

## 8.7 Key Terms

**Service level agreement (SLA):** In cloud computing, a SLA is a contractual agreement between the cloud service provider and a cloud service user. It typically specifies aspects such as the expected uptime of the services provided, support response times and other guaranteed performance criteria, as well as the consequences if these guarantees are not met by the provider.

**Risk Management** is a systematic approach to dealing with inevitable risks in cloud computing. It includes assessing existing risks and their likelihoods and potential impacts, and develops situationally appropriate strategies of dealing with these risks, ranging from risk mitigation approaches to risk transfer and risk acceptance.

**Mobile Device Management (MDM)** is an approach to remotely manage and secure the mobile devices that are often used to access cloud applications, thereby increasing the security of the cloud applications themselves. Typical features of MDM are the ability to enforce security mechanisms on mobile devices accessing cloud applications, the ability to remotely block and erase devices that have been lost or stolen and the creation of separate environments on mobile devices for personal and work use of the device.

---

[22] https://gaia-x.eu/

**Observability:** The goal of observability is to be able to understand the internal state of an IT system in detail. Traditionally, the main mechanism to achieve this was monitoring. Modern cloud infrastructures like GCP extend this by offering additional functionality around logging, tracing and profiling.

**Cloud Migration Strategy:** There are several different ways of migrating an existing application into the cloud, ranging from re-hosting the application, i.e. moving it essentially unchanged from a physical server to a virtual machine in the cloud, to a substantial re-factoring, in which an application is redesigned from scratch to utilize modern cloud computing approaches such as microservice architectures.

**Cutover Strategy:** When an existing IT system is replaced by a new system in general, and when an in-house IT system is migrated into the cloud, and organization has different choices of how to transition from the old to the new system, including a direct cut-over, parallel operation and phased or pilot operations.

**Cloud Computing Challenge:** A cloud computing challenge is something that makes using cloud computing potentially difficult but not impossible in a given situation. Commonly quoted cloud computing challenges include lack of expertise, security concerns and organizational readiness issues.

**Cloud Computing Limitation:** In contrast to challenges that can be overcome, cloud computing also has some limitations that might make its use impractical in certain situations, including applications that have very stringent response time requirements or that are subject to particularly strict government regulations about data security and privacy.

**Cloud Computing Ethics:** While cloud computing in its own right, just like most other technologies, is neither morally good nor bad, the use of cloud computing comes with a number of ethical challenges. Some examples include its potential for magnifying existing biases and sources of discrimination, privacy issues especially in cross-border use of cloud computing, questions around digital sovereignty in the face of increasing industry concentration and environmental impacts.

**Digital Sovereignty** describes the ability of individuals, organizations and countries to be in control about their own data, applications and technologies, without being forced or essentially being forced to give up some of this control by external market forces. The market concentration in cloud computing in which a large percentage of the market share is held by just three US corporations makes this a significant concern for many users outside the USA.

## 8.8 Review Questions

1. What is an SLA?
2. Name some organizational measures organizations take to effectively operate their cloud resources.

3. What is risk management, and why is it important in cloud computing?
4. Explain how cloud provider manage fluctuating workloads of their customers.
5. What is mobile device management?
6. Why is cloud monitoring important? Describe some typical features of cloud monitoring systems.
7. Discuss some of the assessments an organization might perform before migrating applications to the cloud.
8. What are the main cloud migration and cutover strategies?
9. Describe some challenges and limitations of cloud computing.
10. Explain some of the ethical issues the use of cloud computing might raise.

## 8.9 Exercises

The following laboratory exercises contain questions that require written responses and, in some instances, accompanying screenshots. If the exercises have been given as an assignment, please ensure that all answers and requested screenshots are compiled into a separate document for submission to the instructor, as specified by the instructor.

### 8.9.1 Cloud Monitoring

In this lab, we will explore cloud monitoring.

*Objectives*

1. To create resources to monitor
2. To create and test custom alerts and uptime checks
3. To create a custom dashboard

*A. Creating Resources to Monitor*

1. In the "Compute Engine", create a new virtual machine with the name "lab8instance", machine type `e2-small` and Ubuntu 24.04 LTS, otherwise using the default settings.
2. Once the virtual machine is created, connect to it via SSH in a separate browser window.

3. In the hamburger menu, select "Databases", then "SQL". Click on "Create Instance". Use MySQL as database engine.
4. Enter "lab8database" as Instance ID and set the root password to Csis4270. Select "Enterprise" and the edition preset "Sandbox". Then click on "Create Instance".

## B. Enabling Monitoring

1. In the hamburger menu, select "Monitoring" under "Observability".
2. Expand the dropdown on the top right of the screen next to "Set up your project's observability".
3. Below "Get Started with Monitoring", click on "Install an agent".
4. Click on the button "Setup Agents".
5. Click on "List". Select "lab8instance" by checking the checkbox next to it and click on "Install/update ops agents".
6. Read the information provided, then click on "Install Ops Agent".
7. Wait for the agent installation to complete. What is the value below "Agent" in the row "lab8instance"?
8. If the change does not change after reloading the page after waiting a few minutes, repeat steps 5 and 6 and follow the instructions (including clicking on "Run in cloud shell"). Hit enter in the cloud shell to actually run the copied command.
9. What is the output in the cloud shell, indicating the success or failure of the operation?

## C. Creating and Testing an Alert

1. Go back to the Monitoring Overview screen.
2. In the menu on the left, click on "Alerting".
3. Click on "Create Policy".
4. Click on "Select a Metric".
5. In the textbox below "Select a metric", type "GCE VM cpu utilization".
6. Select "CPU utilization" and click on "Apply".
7. Below "Transform Data", change the value for "Rolling window" to 1 min.
8. Click on "Next".
9. For "Threshold value", enter 80 and click on "Next".
10. Click on "Notification Channels", then on "Manage Notification Channels".
11. Next to "Email" click on "Add New" and enter your google email address as "Email Address" and your name as "Display Name".
12. Click on "Save".
13. Close the "Notification Channels" popup.

8.9 Exercises

14. Open the Notification Channels drop down again, select the checkbox next to your name and click on "OK".
15. For "Alert policy name" enter CPUover80%, then click on "Next".
16. Click on "Create Policy".
17. We will now test the alert. Go back to the virtual machine (**NOT the cloud shell!**) and install a stress testing tool with the following command:

    ```
    sudo apt-get install stress
    ```

18. To stress the CPU, run the following command:

    ```
    stress -c 2 &
    ```

19. To see the most busy processes, run the following command (you might have to press enter first):

    ```
    top
    ```

20. What are the two processes that create the most CPU load, and what percentage of the CPU time do they both take up?
21. Wait about five minutes, until you get an email about the alert. What is the subject of the email?
22. Go back to the Monitoring overview. You might have to reload the page. In the "Incidents" section, you should have a new open incident. Expand the view of the incident and include a screenshot of it:
23. Go back to the VM windows. Press "q" to close the top command. Then enter the command

    ```
    ps
    ```

24. How many instances of "stress" are running, and what are the process IDs (PIDs) of the instances?
25. Use the command kill to end all stress processes, e.g.

    ```
    kill 20837
    ```

26. Verify with the command ps that all stress processes are terminated.

## D. Creating and Testing an Uptime Check

1. Before we can create an uptime check, we have to install an application that can be monitored. For this example, we will simply install apache with the following command in the VM:

```
sudo apt-get install apache2
```

2. Then we start apache with the following command:

```
sudo service apache2 start
```

3. Finally, we have to allow http traffic to reach the virtual machine. In the Compute Engine, under VM instances, click on the name of the virtual machine (lab8instance) to go to its detail settings. Click on "Edit" at the top of the screen, and under "Firewalls", check the box "Allow HTTP Traffic". Then scroll to the bottom of the page and click on "Save".
4. Verify that your apache server is running and that you can connect to it by opening the external IP address of the virtual machine in a separate browser window. What is the headline of the page that displays?
5. From the Monitoring Overview page, click on "Uptime checks" in the menu on the left. Click on "Create Uptime Check".
6. Make sure that "HTTP" is selected as protocol and "URL" as resource type. Enter the external IP address of the VM as hostname and select "1 minute" for "Check Frequency". Then click on "Continue".
7. Keep the default settings for "Response Validation" and click on "Continue".
8. Under "Alert & Notification", select your email address under "Notification Channels" and click on "OK". Then click on "Continue".
9. Enter "ApacheIsResponding" as title and click on "Create".
10. Under Monitoring, click on "Uptime Checks" to go to the overview of uptime checks. You should now see the defined uptime check, and green checkmarks indicating that the check succeeded, because the web server responds to requests from several different locations. What are the different locations from which the check is performed? (Note that you will probably have to wait a few minutes for the uptime check to be executed successfully).
11. To test the uptime check, we will simply stop apache on the virtual machine. In the VM window, enter the command

```
sudo service apache2 stop
```

12. Wait for about a minute. Then reload the page. You should now see an exclamation mark next to the uptime check. Click on the uptime check to see details. Insert a screenshot of the failed uptime check:
13. Start apache again in the virtual machine using the command

```
sudo service apache2 start
```

14. Wait a little while. Does the uptime check succeed again if you reload the page?
15. Check your emails. Did you receive a notification about the failed uptime check? What was the subject of the email?

8.9 Exercises

### E. Creating a Custom Dashboard

1. In the Monitoring menu, click on "Dashboards".
2. How many existing default dashboards are there (below "All Dashboards")?
3. Feel free to look at some of them. Then click on "Create Dashboard".
4. Add four different charts, preferably ones that show some data, by using the button "Add Widget" four times.
5. Insert a screenshot of the resulting Dashboard:

### F. Cleaning Up

1. To avoid receiving further emails from the monitoring, go to "Alerting" under "Monitoring". Under "Policies", delete both policies.
2. If you intend to do the Cloud Logging hands-on exercise next, you can skip the rest of this section and continue straight to the next exercise. Otherwise, make sure to follow the next two steps to avoid being charged for the created infrastructure.
3. Shutdown and/or delete the virtual machine.
4. From the hamburger menu, go to "Databases", "SQL", and delete the database lab8database (you might first have to edit its data protection settings to turn deletion protection off).

## 8.9.2 Cloud Logging

In this lab, we explore cloud logging.

### Objectives

1. To create resources to monitor
2. To explore the logging feature

### A. Creating Resources to Monitor

Note: If you just finished the Cloud Monitoring hands-on exercise, and did not delete the created resources at the end of that lab, you can skip this section and continue directly with the section "Examining Log Files".

1. In the "Compute Engine", create a new virtual machine with the name "lab8instance", machine type `e2-small` and Ubuntu 24.04 LTS, otherwise using the default settings.
2. Once the virtual machine is created, connect to it via SSH in a separate browser window.
3. In the hamburger menu, select "Databases", then "SQL". Click on "Create Instance". Use MySQL as database engine.
4. Enter "lab8database" as Instance ID and set the root password to Csis4270. Select "Enterprise" and the edition preset "Sandbox". Then click on "Create Instance".

## B. Examining Log Files

1. In the Monitoring Overview page, click on "Logs Explorer" in the menu on the left.
2. In the Query Builder, click on the Dropdown "All Resources" and select "Cloud SQL Database".
3. Click on the database ID for your lab8database on the right and click on "Apply".
4. Click on "Run Query".
5. If you do not see results, you might have to extend the date range. Insert a screenshot of a log entry that you see (expand an item in the query results):
6. Clear the query and follow similar steps to look at the logs for your "VM Instance" "lab8instance".
7. If you don't see results, you might have to extend the date range. Insert a screenshot of a log entry that you see:
8. In the menu on the left, click on "Logs Storage". How much are the "Current month storage" of your logs?

## C. Cleaning Up

1. Shutdown and/or delete the virtual machine.
2. From the hamburger menu, go to "Databases", "SQL", and delete the database lab8database (you might first have to edit its data protection settings to turn deletion protection off).

### 8.9.3 Cloud Migration Center

In this lab we explore the GCP Migration Center

8.9 Exercises

## *Objectives*

1. Create an initial estimate of costs for a manually defined infrastructure
2. Import sample infrastructure data from a sample AWS deployment
3. Run Total Cost of Ownership (TCO) and license reports for the important infrastructure

## *A. Activate the Migration Center and Get an Initial Estimate*

1. Through the hamburger menu, navigate to Tools->Migration Center
2. Click on "Get Started".
3. Click on "Enable".
4. Select a region (e.g. us-central1). Note that you might have to wait a few minutes for the APIs from the previous step to be enabled and reload the page before a region can be selected.
5. Click on "Next".
6. Click on "Skip".
7. Keep the default migration preferences and click on "Next".
8. Click on "Continue".
9. Click on "Get initial cost estimates".
10. Enter "Test assessment" as Estimate name.
11. Click on "Add to Estimate" below "On-premises".
12. Click on Start Estimate.
13. Below "On-premises", click on "Start".
14. Click on "Next".
15. Assuming we want to migrate two web servers and two database servers with eight CPU cores each, enter 32 for "Number of vCPUs".
16. Enter 10 for "Total storage (TB).
17. Enter 5000 for "CDN data transfer out bandwidth (GB).
18. Click on "Next".
19. Below "Oracle and SP workloads", check the check box next to "Oracle".
20. Enter 50 as "% of total vCPUs running Oracle Database".
21. Enter 0 for the percentages for Oracle Exadata and Oracle Data Warehouse Database.
22. Enter 5 for "Storage for Oracle database (GB).
23. Assuming we are running our infrastructure on Linux only, uncheck the checkbox next to "Windows Server".
24. Click on "Next".
25. Leave the default settings in the "Migration Timeline, pricing and discounts" screen and click on "Submit".
26. Click on "View Details" and insert a screenshot of the result:

## B. Import Sample Infrastructure Data and Create a Group

1. Close the details and go back to the Migration Center.
2. Next, we will import assets an organization might have in AWS from a sample file.
3. In a separate browser window, go to https://cloud.google.com/migration-center/docs/import-data-tables#available_data_templates and download the file vmInfo.csv.
4. Back in the GCP Migration Center, click on "Discover assets".
5. Click on "Add Data".
6. Click on "Upload Files"
7. Enter "Sample AWS infrastructure" a "File import job name".
8. As "File format", select "Asset data from template (CSV).
9. Click on "Select Files to Upload", navigate to the file vmInfo.csv you just downloaded, and click on "Open".
10. Click on "Upload Files".
11. When it says, "The data from your files is ready to import", click on "mport Data".
12. Click on "Confirm".
13. When the import is complete, click on "Go to Assets".
14. Insert a screenshot of servers listed below "Servers to migrate".
15. Click on "Create reports".
16. Click on "TCO and detailed pricing reports".
17. Enter "Basic TCO Report" as report name.
18. Click on "Next".
19. Under "File format", select "AWS (CSV)".
20. Click on "Select files to Upload", navigate to the file you just downloaded and click on "Open".
21. Click on "Upload Files".
22. If you see a warning that some rows cannot be imported, click on "Continue Import".
23. Click on "Confirm".
24. Click on "Assets" on the left and insert a screenshot of the imported assets:
25. Below "Discovery" on the left, click on "Groups"
26. Click on "Create Group".
27. Enter "All Servers" as Group name.
28. Click on "Next".
29. Select all servers by checking the checkbox next to them.
30. Click on "Next".
31. Click on "Create".

## C. Create Pricing and License Reports

1. Below "Reports" on the left, click on "Create Reports".
2. Click on "TCO and detailed pricing reports".
3. Enter "Basic Pricing Report" as Report name.
4. Click on "Next".
5. Select the checkbox next to "All Servers"
6. Click on "Next"Ï.
7. Click on "Generate Report".
8. Click on "Basic Pricing Report" to see its details.
9. Click on "Next" to see a summary of all asset groups.
10. Insert a screenshot below:
11. Click on "Next" twice to proceed to the "Servers" section of the report.
12. Scroll down to see the table of "Monthly cost after server migration" and include a screenshot of that table:
13. Go back to the "Migration Center" overview page and click on "Run reports" again.
14. Click on "License reports".
15. Enter "Basic License Report" as Report name.
16. Click on "Next".
17. Select the checkbox next to "All Servers"
18. Click on "Next".
19. Click on "Generate Report".
20. Click on "Basic License report", then click on "Export to Google Slides" at the top.
21. Once the export is finished, click on "Open Report".
22. In the report, scroll down to page 5 ("Supported licensing Scenarios for Windows") and insert a screenshot of this page below:
23. Go to the next page in the report ("License scenarios assessed monthly TCO") and insert a screenshot of this page below:

# Chapter 9
# Edge Computing, Internet of Things and Cloud-to-Edge Continuum

The convergence of cloud computing and Internet of Things (IoT) has given rise to a new paradigm: edge computing. Edge computing involves processing data closer to its source, at the network's edge, rather than relying solely on centralized cloud data centers. This shift has profound implications for data latency, bandwidth consumption, and real-time decision-making.

In particular, as the number of connected devices continues to grow exponentially, the volume of data generated at the edge is also increasing rapidly. This makes it impractical to send all of this data to the cloud for processing. Edge computing provides a scalable and efficient solution for handling the vast amount of IoT data. In the rest of this chapter, we will discuss the benefits and challenges of this new paradigm, its architecture and, finally, we conclude the chapter with some considerations and introducing future trends.

## 9.1 Introduction

There are several scenarios where real-time decision-making is crucial, one of them is in industrial automation, especially when humans and robots collaborate.[1] In particular, by processing data closer to the source, edge nodes minimize latency, avoiding issues like industrial accidents, reduced production efficiency, and poor product quality. This enables millisecond-level analysis and action without relying on cloud data centers. In collaborative human-robot environments, immediate responses are paramount. For instance, if a robot detects an anomaly or an unexpected human movement within its workspace, a edge-enabled system can instantly trigger a safety protocol, preventing collisions or injuries. Real-time data processing allows robots to adapt dynamically to human actions, ensuring fluid and safe interactions. Furthermore, in tasks requiring precise coordination, edge computing ensures that both human and robot receive and react to information simultaneously, optimizing

---

[1] https://www.controleng.com/fog-computing-for-industrial-automation/

workflow and minimizing potential errors. This responsiveness is not merely about efficiency; it's about safeguarding human workers and ensuring seamless, intuitive collaboration in complex industrial settings.

Before discussing benefits and challenges of edge computing, we first introduce in the next subsections the definition of the key terms: IoT, edge computing and Cloud-to-Edge Continuum.

### 9.1.1 Internet of Things

Internet of Things (IoT) refers to the rapidly growing network of physical objects ("things") that are embedded with sensors, software, and network connectivity, which enables these objects to collect and exchange data.

In simpler terms, it is about connecting everyday objects to the internet, allowing them to communicate with each other and with us. These "things" can range from common household devices like your refrigerator or thermostat to more complex devices like cars, wearable tech, and even industrial machinery.

Some of the key aspects of IoT are:

- Connectivity: IoT devices are connected to the internet, allowing them to send and receive data.
- Sensors: These devices are equipped with sensors that collect data from their environment, such as temperature, motion, or location.
- Data Exchange: The collected data is shared between devices and with larger systems, enabling automation, analysis, and informed decision-making.

IoT has a wide range of applications, including:

- Smart Homes: Automating home functions like lighting, temperature control, and security.
- Wearable Tech: Tracking fitness, health, and providing personalized information.
- Transportation: Connected cars, traffic management systems, and logistics optimization.
- Healthcare: Remote patient monitoring, medical device management, and data-driven healthcare solutions.
- Manufacturing: Industrial automation, predictive maintenance, and supply chain optimization.

IoT is transforming the way we interact with technology and the world around us, creating a more connected and data-driven future.

9.1 Introduction

> **Important IoT Protocols and Standards**
>
> Internet of Things is still an area with rapid innovation. Nevertheless, the field has sufficiently matured to bring out a number of widely supported standards and protocols, promising cross-vendor compatibility. The following list shows just a few of them:
>
> - Zigbee and Z-Wave: Wireless communication protocols for IoT devices that support organizing multiple devices in a mesh.
> - Bluetooth Low Energy: Short-range, low power wireless communication protocol.
> - LoRaWAN (long Range Wide Area Network): Long-range, low power wireless communication protocol.
> - MQTT (Message Queuing Telemetry Transport): Lightweight publish-subscribe protocol that can be used to efficiently communicate between cloud resources and IoT devices, even over unreliable networks
> - CoAP (Constrained Application Protocol): Application-layer communication protocol useful for devices with limited resources (bandwidth, processing power, etc.), thus well suited for IoT devices
> - IEEE 802.1AR: Standard specifying secure device identifiers, allowing for IoT devices that require authentication to communicate securely
> - IETF SUIT (Internet Engineering Task Force Software Update for Internet of Things): Protocol to securely distribute firmware updates to IoT devices
> - Matter: Interoperability standard, specifically focusing on IoT devices used in home automation, with the goal to allow devices by different vendors to work together

## 9.1.2 Edge Computing

Edge computing is a distributed computing paradigm that brings computation and data storage closer to the devices where it is being gathered, rather than relying on a centralized data center or cloud.

Edge computing is becoming increasingly important as the number of connected devices and the volume of data they generate continue to grow. It enables faster, more efficient, and more secure processing of data, leading to a wide range of new applications and services.

### 9.1.3 Cloud-to-Edge Continuum

The Cloud-to-Edge Continuum is a concept that describes the seamless integration and orchestration of computing resources and data processing capabilities across a spectrum, from the edge of the network to centralized cloud servers. It is about creating a unified and flexible environment where applications and data can move and be processed efficiently, regardless of their location.

The Cloud-to-Edge Continuum is a key enabler of digital transformation, allowing organizations to leverage the power of both edge and cloud computing to create innovative applications and services.

## 9.2 Key Benefits and Challenges of Edge Computing

As mentioned before, as any new paradigm, there is a mix of advantages and disadvantages that makes this approach suitable for specific scenarios. Concerning the benefits to use edge computing, the main ones are:

- **Reduced Latency:** By processing data closer to its source, edge computing significantly reduces the time it takes for data to travel to and from the cloud. This is crucial for applications that require real-time responses, such as autonomous vehicles, augmented reality, and industrial automation.
- **Increased Bandwidth Efficiency:** Edge computing can alleviate network congestion by offloading processing tasks from the cloud, reducing the amount of data that needs to be transmitted over the network.
- **Improved Data Privacy and Security:** Processing data at the edge can enhance data privacy and security by minimizing the amount of sensitive information that needs to be transmitted over the network.
- **Enhanced Reliability:** Edge computing can improve system reliability by providing redundancy and fault tolerance at the network's edge.
- **Real-time Decision Making:** Edge computing enables applications to make decisions in real time, without relying on cloud-based processing. This is essential for applications such as smart grids, industrial control systems, and autonomous vehicles.

While edge computing offers many benefits, it also presents several challenges:

- **Complexity:** Implementing and managing edge computing systems can be complex, as it requires coordination between multiple devices, networks, and applications.
- **Security:** Distributing security patches to numerous edge systems presents a significant challenge compared to centralized cloud deployments. The decentralized nature of edge computing necessitates individual updates across a vast network of devices, creating substantial logistical overhead. Failure to consistently and effectively patch these edge instances leaves them vulnerable to exploitation by

## 9.2 Key Benefits and Challenges of Edge Computing

attackers, who can capitalize on known security flaws within the software running on those devices.
- **Cost:** Deploying and maintaining edge computing infrastructure can be expensive, especially in remote or underserved areas.
- **Interoperability:** Ensuring interoperability between different edge computing devices and platforms can be challenging.

In Table 9.1, we present a few real-world scenarios where edge computing can provide benefits; conversely, in Table 9.2 we provide some real-world scenarios where the edge computing should be avoided in favor of cloud computing.

| Scenario | Characteristic | Detail |
|---|---|---|
| Autonomous Vehicles | Real-time Decision Making | Edge computing enables vehicles to process sensor data locally, making split-second decisions to avoid accidents or navigate complex traffic situations. |
| | Reduced Latency | By processing data at the edge, vehicles can react faster to changes in their environment, improving safety. |
| Industrial IoT | Predictive maintenance | Edge devices can monitor equipment health in real-time, predicting potential failures and scheduling maintenance before downtime occurs. |
| | Quality control | Cameras and sensors can analyze products on assembly lines, identifying defects and ensuring quality standards. |
| Healthcare | Remote Patient Monitoring | Wearable devices can process health data locally, triggering alerts for critical conditions and reducing the burden on healthcare providers. |
| | Surgical Robotics | Edge computing can enable real-time image processing and control of surgical robots, improving precision and reducing surgical time. |
| Smart Cities | Traffic Management | Edge devices can analyze traffic patterns in real-time, optimizing traffic flow and reducing congestion. |
| | Smart Grids | Edge computing can enable real-time monitoring and control of energy distribution, improving efficiency and reducing power outages. |

**Table 9.1** Scenarios where the adoption of edge computing brings benefits

It is important to consider the specific requirements of each application when determining whether edge computing is the right solution. A hybrid approach, combining edge and cloud computing, can often provide the best of both worlds. This approach is also called the Cloud-to-Edge continuum. For example, data can be initially processed at the edge for real-time analysis, and then aggregated and stored in the cloud for long-term storage and analysis.

| Scenario | Characteristic | Detail |
|---|---|---|
| Batch Processing of Large Datasets | Data Warehousing | In case of large datasets that need to be processed periodically, a centralized cloud solution might be more efficient. Edge computing is better suited for real-time or near-real-time processing. |
| Highly Sensitive Data | Financial Transactions | For highly sensitive data, centralized cloud solutions with robust security measures may be preferred. While edge computing can improve privacy, it is essential to ensure the security of edge devices. |
| Low-Bandwidth Environments | Remote Areas | In areas with limited network connectivity, edge computing can be useful for local processing. However, if significant data needs to be transmitted to the cloud, it might be more efficient to store and process data locally until connectivity improves. |
| Non-Time-Critical Applications | Email or Web Browsing | For basic applications that do not require real-time processing or low latency, traditional cloud computing is sufficient and often more efficient. |

**Table 9.2** Scenarios where the adoption of edge computing brings disadvantages

## 9.3 Edge Computing Architectures

There are several different edge computing architectures, each with its own advantages and disadvantages:

- **Fog Computing:** Fog computing is a distributed computing paradigm that extends the cloud to the network's edge. It involves deploying computing resources closer to the source of data generation, but at a larger scale than traditional edge computing.
- **Mobile Edge Computing (MEC):** MEC involves deploying computing resources at the edge of cellular networks, such as base stations and radio access networks. This enables applications to be processed and served locally, reducing latency and improving network performance.
- **Industrial Internet of Things (IIoT) Edge Computing:** IIoT edge computing involves deploying computing resources at the edge of industrial networks, such as factories and manufacturing plants. This enables real-time data processing and analysis, improving operational efficiency and productivity.

## 9.4 Future Trends and Opportunities

Edge computing is a rapidly evolving technology with significant potential to transform the way we process and analyze data. As IoT continues to expand and the demand for real-time applications grows, the importance of edge computing will only increase. Future trends and opportunities include:

- **Integration with 5G Networks:** 5G networks will provide the necessary bandwidth and latency to support edge computing applications at a larger scale.
- **Artificial Intelligence and Machine Learning at the Edge:** Edge computing can enable AI and ML models to be deployed closer to the source of data, enabling real-time decision making and analysis.
- **Edge Computing for Smart Cities:** Edge computing can play a key role in enabling smart city applications, such as traffic management, energy efficiency, and public safety.
- **Edge Computing for Industrial Automation:** Edge computing can improve the efficiency and productivity of industrial processes by enabling real-time data analysis and control.
- **Long Range Wide Area Network (LoRaWAN):** is a low-power, wide-area networking protocol designed to wirelessly connect battery-operated "things" to the internet in regional, national, or global networks. In particular, LoRaWAN is designed for applications that require the transmission of small amounts of data and it is able to cover large geographical areas, making it suitable for applications like smart cities, agriculture, and industrial monitoring.

## 9.5 Summary

Edge computing is a rapidly evolving technology that is poised to transform the way we process and analyze data. By bringing computing power closer to the source of data generation, edge computing can enable new applications and services that were previously impractical or impossible. As IoT continues to expand, the importance of edge computing will only grow.

## 9.6 Key Terms

**Internet of Things:** The Internet of Things (IoT) describes the approach of equipping a wide range of devices, vehicles, appliances etc. with networked computational abilities, allowing them to interact and provide functionality that an isolated device could not provide.

**Edge Computing:** In edge computing, data are processed close to their source, i.e. often on the device that created the data, rather than in a centralized cloud computing data center.

**Cloud-to-Edge Continuum:** The cloud-to-edge describes the approach to seamlessly integrate processing of data anywhere between the device on which it is created to servers in centralized cloud data centers, to maximize goals such as efficiency and performance.

**Fog Computing:** In fog computing, data is processed somewhere in between the edge device and the centralized cloud data center. Organizations might operate fog data centers, i.e. small data centers that are in close proximity (e.g. in the same factory) to the edge devices creating the data in order to minimize latency and response time while still benefiting from the advantages of (locally) centralized processing.

**Mobile Edge Computing** is a common edge computing architecture in which computing resources are deployed on base stations or other edge devices of cellular networks.

**Industrial Internet of Things:** Industrial Internet of Things (IIoT) describes the use of fog and edge computing in industrial settings such as in modern manufacturing plants.

**Long Range Wide Area Network:** Long range wide area network (LoRaWAN) is a wireless network protocol designed for the use in a distributed IoT context. It specializes in transmitting small amounts of data efficiently, making it ideal for IoT devices with limited battery life.

## 9.7 Review Questions

1. What is the Internet of Things? Give a few examples of its use.
2. Describe the differences between cloud, fog and edge computing.
3. Name some of the main advantages and disadvantages of edge computing.
4. What are some common edge computing architectures?
5. Identify some future trends and opportunities in fog and edge computing.

## 9.8 Exercises

The following laboratory exercises contain questions that require written responses and, in some instances, accompanying screenshots. If the exercises have been given as an assignment, please ensure that all answers and requested screenshots are compiled into a separate document for submission to the instructor, as specified by the instructor.

### 9.8.1 Streaming IoT Data to Cloud Storage

In this lab you will learn how to configure Cloud IoT Core and Cloud Pub/Sub to create a Pub/Sub topic and registry on Google Cloud.

9.8 Exercises

## *Objectives*

1. Create a Pub/Sub topic
2. Start a Dataflow job
3. Run simulated devices

## *A. Create a Pub/Sub Topic*

First you need to create a Pub/Sub Topic for your streaming data. Go to Google Cloud Platform console and login.

1. On the Navigation menu, look for the Analytics section and click Pub/Sub >Topics.
2. Click Create topic.
3. Type iotlab in Topic ID section:

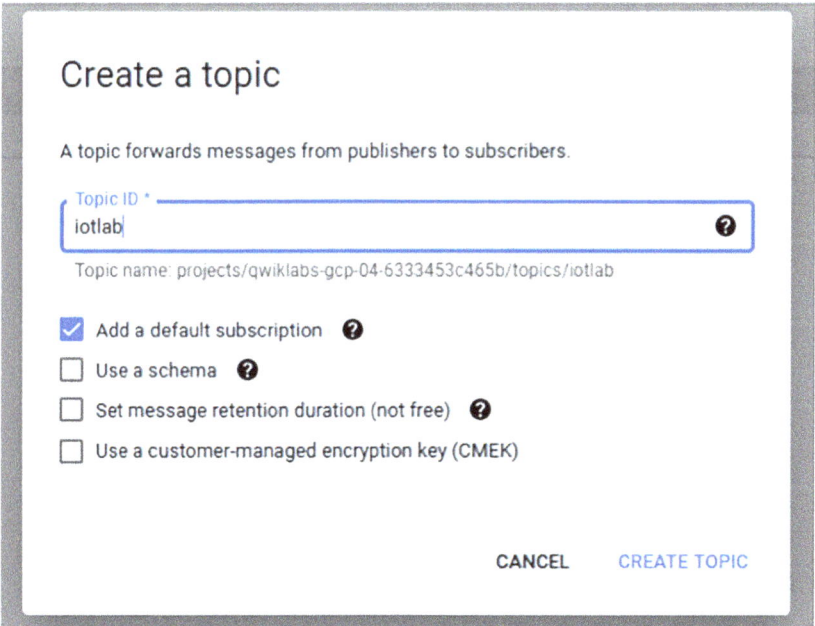

4. Leave the checkboxes as they are.
5. Click Create topic.
6. You now have a Pub/Sub Topic. To allow the project to publish this topic, you need to add the project as a member/publisher.
7. To add members, click Add principal:

324                    9 Edge Computing, Internet of Things and Cloud-to-Edge Continuum

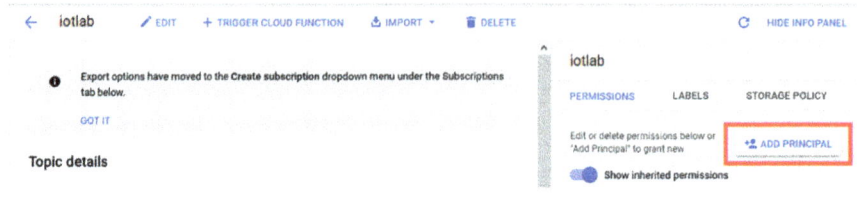

Edit permissions

8. Add the project as a member to the topic: cloud-iot@system.gserviceaccount.com. Select the role of Pub/Sub Publisher, and then click Save to add the member.

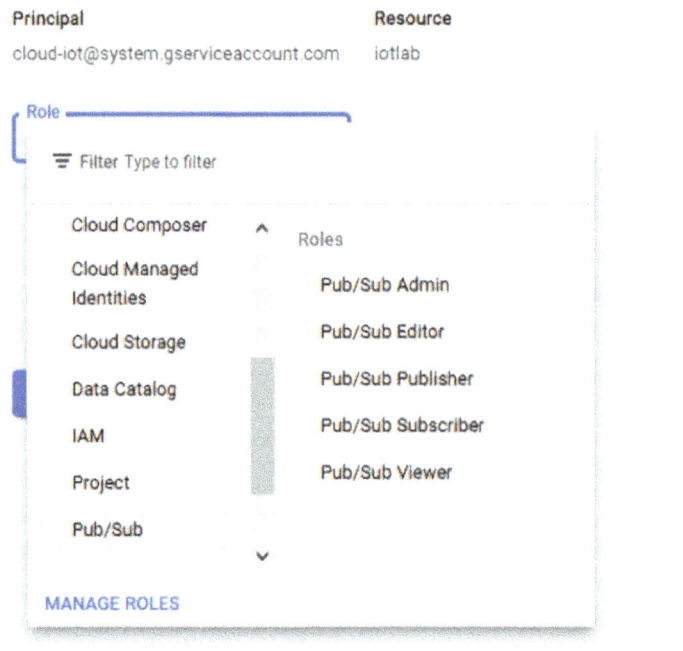

## B. Create Storage

You need to create a storage bucket and folder to store the data streaming from the IoT device.

1. From the Navigation menu, in the Storage section, click Cloud Storage > Browser.
2. Click Create bucket.
3. Bucket names must be unique. Enter a unique bucket name, and then click Create.
4. In the bucket you just created, click Create folder.
5. For Name, type Sensor-Data.
6. Click Create.

## C. Start a Dataflow Job

You now have a device publishing data, and your Google Cloud Project is authorized to receive this data. Now you can start a Dataflow job to save the data to your bucket.

1. On the Navigation menu, in the Analytics section, click Dataflow.
2. Click Create job from template.
3. Enter the following values in the template: Job name = sensor-data, Regional endpoint = us-central1 and Cloud Dataflow template = Pub/Sub to Text Files on Cloud Storage.
4. The template page will expand to display a series of textboxes. Some of the textboxes are optional and some are required. You will only modify the required textboxes:

| Property | Value |
|---|---|
| Input Pub/Sub topic | projects/<project-id>/topics/iotlab |
| Output file directory in Cloud Storage | gs://<bucket-name>/Sensor-Data/ |
| Output filename prefix | output- |
| Temporary Location | gs://<bucket-name>/tmp |

5. Your template should resemble the following:

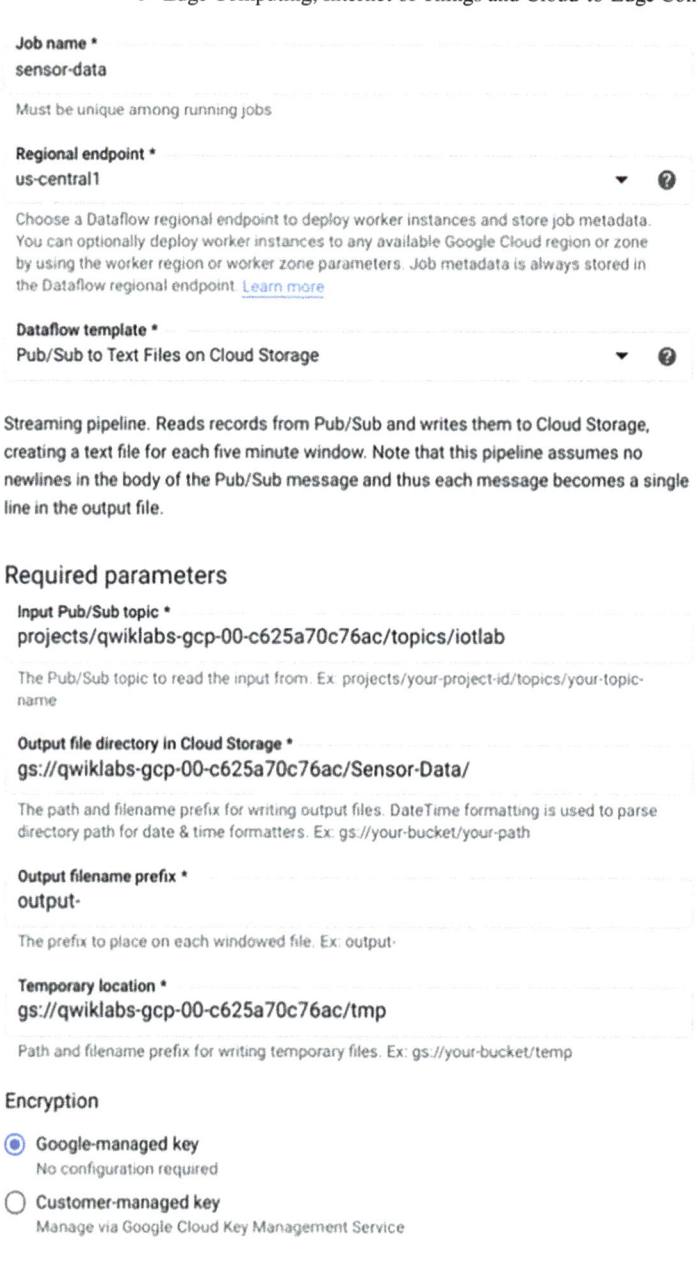

6. Once you have verified that all the fields are properly filled out, click Run job.
7. If the Dataflow job fails the first time, please re-create and run the job.

## D. Device Simulator VM

In your project, a pre-provisioned VM instance named IoT-device-simulator will let you run instances of a Python script that emulate an MQTT-connected IoT device. Before you emulate the devices, you will also use this VM instance to populate your Cloud IoT Core device registry. If you are not following along in a lab environment you can launch a virtual machine, use a physical one or use a real device instead.

1. In the Cloud Console, go to the Navigation menu, look for the Compute section and click on Compute Engine >VM Instances. You will see your VM instance listed as `iot-device-simulator`.
2. Click the SSH drop-down arrow and select Open in browser window.
3. In your SSH session on IoT-device-simulator, enter this command to remove the default Google Cloud SDK installation. (In subsequent steps, you will install the latest version, including the beta component.)

   ```
   sudo apt-get remove google-cloud-sdk -y
   ```

4. Now install the latest version of the Google Cloud SDK and accept all defaults by running:

   ```
   curl https://sdk.cloud.google.com | bash
   ```

5. Enter through all the prompts that follow.
6. End your SSH session on the IoT-device-simulator VM instance:

   ```
   exit
   ```

7. Start another SSH session on the IoT-device-simulator VM instance.
8. Enter this command to make sure that the components of the SDK are up to date:

   ```
   gcloud components update
   ```

9. If you get the error message "Command not found", you might have forgotten to exit your previous SSH session and start a new one. If you get a different error try closing the window and opening a new SSH session.
10. Enter the following command to install the beta components. Enter Y when prompted to continue:

    ```
    gcloud components install beta
    ```

11. Enter through all the prompts that follow.
12. Enter this command to update the system's information about Debian Linux package repositories:

```
sudo apt-get update
```

13. Enter this command to make sure that various required software packages are installed:

    ```
    sudo apt-get install python3-pip openssl git -y
    ```

14. Use pip to add needed Python components:

    ```
    sudo pip3 install pyjwt paho-mqtt cryptography
    ```

15. Enter this command to add data to analyze during this lab:

    ```
    git clone http://github.com/GoogleCloudPlatform/training-data-analyst
    ```

16. In your SSH session on the IoT-device-simulator VM instance, run the following, adding your project ID as the value for PROJECT_ID:

    ```
    export PROJECT_ID=
    ```

17. Your completed command will look like this:

    ```
    export PROJECT_ID=qwiklabs-gcp-d2e509fed105b3ed
    ```

18. You must choose a region for your IoT registry. Set an environment variable containing the us-central1 region with the following command:

    ```
    export MY_REGION=us-central1
    ```

19. Leave this SSH window open. You will come back to it after creating a device registry in the following step.

## E. IoT Core

1. Return to the Cloud Console. From the Navigation menu, in the Analytics section, click IoT Core.
2. Click Create registry.
3. On the Create a registry page, specify the following, and leave the remaining settings as their defaults:

## 9.8 Exercises

| Property | Value |
|---|---|
| Registry ID | iotlab-registry |
| Region | us-central1 |
| Select a Cloud Pub/Sub topic | projects/<project-id>/topics/iotlab |

4. Click Create.

A device registry is a container of devices with shared properties. A registry can have one or more Pub/Sub Topics to which devices in the registry can publish data.

## *F. Create a Cryptographic Keypair*

To allow IoT devices to connect securely to Cloud IoT Core, you must create a cryptographic keypair.
In your SSH session on the IoT-device-simulator VM instance, enter these commands to create the keypair in the appropriate directory:

```
cd {{$HOME/training-data-analyst/quests/iotlab/
openssl req -x509 -newkey rsa:2048 -keyout rsa_private.pem \
    -nodes -out rsa_cert.pem -subj "/CN=unused"
```

This openssl command creates an RSA cryptographic keypair and writes it to a file called rsa_private.pem. When connecting to Cloud IoT Core, each device creates a JWT token signed with its private key, which Cloud IoT Core authenticates using the device's public key.

1. In your SSH session on the iot-device-simulator, type

    ```
    cat rsa_cert.pem
    ```

2. The output will be your certificate. Select and copy the entire certificate (including the begin/end certificate).

```
-----BEGIN CERTIFICATE-----
MIIC+DCCAeCgAwIBAgIJAOJikTScq9oPMA0GCSqGSIb3DQEBCwUAMBExDzANBgNV
BAMMBnVudXN1ZDAeFw0xODA4MTMxNjQ2MTNaFw0xODA5MTIxNjQ2MTNaMBExD
zANBgNVBAMMBnVudXN1ZDCCASIwDQYJKoZIhvcNAQEBBQADggEPADCCAQoCggE
BAL+wLyITE5Tj1H50I63ew3HdvoGty2aOpP04nMy0YZoooAw5o2rj5mkNb/hbkoMTkzo
6/5Jo0zgDYPVRpz2nGAhTfeQzPuvOfPZe7KPpZxYvmSN3pYT9kkiVo9pXwynG7q8kW
72Q9f0pffXS/VElPrC63Y9kcAgOyveZVX61qSokz4DVIj0Z6+1b1utxe2TnxR1q3Hce289
1re6qnxYp6Yuw0gVYtn8HdgEKKMqeSozqJP7dq8EvNkwY8BAUFU2NmuvwK2Z6hB1E
u0DImyhtKRxZ4pUbWuefC+P6GU2fB3rp4pR9Lc7xd5BuWXHgR6f0lV57elL9f1Q/iXippP
8RjhMCAwEAAaNTMFEwHQYDVR0OBBYEFF7808W+vP7vbgg6cS5Fky9xCstNMB8GA
1UdIwQYMBaAFF7808W+vP7vbgg6cS5Fky9xCstNMA8GA1UdEwEB/wQFMAMBAf8w
DQYJKoZIhvcNAQELBQADggEBAD9mSbWQRz8QHI947gGSMrsA+aO4dgWIujkypFw/p
7gSefleCCwGV4Wpfq6zoIjru9bnciWRLHZMKVbhptBDseyBnoPXxnJMgVYBAVzRRMhT
qPeo146Pv99dn3c310M2tkpQeQzP/wE9XFVqEud2sZCKXgXtydIsyTEX3wmG9s9m7f
6TJDknvJ1tOj1R7m+xO6GHPebK29x/r+LzPuYjIDYoG+mxLQU1tDOM3v8QwZ4bneo+HI
BZX6FOBRb+x/fEE3EANCY3J5sKwRCxxXJ6l/Mts7aLUE6MrT8BM0n1fxnY7BX+6dvsJ
H/OeONG2tk3Y0ci/ly245NQyurqa3x35Ws=
-----END CERTIFICATE-----
```

3. Your IoT Core Console page should resemble the following:

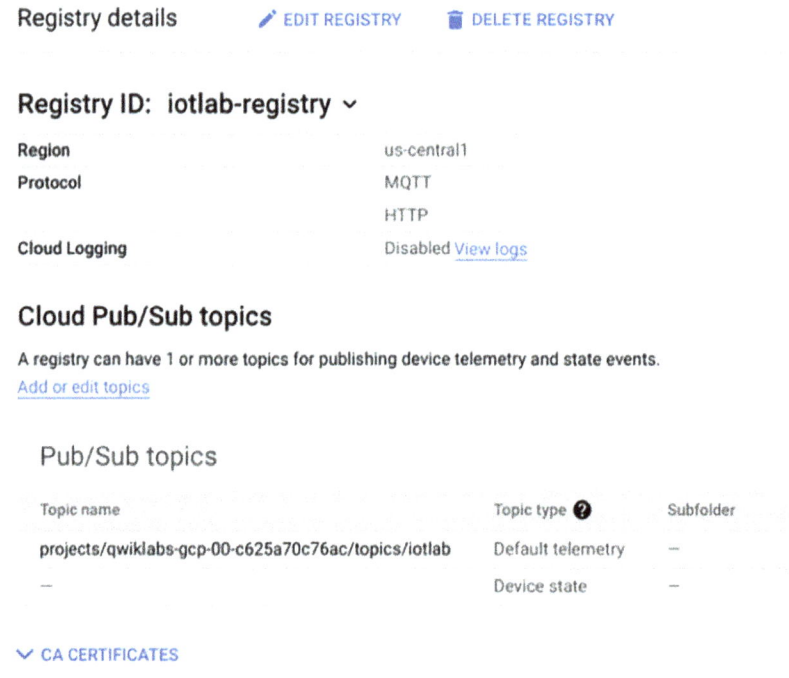

4. From the left-hand menu, select Devices and ensure that the Registry ID is set to iotlab-registry.
5. Click Create a device from the top menu and enter in the following:

9.8 Exercises

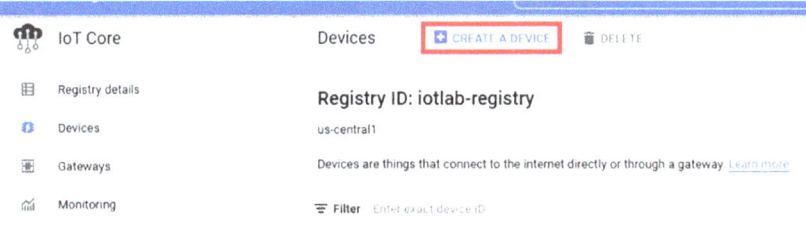

| Property | Value |
|---|---|
| Device ID | `temp-sensor-istanbul` |
| Authentication | `Enter manually` |
| Public key format | `RS256_X509` |
| Public key value | **Paste the certificate that you copied** |

6. Click on the Communication, Cloud logging, Authentication option to see advanced fields.
7. Click Create.
8. You will now add a second device. Hit the back button to return to the device menu and once again click **Create a device**. Then enter the settings.
9. Hit the back button to return to the device overview. Your page should resemble the following:

### Registry ID: iotlab-registry

us-central1

Devices are things that connect to the internet directly or through a gateway. Learn more

| | Device ID | Communication | Last seen | Stackdriver Logging |
|---|---|---|---|---|
| ☐ | temp-sensor-buenos-aires | ✅ Allowed | — | Registry default |
| ☐ | temp-sensor-istanbul | ✅ Allowed | — | Registry default |

Cloud IoT Core documentation

## *G. Run Simulated Devices*

1. In your SSH session on the IoT-device-simulator VM instance, enter these commands to download the CA root certificates from pki.google.com to the

appropriate directory:

```
cd $HOME/training-data-analyst/quests/iotlab/
```

```
curl -LO https://pki.google.com/roots.pem
```

2. Enter this command to run (in background) the first simulated device:

```
python3 cloudiot_mqtt_example\_json.py \
-project_id=\$PROJECT_ID \
-cloud_region=\$MY_REGION \
-registry_id=iotlab-registry \
-device_id=temp-sensor-istanbul \
-private_key\_file=rsa\_private.pem \
-message_type=event \
-algorithm=RS256 -num\_messages=200 > istanbul-log.txt 2>\&1 \&
```

3. Enter the command to run the second simulated device.

```
python3 cloudiot_mqtt_example_json.py \
-project_id=$}}PROJECT_ID \
-cloud_region=$MY_REGION \
-registry_id=iotlab-registry \
-device_id=temp-sensor-buenos-aires \
-private_key_file=rsa_private.pem \
-message_type=event \
-algorithm=RS256 \
-num_messages=200
```

Cloud IoT Core supports two protocols for device connection and communication: MQTT and HTTP. Devices communicate with Cloud IoT Core across a "bridge", either the MQTT bridge or the HTTP bridge. Telemetry data will flow from the simulated devices through Cloud IoT Core to your Cloud Pub/Sub topic. In turn, your Dataflow job will read messages from your Pub/Sub topic and write their contents to your Cloud Storage bucket.

NOTE: Wait for a few seconds for the logs to get generated in the file.

Dataflow is collecting the data published by Pub/Sub and saving it in output files in the bucket and folder specified in the job template. The files are written every 5 minutes, and each begins with the prefix specified in the job template.

1. Return to the Cloud Console. Open the Navigation menu and select Cloud Storage.
2. Select the bucket you created for this project.
3. Select the folder Sensor-Data. Dataflow is writing the data from the device to this folder.
4. Files are written every five minutes. If the folder is empty, wait about 5-10 minutes and periodically click the Refresh Bucket button.

## 9.8 Exercises

5. After refreshing, you will soon see an output file in your directory:

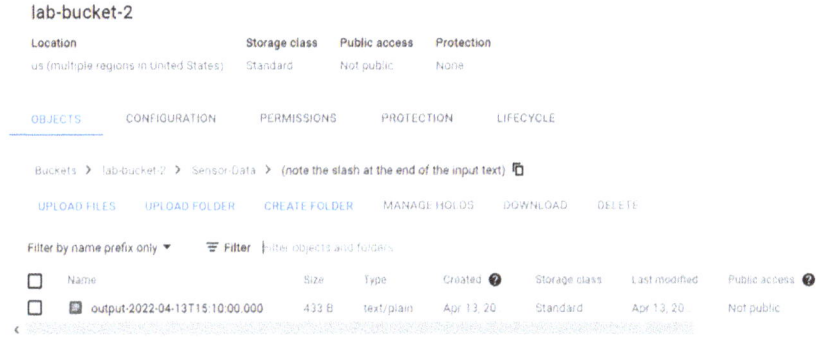

6. Open the file by clicking on its name. Your file contents should be similar to what is shown below. You can click on Download to see the contents:

```
{
    "device": "temp-sensor-buenos-aires",
    "timestamp": 1553631107,
    "temperature": 15.799777248019161
}
{
    "device": "temp-sensor-buenos-aires",
    "timestamp": 1553631108,
    "temperature": 15.787863403464552
}
{
    "device": "temp-sensor-buenos-aires",
    "timestamp": 1553631106,
    "temperature": 15.80888889949552
}
```

## H. Stop the Dataflow Job

In this section you will learn how to stop collecting data through Dataflow by stopping the provisioned job.

1. From the Navigation menu, click Dataflow and select the dataflow you created earlier.
2. Then click the Stop button
3. In the dialog box, select Drain, then Stop Job. It will take a few minutes for the job to stop.
4. Using the back arrow, return to the Dataflow page. Make sure the job status of the sensor-data job is Drained:

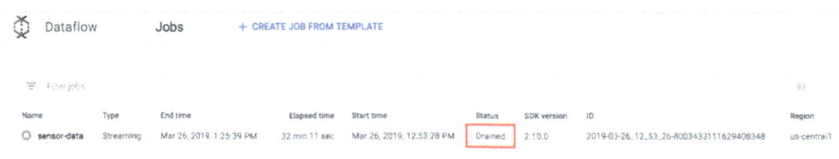

## Conclusion

Congratulations, you made it to the end! Since this may be your first time using these services let's go over what you've done once more. The system has 5 main components.

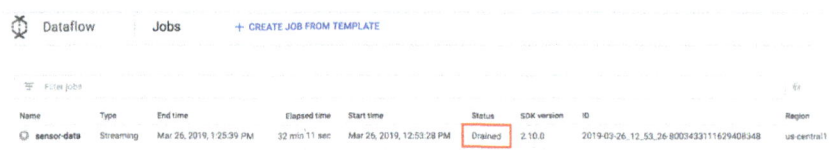

- The Cloud Storage stores the data, there's not much to say about it for this tutorial.
- The Dataflow reads the data from the topic and puts it in the Cloud Storage, it basically acts as a subscriber.
- The Pub/Sub Topic is a MQTT topic which the Dataflow subscribes to and the IoT Core uses for publishing.
- The IoT Core is a service for connecting and managing IoT devices, in this tutorial it's used to allow the simulated devices to publish to the topic. It's slightly more complicated to understand than the rest of the services used here but you don't have to learn everything about it all at once. Here's a brief explanation of what it does in the simple system you created: any device that wants to publish to a

Pub/Sub Topic doesn't directly do so, the IoT Core provides a bridge on which the devices can publish using a device-specific topic. This allows the IoT Core to manage things like authentication and it does this by using Devices and Registries. Devices define real life (or simulated) devices as IoT Cloud resources and let you set a few properties like the public key used for authentication. Registries are containers of devices with shared properties and allow, for instance, to specify one or more Pub/Sub Topics to which devices can publish.
- A Virtual Machine simulates two devices with sensors.

### 9.8.2 Self-driving Cars Using Donkey Car: Training the Model on a Chameleon Node

Donkey Car is an open source program for small self-driving cars. The aim of this lab is to train a self-driving model on a Chameleon Node instead of the local computer, using a specific pathway (Digital pathway) that utilizes Donkeygym—a OpenAI gym wrapper around the Self Driving Sandbox donkey simulator—and Unity to simulate data collection and driving.

### *Objectives*

1. Setting the simulator;
2. Reserving a baremetal Node on Chameleon Cloud;
3. Generating data to train the model.

### *A. Prerequisite*

The Donkey Car simulator is needed to set up a virtual environment on your local machine to drive around and collect data. The prerequisites are:

- Linux or MacOS (if you have a Windows machine—Windows 10 version 2004 or higher -, install the Windows Subsystem for Linux (WSL));
- Python 3.10 or higher (I used Python 3.10.12).

### *A. Setup and Configuration*

Follow the steps provided by CHI@Edge Education in the following link: https://chi-education.gitbook.io/chi-edge-or-education/chi-edge-education/

module-i-autonomous-vehicles/pathways/digital-pathway/simulator-setup. Here some suggestions:

1. If you are having trouble installing the program, try following the official Gym Donkeycar documentation at this link:
   https://pypi.org/project/gym-donkeycar/:

2. As reference, after updating gym-donkeycar with pip install git+https://github.com/tawnkramer/gym-donkeycar the version installed for this tutorial was 1.3.1;
3. If you get the error "Failed building wheel for gym" while installing gym-donkeycar, modify the requirements.py file (located in usr\AppData\Local\Packages\PythonSoftwareFoundation.Python.3.11_qbz5n2kfra8p0\LocalCache\local-packages\Python311\site-packages\wheel\vendored\packaging\requirements.py) as suggested here:

   ```
   def init(self, requirement_string: str) -> None:
   [...]
   try:
               if requirement_string.find('opencv-
                  python>=3.')>=0:
           requirement_string += "0"    # opencv-
               python>=3.0
       parsed = parse_requirement(requirement_string
           )
   ```

4. If you are using WSL, search for its IP address with the ipconfig command on the Windows Powershell and put it on the SIM_HOST variable inside the myconfig.py file:

## 9.8 Exercises

This needs to be done since Windows and WSL don't have a shared localhost. For the same reason, if your connection changes you need to repeat this step.

### *B. Launching the Simulator*

To see if Gym DonkeyCar is correctly set up:

1. from terminal, go to projects/mycar;
2. launch the simulator with: python3 manage.py drive

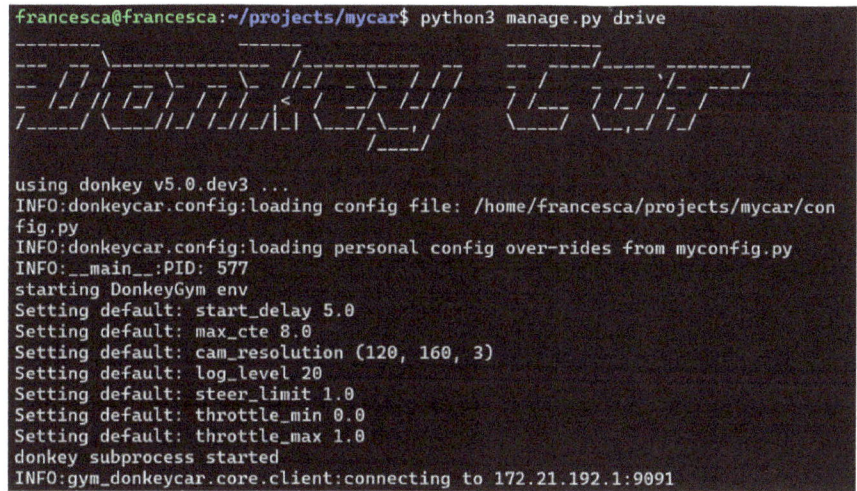

3. connect to http://localhost:8887/drive

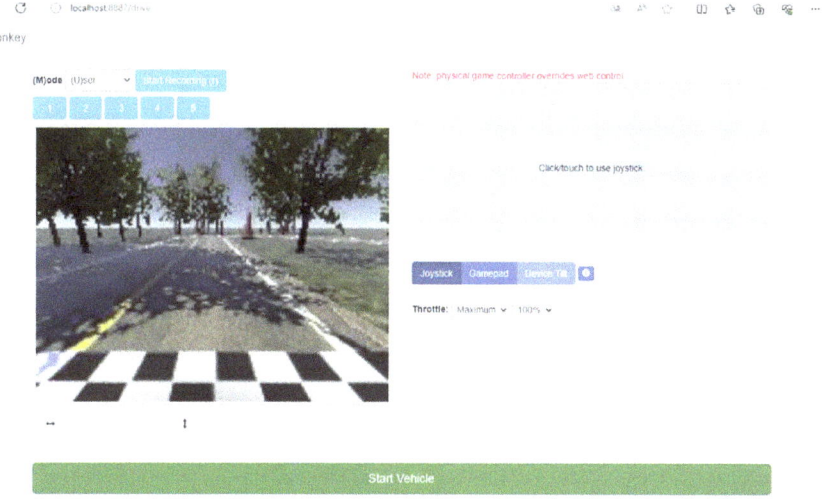

4. If everything works, you should see the donkey_sim window with a car which can be driven from the browser (the result of step #3) clicking on Start Vehicle and then using the light-blue area or connecting a joystick/gamepad. For now, you do not need to modify any parameters.

5. The pathway can be changed clicking on Exit and selecting the preferred track:

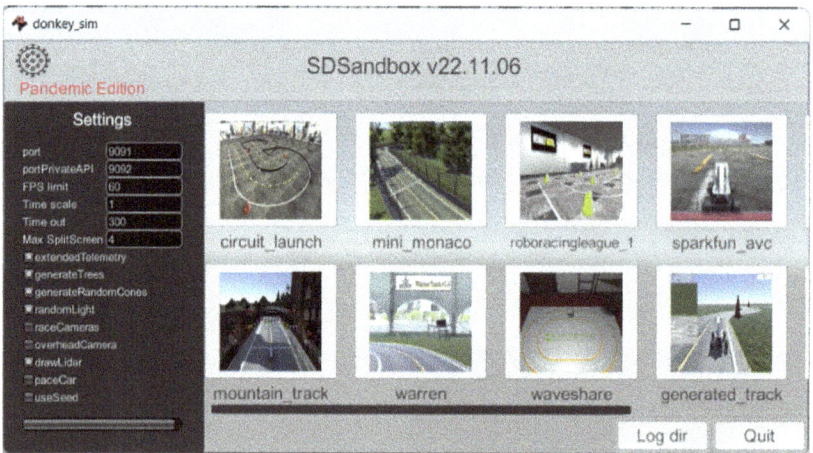

## 9.8 Exercises

### C. Reserving a Baremetal Node on Chameleon Cloud

For this part, you need to create a reservation for a baremetal node on Chameleon Cloud and configure it for training the Donkey car.

1. To reserve the Chameleon instance, use the Trovi artifact[2] and then on click `Launch on Chameleon` button.

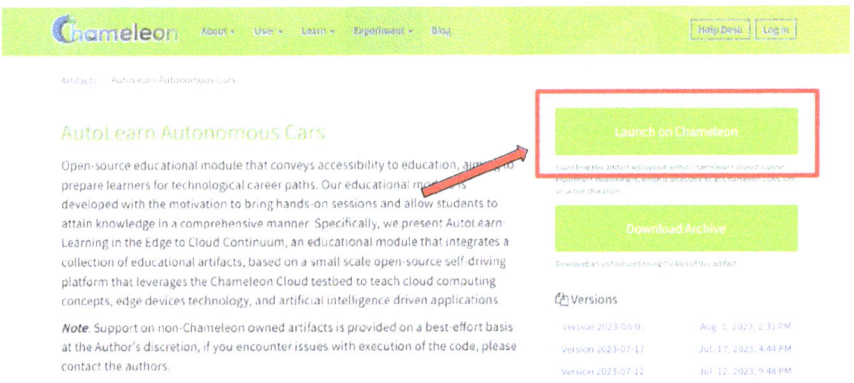

2. After signing in, a Jupyter notebook will open. Open the EdgeracerGuide folder on the left and click on the reserve_baremetal.ipynb file to start modifying it.

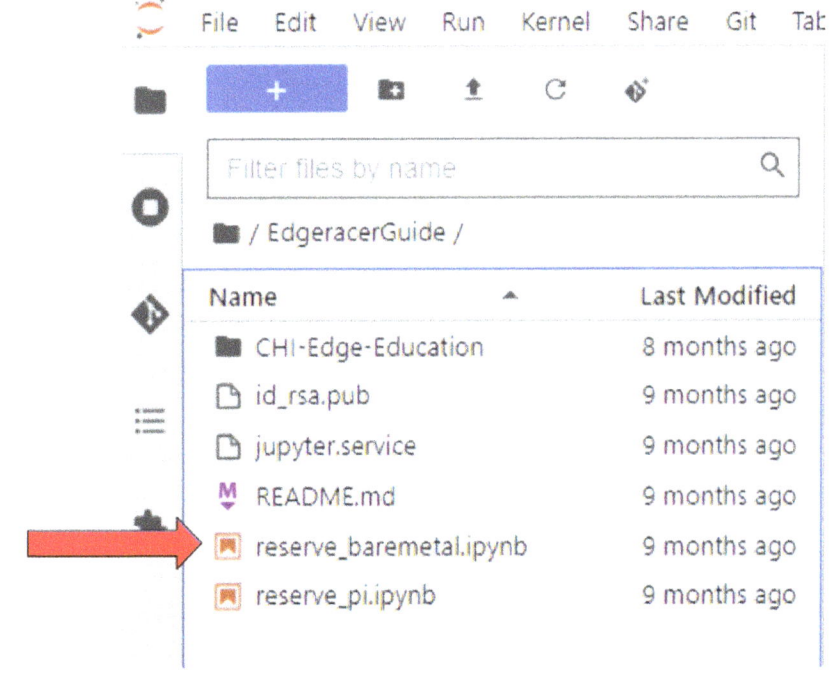

---
[2] https://www.chameleoncloud.org/experiment/share/8800ebd1-411e-4e94-9b62-6883f09188e7

3. Follow all the steps to reserve a baremetal node and launch every cell clicking on the "play" button or pressing Shift+Enter.

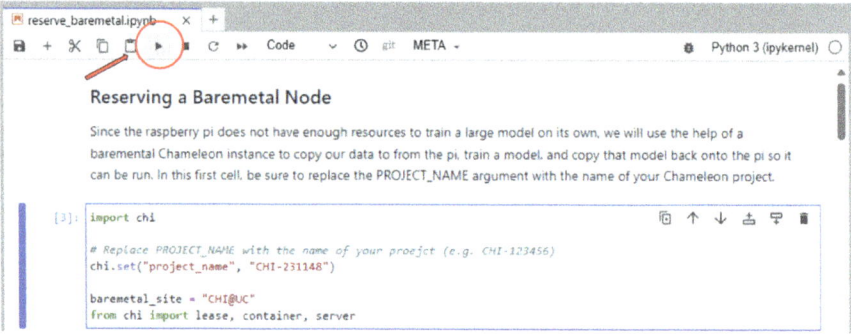

4. Note on Installing Donkeycar and Dependencies step:
   - if it does not run, verify if the Python command and the version used coincide: in this case, I had to change the command from "python ..."İ to "python3 ...";
   - you could possibly get some errors initializing Dialog, Readline and Teletype. This seemed not to have a direct impact on the following steps.

5. As a result, you should see the created instance on your Chameleon Cloud Instances page.

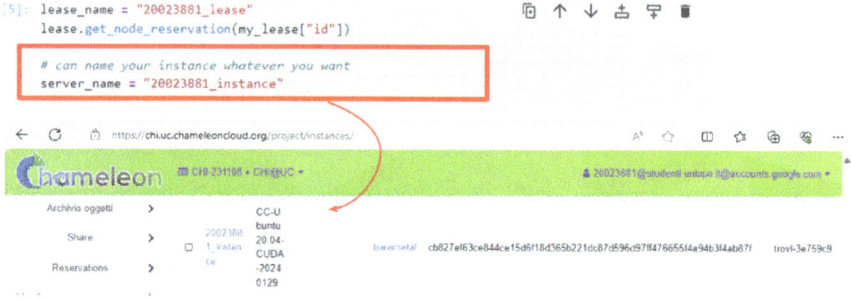

6. Now, you can follow the steps described here[3] to configure the node for training. It is possible to get two errors because Donkeycar already exists and the branch is already up to date with origin/main but everything will work anyway.

---

[3] https://chi-education.gitbook.io/chi-edge-or-education/chi-edge-education/module-i-autonomous-vehicles/pathways/digital-pathway/configuring-chameleon-node-for-training

7. At the end you should get the following output:

```
(.venv) cc@20023881-instance:~/donkeycar$ donkey createcar --path ~/mycar
   _____             _____              _____
___   _____  /_____  __  __  ____/_____ ___
__   / / /  __ \_  __ \_  //_/  _ \_  / /  _  /   _  __ `/_  __/
_  /_/ // /_/ /  / / /  ,<  /  __/  /_/ // /___ / /_/ / /  /
/_____/ \____//_/ /_//_/|_| \___/\__, /  \____/ \__,_/ /_/
                                /____/

using donkey v5.0.dev0 ...
Creating car folder: /home/cc/mycar
making dir /home/cc/mycar
Creating data & model folders.
making dir /home/cc/mycar/models
making dir /home/cc/mycar/data
making dir /home/cc/mycar/logs
Car app already exists. Delete it and rerun createcar to replace.
Car config already exists. Delete it and rerun createcar to replace.
Train already exists. Delete it and rerun createcar to replace.
Calibrate already exists. Delete it and rerun createcar to replace.
Donkey setup complete.
(.venv) cc@20023881-instance:~/donkeycar$
```

## C. Generating Data to Train the Model

1. Sync the previously generated data on your local computer with the node to train it following the CHI@Edge guide here.[4]

   ```
   rsync -r projects/mycar/data cc@192.5.86.253: /mycar/data
   ```

2. check them by listing the content of the data folder:

---

[4] https://chi-education.gitbook.io/chi-edge-or-education/chi-edge-education/module-i-autonomous-vehicles/pathways/digital-pathway/syncing-data-from-local-computer-to-training-node-digital-version

```
cc@20023881-instance:~/mycar/data/data$ ls
catalog_0.catalog           catalog_3.catalog
catalog_0.catalog_manifest  catalog_3.catalog_manifest
catalog_1.catalog           catalog_4.catalog
catalog_1.catalog_manifest  catalog_4.catalog_manifest
catalog_2.catalog           images
catalog_2.catalog_manifest  manifest.json
cc@20023881-instance:~/mycar/data/data$
```

3. Train the model following the steps here.[5] These operations can take a while.
4. Sync the model to your local computer following the steps here.[6]
5. Run the model in the simulator following the steps here. During the simulation, you should see the various windows look like these:

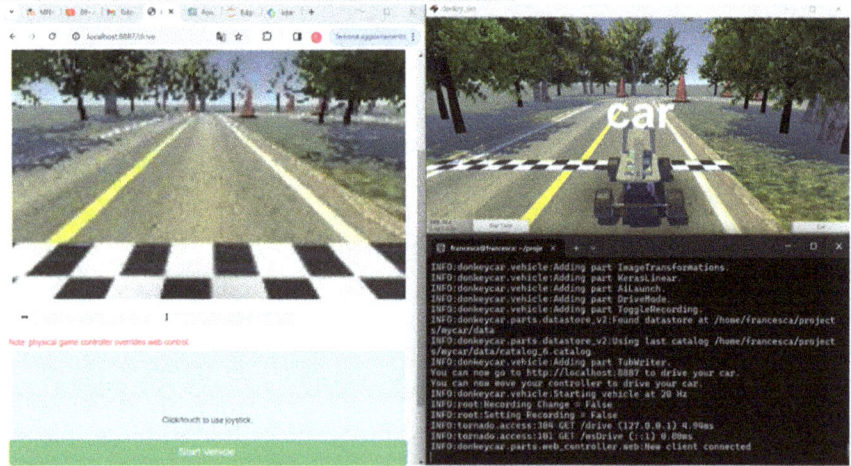

6. By closing the application, you can also see the vehicle statics:

---

[5] https://chi-education.gitbook.io/chi-edge-or-education/chi-edge-education/module-i-autonomous-vehicles/pathways/digital-pathway/training-the-model

[6] https://chi-education.gitbook.io/chi-edge-or-education/chi-edge-education/module-i-autonomous-vehicles/pathways/digital-pathway/syncing-model-to-local-computer

```
^CINFO:donkeycar.vehicle:Shutting down vehicle and its parts...
closing donkey sim subprocess
INFO:donkeycar.parts.tub_v2:Closing tub /home/francesca/projects/mycar/data
INFO:donkeycar.vehicle:Part Profile Summary: (times in ms)
INFO:donkeycar.vehicle:
+--------------------+-------+------+------+------+------+------+-------+
|       part         |  max  | min  | avg  | 50%  | 90%  | 99%  | 99.9% |
+--------------------+-------+------+------+------+------+------+-------+
|       DonkeyGymEnv |  0.74 | 0.01 | 0.04 | 0.03 | 0.04 | 0.13 | 0.36  |
|  LocalWebController|  3.00 | 0.01 | 0.09 | 0.04 | 0.19 | 0.86 | 2.02  |
|               Pipe |  0.43 | 0.00 | 0.01 | 0.01 | 0.01 | 0.03 | 0.16  |
|        ExplodeDict |  0.69 | 0.00 | 0.01 | 0.01 | 0.01 | 0.02 | 0.12  |
|     ThrottleFilter |  0.64 | 0.00 | 0.01 | 0.01 | 0.01 | 0.04 | 0.18  |
|  UserPilotCondition|  0.87 | 0.00 | 0.01 | 0.01 | 0.01 | 0.03 | 0.15  |
|       RecordTracker|  2.75 | 0.00 | 0.02 | 0.01 | 0.01 | 0.47 | 1.58  |
|        FileWatcher |  3.17 | 0.02 | 0.12 | 0.07 | 0.21 | 1.19 | 2.54  |
| ImageTransformations| 0.69 | 0.00 | 0.01 | 0.01 | 0.01 | 0.03 | 0.16  |
|           AiLaunch |  0.81 | 0.00 | 0.01 | 0.01 | 0.01 | 0.03 | 0.13  |
|          DriveMode |  0.47 | 0.00 | 0.01 | 0.01 | 0.02 | 0.03 | 0.11  |
|    ToggleRecording |  5.33 | 0.00 | 0.02 | 0.01 | 0.01 | 0.07 | 3.12  |
|          TubWriter | 10.86 | 0.89 | 4.33 | 4.23 | 6.35 | 8.35 | 9.85  |
+--------------------+-------+------+------+------+------+------+-------+
francesca@francesca:~/projects/mycar$
```

7. For more information about possible extensions of this work visit the CHI@Edge Education dedicated page here.[7]

### 9.8.3 AWS IoT Core Quick Connect

In this lab, you will create your first thing object, connect a device to it, and watch it send MQTT messages. This lab is inspired by "Aws tutorial documentation".[8]

### Objectives

1. Download and run software on a device
2. Connect a device to AWS IoT
3. watch it send MQTT messages

---

[7] https://chi-education.gitbook.io/chi-edge-or-education/chi-edge-education/module-i-autonomous-vehicles/pathways/digital-pathway/possible-extensions

[8] https://docs.aws.amazon.com/iot/latest/developerguide/iot-gs-first-thing.html

## A. *Preliminary Steps*

1. Sign in to the AWS IoT console.[9] In the AWS IoT console home page, on the left, choose Connect and then choose Connect one device.
2. In the Prepare your device section, follow the on-screen instructions to prepare your device for connecting to AWS IoT.
3. In the Register and secure your device section, choose Create a new thing or Choose an existing thing. In the Thing name field, enter the name for your thing object. The thing name used in this example is TutorialTestThing
4. In the Additional configurations section, customize your thing resource further using the optional configurations listed.
5. After you provide your thing object a name and select any additional configurations, choose Next.
6. In the Choose platform and SDK section, choose the platform and the language of the AWS IoT Device SDK that you want to use. This example uses the Linux/OSX platform and the Python SDK. Make sure that you have python3 and pip3 installed on your target device before you continue to the next step.
7. After you choose the platform and device SDK language, choose Next:

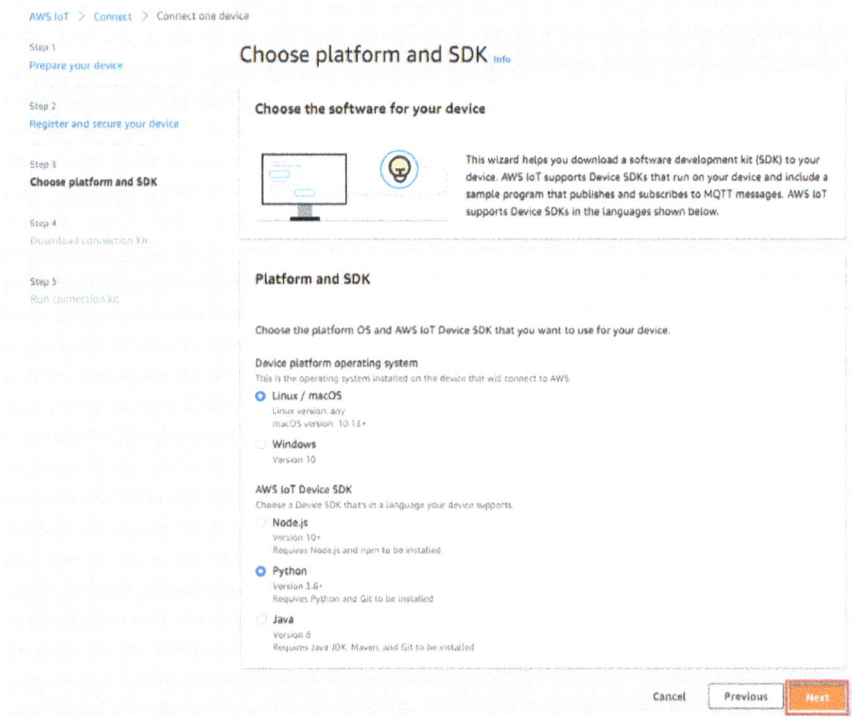

[9] https://console.aws.amazon.com/iot/home

## B. Download Files to Your Device

This page appears after AWS IoT has created the connection kit, which includes the following files and resources that your device requires:

- The thing's certificate files used to authenticate the device
- A policy resource to authorize your thing object to interact with AWS IoT
- The script to download the AWS Device SDK and run the sample program on your device

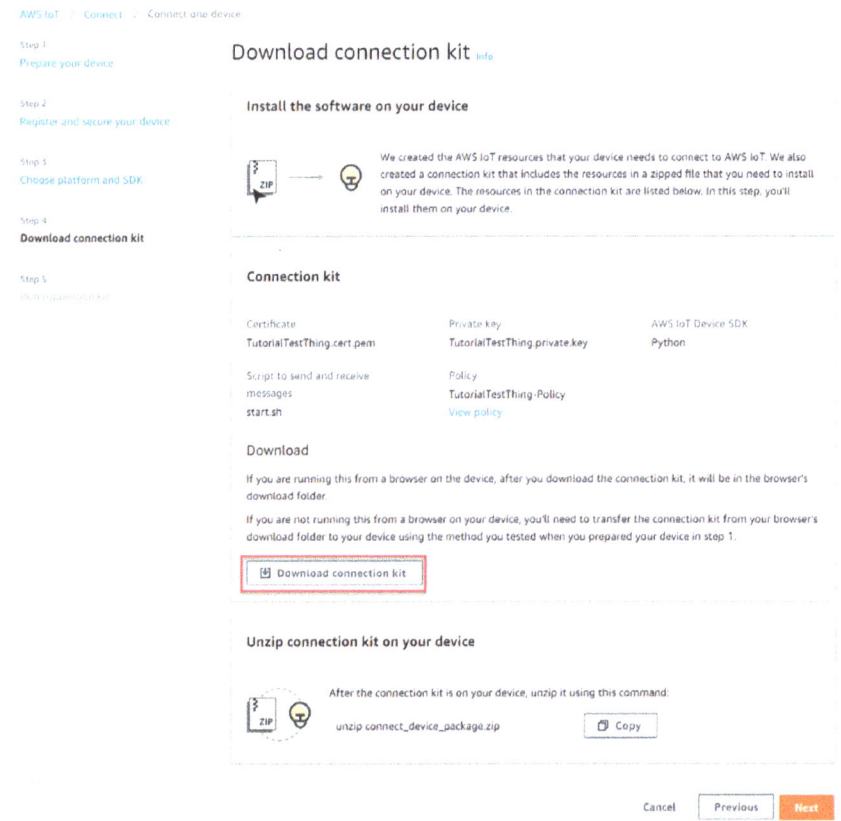

1. When you're ready to continue, choose the Download connection kit for button to download the connection kit for the platform that you chose earlier.
2. If you are running this procedure on your device, save the connection kit file to a directory from which you can run command line commands.
3. If you are not running this procedure on your device, save the connection kit file to a local directory and then transfer the file to your device.

4. In the Unzip connection kit on your device section, enter unzip connect_device_package.zip in the directory where the connection kit files are located.
5. If you are using a Windows PowerShell command window and the unzip command does not work, replace unzip with expand-archive, and try the command line again.
6. After you have the connection kit file on the device, continue the tutorial by choosing Next.

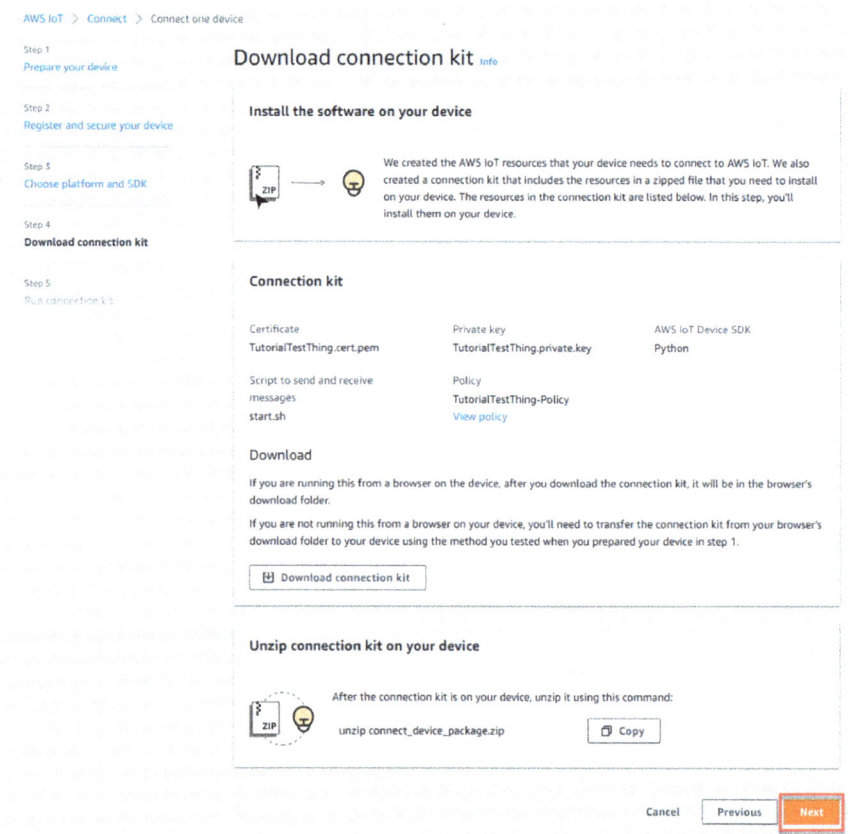

## C. Run the Sample

You do this procedure in a terminal or command window on your device while you follow the directions displayed in the console. The commands you see in the console are for the operating you chose in the preliminary steps. Those shown here are for the Linux/OSX operating systems.

## 9.8 Exercises

1. In a terminal or command window on your device, in the directory with the connection kit file, perform the steps shown in the AWS IoT console.

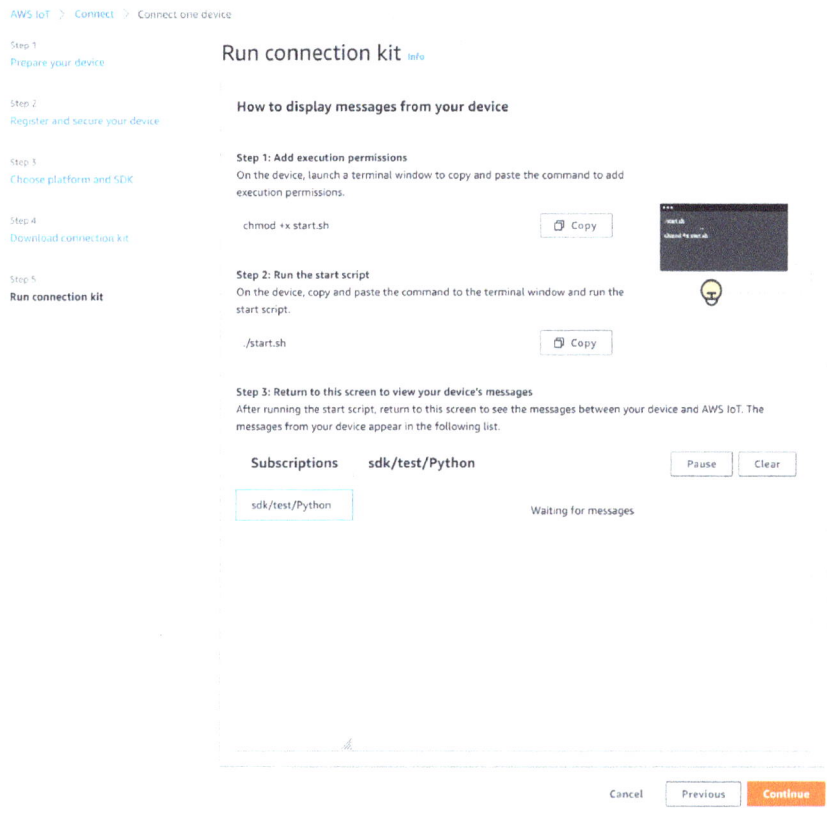

2. After you enter the command from Step 2 in the console, you should see an output in the device's terminal or command window that is similar to the following. This output is from the messages the program is sending to and then receiving back from AWS IoT Core.
3. While the sample program is running, the test message Hello World! will appear as well. The test message appears in the terminal or command window on your device.

```
Running pub/sub sample application...
Connecting to a13hikvzkye6lx-ats.iot.us-east-1.amazonaws.com with client ID 'basicPubSub'...
Connected!
Subscribing to topic 'sdk/test/Python'...
Subscribed with QoS.AT_LEAST_ONCE
Sending messages until program killed
Publishing message to topic 'sdk/test/Python': Hello World! [1]
Received message from topic 'sdk/test/Python': b'"Hello World! [1]"'
Publishing message to topic 'sdk/test/Python': Hello World! [2]
Received message from topic 'sdk/test/Python': b'"Hello World! [2]"'
Publishing message to topic 'sdk/test/Python': Hello World! [3]
Received message from topic 'sdk/test/Python': b'"Hello World! [3]"'
```

4. To run the sample program again, you can repeat the commands from Step 2 in the console of this procedure
5. (Optional) If you want to see the messages from your IoT client in the **AWS IoT console**,[10] open the **MQTT test client**[11] on the Test page of the AWS IoT console. If you chose Python SDK, then in the MQTT test client, in Topic filter, enter the topic, such as sdk/test/python to subscribe to the messages from your device. The topic filters are case sensitive and depend on the programming language of the SDK you chose in Step 1. For more information about topic subscription and publish, see the code example of your chosen SDK.
6. After you subscribe to the test topic, run ./start.sh on your device. After you run ./start.sh, messages appear in the MQTT client, similar to the following:

```
{
    "message": "Hello World!" [1]
}
```

The sequence number encased in [] increments by one each time a new Hello World! message is received and stops when you end the program.
7. To finish the tutorial and see a summary, in the AWS IoT console, choose Continue.
8. A summary of your AWS IoT quick connect tutorial will now appear:

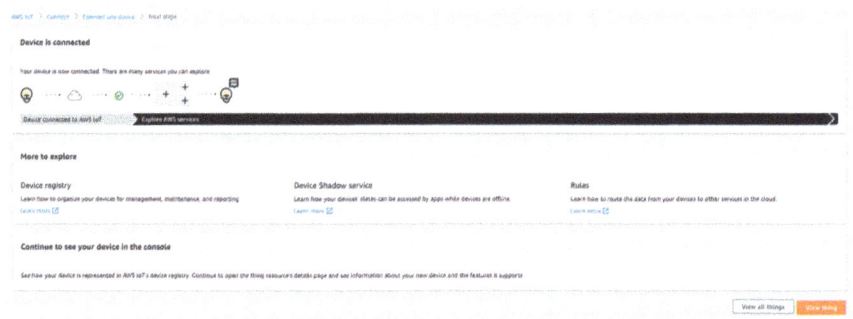

---

[10] https://console.aws.amazon.com/iot/home

[11] https://console.aws.amazon.com/iot/home#/test

# Glossary

**Admin Log:** In GCP, admin logs contain all the administrative actions that modify the configuration or metadata of cloud resources. Admin logs cannot be disabled or deleted, so that attackers who modify cloud resources (e.g. by granting additional permissions or relaxing firewall rules) cannot delete all traces of their actions.

**Agile Development** describes a family of software development methodologies that emphasize iterative development processes that can deal with change well, in contrast to more plan-driven approaches.

**Ansible** is an open source tool that allow users to automate common IT infrastructure tasks. For example, with Ansible it is possible to roll out a software update across multiple virtual machines with a single user interaction.

**API:** An application programming interface (API) is an interface through which user can interact with a service through function or method calls in source code rather than through manual interactions through a graphical user interface.

**App Engine:** The app engine allows users to deploy applications without having to handle the underlying infrastructure (such as virtual machines etc.) It is a way to deploy applications using Platform as a Service (PaaS) in Google Cloud.

**Availability** is one of three critical aspects of IT security, indicating that systems and data are accessible to authorized users.

**AWS:** Amazon Web Services (AWS) is the largest public cloud provider.

**Azure:** Microsoft Azure is the public cloud service offered by Microsoft.

**Basic Role:** GCP has three different basic roles: Reader, writer and admin. As the names indicate, the reader role has read-only access to all resources in a project, the writer role can additionally modify the state of resources, and the admin role can additionally grant or revoke permissions on resources to other roles, set up billing etc. While these basic roles are very simple to understand and use, they typically violate the principle of least privilege and should therefore in most cases not be used in production.

**BigQuery** is a data warehouse operated as a service in GCP.

**Bigtable** is a NoSQL column database operated as a service in GCP.

**Chaos Monkey:** The chaos monkey is a software component that randomly and unpredictably shuts down elements of the (cloud) infrastructure, thereby testing the fault tolerance of the overall system.

**Cloud Armor** is a network security feature in GCP that offers features such as intelligent detection and handling of distributed denial of service (DDoS) attacks.

**Cloud Bursting** describes a common use of hybrid cloud infrastructure in which an application is fully deployed in a private cloud, but configured to use additional resources in a public cloud if the system load exceeds the capacity of the private cloud.

**Cloud Computing** is a practice where a network of remote servers hosted on the internet to store, manage, and process data, rather than a local server or a personal computer.

**Cloud Computing Challenge:** A cloud computing challenge is something that makes using cloud computing potentially difficult but not impossible in a given situation. Commonly quoted cloud computing challenges include lack of expertise, security concerns and organizational readiness issues.

**Cloud Computing Ethics:** While cloud computing in its own right, just like most other technologies, is neither morally good nor bad, the use of cloud computing comes with a number of ethical challenges. Some examples include its potential for magnifying existing biases and sources of discrimination, privacy issues especially in cross-border use of cloud computing, questions around digital sovereignty in the face of increasing industry concentration and environmental impacts.

**Cloud Computing Limitation:** In contrast to challenges that can be overcome, cloud computing also has some limitations that might make its use impractical in certain situations, including applications that have very stringent response time requirements or that are subject to particularly strict government regulations about data security and privacy.

**Cloud Deployment Model:** Cloud deployment models describe who operates the cloud infrastructure for cloud users.

**Cloud Federation** is an approach that allows organizations to integrate applications that are deployed across multiple different cloud environments.

**Cloud Functions** allows users to deploy individual functions written in programming functions like Python or Java along with the specification of what should trigger their invocation.

**Cloud Migration Strategy:** There are several different ways of migrating an existing application into the cloud, ranging from re-hosting the application, i.e. moving it essentially unchanged from a physical server to a virtual machine in the cloud, to a substantial re-factoring, in which an application is redesigned from scratch to utilize modern cloud computing approaches such as microservice architectures.

**Cloud Native:** An application architecture that is specifically designed to leverage cloud APIs to take full advantage of advanced cloud features, in contrast to cloud applications that mirror an architecture as it would be used in a traditional, non-cloud deployment.

Glossary 351

**Cloud Operations Suite:** The GCP Cloud Operations Suite contains numerous abilities necessary to operate complex cloud deployments in production, ranging from monitoring and logging to debugging and error reporting.

**Cloud Service Model:** Cloud service models describe different ways of how the responsibility to operate the different levels of an application (from the underlying operating system at the bottom to the actual software application itself at the top) is broken down between cloud service provider and user.

**Cloud SQL** is a relational database operated as a service by Google Cloud. In contrast to self-hosting a relation database in a virtual machine, using Cloud SQL frees users from database administration activities such as backups, software updates etc.

**Cloud Storage:** GCP Cloud Storage allow users to store files in so-called storage buckets, which provide a flat (not structured by directories) storage location.

**Cloud-to-edge Continuum:** The cloud-to-edge describes the approach to seamlessly integrate processing of data anywhere between the device on which it is created to servers in centralized cloud data centers, to maximize goals such as efficiency and performance.

**Cluster:** A Kubernetes cluster is a number of compute nodes that can be used to deploy container-based applications.

**Community Cloud:** A group of organizations that combine their financial and other resources to host a shared cloud infrastructure exclusively for members of the group operate a community cloud.

**Confidentiality** is one of three critical aspects of IT security, indicating that information is not shared with unauthorized parties.

**Container:** Containers are often used light-weight virtual machines (VMs). They offer similar benefits like VMs such as the ability to package an application with all its dependencies in an easily distributable format. In contrast to VMs, containers do not include a full guest operating system and consequently create less overhead.

**Content Delivery Network:** A content delivery network (CDN) allows organizations to deliver online content to users around the globe with lower latency by taking advantage of servers closer to the end user that cache (parts of) the requested content.

**Control and Data Plane:** An Istio service mesh consists of a data plane in which Istio proxies handle the secure and reliable communication between different services, and a control plane in which these proxies themselves are configured and managed.

**Custom Role:** GCP custom roles allow users to fully specify the individual permissions of a role, allowing full implementation of the principle of least privilege. While custom roles might therefore be the correct choice in situations with particularly stringent security requirements, they come with disadvantages. In particular, role maintenance of custom roles is up to the user, and the complexity of specifying exactly the correct permissions can easily lead to security problems, making predefined roles the better choice in many situations.

**Cutover Strategy:** When an existing IT system is replaced by a new system in general, and when an in-house IT system is migrated into the cloud, and organization has different choices of how to transition from the old to the new system, including a direct cut-over, parallel operation and phased or pilot operations.

**Data Access Log:** In GCP, data access logs record all API calls that affect user data stored in cloud resources. In many systems, data access by users occurs much more frequently than admin activities, which makes full data access logs much larger than admin logs. Therefore, users can configure the level to which user access of data is logged.

**Dataflow** is a fully managed service allowing users to process streams of data in real time with operations that are configured in a declarative fashion, without having to deal with the underlying infrastructure.

**Dataproc** allows users to process large amounts of data in parallel in fully managed compute clusters using tools such as Apache Hadoop or Spark.

**Datastore** is a NoSQL document database operated as a service in GCP.

**Default Service Account:** The GCP Compute Engine and App Engine both feature default service accounts with fairly far reaching permissions (by default with editor level permissions on the whole project). The default service account is great for the prototyping stage of applications, as it frees developers from having to worry about granting sufficient permissions to their virtual machines and applications. However, systems used in production should use more restrictive custom service accounts to respect the principle of least privilege.

**Defense in Depth** is an important principle of IT security that states that IT systems should be redundantly defended with a number of separate security mechanisms, to still protect the system if one or even several of the security mechanisms fail and are overcome by an attacker.

**Demilitarized Zone:** In computer networks, a demilitarized zone (DMZ) is a network segment that is separated from a trusted internal network and an untrusted external network (typically the Internet) by firewalls. Resources such as web servers that need to be accessible from the external network are typically placed in the DMZ, where they can receive some protection from unauthorized accesses, while resources in the trusted internal network are usually not reachable from the untrusted network.

**Detection Coverage** is a measure of the level to which IT security monitoring systems can detect steps taken by attackers. The higher the detection coverage is, the higher are the chances of defenders of detecting and foiling an attacker before they reach their ultimate objective.

**DevOps** is a software development paradigm that emphasizes the need to integrate considerations about the operations of a software system with its development activities, rather than considering the two separate tasks.

**Digital Sovereignty** describes the ability of individuals, organizations and countries to be in control about their own data, applications and technologies, without being forced or essentially being forced to give up some of this control by external market forces. The market concentration in cloud computing in which a large percentage of the market share is held by just three US corporations makes this a significant concern for many users outside the USA.

**Distributed Denial of Service Attack:** In a distributed denial of service (DDoS) attack, an attacker simultaneously floods a target system with fake requests, typically from a number of compromised computers, with the intention of making the target system unavailable to its real users, typically in order to inflict economic harm on the owner of the target system or with the goal to extort a ransom in exchange for stopping the attack.

**Distributed Multi-Cloud Applications:** In a distributed multi-cloud application, different components of the overall application are deployed with different cloud providers, for instance to take advantage of cloud specific features or to optimize cost efficiency.

**DNS:** The domain name system (DNS) is used to map human-friendly domain names such as douglas-college.ca into the IP addresses of the servers behind such domains, allowing users to use names rather than cryptic numbers to specify resources.

**Edge Computing:** In edge computing, data are processed close to their source, i.e. often on the device that created the data, rather than in a centralized cloud computing data center.

**Elasticity** is the property of a cloud to grow or shrink capacity for CPU, memory, and storage resources to adapt to the changing demands of an organization.

**Federated Cloud:** A federated cloud is characterized by multiple cloud providers collaborating and sharing physical resources between themselves. This is typically transparent to cloud service users, i.e. they would not be aware that their cloud resources are not hosted by a single cloud provider, but by a federation of two or more providers.

**Firewall:** A firewall is a network security system that filters network traffic on the basis of defined firewall rules that specify which traffic should be allowed or blocked based on criteria such as direction, source/destination and port/protocol of the network traffic.

**Fog Computing:** In fog computing, data is processed somewhere in between the edge device and the centralized cloud data center. Organizations might operate fog data centers, i.e. small data centers that are in close proximity (e.g. in the same factory) to the edge devices creating the data in order to minimize latency and response time while still benefiting from the advantages of (locally) centralized processing.

**GCP:** The Google Cloud Platform (GCP) is the public cloud service offered by Google.

**Grid Computing** describes the practice of combining computational resources from a distributed number of computers to solve complex computational tasks.

**Hybrid Cloud:** An organization that uses hybrid cloud combines both private and public cloud resources.

**Hybrid Cloud:** A hybrid cloud combines two different types of cloud, most commonly a private and a public cloud, in order to combine the benefits of both.

**Hybrid Cloud:** A hybrid cloud deployment is a multi-cloud deployment that uses different types of cloud deployment models, typically a public and a private cloud.

**Hyperconverged Infrastructure:** Hyperconverged infrastructure is a framework in which the compute, storage and network resources of a number of servers are combined into a unified virtual system, allowing for flexible resource allocation of resources independently of their physical location.

**Hypervisor:** A hypervisor (also called virtual machine monitor or VMM ) is software that allows the creation and management of multiple virtual machines on a single host computer.

**IaaS:** Infrastructure as a service is a cloud service model that provides on-demand access to computing resources such as servers, storage, networking, and virtualization.

**Industrial Internet of Things:** Industrial Internet of Things (IIoT) describes the use of fog and edge computing in industrial settings such as in modern manufacturing plants.

**Infrastructure as Code** describes the approach to build a cloud infrastructure with code rather than by manual interaction with the web-frontend of the cloud provider.

**Infrastructure Manager** is the IaC tool used by GCP to allow users to build their cloud infrastructure with code.

**Integrity** is one of three critical aspects of IT security, indicating that information cannot be deleted or corrupted by accident or unauthorized parties.

**Internet of Things:** The Internet of Things (IoT) describes the approach of equipping a wide range of devices, vehicles, appliances etc. with networked computational abilities, allowing them to interact and provide functionality that an isolated device could not provide.

**IPv4:** The internet protocol in version 4 is the most widely used network protocol for computer networks. It specifies both a way to address individual hosts with 32 bit long addresses as well as a mechanism to send network packets between different hosts.

**IPv6:** The IPv6 protocol is a more modern version of the IPv4 protocol. It uses 128 bit long addresses to overcome one of the main limitations of IPv4, a shortage of available IP addresses.

**Istio** is an open-source service mesh that if frequently used in microservice applications running in Kubernetes clusters.

**Kubernetes** is a widely used open-source container orchestration system, with numerous features such as automatic scaling of applications, health checks that allow for automatic redeployment of failed components etc.

**Kubernetes:** Kubernetes is a cloud orchestration tool. It allows users to declare how cloud applications should be deployed and then handles aspects such as fault tolerance, automatic scaling etc. automatically.

**LAN:** A local area network (LAN) is a computer network connecting a number of devices in a small, localized area such a home, an office or a datacenter.

**Layered Hybrid Cloud:** In a layered hybrid cloud, some layers of an application are deployed in a private cloud, while others are deployed in a public cloud. This can be an attractive alternative to a cloud bursting architecture in cases where an organization wants to use a hybrid cloud to allow for more elasticity of an application than their private cloud infrastructure alone would allow, but still wants to keep certain particularly sensitive parts of the application in house.

**Least Privilege** is an important principle of IT security that states that systems and users should only have the level of access and permissions they require to fulfill their task, and nothing more. The benefit is that an attacker who successfully takes over a system or an account only gains access to a minimal amount of resources.

**Load Balancer:** A load balancer servers as a single point of entry for e.g. users of a web server, and distributes the incoming requests among a number of web server instances. Cloud load balancers can also be configured to react to changing load by scaling the number of virtual machines connected to it up and down as needed.

**Long Range Wide Area Network:** Long range wide are network (LoRaWAN) is a wireless network protocol designed for the use in a distributed IoT context. It specializes in transmitting small amounts of data efficiently, making it ideal for IoT devices with limited battery life.

**Mean Time to Breach (MTTB)** describes the average time it takes an attacker from the start of an attack to achieving their ultimate objective. The goal of security principles like defense in depth, least privilege and separation of duties is to increase the MTTB, giving defenders more time to detect the attack before it succeeds.

**Microservice Architecture:** In a microservice architecture, applications are broken down into a number of small independent services that interact with each other. This has numerous benefits for application development and deployment, but also introduces additional complexity.

**Mobile Device Management (MDM)** is an approach to remotely manage and secure the mobile devices that are often used to access cloud applications, thereby increasing the security of the cloud applications themselves. Typical features of MDM are the ability to enforce security mechanisms on mobile devices accessing cloud applications, the ability to remotely block and erase devices that have been lost or stolen and the creation of separate environments on mobile devices for personal and work use of the device.

**Mobile Edge Computing** is a common edge computing architecture in which computing resources are deployed on base stations or other edge devices of cellular networks.

**Multi-Cloud Native Application:** A multi-cloud native application is an application that is intentionally designed to run on multiple cloud providers to optimize costs, maximize efficiency etc.

**Multi-Cloud System:** A multi-cloud system (MS) is a software system or service that has the goal of helping users of multi- or hybrid cloud deployments integrate and manage their cloud deployments efficiently and effectively.

**Multitenancy** describes the situation in which for example a public cloud provider hosts virtual resources (such as virtual machines) of multiple different client organzitions on the same physical server.

**Node:** A node is one of the physical or virtual machines used in a Kubernetes cluster to run container-based applications.

**Observability:** The goal of observability is to be able to understand the internal state of an IT system in detail. Traditionally, the main mechanism to achieve this was monitoring. Modern cloud infrastructures like GCP extend this by offering additional functionality around logging, tracing and profiling.

**OpenNebula:** is another available open source private cloud platform.

**OpenStack:** is the most widely used open source private cloud platform.

**PaaS:** Platform as a service is a cloud service model that allows user to deploy their applications without worrying about the underlying virtual infrastructure

**Pet vs. Cattle Paradigm:** Traditional IT infrastructures are often characterized by a small number of servers that are individually tended to (pets). In a modern cloud environment, infrastructure elements such as virtual machines should be dynamically allocated and de-allocated based on load, making individual instances less important (cattle).

**Pod:** In Kubernetes, a pod is the smallest unit of computing that can be deployed independently. A pod can contain one or several containers

**Predefined Role:** There are approximately 2000 predefined roles in GCP, each of which gives a set of specific permissions on a specific set of resources. While an individual predefined roles might contain a small number of permissions that an application does not in fact need, carefully selecting predefined roles will typically result in permissions that are quite close to following the principle of least privilege. Therefore, predefined roles are in many cases the best choice for production use.

**Private Cloud:** In a private cloud, an organization operates its own cloud infrastructure in-house.

**Private IP Address:** A private IP address is an IPv4 address that belongs to one of three specific ranges of IPv4 addresses that are not routed across network boundaries and can therefore be used by anybody.

**Project:** Projects are used to control aspects such as billing and access control for resources. In particular, the costs for the resources in a project are paid from a designated billing account, and users often get certain access permission on all the resources of a project.

**Public Cloud:** A public cloud provider offers cloud infrastructure to a range of paying customer organizations.

**RAID:** The acronym RAID stands for redundant array of inexpensive[12] disks. It is usually used in servers to combine multiple physical disks (hard disks or solid state drives) in a larger virtual drive while also storing data redundantly. In most RAID configurations, the failure of a disk can be compensated because of this redundancy, meaning that it causes no server downtime.

**Region:** A region is the geographic location in which cloud services are hosted. Examples for GCP regions are us-central1, europe-north1 or asia-east2.

---

[12] Or alternatively: independent.

Glossary 357

**Replicated Multi-Cloud Applications:** In a replicated multi-cloud application, the application as a whole is deployed across different cloud services, typically to increase redundancy or performance.

**Risk Management** is a systematic approach to dealing with inevitable risks in cloud computing. It includes assessing existing risks and their likelihoods and potential impacts, and develops situationally appropriate strategies of dealing with these risks, ranging from risk mitigation approaches to risk transfer and risk acceptance.

**Role-based Access Control:** The main idea behind role-based access control is that decisions about granting access permissions to resources are not made for individual users, but based on roles. For example, roles such as "accounts payable clerk" are defined along with their required access permissions, and then assigned to all users who hold these roles.

**Router:** Routers are used to connect multiple networks. They use internal routing tables to decide where to forward IP packets based on their destination IP address.

**SaaS:** Software as a service is a cloud service model that offers users ready-to-use software applications hosted in the cloud.

**SAN:** A storage area network (SAN) is a specialized high-speed network connecting a number of servers to a centralized array of storage devices.

**Semi-Private Cloud:** A semi-private cloud provider hosts cloud infrastructure for a range of paying customer organizations. In contrast to a public cloud, this deployment model typically exhibits no multitenancy, i.e. physical resources (such as servers) are not shared between multiple customers.

**Separation of Duties** is an important principle of IT security that states that no individual user or system has full control over an important process. For example, separate accounts should be used by processes that write log entries and by systems that manage the log life cycle (e.g. by archiving and ultimately deleting log entries).

**Serverless Computing** is strictly speaking a misnomer, as all cloud services ultimately run on physical servers. However, a cloud service is called serverless if the underlying physical infrastructure is handled by the cloud provider (e.g. allocation, monitoring, patching etc.). For example, the GCP App Engine can be considered to be serverless.

**Service Account:** In the Google Cloud Platform (GCP), service accounts are used to specify the permissions that a system such as a virtual machine has at runtime. For example, a specific virtual machine might need the ability read files from a storage bucket, in which case a custom service account with a role such as "storage object viewer" would be used.

**Service Level Agreement (SLA):** In cloud computing, a SLA is a contractual agreement between the cloud service provider and a cloud service user. It typically specifies aspects such as the expected uptime of the services provided, support response times and other guaranteed performance criteria, as well as the consequences if these guarantees are not met by the provider.

**Service Mesh:** A service mesh can be used to handle most of the technical and infrastructure tasks of an application using a microservice architecture, such as service discovery, authentication and monitoring.

**Spot Instance:** A spot instance is a heavily discounted virtual machine instance for which the provider reserves the right to shut it down without any significant prior notice if the resources are needed for other purposes.

**Storage Class:** Storage buckets can be assigned to different storage classes—standard, nearline, coldline and archive. The main difference between these storage classes is the trade-off between the cost to store and access data—the former is highest in standard and lowest in archive, while the latter is free in standard and highest in archive.

**Subnet:** Computer networks are often divided into smaller parts called subnets for reasons such as to separate users who need access to different resources on the network or to increase network performance.

**Switch:** A switch is a networking device that connects multiple hosts in a computer network. It uses the MAC address of individual hosts to send data only to the intended destination rather than broadcasting it on the local network (like a hub would do).

**TCP:** The transmission control protocol is one of the most widely used transport protocols in computer networks, allowing for reliable communication in IP networks.

**Terraform** is a widely used infrastructure as code tool that allows users to declaratively specify and provision their cloud resources.

**Vendor Lock-In** describes the situation in which an organization finds it hard to switch from one service provider to another one, for example because the services are not compatible. In cloud computing, this is generally not a contractual lock-in, but one that is created by the practical difficulties or costs from switching providers.

**Vertex AI** is Google Cloud's integrated platform for artificial intelligence (AI) tasks.

**Virtual Private Cloud:** The different resources a user created in the cloud are connected via a virtual private cloud (VPC), which is a virtual (software defined) computer network that is not visible to other cloud users.

**Virtual Private Cloud:** In GCP, a virtual private cloud (VPC) is a private virtual network that is automatically created to connect all the cloud resources a user creates in a project, regardless of which region they reside in. It by default contains a subnet for each region in GCP, abstracting away the complexity of the underlying physical network infrastructure from the user.

**Virtualized Data Center:** In virtualized data centers, individual applications are not run directly on physical servers. Instead, virtualization software is deployed on the physical infrastructure, and applications are deployed in virtual machines.

**WAN:** A wide area network (WAN) is a computer network connecting devices and often entire LANs across a large geographic area.

**Zone:** Each region contains several zones. For example, us-cental1 includes zones such as us-central1-a, us-central1-b and us-central1-c. The datacenters hosting the different zones in a region are in different physical locations.

GPSR Compliance
The European Union's (EU) General Product Safety Regulation (GPSR) is a set of rules that requires consumer products to be safe and our obligations to ensure this.

If you have any concerns about our products, you can contact us on

ProductSafety@springernature.com

In case Publisher is established outside the EU, the EU authorized representative is:

Springer Nature Customer Service Center GmbH
Europaplatz 3
69115 Heidelberg, Germany

www.ingramcontent.com/pod-product-compliance
Ingram Content Group UK Ltd.
Pitfield, Milton Keynes, MK11 3LW, UK
UKHW022203230426
470311UK00001BA/9